MALMESBURY ABBEY 670–1539

Malmesbury Abbey 670–1539
Patronage, Scholarship and Scandal

Tony McAleavy

THE BOYDELL PRESS

© Tony McAleavy 2023

All Rights Reserved. Except as permitted under current legislation no part of this work may be photocopied, stored in a retrieval system, published, performed in public, adapted, broadcast, transmitted, recorded or reproduced in any form or by any means, without the prior permission of the copyright owner

The right of Tony McAleavy to be identified as the author of this work has been asserted in accordance with sections 77 and 78 of the Copyright, Designs and Patents Act 1988

First published 2023
The Boydell Press, Woodbridge

ISBN 978 1 78327 714 8

The Boydell Press is an imprint of Boydell & Brewer Ltd
PO Box 9, Woodbridge, Suffolk IP12 3DF, UK
and of Boydell & Brewer Inc.
668 Mt Hope Avenue, Rochester, NY 14620–2731, USA
website: www.boydellandbrewer.com

A CIP catalogue record for this book is available
from the British Library

The publisher has no responsibility for the continued existence or accuracy of URLs for external or third-party internet websites referred to in this book, and does not guarantee that any content on such websites is, or will remain, accurate or appropriate

For Billy, Maisie and Ned

CONTENTS

List of Illustrations	ix
Acknowledgements	xi
Abbreviations	xiii
Foreword by Rod Thomson	xv
Prologue: Before the monastery	1
1. From Máeldub to Aldhelm	5
2. Aldhelm's community	23
3. Royal patronage and exploitation (710–960)	35
4. Malmesbury and the late Anglo-Saxon Benedictine reform movement	47
5. Responding to the Conquest (1066–1100)	61
6. William of Malmesbury and Queen Matilda	75
7. The ascendancy of Bishop Roger of Salisbury	89
8. The Abbey and the Anarchy	109
9. The dispute with the bishops of Salisbury (1142–1217)	123
10. A self-confident age: the Abbey in the thirteenth century	141
11. The Despenser years and the criminal career of Abbot John of Tintern	159
12. Thomas of Bromham and the *Eulogium Historiarum*	177
13. After the Black Death	193
14. The abbots of the fifteenth century	201
15. The Tudor Abbey	213
Epilogue: After the departure of the monks	235
Bibliography	241
Index	255

ILLUSTRATIONS

1. South front of Malmesbury Abbey (Photo: Christina Staff, with her permission) — xvi
2. Malmesbury Abbey from William Dugdale's *Monasticon Anglicanum*, 1655 (Author) — xvi
3. South porch (Photo: Toby James, with his permission) — xvii
4. Sculptural bands on the exterior of the porch (Photo: Toby James, with his permission) — xvii
5. Adam and Eve sculpture in the south porch (Photo: Toby James, with his permission) — xviii
6. The entombment of Christ in the south porch (Photo: Toby James, with his permission) — xviii
7. Sculptures of apostles in the interior of the south porch (Photo: Toby James, with his permission) — xix
8. Christ in Majesty tympanum south porch doorway (Photo: Christina Staff, with her permission) — xx
9. Ruins of south transept (Photo: Toby James, with his permission) — xx
10. Drawing of ruined west front by F. Nash, 1806 (Athelstan Museum Malmesbury, with permission) — xxi
11. Blocked off processional doorway linking the church to the cloisters (Photo: Toby James, with his permission) — xxii
12a. Architectural drawing of internal elevation of south side of the nave, *Society of Antiquaries*, 1816 (Author) — xxiii
12b. South side of the nave (Photo: Christina Staff, with her permission) — xxiii
13. Dogs' heads sculpture (Photo: Christina Staff, with her permission) — xxiii
14. Romanesque detail at arcade and triforium levels (Photo: Christina Staff, with her permission) — xxiv
15a. Romanesque capital with palm leaves (Photo: Christina Staff, with her permission) — xxiv

Illustrations

15b. Blind arcading on Abbey exterior (Photo: Christina Staff, with her permission) — xxiv

16. View of fourteenth-century church roof with lierne vaulting (Photo: Toby James, with his permission) — xxv

17. Fourteenth-century roof bosses (Photo: Toby James, with his permission) — xxvi

18. View of fourteenth-century clerestory windows set above Romanesque work (Photo: Christina Staff, with her permission) — xxvii

19. Tiles from the cloister with Despenser arms, *Archaeologia* 1913 (Author) — xxvii

20. Tiles from the cloister with the initials of Abbot Thomas Bristow, *Archaeologia* 1913 (Author) — xxviii

21. The tomb of Æthelstan (Photo: Toby James, with his permission) — xxix

22. Tudor stone screen in the south aisle (Photo: Toby James, with his permission) — xxix

23. The high altar and Tudor screen (Photo: Toby James, with his permission) — xxx

24. Detail of Tudor screen frieze (Photo: Toby James, with his permission) — xxx

25. Late medieval roof boss depicting the wounds of Christ (Photo: Christina Staff, with her permission) — xxxi

The author and publisher are grateful to all the institutions and individuals listed for permission to reproduce the materials in which they hold copyright. Every effort has been made to trace the copyright holders; apologies are offered for any omission, and the publisher will be pleased to add any necessary acknowledgement in subsequent edition

ACKNOWLEDGEMENTS

I owe a huge debt to Michael Winterbottom and Rod Thomson for their contribution to this book. In 2017, after several years of intermittent research into the history of the Abbey, I had the immense good fortune to meet both Michael and Rod when they spoke at a conference in Malmesbury that I had organised. Soon afterwards Michael and I began to look together at untranslated documents within the Malmesbury cartulary and, together with Rod, we began discussing the shape of a possible book about the Abbey. Since then, Michael has enriched this work beyond measure with many impeccable translations of previously neglected Latin documents and much wise advice on matters of content, structure and style. He has been extremely generous with his time and unerringly correct in his judgements on the strengths and weaknesses of my draft material. Rod has also been unfailingly supportive of the project and, like Michael, a source of authoritative guidance. I have also made extensive use of the definitive editions of several of the works of William of Malmesbury produced by Michael and Rod and their many perceptive articles about the Abbey's great historian.

Michael's translations can be found throughout the work. His renderings of the accounts of William of Malmesbury and Faricius of Arezzo relating to the history of the Abbey feature prominently in the early chapters. New translations by Michael of documents from the Malmesbury cartulary are at the core of those chapters describing the life of the Abbey between 1100 and 1300 and these are supplemented by his original translations of material from the letters of Gilbert Foliot, Herbert of Bosham and Peter of Blois. Most of the material from the *Eulogium Historiarum* used in the book was translated by Michael and he was also responsible for the 1527 visitation report which revealed a breakdown in discipline within the community.

In addition to Michael's translations, later chapters in the book include some hitherto unpublished legal documents from the National Archives which were skilfully translated by Simon Neale. I am very grateful to Simon for helping me to unlock these sources and to reveal, for example, the full extent of the criminal career of Abbot John of Tintern and the strange case of the rebellion of John Dyer in 1450.

Acknowledgements

The book is greatly enriched by the excellent photographs of the Abbey taken by Christina Staff and Toby James. Thanks to Philip Barras for his meticulous reading of the draft manuscript. Thanks to Deborah Clogg and Peter Holland for their kindness in giving me access to the collection of the Athelstan Museum, including the splendid watercolour of the Abbey by Turner which is on the cover of the book. I am very grateful to Richard Barber of Boydell & Brewer for his support and editorial wisdom. Sarah Thomas edited the manuscript thoughtfully and with meticulous attention to detail and thereby greatly improved the book.

I have sought to build upon several valuable previous studies of Malmesbury Abbey by Harold Brakspear, Richard Luce, Aelred Watkin and Ron Bartholomew, and the extensive bibliography signals my debt to many other historians who have taken an interest in particular facets of the history of the Abbey. I would like to express my admiration for the work of a large number of scholars: Michael Lapidge, Andy Orchard, Jesse Billett and Emily Thornbury for the way they have transformed our understanding of the world of Aldhelm; Susan Kelly for her magisterial analysis of the monastery's pre-Conquest charters; Lois Huneycutt for her insightful reflections on the relationship between Malmesbury and Queen Matilda of Scotland; Malcolm Thurlby for his brilliant re-evaluation of the role of Bishop Roger of Salisbury in the building of the twelfth century church; the late Roger Mynors for his remarkable discoveries of previously unknown letters from William of Malmesbury and the lost ending of *Gesta Stephani*; Andrew Dunning for unearthing the story of the fraternal relationship between Malmesbury Abbey and Cirencester Abbey; Nigel Berry for his forensic assessment of the economics of the Abbey under the rule of Abbot William of Colerne; Nigel Morgan for his discovery of the fourteenth-century Malmesbury psalter and prayer book at Sankt Gallen and his work on liturgical practice at Malmesbury; Julian Luxford for his study of the seals of Malmesbury and Pilton and his insights concerning the late medieval tomb of Æthelstan; Trevor Russell Smith for his study of the late medieval Malmesbury manuscript in Yale University; Martin Heale for his analysis of the role of Thomas Cromwell in Abbey affairs in the 1530s; David Robinson and Richard Lea for their study of the Tudor period stone screens at the Abbey; Barry Dent for his work on the dating of the iconography of the Tudor frieze; and James Carley and Pierre Petitmengin for their account of John Leland's appropriation of Malmesbury manuscripts.

My greatest thanks go to my wife, Chris, for her encouragement, support, insights and tolerance.

Tony McAleavy
Malmesbury
February 2023

ABBREVIATIONS

Aldhelm, *Poetic Works*	*Aldhelm: The Poetic Works*, trans. Michael Lapidge and James Rosier (Woodbridge, 2009)
Aldhelm, *Prose Works*	*Aldhelm: The Prose Works*, trans. Michael Lapidge and Michael Herren (Woodbridge, 2009)
ASC	*The Anglo-Saxon Chronicles*, ed. and trans. Michael Swanton (London, 2000)
Berry	Nigel Berry, 'The Estates and Privileges of Malmesbury Abbey in the Thirteenth Century', unpublished doctoral thesis, University of Reading (1989)
Cal. Close	Calendar of Close Rolls
Cal. Papal Registers	Calendar of Papal Registers Relating to Great Britain and Ireland
Cal. Pat.	Calendar of Patent Rolls
Collectanea	John Leland, *De Rebus Britannicis Collectanea*, ed. Thomas Hearne, 6 vols. (London, 1770)
Eulogium	*Eulogium Historiarum Sive Temporis: Chronicon ab orbe condito usque ad annum domini MCCCLXVI a monacho quodam Malmesburiensi exaratum*, ed. Frank Scott Haydon, 3 vols. (London, 1858–63)
Faricius, *Vita*	Faricius, *Vita S. Aldhelmi* Michael Winterbottom, 'Faricius's Life of Aldhelm, Translation and Commentary', *Wiltshire Archaeological and Natural History Magazine*, 115 (2022): 2–45
Gesta Stephani	*Gesta Stephani*, ed. and trans. K. R. Potter, introduction by R. H. C. Davis (Oxford, 1976)
GP I	William of Malmesbury, *Gesta Pontificum Anglorum: The History of the English Bishops*, ed. and trans. Michael Winterbottom (Oxford, 2007)

Abbreviations

GP II	Rodney M. Thomson, *Gesta Pontificum Anglorum: The History of the English Bishops 2: Introduction and Commentary* (Oxford, 2007)
GR I	*William of Malmesbury: Gesta Regum Anglorum*, ed. and trans. R. A. B. Mynors, Rodney M. Thomson and Michael Winterbottom (Oxford, 1998)
GR II	Rodney M. Thomson, *William of Malmesbury: Gesta Regum Anglorum: General Introduction and Commentary* (Oxford, 1999)
HE	Bede, *Historia Ecclesiastica Gentis Anglorum. Bede's Ecclesiastical History of the English People*, ed. and trans. B. Colgrave and R. A. B. Mynors (Oxford, 1969)
Heads of Houses	C. N. L. Brooke, David Knowles, Vera London, David M. Smith, *Heads of Religious Houses in England and Wales*, 3 vols. (Cambridge, 2001–8)
Historia Novella	*William of Malmesbury: Historia Novella: The Contemporary History*, trans. K. R. Potter; ed. Edmund King (Oxford, 1998)
Kelly, *Charters*	Susan Kelly, *Charters of Malmesbury Abbey* (London, 2005)
Lapidge, 'Career'	Michael Lapidge, 'The Career of Aldhelm', *Anglo-Saxon England*, 36 (2007): 15–69
L. & P. Hen. VIII	Letters and Papers of Henry VIII
Orchard, *Poetic Art*	Andy Orchard, *The Poetic Art of Aldhelm* (Cambridge, 1994)
ODNB	Oxford Dictionary of National Biography
RM	*Registrum Malmesburiense: The register of Malmesbury Abbey*, ed. J. S. Brewer and Charles Trice Martin, 2 vols. (London, 1879)
Thomson, *William*	Rodney M. Thomson, *William of Malmesbury* (Woodbridge, second edition 2003)
TNA	The National Archives
WANHM	*Wiltshire Archaeological & Natural History Magazine*

FOREWORD

Malmesbury Abbey is famous, not only for its continuous longevity (part of it still survives today as the town's parish church), but, even more so, for its having given home to two individuals who were outstanding on the European stage: Aldhelm and William of Malmesbury. In fact, were it not for the writings of these two men, especially William, we should know far less and be much less interested in the Abbey. As it is, our knowledge is very 'spotty', and it is to Tony McAleavy's credit that he has not concealed the existence of the gaps, while doing his best to fill them. He sheds light on less well-understood phases of the monastery's history, such as the late Saxon period when celibate monasticism was restored, and the fourteenth century when the monks became entangled in national politics during the reign of Edward II. He gives us, for example, an excellent account of a chronicle written at Malmesbury in the mid-fourteenth century, the *Eulogium Historiarum*, and identifies, for the first time, its author as Thomas of Bromham. The misdeeds of John of Tintern, abbot in the fourteenth century, have received no previous scholarly attention, and Tintern is a splendid addition to the medieval gallery of 'criminous clerks'. Thus, the text both synthesises findings from previous Malmesbury scholarship and includes significant new findings based on fresh research. It is greatly enriched by the excellent translations of Michael Winterbottom, many of which have not been previously published.

Tony McAleavy has given us the first connected, scientifically based history of the house, and it will be fundamental to any further research upon it. What remains to be done? It is most unlikely that many more literary sources will emerge, and expansion in our knowledge will only come through archaeology. William peppers the site with Anglo-Saxon churches of which nothing remains above ground, and which were thoroughly demolished after the Norman Conquest. There is much still to be discovered among the ruins and remains.

Rod Thomson

1. The surviving fragment of the conventual church was built in the twelfth century and partially remodelled in the fourteenth century. No traces remain above ground of the pre-Conquest monastery, and little is known about its layout.

2. William Dugdale's *Monasticon Anglicanum*, published in 1655, contained an early attempt to represent accurately the remains of Malmesbury Abbey.

3. The central core of the south porch dates from the twelfth century. It was rebuilt externally with the addition of angle buttresses in the fourteenth century.

4. The twelfth-century porch is richly decorated with sculpture. The entrance arch has bands with lozenges depicting episodes from the Bible. The inner arch contains scenes from the New Testament while the central and outer arches reference stories from the Old Testament.

5. South porch sculptures: Eve gives fruit to Adam.

6. South porch sculptures: Nicodemus and Joseph of Arimathea place the body of Jesus in the tomb.

7. The interior east and west walls of the south porch are decorated with sculpture representing the apostles in the company of angels.

8. The door inside the south porch is crowned with a tympanum showing Christ in Majesty, flanked by angels.

9. The ruined south transepts of the conventual church.

10. This nineteenth-century engraving shows the ruined west front of the Abbey church.

11. On the north side of the church is a fifteenth-century processional archway set within an earlier twelfth-century doorway. This entrance linked the cloister area with the monastic church.

12a & b. The internal elevation of the south side of the nave as shown (left; a) in an engraving of 1816 and today (right; b). The twelfth-century work survives at arcade and galley levels while the Romanesque clerestory was replaced in the fourteenth century.

13. The 'stops' of the twelfth-century arcade mouldings were ornamented throughout with distinctive carvings of dogs' heads.

14. The Romanesque work involved both round arches at triforium level with innovative use of pointed arches at arcade level.

15a & b. Features of the twelfth-century work such as stylised palm leaves as capitals (left; a) and elaborate blind arcading (right; b) are consistent with the idea that Bishop Roger of Salisbury was responsible for the design of the twelfth-century work at the Abbey.

16. In the fourteenth century the conventual church was transformed at clerestory and roof level with the addition of new elevated windows and a new stone roof with lierne vaulting.

17. The fourteenth-century lierne roof was decorated with elaborate bosses.

18. The fourteenth-century clerestory windows set above the Romanesque work were possibly designed by Thomas of Witney.

19. Encaustic tiles uncovered in the cloisters suggest that the Despenser family was involved in the decision to rebuild the church in the early 1320s. The tiles include a version of the Despenser arms.

20. The cloisters were remodelled in the fifteenth century during the abbacy of Thomas Bristow and tiles decorated with his initials – T B – have been found in the area.

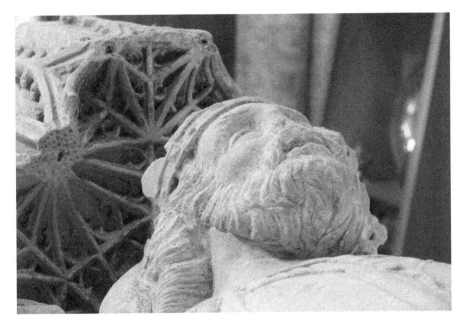

21. The monks were immensely proud that they possessed the remains of Æthelstan, the first king of all England.

22. In around 1500 Abbot Thomas Olveston commissioned new stone screens for the Abbey church. Here is the screen in the south aisle.

23. Behind the altar of today's parish church is a Tudor frieze with heraldic decorations and an archway which originally linked the nave to the crossing and monastic choir.

24. The frieze behind the high altar of the parish church is decorated with the Tudor emblems of the portcullis and the rose, together with the pomegranate of Catherine of Aragon.

25. A late medieval roof boss from Malmesbury showing the five wounds of Jesus.

Prologue: Before the monastery

Malmesbury Abbey is one of England's great medieval sites.[1] Its significance is considerable but often underestimated: a Christian community lived and worshipped on this site more or less continuously for over eight centuries – from around 670 to 1539 – and during these years the Abbey was an important national institution for a shifting combination of religious, artistic, cultural and political reasons. By 700 the monastery was one of the leading centres of higher learning in Britain and Ireland, with a library that could match any in western Europe. The large fragment of the Abbey church that still survives today is a masterpiece of twelfth-century Romanesque architecture and the south porch contains some of the finest sculpture of the period in England. Malmesbury had many links with royalty, both before and after the Conquest: it was originally endowed jointly by the royal houses of both Wessex and Mercia; Æthelstan chose the place as his mausoleum; Edmund Ironside was married there; Queen Matilda, wife of the Conqueror, was a patron; and Henry I gave control of the monastery to his wife, Matilda of Scotland, as part of her dower.

The monastery produced two great writers: Aldhelm, the first English 'man of letters' (died c. 709), and William of Malmesbury, the most learned English historian of the high Middle Ages (died c. 1143). The place was also home to many other now largely forgotten individuals who led surprisingly interesting lives, such as: Faricius of Arezzo, the Italian monk who became the personal physician to Henry I; William of Colerne, the farming abbot who transformed the economic fortunes of the Abbey in the thirteenth century; Thomas of Bromham, the chronicler and English nationalist who envisaged a messianic role for the Black Prince; and John of Tintern, the criminal abbot who lived openly with his lover in the 1340s and was accused by local people of arson and murder.

The monastery was established in the seventh century in unsettled times, and perhaps it is unsurprising, therefore, that the most striking

---

[1] 'Malmesbury Abbey' is deployed here, and at different stages in this book, as the name of the medieval religious institution that existed in Malmesbury between the seventh and the sixteenth centuries. In reality the religious community in Malmesbury was not called 'Malmesbury Abbey' by contemporaries before the Norman Conquest and the first recorded use of the term is in a letter written by Queen Matilda, wife of Henry I, to Archbishop Anselm in 1106.

features of the topography of the site are its strong natural defences. The historic centre of Malmesbury is built on a plateau which tops an elevated promontory of oolitic limestone. Visitors, including those intent on attack and plunder, encountered steep slopes on almost all sides as they approached the monastery, and the place is virtually encircled by two branches of the Bristol Avon which join together just beyond Malmesbury. The medieval monastery precinct occupied the northernmost section of the promontory with the surviving remains of the Abbey church in the north-west area.

The history of the Malmesbury community can be traced through the study of substantial surviving documentary sources: from the extant works and correspondence of Aldhelm, to the eyewitness testimony of the Tudor antiquary, John Leland, who visited Malmesbury around the time of the Dissolution. There are, of course, huge gaps in the evidence but, overall, we are fortunate to have access to a great body of primary source material. By contrast, little documentary evidence survives relating to the history of Malmesbury before the monastery. People have long speculated about human habitation in prehistoric Malmesbury, and Leland claimed that there had been an ancient 'castelle' or fortress on the site before the arrival of the monks.[2] He derived his information from the chronicle, *Eulogium Historiarum*, written in the 1360s by a Malmesbury monk called Thomas of Bromham, who stated precisely, but without any supporting evidence, that a fort had been built in 642 BC by a British king called Dunwallo Molmuncius. In the terminology of modern archaeology, Leland and Bromham were promoting the idea that there was an Iron Age hillfort on the site of the future monastery. Bromham claimed that the structure was still, in some measure, intact over a thousand years later and was not destroyed until the time of a barbarian king called Gurmundus who lived in the sixth century AD.[3]

In fact, Bromham's account was almost certainly a work of fiction, inspired by his reading the *Historia Regum Britanniae* of Geoffrey of Monmouth, where he encountered tales of characters called Dunwallo and Gurmundus. Monmouth's *Historia* said nothing about the involvement of these figures in the early history of Malmesbury, and Bromham, it seems, simply invented his account of the foundation of the place. None of the specific details of the prehistory of Malmesbury, as recounted by the author of the *Eulogium Historiarum*, can be trusted, and until recently there was little archaeological evidence that could be used to supplement his highly unreliable account. The situation changed dramatically following two archaeological excavations which were carried out near the medieval East Gate of the town in 1998–2000 and 2005–6.[4] Both investigations

[2] John Leland, *The Itinerary of John Leland* I (London, 1907), 131.
[3] *Eulogium* III CVIII (ed. Haydon 61).
[4] T. Longman, 'Iron Age and Later Defences at Malmesbury: Excavations

Prologue: Before the monastery

showed that people using worked flints were present on the promontory in the late Neolithic or Bronze Age, and that a major hillfort was built on the site during the early Iron Age. The fort was encircled by substantial ramparts, and by the middle Iron Age, a second set of ramparts had been added making the place a formidable defensive structure.

The archaeology revealed that the main development of the defences of the hillfort took place c. 700–400 BC; what happened next is not clear, but it seems highly likely that there was some occupation of the site during the Roman centuries. In 1887 it was recorded that a Roman hypocaust system had been discovered and removed from a site in the 'abbey grounds'.[5] More recently Roman pottery was found residually in later medieval strata during the East Gate excavations and in other archaeological investigations in the Malmesbury area. In 2001 a Roman villa was discovered just a mile to the north-east of Malmesbury.[6] This stone-built house, equipped with hypocausts and mosaic pavements, was constructed in the third or fourth century. Aerial photography indicated the existence of a track that went from the villa in the direction of Malmesbury, suggesting that there was some sort of settlement within the hillfort site.

The excavations of 1998–2000 and 2005–6 provided no firm evidence of any attempts to reoccupy the hillfort in the unsettled times after the departure of the Roman legions. However, reoccupation is entirely possible since the archaeological evidence base remains extremely limited. In the sixth or early seventh century, the West Saxons took control of the Malmesbury area and displaced the previous British rulers. There is some debate about how and when this happened. One apparently fixed point is the entry in the Anglo-Saxon Chronicle relating to the Battle of *Dyrham* in 577, which describes how two West Saxon rulers defeated the Britons near Bath and took control of the former Roman settlements in the area.

> 577. Here Cuthwine and Ceawlin fought against the Britons and they killed three kings, Coinmagil and Candidan and Farinmagil, in the place which is called Dyrham; and took three cities: Gloucester and Cirencester and Bath.[7]

The traditional interpretation of this entry is that the victory at *Dyrham* allowed the West Saxons to subjugate the British people in these territories and since Malmesbury is situated between Bath and Cirencester,

---

1998–2000', *WANHM*, 99 (2006): 104–64. M. Collard and T. Harvard, 'The Prehistoric and Medieval Defences of Malmesbury: Archaeological Investigations at Holloway, 2005–2006', *WANHM*, 104 (2011): 79–94.

5   G. Esdaile, 'On the Roman Occupation of Britain', *Archaeological Journal*, 44 (1887): 53.

6   J. Hart et al., 'A New Roman Villa near Malmesbury', *WANHM*, 98 (2005): 297–306.

7   ASC s.a. 577 (ed. Swanton 19).

Malmesbury Abbey 670–1539

the Chronicle account is consistent with the idea of the Saxon takeover of north-west Wiltshire at this time. While modern scholars have urged caution regarding the battle and its significance, some archaeological evidence has come to light indicating that by around 600 West Saxon kings were indeed in control of the Malmesbury area.[8] In 1975 aerial photographs revealed extensive crop marks near Cowage Farm, two miles outside Malmesbury; an excavation followed in 1983, which showed that the site was once dominated by a group of substantial timber buildings, built with great care and with foundations dug deep into the limestone.[9] The site was officially designated as an archaeological site of national importance, and archaeologists now believe that the Cowage Farm complex constitutes a significant example of a regal 'great hall complex': a settlement type that was established by emergent Anglo-Saxon ruling dynasties in the late sixth and early seventh centuries. At the heart of the site was a large timber hall, probably intended to provide a setting for assemblies hosted by the peripatetic West Saxon royalty. The hall was surrounded by several other buildings and fenced enclosures, carefully laid out on a grid plan, and the place was occupied for an extremely long time stretching from before and after the conversion of the West Saxons to Christianity in the mid-seventh century. Later additions to the buildings included a small apsidal church, which can be seen clearly in the crop mark photographs. Two samples of carbonised timber were recovered and subjected to carbon dating, which produced dates in the ranges of 560–670 and 680–900. These dates are consistent with the view that the place was occupied in both the pagan and Christian periods.[10]

It is possible to reconstruct a likely sequence of events at Cowage Farm, which began as a pagan-era royal site in the earliest days of Saxon control of north Wiltshire. It was initially a place of grand royal assembly; here the kings of the West Saxons received food renders from their subjects and feasted with their warriors in the great hall. It seems likely that in the late seventh century the hall and the associated buildings were granted to Aldhelm as part of a substantial royal endowment of land that he received for his monastic community. The place was transformed into a monastic grange, an agricultural centre for the estate of the new monastery, and the rediscovered 'crop mark' church was built to indicate its affiliation with the nearby religious community.

---

[8]   See Patrick Sims-Williams, 'The Settlement of England in Bede and the Chronicle', *Anglo-Saxon England*, 12 (1983): 1–41.

[9]   John Hinchliffe, 'An Early Medieval Settlement at Cowage Farm, Foxley, near Malmesbury', *Archaeological Journal*, 143 (1986): 240–59.

[10]   A. Bayliss et al., *Radio Carbon Dates from Samples funded by English Heritage* (Swindon, 2013), 127.

1

From Máeldub to Aldhelm

The story of the earliest days of the monastery at Malmesbury is obscure. The most important figure in the history of the monastic community of Malmesbury was St Aldhelm, who died 709–10 and was recognised during his own lifetime as a scholar and ecclesiastic of national significance. The later tradition of the house held that Aldhelm was not the first abbot, and instead an Irish holy man called Máeldub was revered as the founder of the community. Over four hundred years after Aldhelm's death, William of Malmesbury set out to explain how the monastery of Malmesbury was established by this Irish missionary.

> It had been founded by one Meldum, also called Meildulf, an Irishman, a learned philosopher and professed monk, who went there in voluntary exile from his homeland, and, captivated by the agreeable woodland which at that period flourished exceedingly there, he began to practise the life of a hermit. When he ran short of what he needed to live, he took on boys as pupils, so that their generosity might make good the slenderness of his means. As time went on they followed in their master's footsteps by becoming monks instead of students, and came to form a sizeable convent.[1]

According to William, it was this pre-existing community that Aldhelm joined and ultimately came to lead. It has been suggested that William may have invented some of the detail of his account of the career of Meldum.[2] If the Irishman had indeed been the teacher of Aldhelm one might expect a reference to him in the extensive surviving works of Aldhelm; but there is none. Although understandable doubts have been raised about the Meldum/Máeldub story, there is evidence to suggest that a religious community at Malmesbury was founded by an Irish monk with a name similar to this and that he may well have been Aldhelm's earliest teacher. One early reference to a version of the placename, 'Malmesbury', comes from Bede's *Historia Ecclesiastica*, in which he described Aldhelm

---

1 William of Malmesbury's *Gesta Pontificum* is a key source for the early history of the community and will be referenced many times in the early chapters of this study. Written in around 1125 the fifth and final book of the *Gesta Pontificum* is, in effect, a history of Malmesbury from the time of Aldhelm to William's own time. For the story of Meldum/Máeldub, see *GP I* V.189.2–3. (ed. Winterbottom 503–5).
2 Michael Lapidge, *Máeldub*, ODNB (2004).

as the abbot of a monastery called *Maildubi Urbs*, which means literally 'the city of Maildub'.[3] The name 'Maildub' appears to be a rendering of an authentic Old Irish personal name, Máeldub.[4] Bede was a careful historian and although he was based in Northumbria, he took steps to make sure that his information about the history of the faraway West Saxons was correct. His key source for information about Wessex was Bishop Daniel of Winchester, whose contribution was acknowledged in the introduction to the *Historia*.

> [...] the most reverend Bishop Daniel of the West Saxons, who is still alive, sent to me in writing certain facts about the history of the Church in his province [...][5]

It is highly likely, therefore, that Daniel called Aldhelm's monastery *Maildubi Urbs* and used this term when writing to Bede. Since Daniel had been a monk of Malmesbury and disciple of Aldhelm before he became a bishop in 705 or 706, it seems inconceivable that Daniel would have used a term different to that employed by Aldhelm when describing the place where they had lived together.[6] On this basis, there is a strong case for thinking that Aldhelm called his own community *Urbs Maildubi* or 'the city of Maildub', thereby acknowledging the name of the founder of the community. Early charter evidence is consistent with this theory: a diploma with fundamentally authentic elements was issued to Aldhelm in 685, and it described his community as 'the monastery called *Maeldubesburg*'.[7] This is a formulation similar to Bede's; *Maeldubes Burg* looks like an Old English version of *Maildubi Urbs* and its inclusion in this charter suggests that it was a name that Aldhelm used and approved.

Another early source indicates that Malmesbury monks in the years immediately after the death of Aldhelm called their community by a term comparable to that used by Bede. In a ninth-century codex that survives in Vienna there is a copy of a letter sent from an anonymous monk of Malmesbury in the mid-eighth century to Lullus, missionary to the German people and associate of St Boniface. The author of the letter and Lullus had both been at Malmesbury around 730, and Lullus was asked to remember the happy time they had spent together in *Maldubia Civitatis*.[8] 'Civitas', like 'urbs', is a Latin word for 'city'. The Vienna codex term

---

3   *HE* V.18 (ed. Colgrave & Mynors 513–17).
4   Lapidge, *Máeldub*.
5   *HE* Preface (ed. Colgrave & Mynors 5).
6   The date traditionally given for Aldhelm's elevation to the episcopate is 705. Michael Lapidge considered that the correct date was possibly 706. See Aldhelm, *Prose Works*, 10.
7   Kelly, *Charters*, 139.
8   *Die Briefe des Heiligen Bonifatius und Lullus*, ed. Michael Tangl (Munich, 1989), 273–4.

Maldubia Civitatis, Bede's *Maildubi Urbs* and the Old English placename *Maeldubes Burg* used in the 685 charter can all be seen as versions of the same name for the monastery: it was known as 'the city of Máeldub'. Why would this be the commonly and consistently recognised term for the monastery unless Máeldub had a particular significance to Aldhelm and his disciples as the name of the founder? Of course, Aldhelm's Malmesbury was not a city, it was a *monasterium*; but the convention of describing a large monastic community as a 'city' was common in Ireland from the seventh century onwards and the use of this word is also suggestive of Irish influence and presence.[9]

Máeldub as *peregrinus*

The arrival of Máeldub in the Malmesbury area in the mid-seventh century is consistent with contemporary trends in Irish spirituality and missionary endeavour. From the sixth century onwards the tradition of *peregrinatio*, or spiritually motivated travel overseas, became an established part of Irish religious tradition. *Peregrinatio* inspired, for example, Columbanus, who left Ireland with several companions and founded monasteries across Francia and northern Italy. The letters of Columbanus, written in the early seventh century, express the view that the renunciation of one's native land was a noble act and a means of finding God.[10] Columbanus was the greatest of the Irish *peregrini* but there were several others, such as Columba of Iona and Aidan, the apostle to the Northumbrians. Perhaps the closest parallel with the career of Máeldub is provided by the more modest story of the Irish monk, Fursey, and the way he established a monastery in East Anglia during the 630s before moving on to Francia. Bede recounted how Fursey left his Irish homeland with some companions and eventually arrived in the land of the East Angles. Here Fursey was required to win the endorsement of Sigberct, the East Anglian king, before founding a monastic community in his realm.[11] It seems entirely possible that, just as Fursey's journey took him to East Anglia, where he established a monastery, Máeldub's *peregrinatio* resulted in his arrival among the West Saxons and the foundation of a religious community at Malmesbury. If one assumes that Máeldub did exist, he arrived in Malmesbury at a time when the West Saxons were still in the

---

9   See for example, the *Vita Sanctae Brigitae*, written by an Irish monk called Cogitosus in the years 650–75 in which the monastery at Kildare was called a 'monastic city'. See Cogitosus, 'Cogitosus's Life of St Brigit', ed. Sean Connolly, Sean and Picard, J.-M., *The Journal of the Royal Society of Antiquaries of Ireland*, 117 (1987): 5–27.

10 E. Johnston, 'Exiles from the Edge? The Irish Contexts of Peregrinatio', in *The Irish in Early Medieval Europe* (London, 2016), 38–52.

11 *HE* III.19 (ed. Colgrave & Mynors 269–77).

early stages of conversion to Christianity. According to the much later *Eulogium Historiarum*, Máeldub founded the monastery in 637.[12] There is no reason at all to take this specific date seriously, but it is possible that both Irish and Roman missionaries were more or less simultaneously attempting to convert the West Saxons. Bede told how, in 635, Birinus, a missionary sent from Italy with the endorsement of the papacy, baptised Cynegils, the king of the West Saxons at Dorchester-on-Thames.[13]

Aldhelm's family and education

Aldhelm transformed the city of Máeldub, making Malmesbury a major centre of learning. It seems highly likely that in the late 670s, at precisely the same time when Aldhelm was establishing Malmesbury's reputation for scholarship and spirituality, his own father was king of the West Saxons. We know little about the circumstances of Aldhelm's birth; it is sometimes said that he was born around 640 but this is purely conjectural and is based simply on William of Malmesbury's guess that the saint was about seventy years old when he died.[14] There is now a scholarly consensus that Aldhelm was a member of the royal house of the West Saxons. William of Malmesbury is the key source for understanding Aldhelm's genealogy, and in this context it is necessary to consider carefully William's statement that, according to the 'Handbook' of Alfred the Great, the father of Aldhelm was one 'Kenten' who was 'closely related' to King Ine.[15] Unfortunately, the Handbook is no longer extant, but there is little doubt that it did exist and was a reliable source. 'Kenten' is not known as an Old English name, but it could easily be a corruption of 'Centwine', and one King Centwine was undoubtedly a close relative of Ine. Centwine ruled as king of the West Saxons from around 676 to around 685, when he abdicated and became a monk. Rodney Thomson concluded that Centwine 'must surely have a good claim to be considered as Aldhelm's parent'.[16] The name of Aldhelm's mother is not known; however, we do know from Eddius Stephanus, biographer of St Wilfrid, that Centwine was married during the early 680s to a sister of Queen Eorminburg, wife of King Ecgfrith of Northumbria.[17] This unnamed

---

[12] *Eulogium* 'Chronicon Brevius' (ed. Haydon III 279).

[13] *HE* III.7 (ed. Colgrave & Mynors 233–7).

[14] *GP* I V 189.3 (ed. Winterbottom 503–5).

[15] Rodney Thomson has tracked the way that William altered his opinion about Aldhelm's family, moving from an originally sceptical position to a positive view of the genetic link between Aldhelm and the royal family. See *GP II*, 247–9.

[16] In 2007, the same year that Thomson published his views, Michael Lapidge came to a similar conclusion, arguing that Aldhelm was by birth a prince and the son of Centwine. See Lapidge, 'Career', 17–18.

[17] *Vita S. Wilfridi*, c. 40 (ed. B. Colgrave, *The Life of Bishop Wilfrid by Eddius*

From Máeldub to Aldhelm

queen of the West Saxons was, therefore, either Aldhelm's mother or his stepmother.[18] Aldhelm's childhood was a time of transition for the West Saxon people as they moved, somewhat erratically, from paganism to Christianity. The West Saxon royalty first embraced Christianity in 635 when King Cynegils was baptised, and the Northumbrian ruler, King Oswald, was present, acting as godfather.[19] Cynegils was succeeded by his son, Cenwalh who remained unbaptised for several years. When Cædwalla became king around 685, he was, at least technically, still a pagan since he was not baptised until shortly before his death in Rome in 689.

As a prince of the royal house of Wessex, Aldhelm doubtless had easy access to the resources needed to fund a prolonged and expensive education. There were two distinct phases to Aldhelm's educational journey: an initial 'Irish' period followed by a 'Mediterranean' stage. We know for sure that the 'Mediterranean' education took place in Canterbury in the early 670s, where Aldhelm has access to teaching that was similar to that provided in the best contemporary schools of Rome and Constantinople, but the earlier 'Irish' phase is much more of a mystery. There is a good chance that he was a student of the Irish *peregrinus*, Máeldub, and some evidence for this theory is provided by an authentic letter from an anonymous Irish student who wrote to Aldhelm, asking to be taken on as a student and saying that Aldhelm had been 'nourished by a certain holy man of our race'.[20] It is also possible that Aldhelm spent time in the mid-660s undertaking higher study in an Irish context beyond the city of Máeldub. The evidence for this comes from Aldhelm's great composite work known as the *Epistola ad Acircium*, which was dedicated to one *Acircius*, a playful nickname Aldhelm gave to his friend, Aldfrith, king of Northumbria (685–705).[21] According to Bede, Aldfrith spent many years 'pursuing his studies in the regions of the Irish, suffering a self-imposed exile to gratify his love of wisdom'.[22] In around 686 Aldhelm sent a literary gift to Aldfrith in the form of the *Epistola ad Acircium*, and in the introduction he explained, in a somewhat convoluted way, that about twenty years earlier – that is to say around 666 – a bishop had provided the sacrament of confirmation to Aldfrith in Aldhelm's

---

    Stephanus (Cambridge, 1927), 80.

18 According to Bede, Eorminburg had another sister who was the abbess of Carlisle and a friend of St Cuthbert. See *HE* IV.26 (ed. Colgrave & Mynors 429–30).

19 *HE* III.7 (ed. Colgrave & Mynors 233–5).

20 Aldhelm, *Prose Works*, 146.

21 As Thomson has pointed out, William of Malmesbury cleverly identified Acircius as Aldfrith. See *GP II* 256.

22 *HE* V.18 (ed. Colgrave and Mynors 514–15).

Malmesbury Abbey 670–1539

presence.[23] Aldhelm took part in the ceremony and became some sort of spiritual sponsor to Aldfrith.

Since Aldhelm knew Aldfrith as a young man, and Aldfrith studied with Irish masters, it seems likely that Aldhelm encountered Aldfrith when they were both studying in an Irish monastic and academic setting. This has led to some speculation as to precisely where the two men might have been students together, and both Bangor in the north of Ireland and Iona have been proposed as likely locations.[24] It would not be at all surprising if Aldhelm had indeed travelled to a major Irish monastery for the purpose of study before he received instruction in Canterbury because there was a considerable traffic of English students to Ireland in the late seventh century.[25] We know that Heahfrith, one of Aldhelm's own students at Malmesbury, had previously spent substantial time in Ireland. A letter survives from Aldhelm to Heahfrith who was just beginning advanced studies at Malmesbury, having previously studied 'in the north-west part of the island of Ireland'. In this letter Aldhelm mentioned how 'thronging students by the fleet-load' could be seen travelling from England to Ireland.[26] There has been some debate about the influence of Aldhelm's Irish education on his mature work as a writer of Latin prose and verse. Michael Winterbottom demonstrated that Aldhelm's prose style owed little to Irish literary models; for example, Aldhelm's long, complex rhythmical sentences in his prose treatise on virginity were different from the Irish texts that he may have encountered and point rather to the influence of the Mediterranean phase of his education.[27] While his prose was dissimilar that of Irish authors, Andy Orchard has argued that aspects of Aldhelm's poetry do reflect Irish influences.[28] Much of his poetry was in hexameters, but on occasion he used an octosyllabic verse-form with frequent rhyme and alliteration that can be traced back to Irish exemplars.

The arrival of Theodore of Tarsus as archbishop of Canterbury in England in 669 was an event of huge significance in the life of Aldhelm,

---

23 Aldhelm, *Prose Works*, 34.
24 For Iona, see Lapidge, 'Career', 22–7. For Bangor, see Ireland, Colin A., 'Where was King Aldfrith of Northumbria Educated? An Exploration of Seventh-Century Insular Learning', *Traditio*, 70 (2015): 29–73.
25 Bede described how several Anglo-Saxon clerics went to Ireland for spiritual and academic reasons. Willibrord, who became a missionary to the Frisians in the 690s had lived for some time in Ireland. See *HE* III.13 (ed. Colgrave & Mynors 253). A whole community of English monks was established at Mayo, see *HE* IV.4 (ed. Colgrave & Mynors 346–8).
26 Aldhelm, *Prose Works*, 161.
27 Michael Winterbottom, 'Aldhelm's Prose Style and its Origins', *Anglo-Saxon England*, 6 (1977): 39–76. Reprinted in Michael Winterbottom, *Style and Scholarship: Latin Prose from Gildas to Raffaele Regio* (Florence, 2020).
28 Orchard, *Poetic Art*, 19–72.

From Máeldub to Aldhelm

and in 670 Theodore was joined by his friend and close associate, Hadrian, who became abbot of the monastery of St Peter and St Paul (later known as St Augustine's) in Canterbury. Theodore and Hadrian established a school of advanced study, and word soon spread across the English Church about the remarkable quality of their teaching.[29] Bede described how the instruction of Theodore and Hadrian at Canterbury soon 'attracted a crowd of students into whose minds they poured the streams of wholesome learning', and one of the students who made his way to Canterbury was Aldhelm. Theodore was extraordinarily learned and had access to an exceptional range of Latin and Greek texts and, as a result, Aldhelm had the immense good fortune to study with a master whose teaching constituted 'the apogee of biblical scholarship in the Latin west between late antiquity and the twelfth century'.[30] Unsurprisingly, Aldhelm was extremely enthusiastic about his experience at Canterbury and while there he wrote a letter to a bishop, probably Leuthere bishop of the West Saxons, extolling the virtues of the Canterbury curriculum. Quoting St Jerome, he suggested that his previous education, which was of course Irish, now appeared to him to be almost worthless, and he wrote that he was beginning to learn properly for the first time.

> [...] I began to disparage all my earlier laborious studies, whose secrets I had imagined I had long since mastered; and (to take this opportunity of using an epigram of St Jerome): *I who previously thought myself to have a smattering of knowledge now started to be a pupil all over again.*[31]

Aldhelm's letter to Leuthere was an apology for his absence from Wessex at Christmas and his excuse for missing the celebrations (presumably in Malmesbury) was that he was too busy with his studies in Canterbury.

> I confess, most blessed bishop, that I long ago resolved, if the vicissitudes of the fleeting years allowed, to have the joy of celebrating the next Christmas season there in the society of my brethren, and afterwards, if I lived, to enjoy your Charity's company. But because we could not do this, held up as we were by various impediments, which the bearer of this letter will announce in person, I must beg you to forgive me amid my problems.[32]

29 *HE* IV.2 (ed. Colgrave & Mynors 333–7).
30 Michael Lapidge, *Aldhelm*, ODNB (2004).
31 *GP* I V 195.6 (ed. Winterbottom 517).
32 *GP* I V 195.2–3 (ed. Winterbottom 515).

Aldhelm's rejection of Irish culture and Church traditions

After his Canterbury education Aldhelm positioned himself unequivocally with those who argued that contemporary religious practices promoted by the papacy were superior to those prevalent in Ireland. He concluded that the Roman traditions represented a purer form of Christianity, and this enables us to understand why Aldhelm made no reference in his extant writings to his first teacher, Máeldub: Aldhelm wanted to be known as an adherent of Roman ways and sought to distance himself from any Irish connections. A combination of factors led Aldhelm to have doubts about the practices of Irish Christianity and the quality of Irish scholarship. At about the time of his 'Irish' education the English Church was aligning itself decisively with Rome, and the Irish method for the calculation of Easter was rejected at the Synod of Whitby in 664. The great protagonist of the 'Roman' case at Whitby was Wilfrid, who later became Aldhelm's friend. After studying in Canterbury Aldhelm concluded that Wilfrid was right: the Roman ways were closer to the pristine practices of the early Church, and the education provided by Roman teachers was greatly superior to that on offer in Irish monastic schools. Aldhelm made clear his view of the relative inferiority of Irish scholarship in his letter to his student, Heahfrith: there was no longer any reason for English students to seek out an Irish education because a superior Mediterranean curriculum was on offer from Theodore and Hadrian.

> Here in the fertile soils of Britain, teachers who are citizens of Greece and Rome [...] are able to unlock and unravel the murky mysteries of the heavenly library to the scholars who are eager to study them.[33]

Aldhelm also wrote to a former Malmesbury student, Wihtfrith, who was just about to go to study in Ireland: once again the tone of the letter was extremely negative about Irish scholarship. He criticised the Irish curriculum for placing too much emphasis on the study of pagan literature, which was often obscene, rather than on consideration of the Christian scriptures. Highlighting the moral dangers of life in Ireland, Aldhelm alleged that students there sometimes succumbed to the temptations of Irish prostitutes 'decked out with gleaming gold anklets and delicate bracelets, like chariot horses in their proud trappings'.[34]

In his rejection of Irish religious and cultural traditions, Aldhelm was probably influenced by another factor: his sense of his Germanic ethnicity. He took manifest pride in the way he had personally contributed to the flourishing of a new Latin-based intellectual culture among the Saxon people and concluded his treatises on poetic metre with a boast that he

---

[33] Aldhelm, *Prose Works*, 163.
[34] *GP I* V 214.4. (ed. Winterbottom 541–3).

From Máeldub to Aldhelm

was the first 'Germanic' person to set down the principles of quantitative verse composition.

> [...] no one born of the offspring of our race and nourished in the cradles of a Germanic people has toiled so mightily in a pursuit of this before our humble self and has committed to the structure of letters the statements of earlier minds regarding the discipline of the metrical art [...][35]

Given his own literary achievements, Aldhelm felt no need to be in awe of Irish culture. Pride in his own level of accomplishment – and antagonism towards the Irish – is evident in a fragment of correspondence that survives between Aldhelm and an Irish monk called Cellanus who was living at the monastery of Peronne in Francia. Cellanus had written to Aldhelm complimenting him on his literary style, and it seems likely that Aldhelm felt patronised by the Irishman's praise for the surprising achievements of a Saxon working in the remote setting of Malmesbury.

> To my lord rich in literary studies, and distinguished for little effusions that flow with honey, Aldhelm the abbot, who marvellously enough finds on Saxon shores a treasure which some can scarce win by sweat and toil under foreign skies [...] As though by winged flight there has come to the ears of our poverty the encomiastic report of your mastery of Latin [...][36]

Aldhelm's annoyed, ironic response verged on sarcasm.

> I am surprised that from the famous and flower-laden countryside of the Franks my wise brother should take the trouble to address me, a midget of so little worth, born of Saxon stock, and nurtured in the soft cradles of infancy beneath the Pole Star.[37]

The patronage of the West Saxons

In Aldhelm's collection of verse church dedications, known today as *Carmina Ecclesiastica*, there is a poem written to celebrate a new monastic church ruled over by a woman who was perhaps his sister or half-sister, Abbess Bugga or Osburga.[38] This poem is, in part, a song of praise of Aldhelm's family, the rulers of the West Saxons. Aldhelm extolled the virtues of three successive kings of Wessex, whose reigns coincided with his abbacy in Malmesbury: Centwine, Cædwalla and Ine. These kings

35 Aldhelm, *Prose Works*, 45.
36 *GP I* V 191.2–4 (ed. Winterbottom 509–11).
37 *GP I* 188.4 (ed. Winterbottom 503).
38 Aldhelm, *Poetic Works*, 47–9.

ruled wisely and deserved respect for their victories in just wars waged against the Britons. Centwine was praised for his success in three major military campaigns, while Cædwalla was 'renowned in war and arms [...] a powerful occupant of the throne and its rightful heir'. Ine took up 'the noble sceptre' and was acclaimed by 'all peoples'.[39] Unsurprisingly, Aldhelm made no reference to the more brutal aspects of the rule of his relatives, such as the genocide of the people of the Isle of Wight by Cædwalla in 686, which was recorded by Bede using information provided by Aldhelm's disciple, Daniel.[40]

In his description of Centwine's abdication and retirement, Aldhelm explained how the king made generous gifts of land to new monasteries. Although specific beneficiaries are not named, it would be strange if the community at Malmesbury had not benefitted from the royal largesse of his own father.

> Centwine formerly wielded justly the government of the [West] Saxons, until, rejecting the summits of this temporal realm, he abandoned his worldly wealth and the reins of power by granting many estates to recently established churches in which Christian worshippers now keep their monastic vows [...] he ruled his kingdom happily for several years until, having been converted, he retired to a holy [monastic] cell.[41]

It is possible that Aldhelm's father, Centwine, after retiring, came to spend his final years with his son at Malmesbury, and it is highly likely that the Malmesbury community was a beneficiary of his patronage and that of his successors, Cædwalla and Ine. The Abbey's medieval cartulary contained charters that were supposedly issued in favour of the monastery during Aldhelm's lifetime. Some of these documents are of questionable authenticity, but one diploma of Ine, dated to 701, has been assessed as being 'fundamentally authentic'.[42] Archaeological evidence relating to Aldhelm's endowment has also recently come to light. As we saw in the Prologue, the Cowage Farm complex at Foxley near Malmesbury began as a Saxon pagan royal site, and it was subsequently transformed into an early Christian period site with ecclesiastical features and probable agricultural functions.[43] The cropmark evidence indicates that at some point a church

---

[39] Aldhelm, *Poetic Works*, 48.
[40] *HE* IV.16. (ed. Colgrave & Mynors 383–5).
[41] Aldhelm, *Poetic Works*, 48.
[42] See Kelly, *Charters*, 151. For evidence that Centwine may have given land to Malmesbury see Kelly, *Charters*, 145.
[43] For a discussion of the significance of Cowage Farm, see J. Blair, *The Church in Anglo-Saxon Society* (Oxford, 2005), 213–14 and J. Blair, *Building Anglo-Saxon England* (Oxford, 2018), 120–31. In *The Church in Anglo-Saxon Society*, Blair suggests a possible relationship between the 'crop mark' church and a nearby extant medieval church. The two churches together perhaps formed a 'bi-polar axial arrangement encapsulating the settlement'.

was added to the complex, located within a rectangular enclosure and built on an east-west axis with an apsidal projection at the east end, which presumably housed the altar. John Blair saw the changing function of Cowage Farm as an instance of a broader trend towards the 'monasticisation' of previously secular royal sites.[44] It seems likely that West Saxon royalty, including perhaps Aldhelm's father, granted the Cowage Farm complex to his fledgling monastery.

The Mercian connection

Although by birth a prince of the house of Wessex, and a man who was successful in winning West Saxon patronage, Aldhelm also made determined efforts to ensure support from the rulers of Mercia. This was an astute move because, located as it was in the extreme north of Wessex, Aldhelm's community in Malmesbury was vulnerable to Mercian aggression. Two very early Mercian land grants to Aldhelm survive, both containing authentic elements, and both issued in the presence of Theodore, archbishop of Canterbury and Aldhelm's former teacher.[45] One of these charters, dating from 680 or 681, was issued by the powerful Mercian king, Æthelred of Mercia, and granted Aldhelm and his community land near Tetbury on the Mercian side of the border.

> [...] I Æthelred, king of the Mercians, at the request of my patrician and relative, Cenfrith, and for the prayers of the brothers who serve God at *Meldubesberg,* have gladly granted to Abbot Aldhelm fifteen hides next to the monastery of *Tette.* If anyone wishes to increase and multiply this gift may God increase his part in the book of life.[46]

Æthelred's grant contains an intriguing reference to the presence nearby of another monastery, ruled over apparently by a woman. The estate gifted to Aldhelm was located near 'the monastery of *Tette',* and while nothing else is known of this institution *Tette* is undoubtedly an Old English female personal name. The obvious explanation is that a double monastery, founded by one Abbess Tette, was operating just five miles away from Aldhelm's male community.

A second charter, dated 685, was granted in the 680s by a Mercian sub-king called Berhtwald, with the endorsement of his overlord, King Æthelred, and this gave Aldhelm's community land at Somerford Keynes in modern Gloucestershire.

> [...] I, Berhtwald, king under the Lord, for the salvation of my soul and for the forgiveness of the crimes I have committed, have decided

---

44 Blair, *Building,* 131–5.
45 The two 'Mercian' charters are discussed in Kelly, *Charters,* 134–41.
46 Kelly, *Charters,* 134.

Malmesbury Abbey 670–1539

to confer and bestow on Abbot Aldhelm land to the east of the River Thames, near the ford called Somerford, fourteen hides: with the provision that that this portion of land should be free for all time of the servitude of lay powers, to supply the needs of the monks who serve God in the monastery called Maeldubesburg.[47]

The charter concluded with a deferential reference to the authority of Æthelred and a pronouncement of anathema against any who questioned or challenged the grant.

> And to confirm this gift for ever the more firmly and surely, I have summoned King Æthelred also, that excellent monarch, to be witness, for it is by his consent and confirmation that this act of liberality has been carried out. But if anyone should try to oppose this gift, or rely on a tyrant's power to assault it, let him know that he will answer for it before Christ at the terrible judgement of all men.[48]

The gift of Somerford Keynes suggests that Aldhelm's benefactor, the sub-king Berhtwald, had some sort of control on behalf of his overlord over those parts of Gloucestershire immediately to the north of Malmesbury.

It was economically and politically beneficial for Aldhelm to cultivate the favour of Æthelred of Mercia and his subordinates such as Berhtwald. Not only did he gain valuable resources by winning support from the powerful Mercian king, Aldhelm also reduced the danger of armed attack on the monastery and its lands. At the beginning of his reign Æthelred demonstrated that he was capable of highly aggressive behaviour towards Church institutions in the lands of those he considered his enemies. Bede outlined how he had attacked churches and monasteries in Rochester in 676, just a few years before the grant to Aldhelm.[49] Aldhelm, who had been a student in Canterbury just a couple of years earlier, knew Kent well and would have heard the shocking news from Rochester.

Can it be a coincidence that on two occasions Archbishop Theodore was present when Aldhelm received generous gifts of land from Æthelred of Mercia and his followers? Is it possible that Theodore played an active part in a campaign to persuade the Mercian king to endow Aldhelm's community? As we have seen Aldhelm had been a student of Theodore's in Canterbury during the previous decade, and greatly admired the archbishop. In a letter to a friend, Aldhelm described Theodore, in the most fulsome terms, as a man who should be likened to 'the flaming

---

47 *GP* I V 204.2 (ed. Winterbottom 531). See also Kelly, *Charters*, 138–41. William used the placename *Maldumesburg*. Having consulted a range of manuscript witnesses Kelly preferred the reading *Maeldubesburg*. This is the charter mentioned above as evidence for the use of the early placename *Maeldubes Burg*.

48 *GP* I V 204.2 (ed. Winterbottom 531).

49 *HE* IV.12 (ed. Colgrave & Mynors 369).

From Máeldub to Aldhelm

sun and moon', when compared with other teachers who were mere 'twinkling stars'.[50] Theodore, doubtless, saw Aldhelm as one of his most talented and influential protégés, and we know that he was keen to build bridges between the independent and combative Anglo-Saxon kingdoms. In 679 Theodore brokered a peace deal between Mercia and Northumbria.[51] Bede praised Theodore, recounting how he 'smothered the flames' of bitter conflict with 'his wholesome advice'.[52] It is possible, therefore, that Theodore endorsed Aldhelm's vision for a jointly endowed religious community at Malmesbury as a way of both cementing peace between Mercia and Wessex and protecting the border monastery.

West Saxon and Mercian endorsement of the 'privilege' of Pope Sergius

There is little doubt that Aldhelm visited Rome during his time as abbot of Malmesbury.[53] Michael Lapidge has suggested that Aldhelm probably travelled as part of the entourage of King Cædwalla who, following his abdication, went to Rome in 688.[54] In a surviving poem Aldhelm provided a graphic account of Cædwalla's journey, perhaps based on his eyewitness perspective as the king's travelling companion.

> [...] he [Cædwalla] furrowed the swelling waters with the curved keel [of his boat] and traversed the briny expanses of the sea by oar. The frozen sails crackled in the windy blasts until the ship touched the shore with its untried prow; thereafter he crossed on foot the stormy Alps, closed in by massy glaciers and mountain peaks.[55]

As we shall see, after the Conquest the Malmesbury monks of Malmesbury claimed institutional exemption from episcopal control based on a tradition that when in Rome, Aldhelm had obtained a charter or 'privilege' from Pope Sergius I. Later medieval versions of this document are still extant, and there are grounds for thinking that these contain fundamentally authentic elements.[56] Writing in the 1090s Faricius, then a Malmesbury

---

50 Aldhelm, *Prose Works*, 163.
51 *HE* IV.21 (ed. Colgrave & Mynors 401).
52 Ibid.
53 An authentic letter to Aldhelm from an Irish student states that Aldhelm was known to have visited Rome, see Aldhelm, *Prose Works*, 146. Aldhelm appears to have brought back from Rome a mid-seventh-century guidebook to the main pilgrimage sites in Rome which was preserved at Malmesbury and incorporated by William of Malmesbury in his *Gesta Regum*. See *GR* I IV 352.1–13 (ed. Mynors, Thomson & Winterbottom 615–21).
54 Lapidge, 'Career', 15.
55 Aldhelm, *Poetic Works*, 48.
56 For a summary of the debate about the authenticity of the grant of Sergius, see Kelly, *Charters*, 7. Circumstantial evidence is consistent with the granting

Malmesbury Abbey 670–1539

monk, described how Aldhelm sought ratification of the papal charter from both the West Saxon and the Mercian authorities.

> The holy man brought this charter of liberty back to the monasteries specified above, and showed it to two kings currently ruling in England, his uncle Ine king of the Saxons, and Æthelred king of the Mercians. These men, very active kings full of zeal for God, gave them their authoritative approval, for they knew that the pope had afforded them his incorruptible sanction. And they decreed that, whatever kind of foray or war disturbed their borders, the places belonging to the holy and knowledgeable Aldhelm should be free from all service; and they left [instructions], in documents written in their own hand, for the same policy to be continued there by their successors.[57]

Faricius, and his younger contemporary William of Malmesbury had access to a document in the monastery archive, which purported to be the 'privilege' issued by Sergius. This was, of course, written in Latin, but the earliest surviving version of the text is an Old English translation, dating from around 1050, which survives in a manuscript held by the British Library.[58] The Old English 'privilege' contains a postscript stating that Aldhelm sought endorsement of the autonomous status of the monastery at Malmesbury from both the Mercian and West Saxon kings.

> I, Aldhelm, brought to Ine the King of the West Saxons and to Æthelræd the King of the Mercians these *privilegia* that are privileges which the apostolic Pope Sergius wrote for the monasteries of the apostles St Peter and St Paul, and they agreed and they settled it so that whether there is peace or war between the Saxons and Mer[cians] that the monastery be [text missing] in peace [...][59]

The kingdom of Mercia had long gone by the time that the eleventh-century version of the 'privilege' was transcribed. There was no obvious motive for the monks of the period to fabricate the idea of joint endorsement by the two monarchs, and the eleventh-century evidence therefore supports

---

of the privilege by Sergius. Exemption privileges were granted by the popes of the late seventh century to other monasteries in England. Bede described how the new foundation of St Peter's, Wearmouth, in Northumbria was granted a charter by Pope Agatho in the years 678–80, exempting the minster from external interference. The slightly later foundation of St Paul's minster at Jarrow was given similar privileges by Pope Sergius in 701. It is certainly possible, therefore, that Aldhelm visited Rome and obtained some sort of grant of exemption from Sergius.

[57] Faricius, *Vita*, VIII.6–7 (ed. Winterbottom 12).
[58] British Library, MS. Cotton Otho C 1/1.
[59] Christine Rauer, *Translation of the Old English Version of Pope Sergius's Bull for Malmesbury*, available online: https://www.st-andrews.ac.uk/~cr30/sergius/.

From Máeldub to Aldhelm

the view that Aldhelm conceived his monastery as a joint West Saxon and Mercian foundation.

Aldhelm's early years as abbot

William of Malmesbury preserved a charter supposedly dating from 675 which stated that Bishop Leuthere of the West Saxons confirmed Aldhelm's appointment as abbot, and this date is often given as the commencement of his abbacy. However, the charter in question is now regarded as, in large measure, a twelfth-century fabrication; indeed, it is possible that William himself was involved in the forgery.[60] So is it possible to work out when Aldhelm took over the running of the monastery?[61] There is some other evidence which is consistent with Aldhelm becoming abbot around 675, and this can be found in a letter he sent to the abbots of Mercia and Northumbria who were associated with the controversial and divisive Northumbrian bishop, Wilfrid. There was tension between Wilfrid and both Ecgfrith, the king of Northumbria, and Archbishop Theodore, and in 677 Theodore deposed Wilfrid as bishop, dividing his large see into three dioceses with newly appointed bishops. The dispute prompted Aldhelm to write to the heads of monasteries associated with Wilfrid urging them to remain loyal to their master and if necessary to join him in exile. Excerpts from his letter have survived, and although it is undated, it has been argued convincingly that it was written in 677.[62] Public support for Wilfrid was problematic for Aldhelm because it set him, to some extent, at odds with his teacher, Archbishop Theodore. It seems highly unlikely that Aldhelm would feel free to intervene in this sensitive matter unless he had left Canterbury, and now had some standing in the Church in his own right as the abbot of Malmesbury.

William of Malmesbury preserved part of the text of the letter to Wilfrid's abbots and included it in his *Gesta Pontificum*: it was sympathetic to Wilfrid's cause and authoritative in tone. The style and contents of the letter are consistent with the idea that Aldhelm had abbatial status at the time of writing, and this gave him the authority to lecture Wilfrid's abbots. Aldhelm argued strongly that the abbots had a duty to stand by their ecclesiastical lord, Wilfrid, in his time of need. If one accepts that this letter was written in 677, by which time Aldhelm was abbot

---

60 Kelly, *Charters*, 127.
61 See Lapidge, 'Career', 66. Lapidge suggested that Aldhelm might not have become abbot until as late as 682–5. He came to this conclusion on the basis of his view that there is no surviving charter which proves incontestably that Aldhelm was abbot of Malmesbury before 685. This is debatable. Kelly considered that a charter of 681 was fundamentally authentic. See Kelly, *Charters*, 136.
62 Aldhelm, *Prose Works*, 151.

Malmesbury Abbey 670–1539

of Malmesbury, it is reasonable to assume that he had been in post for at least a couple of years, making it plausible that he became abbot in around 675. The letter to Wilfrid's abbots is also interesting because it articulates Aldhelm's own conception of his role as abbot at the beginning of his career at Malmesbury. Like Wilfrid, he was the father of the monks and should provide a mix of support, instruction and correction. In return for paternal care, he expected unconditional obedience and loyalty.

> [...] by his nourishment, teaching, and discipline [Wilfrid] has brought you with a father's affection through to the flower of adulthood, and who, like a nurse warming the beloved foster-children she carries folded in her enveloping arms, has cherished you in his affectionate bosom and clasped you in his merciful embrace?[63]

The lives of Aldhelm and Wilfrid intersected again in 681 when the dispute between Bishop Wilfrid and King Ecgfrith was renewed. On this occasion Wilfrid fled with several companions from Northumbria to southern Mercia where he was given shelter by one Berhtwald, almost certainly the Mercian sub-king mentioned above who acted as patron to Aldhelm. Berhtwald permitted Wilfrid to establish a monastery on his lands.[64] Since Berhtwald's sphere of control was an area immediately to the north of Malmesbury, it seems that for a while Wilfrid and Aldhelm lived in close proximity, and unless Aldhelm was away on business, he must surely have spent time in the company of his new neighbour, Wilfrid. The two men had much in common as advocates of Roman learning and traditions, and there was, in all likelihood, a fraternal relationship between their neighbouring monastic families. However, Wilfrid did not remain long in southern Mercia. Wishing to curry favour with Ecgfrith, King Æthelred ordered his subordinate, Berhtwald, to expel Wilfrid, who moved south and sought protection in Wessex from Centwine, Aldhelm's father. It seems likely that Aldhelm was involved in an attempt to provide sanctuary for his friend, and perhaps Wilfrid based himself at Malmesbury for a while. The plot then thickened as Centwine's wife became involved and insisted that Wilfrid should not be permitted to remain in Wessex. She did this to express solidarity with her sister, Queen Eorminburg of Northumbria, who disliked Wilfrid.[65] This story hints, intriguingly, at a serious family argument; with Aldhelm and his mother or stepmother taking opposite sides in a fierce dispute about how Bishop Wilfrid should be treated.

---

63 *GP* I V 192.3–4. (ed. Winterbottom 509–11).
64 *Vita S. Wilfridi* c. 40 (ed. Colgrave 81).
65 Ibid.

The public career of Aldhelm

As the abbot of an important monastery sponsored by the kings of both Wessex and Mercia and a prince of the royal house of Wessex, Aldhelm inevitably became involved in public affairs. His responsibilities would, on many occasions, take him away from Malmesbury. We know that Aldhelm attended Church synods, and in the introduction to the prose *De Virginitate* he complained about the burdens of his ecclesiastical responsibilities. He told Abbess Hildelith of Barking, for whom the work was composed, that he had received letters from her 'while proceeding to an episcopal convention accompanied by brotherly throngs of associates'.[66] Towards the end of the same work, Aldhelm apologised to Hildelith for the excessive length of time taken writing the treatise.

> I confess to Your Kindness, that I have not been able to write this little work, even though it's very small, and send it to you as quickly as you wished, since I have been weighed down with the burden of pastoral care and overwhelmed with the weight of worldly business, [and] because the demanding responsibilities of ecclesiastical administration did not allow any space of undisturbed peace and a leisured interval for writing, and the noisy bustle of practical matters interrupted it.[67]

Aldhelm joined other ecclesiastical dignitaries at important events. Abbots were expected to attend the king's council or witan as well as ecclesiastical synods. Largely trustworthy charters indicate his presence on two occasions when the king of the West Saxons made major grants of land to other religious houses.[68]

The laws of Ine, ratified by his witan, distinguished between the rights of the Saxons when seeking legal redress and the lesser rights of the king's British subjects.[69] The law code is a reminder that Aldhelm's Malmesbury was in a recently conquered region where the victors and the vanquished were still distinct linguistic groups. There was probably some tension between the local British clergy and the Malmesbury monks on the contentious issues of the calculation of Easter and the correct shape of the clerical tonsure. On one occasion Aldhelm was asked by a major Church synod to communicate with the British king, Geraint, who ruled over 'Dumnonia', an area roughly equivalent to modern Devon and Cornwall. The synod wanted to enjoin conformity with

---

66   Aldhelm, *Prose Works*, 59.
67   Aldhelm, *Prose Works*, 129–30.
68   See the Electronic Sawyer: https://esawyer.lib.cam.ac.uk/about/index.html. Sawyer 235 (Farnham) and Sawyer 248 (Glastonbury). Sawyer 235, dated 688, was also witnessed by Wilfrid, who had recently been restored to the episcopate by Aldhelm's old friend, King Aldfrith of Northumbria.
69   For the Laws of Ine, see Stefan Jurasinski and Lisi Oliver, *The Laws of Alfred: The Domboc and the Making of Anglo-Saxon Law* (Cambridge, 2021).

the Roman traditions concerning Easter and the tonsure on the clergy subject to Geraint's authority. Aldhelm was asked to write to Geraint to persuade him of the correctness of Roman ways, and the text of the letter survives.[70] Aldhelm's letter was skilfully constructed: anxious not to present himself as a representative of the West Saxons, the historical enemies of the rulers of Dumnonia, he explained that he was instructed to act by a synod attended by an enormous number of bishops drawn from 'almost the entirety of Britain'.[71] He criticised Geraint's own clergy for using the wrong tonsure and calculating Easter incorrectly, but he saved his greatest scorn for the unorthodox practices of the British churches across the Bristol Channel in Dyfed. Geraint was being asked to choose between the purity of Roman traditions and the corrupt practices of his neighbours in nearby Dyfed. Aldhelm reminded Geraint that the Roman ways had the blessing of St Peter, and, quoting his own poetry, he pointed out that Peter was the keeper of the keys to Heaven.[72] The spiritual threat was clear: comply with my request and impose Catholic orthodoxy on your clergy, or risk exclusion from Heaven.

On the death of Bishop Hædde in 705 or 706, the large diocese of Wessex was divided in two with sees established in both Winchester and Sherborne. Aldhelm became bishop of Sherborne while his Malmesbury disciple, Daniel, was appointed to Winchester. The new diocese of Sherborne covered, according to the Anglo-Saxon Chronicle, the lands 'to the west of the Wood', meaning Selwood Forest.[73] This cannot have been an easy assignment for Aldhelm as the territory assigned to him had only recently been conquered by the West Saxons. Bede, no doubt using information provided by Daniel, recorded that Aldhelm ruled his diocese 'most energetically', and perhaps this was a reference to the zeal with which he imposed Roman traditions on the recalcitrant British clergy.

[70]   Aldhelm, *Prose Works*, 155–60.
[71]   Aldhelm, *Prose Works*, 155.
[72]   Aldhelm, *Prose Works*, 159.
[73]   ASC s.a. 709 (ed. Swanton 41).

2

Aldhelm's community

No trace remains above ground of Aldhelm's monastery, and the precinct has not been subject to any modern archaeological investigation.[1] We are forced therefore to rely on clues found in documentary sources, such as the works of Aldhelm and William of Malmesbury, when trying to reconstruct the early monastic campus. In the *Gesta Pontificum* William stated that a 'very small church' reputed to have been built by Máeldub was extant until his own time, and he also described how Aldhelm built new churches for the community.

> The monastery, as I have said, centred on St Peter's church. But a noble mind is incapable of taking a rest from activity, and Aldhelm set about a second foundation in the precincts of the same convent, in honour of Mary Mother of God. So he built this second church, and yet another next to it dedicated to St Michael; of this I have seen traces. As to the greater one, its whole fabric stood, famous and unimpaired, even in our day, larger and fairer than any old church that was to be seen anywhere in England.[2]

In another part of the *Gesta Pontificum* William stated that the chief monastic church was dedicated not just to St Peter but jointly to 'the chief of the apostles, Peter and Paul', and this church 'was from of old the centre, the place at which the monks came together'.[3] William's account of the monastic campus is consistent with early English and contemporary Frankish usage, with two main monastic churches 'one dedicated to an apostle or martyr, the other to St Mary'.[4] William indicated that, in addition, there were at least two other smaller churches: the chapel of Máeldub and a church dedicated to St Michael, which was probably a mortuary chapel, given that such chapels were often dedicated to St Michael, an archangel who could act as a guide to the dead on their journey to Heaven. Significantly William preserved the tradition that Aldhelm was initially buried in St Michael's.[5]

---

[1] The Anglo-Saxon churches at Malmesbury are discussed by Thomson in *GP II* 330–3.

[2] *GP I* V 216.1 (ed. Winterbottom 545).

[3] *GP I* V 197.3 (ed. Winterbottom 521).

[4] For this, see Thomson in *GP II* 270.

[5] Ibid.

Malmesbury Abbey 670–1539

One of Aldhelm's poems supports the idea that he built a substantial church at Malmesbury which was dedicated jointly to St Peter and St Paul. This source also gives us some flavour of the collective worship in the church. Following Roman practice, it was the tradition at the time of Aldhelm to celebrate the dedication of a new church with a poetic inscription known as a 'titulus' which was placed at the church door. Aldhelm wrote several tituli and one of these was preserved by Faricius in his eleventh-century life of the saint.[6] Faricius assumed that this titulus was a description of St Peter's in Rome, but William of Malmesbury, who also knew the poem, concluded that Aldhelm wrote it for the main monastic church at Malmesbury. Modern scholars consider William's explanation to be correct.[7] We have, therefore, almost certainly, the text of the inscription that greeted those entering Aldhelm's newly built church of St Peter and St Paul at Malmesbury. While versions of the poem exist in both the *Vita* of Faricius and in William's *Gesta Pontificum*, the following is the earlier rendition given by Faricius:

> Here flourishes the notable glory of a new church
> Which emblazons the bright standards of a holy triumph.
> Here Peter and Paul, who bring light to the darkness of this world,
> Outstanding fathers, who guide the reins of the people,
> Are worshipped with constant hymns in the blessed hall.
> O you [Peter] who keep the keys of heaven, who unlock the gate to the sky,
> Who open the dazzling realms of the Thunderer's heaven,
> Listen mercifully to the vows of your peoples when they pray,
> Who bedew their wasted faces with floods of tears.
> Accept the sighs of those who groan for the sins they have committed,
> Who burn away the sins of their life with flaming prayer.
> Lo, Great Teacher (called Paul after your change of name,
> But Saul when you desired to prefer the ancient rites to Christ)
> Who began to perceive clear light after darkness:
> Now open your ears in kindness to hear the voices of those who pray,
> And as their protector hold out your hand like Peter to the trembling,
> Who throng in great numbers the holy threshold of the hall,
> So that here enduring forgiveness may be granted for sins,
> Flowing from generous Love and the fountain on high,
> Which never at any time grows dry for the peoples who merit it.[8]

---

6 Faricius probably came across the poem in a 'sylloge' – an anthology of tituli – compiled by Milred, the eighth-century bishop of Worcester. See the discussion by Thomson in *GP II* 259 and Patrick Sims-Williams, 'Milred of Worcester's Collection of Latin Epigrams and its Continental Counterparts', *Anglo-Saxon England*, 10 (1982): 21–38. The Milred manuscript was seen at Malmesbury by John Leland in the early sixteenth century, and a fragment is preserved at the University of Illinois Urbana-Champaign in the USA.

7 See discussion in *GP II* 259.

8 Faricius, *Vita*, VII.4–7 (ed. Winterbottom 10–11). William's version is in

The titulus reveals aspects of Aldhelm's views about monastic worship. Collective prayer was dominated by the cult of the saints and underpinned by belief in the intercessory power of important saints such as Peter and Paul. As the keeper of the keys to Heaven, Peter had a special status, while Paul as the divinely inspired first theologian of Christianity – the 'Great Teacher' – was also a powerful figure in Heaven. The titulus indicates that the monastic liturgy was penitential: the aim of the monks was 'to burn away the sins of their life with flaming prayer' to God via these powerful saints.

A Benedictine community?

Aldhelm was aware of St Benedict's life and Rule, and he included Benedict as one of the male and female virgins who were praised in his two treatises on virginity. While the prose version, written first, made somewhat vague reference to Benedict's achievements, the verse work on virginity was much more concrete and recounted miraculous incidents in the saint's life that were taken from Gregory the Great's *Dialogi*. Aldhelm concluded this account with a brief reference to Benedict's Rule.

> He was the first to set forth in the struggle of our life the way in which
> the monasteries might hold to a desired rule, and the way in which a
> holy man might hasten, ascending by the right path, to the lofty heights
> of the heavens.[9]

Despite this mention there is no evidence at all that Aldhelm imposed the Rule of St Benedict on the community in Malmesbury, and it would be anachronistic to call a monastery such as Aldhelm's Benedictine. Indeed one aspect of life at Aldhelm's Malmesbury, the prevalence of temporary community membership for educational purposes, has been described as being 'very un-Benedictine'.[10] Benedict stressed 'stabilitas', the lifelong commitment of the monk to a particular community, but life at Aldhelm's Malmesbury was different because young men often went there without necessarily promising to stay for life; some did stay but others departed, either to pursue Church careers or re-enter secular society. The tradition of providing a temporary home for the sons of the elite was perhaps influenced by the Irish tradition of fostering, whereby older boys and

---

GP I V 197.4–5 (ed. Winterbottom 521–3). For the ways in which William sought to 'improve' Aldhelm's text, see Michael Winterbottom, 'William of Malmesbury: versificus', in *Anglo-Latin and its Heritage*, eds. S. Echard and G. R. Wieland (Turnhout, 2001), 109–27. Reprinted in Michael Winterbottom, *Style and Scholarship: Latin Prose from Gildas to Raffaele Regio* (Florence, 2020).

9   Aldhelm, *Poetic Works*, 122.

10 Emily V. Thornbury, *Becoming a Poet in Anglo-Saxon England* (Cambridge, 2014), 147.

young men from aristocratic families joined the household of another chieftain in order to complete their education.[11] The temporary presence in the monastery of the sons of the nobility had parallels elsewhere in the early Anglo-Saxon Church. Aldhelm's friend and contemporary, Bishop Wilfrid, also welcomed young noblemen into his monasteries, without any assumption that they had committed to a life in the Church and this phenomenon was commented upon by Wilfrid's biographer.

> And also secular chieftains, noble men, gave him their sons to be instructed, so that they might serve God if they so chose, or, if they preferred, might be commended to the king as warriors when they were grown up.[12]

Aldhelm's surviving correspondence enables us to understand a little more about the nature of 'fostering'. One of Aldhelm's students at Malmesbury was called Æthilwald; he eventually left Malmesbury, probably returning to the life of a young nobleman. Later Æthilwald wrote to thank Aldhelm for his upbringing.

> To the most holy Abbot Aldhelm, bound to me by the inextricable bonds of glowing charity, Æthilwald, humble fosterchild of your loving Paternity, [wishes] the perpetual well-being of salvation in the Lord [...] You brought me forward from the very cradles of tenderest infancy, by nourishing, loving, and gradually restoring me with the more delicate foods of knowledge as far as vigorous adolescence [...][13]

Æthilwald recalled his education with great fondness; he had enjoyed spending time with Aldhelm 'in the pursuit of learning'. His experience was special because this tranquil period of study took place when much of the country was embroiled in war: 'this most pitiable country was being savagely ravaged by the successive mounting of large and savage attacks'.[14] Although no longer able to study in person in Malmesbury, Æthilwald wanted to continue his education by correspondence and sent Aldhelm some of his own poems for the critical appraisal of his master. Remarkably, several of these poems survive. One was written in praise of Aldhelm and in it the former student was flattering in his portrayal, proclaiming grandly: 'I sing of the most exalted and most famous Aldhelm'. For Æthilwald, Aldhelm and his works illuminated the world like the sun, the moon and the stars, and Heaven was full of talk of his virtues. His master's poems were 'bejewelled ornaments [...] wreathed with pure gold'.[15] A letter from Aldhelm to Æthilwald, which is full of

11 See Thornbury, *Becoming a Poet*, 144–5.
12 *Vita S. Wilfridi* c. 21 (ed. Colgrave 44).
13 Aldhelm, *Prose Works*, 164–5.
14 Ibid.
15 Brent Miles, 'The "Carmina Rhythmica" of Æthilwald: Edition, Translation,

fatherly advice, also survives. The young man had resumed a secular life and Aldhelm had no difficulties with this in principle. He addressed his former student extremely affectionately but was concerned that Æthilwald might be led astray by some of the temptations of an aristocratic lifestyle.

> And so, my dearest son, though you are young in years, you should in no wise put yourself too much at the mercy of the vain delights of this world, whether in the excessive practice of daily drinking bouts and parties, taken to disgraceful extremes, or in blameworthy wanderings on horseback, or in any of the damnable pleasures of the body.[16]

While Æthilwald did not pursue a Church career, other alumni left Malmesbury to take up senior ecclesiastical posts elsewhere. Pehthelm, for example, became the first bishop of Whithorn, faraway in southern Scotland.[17] Perhaps Aldhelm's most distinguished Malmesbury disciple was Daniel, who left to become bishop of Winchester in 705–6. Daniel must have been a relatively young man when promoted because he held episcopal office for almost forty years. Daniel went on to have a notable career, and he acted as a mentor and guide to Boniface in his missionary work in Germany, providing him with an introductory letter when he set off to the continent as a missionary in 718. This self-confident letter called upon the secular and ecclesiastical authorities to provide hospitality to Boniface, and surely reflects the influence of Daniel's education by Aldhelm with its learned biblical references and its emphasis on the particular importance of hospitality to travellers.[18]

Celebrating the Divine Office in Aldhelm's Malmesbury

Aldhelm's references in his work to liturgical practice shed important light on the religious life of English monastic communities at the end of the seventh century. At Aldhelm's Malmesbury the Divine Office – the chanting of the whole Book of Psalms each week – was the main form of collective worship. There is no evidence to suggest that Aldhelm followed the guidance on the Office set out in the Rule of St Benedict.[19] Instead, he appears to have observed the conventions followed in seventh-century Roman basilicas. Aldhelm emphasised the importance of the Divine Office in his treatise, *De Metris*, alluding to Psalm 119 with its reference to the need to praise God 'seven times a day' and comparing the Divine

---

and Commentary', *The Journal of Medieval Latin*, 14 (2004): 95.

16 *GP I* V 193.1–2 (ed. Winterbottom 513).

17 Pehthelm as bishop corresponded both with Bede and Boniface, offering the missionary to the Germans advice on canon law. See *HE* V.13 (ed. Colgrave & Mynors 502–3).

18 Tangl, *Die Briefe*, 16.

19 See J. Billett, *The Divine Office in Anglo-Saxon England* (Woodbridge, 2014), 84.

Malmesbury Abbey 670–1539

Office to 'a revenue owed to the state or a payment to the treasury'.[20] One distinctive feature of Roman, but not Irish, practice was the division of the participants in the Divine Office into two choirs who stood opposite each other and chanted alternate verses of the psalms. Aldhelm's poetry confirms that he was familiar with this antiphonal chant, and he almost certainly employed it in Malmesbury. In his *Carmen Rhythmicum* Aldhelm described the dual choir in action during the 'hour' of matins:

> When the fourth cockcrow – as if it were the fourth vigil of the night – had roused the slumbering masses with its clarion calls, then standing in two responding ranks we were celebrating matins and the psalmody of the Divine Office.[21]

Aldhelm's friend, Wilfrid, also insisted that the double choir should be used in the monasteries that were loyal to him. Aldhelm doubtless agreed with Wilfrid that the use of antiphonal chant was one of several ways in which Roman practice was superior to Irish traditions. For Wilfrid, this way of worship was closer to the original practice of the early Church, and he contrasted it with the corrupt practices of the Irish Church.[22] Aldhelm's Malmesbury was an all-male community. His poems indicate that he was familiar with liturgical practice in a dual monastery where monks and nuns were governed by an abbess who was possibly his own sister or half-sister. In one of his poetic 'tituli' Aldhelm wrote in praise of observance at this double monastery: antiphonal singing was used, with one choir of monks and another of nuns taking turns, and complemented by solo contributions from an expert precentor.

> May antiphons strike the ear with their pleasing harmonies and the singing of psalms reverberate from twin choirs; may the trained voice of the precentor resound repeatedly and shake the summit of heaven with its sonorous chant! Brothers, let us praise God in harmonious voice, and let the throng of nuns also burst forth in continual psalmody![23]

The curriculum for advanced study at Malmesbury

Malmesbury, at the turn of the seventh and eighth centuries, was an important academic centre, and the education provided by Aldhelm as the leading teacher was probably modelled on the style and content of the teaching he had experienced as a student at Canterbury in the early 670s. Both Aldhelm and Bede provide some details about the focus of

---

20 Translation from Billett, *Divine Office*, 102–3.
21 Aldhelm, *Poetic Works*, 178.
22 *Vita S. Wilfridi* c.47 (ed. Colgrave 99).
23 Aldhelm, *Poetic Works*, 48–9.

28

Aldhelm's community

academic study in the school of Theodore and Hadrian. Aldhelm sent a letter to Bishop Leuthere describing the course content at Canterbury. Taking it for granted that the bishop knew he was engaged in scriptural study, Aldhelm explained that he was learning about poetry, the stars, 'computus' (the calculation of Easter and other moveable feasts) and Roman civil law.[24] Bede made similar observations about the Canterbury curriculum, stating that Theodore and Hadrian 'gave their hearers instruction not only in the books of holy scripture but also in the art of metre, astronomy and computus'.[25] Aldhelm was intrigued by the challenge of understanding the principles of quantitative Latin verse, commenting that mastering the metre of Latin verse was 'something much more complex' than understanding Roman law. He considered himself fortunate that his teachers, Theodore and Hadrian, were experts in the art of metrical analysis.

> The student of this subject finds himself faced by obscurity the more labyrinthine just because so few are to be found who are able to teach it.[26]

One interesting subject area where Bede and Aldhelm used different terminology concerned the study of the stars. Bede called this part of the curriculum 'astronomica' but Aldhelm told his bishop that he was studying 'astrologica'. Were Theodore and Hadrian teaching about the astronomical science of the stars or the predictive power of astrology or both? Aldhelm was coy about the details, perhaps fearful that his study of 'this dark and deep art' should be seen as morally questionable and akin to sorcery.

> But as to the Zodiac and the way in which the twelve signs revolve with the movement of the heavens, I think I should keep silent, lest this dark and deep art, which needs long and systematic explanation of its subject matter, should be cheapened and brought into disrepute by being divulged in a common or garden course of interpretation, especially considering that skill in astrology and the complicated reckoning of the horoscope require the devoted research of a master hand.[27]

While Aldhelm definitely taught scriptural exegesis and metrical poetry at Malmesbury, and probably provided instruction in the computus, there is no evidence that he taught either Roman law or astrology. His letter to

---

24 There is evidence that Theodore had studied some jurisprudence as a student in Constantinople. See Bernhard Bischoff and Michael Lapidge, *Biblical Commentaries from the Canterbury School of Theodore and Hadrian* (Cambridge, 1994), 62.

25 *HE* IV.2 (ed. Colgrave & Mynors 333).

26 *GP* I V 195.4 (ed. Winterbottom 515).

27 *GP* I V 195.7 (ed. Winterbottom 517).

Leuthere expressed some worries about the moral risks of astrology if it was not approached in the right way. Perhaps these anxieties increased over time. He condemned the folly of Zodiac astrology in the introduction to his *Epistola ad Acircium* which was finished no earlier than 686, long after he had graduated from Canterbury.[28] In this work Aldhelm criticised the folly of those astrologers who based their predictions on 'the circle of the Zodiac among the twelve constellations'.

> [...] the astrologers in their laughable stupidity think they have knowledge of fate fortune or birth [...][29]

In addition to the testimony of Bede and Aldhelm there are other sources that help us to understand the nature of the teaching at Canterbury (and later Malmesbury). Several manuscripts preserve lecture notes made by English students as they listened to the biblical commentary of Hadrian and Theodore. The fullest collection of such notes exists in an eleventh-century manuscript held in Milan, and these confirm that Theodore and Hadrian adopted the approach of the Antioch school of scriptural study which encouraged a literal rather than an allegorical reading of biblical texts.[30] This was the way that Aldhelm was taught and, presumably, the way he proceeded to teach at Malmesbury.

There is no evidence that Aldhelm was one of the English students whose lecture notes survive in Milan. It is possible, however, that Aldhelm was personally involved in the writing of certain surviving glossary texts. These were guides to the vocabulary of those classical and patristic works that were studied in Canterbury and subsequently at Malmesbury. They provided English students with explanations of difficult Latin words and often included Old English interpretations of the highlighted Latin 'lemmata'. One important glossary held in Leiden sheds light on the Canterbury 'reading list' and Aldhelm's teaching at Malmesbury. Aldhelm's surviving body of work contain extensive references to works that were glossed in the Leiden text.[31] It seems likely that Aldhelm, together with other students of Theodore and Hadrian, personally contributed to the writing of the Leiden Glossary when he was a student in Canterbury in the 670s.[32] A second glossary survives, dating from the later period when Aldhelm was teaching at Malmesbury. This is known as the Épinal-Erfurt Glossary because it

---

28 Lapidge, 'Career', 25.
29 Aldhelm, *Prose Works*, 43.
30 Bischoff and Lapidge, *Biblical Commentaries*, 190–242.
31 See Lapidge, 'Career', 34. These texts included guides to Latin grammar by Donatus and Phocas, a treatise on physics, astronomy and geography by Isidore of Seville, religious and ecclesiastical histories by Orosius and Eusebius, biblical commentary by Jerome and several lives of early saints.
32 Lapidge, Michael, *The Anglo-Saxon Library* (Oxford, 2006), 88–91.

Aldhelm's community

survives in two early manuscripts held in Épinal in France and Erfurt in Germany. It contains over 3000 'lemmata' or key words, and, for about one third of these words, Old English interpretations were provided. The Épinal-Erfurt text derives in part from the Leiden Glossary but also contains additional material, some of which relates to difficult words found in Aldhelm's own work.[33] The Épinal manuscript is particularly interesting because it has been dated to around 700, when Aldhelm was still alive.[34] Palaeographical analysis suggests that it was written in southern England, and the manuscript may have been produced in Malmesbury under Aldhelm's supervision.

The texts drawn on in the Épinal-Erfurt Glossary indicate that Aldhelm's instruction at Malmesbury was a modified version of the Canterbury curriculum, with Aldhelm's own work added to the 'reading list'. The compilers of Épinal-Erfurt thought that native English-speaking students needed help with more abstruse examples of Latin vocabulary. Thus, while the earlier Leiden Glossary contained 250 Old English glosses, the Épinal-Erfurt Glossary had more than 1000 Old English interpretations. It is highly likely that Aldhelm was personally responsible for many of the Old English words used in Épinal-Erfurt, particularly those related to the works of his hero, Virgil.[35]

At Malmesbury Aldhelm taught the appreciation and writing of Latin verse, introducing his students to a range of pagan and Christian Latin poets.[36] He understood that quantitative verse was difficult for English students as non-native speakers of Latin, and his own composite work, *Epistola ad Acircium*, provided a guide for those interested in reading and composing Latin verse. This text included two treatises concerning verse composition: *De Metris* explored the varieties of metrical 'feet' and the composition of hexameter verse, while *De Pedum Regulis* provided long lists of Latin words that exemplified different metrical principles. Between the two treatises Aldhelm inserted his *Aenigmata* or *Riddles*. This collection of one hundred short poems was a serious literary endeavour in its own right, but it also provided his students with an anthology of exemplars of technically correct Latin hexameter verse.

---

33 Lapidge, 'Career', 41–2.
34 Michael W. Herren and Hans Sauer, 'Towards a New Edition of the Épinal-Erfurt Glossary', *The Journal of Medieval Latin*, 26 (2016): 125–98.
35 Ibid.
36 It is also possible that Aldhelm also encouraged his students in Malmesbury to write English poetry. According to William of Malmesbury, Alfred the Great in his lost Handbook identified Aldhelm as the greatest ever writer of English verse. See *GP I* V 190.3 (ed. Winterbottom 507).

The library at Aldhelm's Malmesbury

Aldhelm assembled a magnificent library in Malmesbury, containing 'astonishing rarities'.[37] He made hundreds of references or allusions in his works to texts written by other authors. Some caution is needed; Aldhelm liked to show off his breadth of reading, and some quotations and references he used were probably derived second-hand from the works of others. Despite this caveat, it is clear that he had direct access to an extraordinary range of texts: unusually for this period, Aldhelm had read Seneca's tragedies; one late Latin author, Paulus Quaestor, who is quoted by Aldhelm is otherwise entirely unknown;[38] and the existence of a lost poem by Lucan is known only from a single quotation in Aldhelm.[39] Aldhelm's library in Malmesbury was known during his lifetime for containing books that were difficult to obtain. A letter survives from an anonymous Irish student who applied to study at Malmesbury and used the opportunity to ask to borrow an obscure book, but only on short-term loan so as not to inconvenience Aldhelm.

> I also candidly declare this to you: I desire to read a certain book which I do not have, and this is for a period of no longer than two weeks; moreover, I mention this brief period, not because I do not have no more need of it, but so that this request may not cause annoyance to your mind. I shall obtain a messenger and horses, I imagine.[40]

The library doubtless contained much scriptural commentary and other patristic works, but there were also many works of poetry by both pagan and Christian authors. Aldhelm was familiar with secular verse by a range of non-Christian writers including Ovid, Lucan and Statius, but the pagan poet held in esteem above all by Aldhelm was Virgil. Over 130 quotations from Virgil have been identified in Aldhelm's treatises on poetic metre. His students were encouraged to admire Virgil's style and that of other pagan writers but also to consider the Latin poetry by Christian writers such as Sedulius, Juvencus, Fortunatus and Arator.[41] Perhaps the most influential Christian poet whose verse was subject to analysis at Aldhelm's Malmesbury was Caelius Sedulius, a fifth-century writer whose principal work, *Carmen Paschale*, celebrated the life of Christ and the prefiguring of Christ in the Old Testament.[42] Sedulius produced both a verse and a prose version of this work, and this example of an *opus*

---

[37] Lapidge, *Anglo-Saxon Library*, 93–7.
[38] Orchard, *Poetic Art*, 127.
[39] Orchard, *Poetic Art*, 140. Aldhelm also quoted from a little known 'Sybilline' poem that survives in full in a single ninth-century manuscript held in Leipzig. See Bischoff and Lapidge, *Biblical Commentaries*, 185.
[40] Aldhelm, *Prose Works*, 164.
[41] Orchard, *Poetic Art*, 161.
[42] Orchard, *Poetic Art*, 164.

Aldhelm's community

geminatum or 'twin work' provided Aldhelm with a model for his own parallel verse and prose works on virginity. Students at Malmesbury had without doubt access to the *Carmen Paschale* of Sedulius, and when Æthilwald, Aldhelm's former student, wrote to his erstwhile teacher he made explicit his admiration for the style of Sedulius.

> [...] the famous poet and inhabitant of the city of Rome, Sedulius, learned in speech, diligently wrote with a grating reed-pen and recorded in honeyed hexameter verses on sacred papers [...][43]

There is a good chance that one manuscript from Aldhelm's library remained at Malmesbury for the following eight centuries and was there until the Tudor period: fragments of this precious document survive today in the British Library. The work was a biblical commentary known as *Instituta Regularia Divinae Legis*, compiled by Junilius Africanus in the sixth century. Aldhelm was probably familiar with this text because it was one of the works of the Antioch school taught at Canterbury.[44] He was struck by the way that Junilius formatted his work as a dialogue between master and student, using Greek letters to indicate clearly the respective contributions of the two individuals, and he copied this device for his treatise on poetic metre, *De Metris*, duly acknowledging his model. The *Instituta* of Junilius was dedicated to one 'Primasius'. Aldhelm's copy contained the incorrect information that Primasius was pope. For this reason, Aldhelm erroneously stated in *De Metris* that the work was dedicated 'to Primasius, bishop of the Apostolic See'. In fact, Primasius was never pope and was merely bishop of Hadrumetum (now Sousse in modern Tunisia). In 1533, just six years before the Dissolution, John Leland visited Malmesbury Abbey and noted the more interesting texts in the library.[45] These included a work that Leland listed as 'Junilius ad Primasius papam', that is to say' 'Junilius [dedicated] to Pope Primasius'.[46] This was in all probability the same manuscript that Aldhelm had used many centuries earlier.

---

43 Miles, '"Carmina Rhythmica" of Æthilwald', 92.
44 Bischoff and Lapidge, *Biblical Commentaries*, 243.
45 Leland, *Collectanea* (ed. Hearne III 157). See below pp. XX for more detail about Leland's visit.
46 Ibid. For a discussion of this, see Thomson, *William*, 103–4.

3

Royal patronage and exploitation (710–960)

After Aldhelm's death much of the community's history is obscure for several centuries, although there is some evidence that the monastery continued to function in a recognisably 'Aldhelmian' manner for a while. The key source for understanding the period 710–50 is the correspondence of Lullus, later archbishop of Mainz and a missionary, with St Boniface, to the German people. Lullus was a student at Malmesbury in the early 730s before setting off on a journey that took him first to Rome and ultimately to Germany. Letters to and from Lullus, together with other documents with Malmesbury connections, were preserved by Lullus and survive in a ninth-century codex held in Vienna.[1] This manuscript is famous for its collection of the letters of Boniface, but it also provides vital clues for an understanding of life in Malmesbury in the first half of the eighth century. The Vienna codex contains an undated letter sent to Lullus in Germany many years after he had left England, perhaps in the 750s, and written by an anonymous Malmesbury monk, who reminisced about the 'good old days' of the early 730s when he and Lullus had both been young members of the Malmesbury community.

> [...] do not forget but recall to memory in your most learned mind our former friendship, which we shared in the monastery at Malmesbury, when Abbot Eaba fostered you with loving care. I remember this token, that he nicknamed you 'Little'.[2]

This letter implies that Abbot Eaba's relationship with Lullus in the 730s had been fundamentally educational, and the reference to 'fostering' is similar to the language used decades earlier by Æthilwald when he described his relationship with Aldhelm and his time at Malmesbury. In the 730s, as in the 690s, it seems that some students joined the Malmesbury community temporarily for 'fosterage' or temporary educational purposes and did not make a lifelong commitment to the place. The correspondence of Lullus also reveals that before he came to Malmesbury he was a member of an entirely different monastic community, headed by an abbess called Cyneburg. In a letter dated to 739–41, Lullus and two friends wrote from Germany to one Abbess Cyneburg, thanking

---

1   Vienna, Österreichische Nationalbibliothek MS 751.
2   Translation in Orchard, *Poetic Art*, 64.

Malmesbury Abbey 670–1539

her for her role in their early education and promising that if they ever returned to Britain they would re-join her community and offer her their obedience and loyalty.[3] Cyneburg has been provisionally identified as the head of a double monastery of men and women located in what is now the Worcestershire village of Inkberrow.[4] The letter to Cyneburg helps us to make sense of Lullus' career, and there is no sense at all of Benedictine 'stabilitas' in his academic and spiritual journey. Having begun his monastic and academic career at Inkberrow, he transferred to Malmesbury, presumably because of its reputation for advanced study based on the curriculum established by Aldhelm and once he had completed his studies, he moved on.[5] The time spent by Lullus in Malmesbury was relatively brief but its impact was profound, and he became a huge admirer of Aldhelm. In around 745–6 Lullus wrote from Germany to Dealwine, his former Malmesbury teacher ('iamdudum magistro'), requesting that Dealwine should arrange the copying and despatch of several texts by Aldhelm.

> [...] send me some works of Bishop Aldhelm, either in prose or metre or rhythmical verse to soothe my stay abroad.[6]

Lullus wrote from Germany assuming that his old Malmesbury teacher was still active in the 740s, a decade after his own departure from England, and that Dealwine continued to have access to major Aldhelmian texts in the Malmesbury library. It seems highly likely that Dealwine complied with the request and was able to send some of the works of Aldhelm to Lullus in Germany.[7] During his Malmesbury education in the 730s Lullus had studied Aldhelm's prose and verse works closely. The Vienna codex contains many of the letters of Lullus together with a few of his own verse

---

3 Tangl, *Die Briefe*, 78.
4 Patrick Sims-Williams, 'Cuthswith, Seventh-Century Abbess of Inkberrow, near Worcester, and the Würzburg Manuscript of Jerome on Ecclesiastes', *Anglo-Saxon England*, 5 (1976): 1–21
5 Coming almost certainly from Worcestershire, Lullus was Mercian. His correspondence provides information about his family background. Lullus was from a prosperous slave-owning family. His letters reveal that when he decided to leave Malmesbury and go to Rome his father used this as the opportunity to emancipate two named slaves.
6 Translation from Orchard, *Poetic Art*, 20
7 Several of Aldhelm's works survive solely in the Vienna Codex and were perhaps the texts sent in response to Dealwine's letter These works include the major poem known today as the *Carmen Rhythmicum*. This distinctive work, presented in 200 lines of octosyllabic verse, describes a journey made by Aldhelm through Cornwall and Devon. Lullus also preserved unique witnesses to four octosyllabic poems by Aldhelm's student Aethilwald and several letters to and from Aldhelm.

Royal patronage and exploitation (710–960)

compositions, and this body of work is replete with Aldhelmian references and echoes.[8]

Further evidence of Aldhelm's influence on the intellectual life of the community at Malmesbury can be found in the anonymous Latin prose text known as *Liber Monstrorum*.[9] This is a compendium of stories about monstrous creatures taken largely from Greek and Roman sources and has been dated to the period 700–50. The writer almost certainly had access to Aldhelm's library at Malmesbury.[10] He may have studied with Aldhelm or spent time at Malmesbury during the decades following Aldhelm's death. *Liber Monstrorum* drew upon many of the same sources as Aldhelm, and the work also echoes many of the characteristics of Aldhelm's prose style: convoluted sentence structure, fondness for alliteration and a penchant for particularly obscure vocabulary.

Taken together, the correspondence of Lullus and the text of *Liber Monstrorum* suggest that Malmesbury continued to operate as a centre of advanced scholarship until the middle decades of the eighth century. Bishop Daniel's decision in the early 740s to retire to Malmesbury is also consistent with this picture of Aldhelmian continuity. William of Malmesbury preserved the tradition that Daniel stood down as bishop of Winchester after almost four decades of episcopal service and moved back to Malmesbury where he eventually died.

> Daniel long out-lived Aldhelm, for his reign [as bishop] lasted forty-three years. Later, so that he could crown a green old age with a period of holy leisure, he gave up his office while still living, and until his death was a monk of *Meldunum*, according to a genuine report that has percolated to us down the generations.[11]

If this account is true, Daniel saw the monastery of the 740s as a suitable retirement home and an institution that was still true to the spirit of his master, Aldhelm.

The years of Mercian authority

After Daniel's death the lack of evidence severely limits our knowledge of the religious, intellectual and economic life of the monastery. The political context is a little clearer, and during the eighth century the monastery became subject to the authority of the kings of Mercia. The

---

8 The Aldhelmian influences in the works of Lullus are described in Orchard, *Poetic Art*, 64.

9 Andy Orchard, *Pride and Prodigies* (Toronto, 1995), 86–115.

10 Michael Lapidge, 'Beowulf, Aldhelm, the Liber monstrorum and Wessex', *Studi medievali*, 23 (1982): 151–92. Lapidge demonstrated that both writers had read a particularly obscure and now lost poem, *Orpheus*, by Lucan.

11 *GP* I II 75.11–12 (ed. Winterbottom 253).

Malmesbury Abbey 670–1539

evidence discussed in Chapter One concerning the early charters and the 'privilege' of Sergius suggested a degree of parity of power and influence over the Malmesbury community between the West Saxon and Mercian kings during the late seventh century. This situation changed after Aldhelm's death as the Mercian kings became the dominant force. The Mercian ruler, Æthelbald, asserted some level of control over much of Wessex following the abdication of Ine of Wessex in 726. According to the anonymous letter from Malmesbury addressed to Lullus, the abbot of Malmesbury in the 730s was called Eaba, and it is highly likely that he was obliged to recognise Æthelbald's authority and attended the court of the Mercian king. Three charters of Æthelbald are attested by an abbot with a similar name to Eaba, and several scholars have considered that this was the abbot of Malmesbury.[12] One charter witnessed by an abbot called Ibe (probably a version of the name 'Eaba') can be dated to 736; the abbot's name as witness is listed prominently, fifth in order of precedence.[13]

It is difficult to know how Malmesbury fared during Æthelbald's reign. The king had a reputation among contemporaries for aggressively appropriating the resources of religious houses, and in 745–6 the English missionary to Germany, Boniface wrote to Æthelbald condemning this behaviour.[14] However, since the abbot of Malmesbury appears to have been a member of his witan or council, the monastery may have received a degree of protection. Æthelbald's long reign ended in 757, when he was murdered by members of his own bodyguard. Shortly before his death, he made a grant of land in Tockenham in Wiltshire, possibly to the community at Malmesbury. The document only survives in fragmentary form but the witness list is extant and shows that the agreement was attested by Hereca, the abbot of Malmesbury.[15] The Tockenham grant, although issued by the Mercian king, was endorsed by Cynewulf, the king of Wessex. Cynewulf was clearly subordinate to Æthelbald and was obliged to acquiesce in Æthelbald's decision to dispose of land in an area which was historically part of Wessex. Æthelbald's hegemonic power was explicitly referenced in the charter which described him as 'king, not only of the Mercians but also of the surrounding peoples'. In the aftermath of the assassination of Æthelbald, Mercia appears to have briefly lost control over the Malmesbury area and Cynewulf of Wessex was no longer subject to Mercian hegemony. In 758, just a year after he played a subordinate

12 The evidence is summarised in Kelly, *Charters*, 108–9.
13 Sawyer 89. See: https://esawyer.lib.cam.ac.uk/charter/89.html.
14 Tangl, *Die Briefe*, 146–55.
15 Kelly, *Charters*, 294–9; Sawyer 96; British Library, MS Cotton Ch VIII 3. Digitised image available at: http://www.bl.uk/manuscripts/Viewer.aspx?ref=cotton_ch_viii_3_f001r. Abbot Hereca sent good wishes to Lullus via the anonymous letter from Malmesbury preserved in the Vienna codex.

Royal patronage and exploitation (710–960)

role in the issuing of the Tockenham grant, Cynewulf was free to make a gift to the Malmesbury community without any hint of Mercian overlordship. He granted land at Rodbourne and *Mearcdaeno*, a place which cannot be certainly identified, and Abbot Hereca of Malmesbury was listed as a witness.[16]

Offa became king of Mercia in 757 and pursued an aggressive policy towards his English and Welsh neighbours. For the most part, Cynewulf was able to maintain his independence, although, according to the Anglo-Saxon Chronicle, he suffered a reverse in the upper Thames in 779 and may then have lost lands in northern Wessex. Cynewulf's successor, Beorhtric, was unsuccessful in his attempts to resist Mercian power, and this led to his acceptance of Offa as overlord and the appropriation of some Malmesbury estates by Offa. William of Malmesbury was aware that Offa had seized lands belonging to Malmesbury, noting this in his *Gesta Regum* as one of many examples of the Mercian king's abuse of Church property.

> Nor did Offa's greed stop there; the estates of many churches, Malmesbury among them, fell victim to his widespread depredations.[17]

Offa died in 796, and there was a brief rapprochement between his immediate successor, Ecgfrith and Beorhtric, king of Wessex. An apparently authentic charter relating to Purton, and dating to immediately after Offa's death, indicates that Ecgfrith agreed to hand back some Malmesbury land previously seized by Offa. The charter names the abbot as Cuthbeorht, and this man is the last known head of the community before Abbot Ælfric re-established a celibate monastic community in Malmesbury in the 960s.

> I Ecgfrith, king of the Mercians, in the first year of the reign that God has granted me, have at the request of Brihtric king of the West Saxons and of Archbishop Æthelheard returned land amounting to thirty-five hides in the place called æt Purton, to the east of the wood called Braydon, to Abbot Cuthbeorht and the brethren of the monastery of Meildulf, for the forgiveness of my sins, and for the rest of the soul of my father Offa, who in his lifetime took it from them.[18]

There was a significant 'catch' to the restitution of Purton. The text recognised that Offa had unlawfully seized the property and that it should be restored, but the Malmesbury community was obliged to pay the large sum of two thousand silver shillings; the community was buying back its property from the family of the man who had stolen it.

---

16 Kelly, *Charters*, 110.
17 *GR I* 87.3 (ed. Mynors, Thomson & Winterbottom 123).
18 *GP I* V 235. 2 (ed. Winterbottom 581).

I give the aforesaid land on the understanding that it shall be free of lay services to kings, so that it may be devoted to the needs of the brethren who serve God in the aforesaid monastery, that my memory may be preserved for ever with them in the holy prayers uttered in that holy place. But in addition the abbot and brethren of the same monastery have given me in payment for the land two thousand shillings in pure silver.[19]

The 'protection' of the kings of Wessex

The century of Mercian hegemony and aggression that followed the age of Aldhelm came to an end in 825 when, at the Battle of *Ellandun*, probably fought not far from Malmesbury, Ecgberht of Wessex defeated Beornwulf of Mercia. The tradition was preserved at Malmesbury that Ecgberht's son, Æthelwulf, was a generous patron and presented a magnificent shrine for the relics of Aldhelm.[20] The Malmesbury cartulary contained several charters supposedly issued in favour of Malmesbury by King Æthelwulf.[21] However, the clauses in the charters that relate to Malmesbury are now thought to be later forgeries and other evidence suggests a story of exploitation rather than patronage. The ending of Mercian overlordship led not to a period of significant royal largesse from the West Saxon rulers but to the start of a long phase of control over religious communities such as Malmesbury. The 830s and 840s were a time of increasing disorder and instability, resulting from recurrent Viking raids and, in this troubled context, some historians consider that Ecgberht and Æthelwulf circumscribed the institutional independence of the minsters of Wessex. Religious communities surrendered control over their estates in return for a promise of royal protection. In 838 Ecgberht and Æthelwulf held a council at Kingston at which several minsters placed themselves under the control of the kings of Wessex.

> [...] the communities of free monasteries, which were long ago established under the rule and lordship of abbots and abbesses [...] have chosen me and my father, King Ecgberht, for protection and lordship on account of their own very great needs [...][22]

It seems likely that Malmesbury was subject to this arrangement and that the new system of royal control persisted for many years.[23] In the

---

19 *GP* I V 235. 3 (ed. Winterbottom 581–2).
20 *GP* I V 236.1. (ed. Winterbottom 583).
21 See Kelly, *Charters*, 115.
22 Translation available at: https://esawyer.lib.cam.ac.uk/charter/1438.html.
23 Kelly, *Charters*, 17–18. Kelly characterised the minster at Malmesbury in the ninth century as probably 'submitting to the lordship of the West Saxon kings in return for protection'.

Royal patronage and exploitation (710–960)

aftermath of the defeat of the Vikings by King Alfred at the Battle of Edington in 878, Malmesbury was designated as a 'burh' or fortress, as part of a network of defences intended to protect the borders and coastline of Wessex from Danish incursions.[24] With its steep slopes, surviving Iron Age defences and encircling streams, Malmesbury was eminently suitable as a fortress, and in the late ninth and early tenth centuries it housed a large military garrison, manned on a rotational basis by conscripts drawn from the communities of north Wiltshire. The early tenth-century document known since the Victorian period as the Burghal Hidage indicates that, at any one time, the garrison strength was 1200 men. This development changed the character of Malmesbury, from a largely religious settlement to a place teeming with soldiers. William of Malmesbury rightly saw that the reigns of Alfred and his son, Edward the Elder, were not a time of great patronage.

> King Alfred and his son Edward contributed nothing to this monastery, save what may be reckoned an exchange rather than a gift.[25]

The later medieval Abbey cartulary preserved a charter issued by Alfred the Great, probably dating from the 890s, and by this time the Malmesbury minster was located within a militarised zone. Alfred's diploma does not describe a gift of land to the community; on the contrary, the purpose of the charter was to hand the minster's land over to Dudig, one of Alfred's thegns, under a long lease. It was an act of royal appropriation in the middle of a military crisis. The grant to Dudig was approved by Alfred and witnessed by a nobleman called Æthelhelm, whose grand title was given in Latin as 'dux'. This was a translation of the Old English word 'ealdorman', meaning the king's representative in the shire, and Æthelhelm 'dux' was the ealdorman of Wiltshire. He was an important man, and Alfred showed his trust in Æthelhelm by sending him as his envoy to Rome in 887.[26] The witness list of the Malmesbury charter also illustrates Æthelhelm's high status by placing him in the order of precedence above the king's sons. Since the garrison of Malmesbury *burh* was his responsibility, it is likely that Æthelhelm was the driving force behind the decision to reward the thegn, Dudig, with land taken from the local minster.

In 893 a Danish army crossed England from east to west, passing to the north of the stronghold of Malmesbury as the force moved through the upper Thames valley and then across to the River Severn, before turning north. The Anglo-Saxon Chronicle stated that Æthelhelm went

---

24 David Hinton, 'The Fortifications and their Shires', in *The Defence of Wessex: Burghal Hidage and Anglo-Saxon Fortifications*, ed. D. Hill (Manchester, 1996), 151–9.

25 *GP* I V 241.1 (ed. Winterbottom 591).

26 ASC s.a. 887 (ed. Swanton 80).

Malmesbury Abbey 670–1539

after the Danes, having first summoned 'the king's thegns who were occupying the fortifications, from every stronghold east of the Parrett'.[27] This presumably included forces drawn from the *burh* of Malmesbury. The army led by Æthelhelm caught up with and then encircled the Danish army at a place in Wales called Buttington. The Danes were defeated, but not before both sides had received heavy casualties. With Æthelhelm acting as general, there is a good chance that the thegn, Dudig, and men drawn from the Malmesbury area fought at the bloody Battle of Buttington.

Ealdorman Ordlaf: 'lord and governor' of the church at Malmesbury

Ealdorman Æthelhelm appears to have been able to dispose of minster property at Malmesbury as he wished. His death in 897 was considered sufficiently important to be recorded by the annalists of the Anglo-Saxon Chronicle, and he was replaced as ealdorman of Wiltshire by Ordlaf. It seems that Ealdorman Ordlaf took a particular interest in Malmesbury, and the later Abbey cartulary indicates that Ordlaf, like his predecessor, had control over minster resources.[28] Writing two centuries later, William of Malmesbury had a sense of Ordlaf's importance, recounting how Ordlaf was buried at Malmesbury and implying that the tomb was still visible.[29]

> As time went on, under Edward, Alfred's son, the powerful *dux* Ordlaf bought the land from Dudig and gave it to the monastery in exchange for another piece of land. Ordlaf, being a good man of peaceable inclination, gave instructions when he was dying that both should be restored with no objections raised. For this he was rewarded with a noble tomb and lasting memory in the place.[30]

William stated that the impressive monument was a consequence of the community's gratitude to Ordlaf for his generosity. This was speculation on William's part, and it seems much more likely that the tomb reflected Ordlaf's power rather than any warm feelings towards him. Ordlaf would never be forgotten according to William, and the ealdorman has, in fact, achieved a form of immortality because he wrote the so-called Fonthill Letter which is 'the earliest surviving letter in the English language'.[31] Dating from around 920, but describing events that had

---

27 ASC s.a. 894 (893) (ed. Swanton 87).
28 Kelly, *Charters*, 204.
29 *GP* I V 242 (ed. Winterbottom 591).
30 Ibid.
31 Simon Keynes, 'The Fonthill Letter', in *Anglo-Saxon Kingdoms*, ed. Claire Breay and Joanna Story (London, 2018), 190–1.

Royal patronage and exploitation (710–960)

taken place about twenty years earlier, the Fonthill Letter sheds light on Ordlaf's character and behaviour. He was powerful and influential, with easy access to King Alfred and later to his son, King Edward. The letter reveals a dark side to Ordlaf's personality. He required a substantial bribe in the form of a gift of a landed estate in Fonthill, in south Wiltshire, in return for a commitment to help his godson Helmstan, who was in trouble with the law due to an accusation of theft.[32] To avoid punishment Helmstan needed to assert his innocence by a solemn oath, supported by the testimony of others. Ordlaf was only prepared to help if Helmstan granted him the long-term ownership of five hides of land in Fonthill. In this way Ordlaf secured title to his godson's land. Later, after Helmstan was found guilty of another crime, Ordlaf took possession of the property which he promptly exchanged with the bishop of Winchester for an estate in Lydiard, not far from Malmesbury.

The Malmesbury cartulary contained charters relating to an exchange of land between Ordlaf and the Malmesbury community, and there are echoes in Ordlaf's Malmesbury charters of the unscrupulous practice and self-interest suggested by the Fonthill Letter.[33] Ordlaf granted an estate at Chelworth to the community in return for property at Mannington in Lydiard. The deal was lopsided: Ordlaf received five hides in return for the transfer of four hides. The charters contain some additional intriguing details: control of Chelworth, which had been undisputed community property until it was leased to Dudig, would revert in perpetuity to the heirs of Ordlaf who was referred to as the minster's 'lord and governor'.[34] This crucial detail was removed by William of Malmesbury from the version of the charter that he included in the *Gesta Pontificum*. The arrangement was exceptionally good for Ordlaf and his family. He handed over Chelworth to the minster in return for a long lease on a larger property in Lydiard, conveniently close to the other property he had secured from the bishop of Winchester by means of the Fonthill transactions. At the same time, he asserted his heirs' long-term right to the reversion and ownership of Chelworth. This clever, self-interested dealing is consistent with the evidence from the Fonthill Letter. It seems that Ordlaf used his power as the king's representative in Malmesbury to build up a block of landed property for his family in north Wiltshire.

---

32 S. Keynes, 'The Fonthill Letter', in *Words, Texts and Manuscripts: Studies in Anglo-Saxon Culture*, ed. M. Korhammer et al. (Munich, 1992), 53–97.

33 See Kelly, *Charters*, 199–208. Ordlaf features in three diplomas in the Malmesbury cartulary (Kelly's charters 21–3). One charter, Kelly 23, can be discounted as a later forgery. Kelly 21 and 22 appear to contain some authentic material. The two charters mirror each other. In Kelly 21, Ordlaf granted the estate at Chelworth to the community in return for property at Mannington in Lydiard; in Kelly 22, the community agreed to this swap.

34 Kelly, *Charters*, 204.

The clause in the charter describing Ordlaf as the minster's 'lord and governor' seems authentic. The monks who later curated the cartulary had no reason at all to invent any notion that a layman once controlled the monastery, and the use of the epithet indicates that by around 900 the community was under the control of a powerful, acquisitive nobleman whose authority derived from that of the king.

Æthelstan's generosity towards Malmesbury

Malmesbury is still renowned today as the burial place of King Æthelstan, following his death at Gloucester in 939. The connection between the community and Æthelstan was a source of great pride throughout the Middle Ages, and a late medieval effigy of the king can still be seen in the Abbey church. Writing in the twelfth century William of Malmesbury described how the earlier sepulchre of Æthelstan visible in his day bore a poetic inscription which he transcribed: these words were probably written by William himself.[35]

> Here lies one honoured by the world and grieved by his land:
> Path of rectitude, thunderbolt of justice, model of purity.
> His spirit has gone to heaven, its covering of flesh dissolved:
> An urn receives those triumphant relics.[36]

Inspired by the Malmesbury connection, William sought to find out everything he could about Æthelstan, and wrote extensively about him in both the *Gesta Regum* and the *Gesta Pontificum*. These works celebrated Æthelstan's victory at the decisive Battle of *Brunanburh* in 937 during which St Aldhelm miraculously provided the king with a sword which he used to glorious effect.[37] After the battle Æthelstan insisted that the bodies of his fallen cousins should be buried close to Aldhelm's remains in the church of Malmesbury, and the saint's intervention led to a flurry of gifts for Malmesbury.

> From that day forth he lavished on the monastery many estates, many palls, a gold cross, phylacteries, also of gold, and a fragment of the Lord's cross which he had been sent by Hugh king of the Franks.[38]

William recounted how Æthelstan went to great lengths to obtain relics for Malmesbury from as far afield as Brittany and Normandy, including the miracle-working relics of St Paternus, a sixth-century bishop of

---

[35] Winterbottom, 'William of Malmesbury: versificus', 109–27. Reprinted in Winterbottom, *Style and Scholarship*.
[36] *GP* I V 246.5 (ed. Winterbottom 595).
[37] *GR* I II 131.1–7 (ed. Mynors, Thomson & Winterbottom 207–9).
[38] *GP* I V 246.2 (ed. Winterbottom 593).

Royal patronage and exploitation (710–960)

Avranches.[39] These relics were venerated for an extremely long time: a Tudor prayer book from Malmesbury indicates that prayers to Paternus were still being said as part of the Litany of the Saints in 1521, almost six hundred years after the original gift of Æthelstan.[40] In the *Gesta Regum* William of Malmesbury claimed that Æthelstan had given many large estates to the community. In fact, the exact scale of Æthelstan's patronage is difficult to ascertain because his charters granting lands to Malmesbury are all later forgeries.[41] One charter, quoted in the *Gesta Pontificum*, is a summary fabrication synthesising other forgeries, which was probably produced by William himself. While the surviving charters are forgeries, it is entirely possible that Æthelstan did indeed grant many of the estates itemised in these documents, which included some lands held by Malmesbury after the Conquest such as Norton and Little Somerford. Malmesbury was, to some extent, a surprising choice as Æthelstan's mausoleum; no king had been buried there before, and his own father and grandfather were both interred at the New Minster in Winchester. So why Malmesbury? William claimed that Æthelstan's profound affection for Malmesbury was the result of devotion to the cult of Aldhelm based on his kinship with the saint and the miraculous events at Brunanburh. There is no reason to doubt that this was one factor but Sarah Foot has suggested another possible reason: Malmesbury, with its proximity to Mercia and its West Saxon heritage, symbolised his status as the king of all the English.[42]

We know little about the history of the Malmesbury community during the two decades following Æthelstan's death, and the post-Conquest institutional memory of the monastery was particularly confused about the reign of King Eadwig (955–9). There is a charter of Eadwig in the Malmesbury cartulary, which confirms the minster's landholdings, but it is now considered to be a later forgery.[43] The Malmesbury monks of the Norman period had a negative view of Eadwig, and writing in the 1090s, the monk of Malmesbury, Faricius of Arezzo, criticised Eadwig's anti-monastic depredations.

> Eadwig [...] went astray in his feckless infancy, having no upright man to advise him. Hence he frittered away and divided the realm, distributing the property of the churches among intestine plunderers.[44]

---

39   *GP* I V 247.1 (ed. Winterbottom 595).
40   *English Monastic Litanies of the Saints after 1100*, I ed. N. J. Morgan (Woodbridge, 2012), 133.
41   Kelly, *Charters*, 211–27.
42   Sarah Foot, *Æthelstan: The First King of England* (London, 2011), 187.
43   Kelly, *Charters*, 227–31.
44   Faricius, *Vita*, XIV.2 (ed. Winterbottom 16).

A generation later William of Malmesbury endorsed this hostile view, believing incorrectly that Eadwig had ejected celibate monks from the minster and installed secular clerics in their place. He assumed wrongly that some version of Benedictine monasticism had been practised continuously in Malmesbury from the 670s until the reign of Eadwig.

> [...] he inflicted woes they did not deserve on all monks throughout England, first stripping them of their revenues, and then even sending them into exile. Indeed he went so far as to make the monastery of *Meldunum* a stable of clerics, 245 years after the passing of father Aldhelm and 275 after Leuthere had appointed him abbot there.[45]

The post-Conquest narrative in Malmesbury about Eadwig was contradictory. While Faricius and William both vilified Eadwig as an immoral man and the enemy of monasticism, they also suggested that his reign was a time when the cult of Aldhelm was being promoted. Faricius described, for example, how during the brief years of Eadwig's rule the saint's body was 'placed with all honour in a silver shrine', decorated with images illustrating stories of Aldhelm's miracles 'engraved on gilded plates'.[46]

---

[45] *GP I V* 251.1–2 (ed. Winterbottom 603).
[46] Faricius, *Vita*, XIV.4 (ed. Winterbottom 16).

4

Malmesbury and the late Anglo-Saxon Benedictine reform movement

The monastery at Malmesbury was in effect re-founded in the 960s as part of a wider programme of Benedictine reform in southern England promoted by King Edgar (959–75). This development involved a radical change to the Malmesbury community: the married clergy were evicted and replaced by celibate monks who followed the Rule of St Benedict under the authority of an abbot. The changes were part of a wider campaign to establish Benedictine monasticism as the form of religious life followed in a relatively small but elite and wealthy network of royal monasteries. The intellectual leaders of the movement were Dunstan (archbishop of Canterbury and previously abbot of Glastonbury) and Æthelwold (bishop of Winchester and previously abbot of Abingdon). The Benedictine campaign was linked to developments in monasticism in continental Europe, particularly in northern Francia.

With sponsorship from Edgar, and guidance from Dunstan and Æthelwold, Malmesbury became an important institution within the new network of Benedictine houses. It is possible that the Malmesbury monks, including the abbot, Ælfric I, were recruited from Dunstan's Glastonbury. Certainly, Dunstan took a close personal interest in Malmesbury, and Faricius provided a detailed account of Dunstan's 'loving regard' for Malmesbury.

> Dunstan, hearing of the works of so great a man [Aldhelm], and seeing every day the frequent miracles he performed, began to pay loving regard to that monastery above all others, excepting only the one [Glastonbury] in which he had himself been enthroned as abbot. He began to put there from his own property many things suitable for service in church. Many are kept in the place to this day, together with his curses to be seen written on them in verse against anyone daring to remove them to the detriment of the church.[1]

William of Malmesbury endorsed this view and copied out one of Dunstan's 'curses' which was inscribed on an organ.

---

[1]   Faricius, *Vita*, XV.1–2 (ed. Winterbottom 16).

I, Bishop Dunstan, give this organ to St Aldhelm;
May he who wishes to remove it from here lose his share in
the eternal kingdom.[2]

The exact sequence of the events whereby Edgar and Dunstan relaunched celibate monasticism in Malmesbury is unclear, and William of Malmesbury misunderstood the chronology. The monastery preserved in its cartulary a charter of 974, granted by Edgar in favour of Malmesbury, which confirmed ownership of an estate at Eastcourt.[3] William mistakenly saw this as a document that was issued at the time of the return of monks to Malmesbury which he, therefore, dated to 974. However, Abbot Ælfric of Malmesbury appears frequently as a witness to several charters relating to places other than Malmesbury from as early as 963, indicating that the re-establishment of Malmesbury almost certainly took place during the early years of Edgar's reign, between 959 and 963.

The post-Conquest monastery celebrated the connection of the house with Dunstan. It seems likely that Æthelwold also played a major role in the re-establishment. The charter relating to Eastcourt stated that the secular clerics who lived at Malmesbury were forcibly ejected from their minster to allow celibate monks to be installed. This is exactly what happened, at Æthelwold's behest, at Winchester. Æthelwold may have assisted in the drafting of the charter. The document also contains what, at face value, is a personal statement of Edgar's motivation driven by a mix of self-confidence and piety.

> Hence I Edgar, king of all Albion, raised, by God's bountiful grace, higher than any of my forefathers, thanks to my subjugation of the kings who dwell round about on the sea coast or in islands, have often given careful thought as to what part of my empire in particular I should give to the Lord, the King of Kings, to mark my awareness of the great honour that I enjoy. So it was that the goodness of God, which fosters my pious devotion, suddenly suggested to my wakeful mind as I brooded on this question the idea that I should restore all the holy monasteries in my kingdom.[4]

The charter painted a bleak picture of the existing state of the monasteries and by implication the decayed physical and moral condition of the religious house at Malmesbury before the changes.

> They had fallen into ruin for all to see, with moss-grown shingles and planking crumbled down to the framing beams; but equally (and this matters more) they had been neglected inwardly, for they had become

2   *GP I* V 255.2 (ed. Winterbottom 609).
3   *GP I* V 252.1–5 (ed. Winterbottom 605–7). Susan Kelly considered it 'an unconventional but authentic diploma of Edgar'. See Kelly, *Charters*, 236.
4   *GP I* V 252. 1–2 (ed. Winterbottom 605).

almost empty of God's service. I therefore cast out secular clerics not subject to the discipline of any religious rule, and over many places appointed shepherds of a holier kind (wearers, that is, of the monastic habit), providing them with a plentiful supply of money from the treasury to enable them to restore the ruinous parts of their churches.[5]

This passage needs to be approached with considerable caution. Dunstan and Æthelwold were seeking to justify their 'reforms', and we cannot be sure that the charter accurately depicts the status quo before the changes. What we do know is tha the new Benedictine house in Malmesbury was an institution of importance. Abbot Ælfric I featured prominently as a witness in diplomas issued by King Edgar and was given high precedence.[6] William of Malmesbury pointed out that an unnamed abbot of Malmesbury, presumably Ælfric, was sufficiently well known to be mentioned in writing by Abbo of Fleury.[7] The charter of 974 celebrated Edgar's generosity and his intention to ensure 'a plentiful supply of money' for the monastery. The king encouraged the restitution of lands originally held by Aldhelm but subsequently alienated. The Eastcourt estate was, according to the charter, part of the community's historic endowment and had been illegally possessed by a man called Æthelnoth. Further evidence of royal action to restore the community's lost land is provided by the surviving will of Ælfheah, ealdorman of Hampshire, who died in around 971. He appears to have been under some pressure from Edgar to use his will to restore those of his estates which had been previously in monastic hands, and his will granted the Malmesbury community a large estate of twenty hides in nearby Charlton.[8]

Either during Edgar's reign or shortly after, the monastic community used forgery as a means of justifying claims to supposedly appropriated lands.[9] At this time, two authentic ninth-century charters of Æthelwulf were altered, and a list of 'lost' Malmesbury estates was added. According to Susan Kelly the description of property in one charter 'may represent interpolations made in the second half of the tenth century, as part of a campaign to secure lost and vulnerable estates that had formed part of the early endowment'.[10] Similarly, another charter which was purportedly granted by Æthelwulf in 844 listed, among other property, the estate at Charlton, eventually bequeathed by Ealdorman Ælfheah to the community at Malmesbury. The use of forgery to reclaim lost lands

---

5   Ibid.
6   Simon Keynes, 'Edgar, *rex admirabilis*', in *Edgar, King of the English, 959–975: New Interpretations*, ed. Donald Scragg (Woodbridge, 2014), 3.
7   *GP* I V 252.2–3 (ed. Winterbottom 605). See Abbo of Fleury, *Passio S. Edmundi*, praef., in *Three Lives of English Saints*, ed. M. Winterbottom (Toronto, 1972), 67.
8   Dorothy Whitelock, *Anglo-Saxon Wills* (Cambridge, 1930), 22–5.
9   Kelly, *Charters*, 83.
10   Ibid.

was perhaps undertaken, in a collusive way, with Glastonbury monks who also wanted to see the restoration of their lost estates.[11]

Royal intercession and the *Regularis Concordia*

Æthelwold wished to standardise the conduct of the religious life in the reformed communities. In around 970 the abbots and abbesses of the royal Benedictine houses met at a synod in Winchester and endorsed an extremely detailed set of regulations known as the *Regularis Concordia* ('the agreement about the Rule'). This provides us with a mass of fascinating detail about life in a monastery such as Malmesbury during the reign of Edgar. The *Regularis Concordia* emphasised that the overriding function of the participating monastic communities was to intercede with God on behalf of the royal family of Wessex. The introduction to the text stressed that prayers for the king had to be chanted particularly carefully and slowly so that God would not be provoked to anger. The reformed houses were placed under the special protection of the royal family (with the queen taking responsibility for the nunneries) and the heads of the houses could expect to have personal contact with royalty.

> As often therefore as it shall be to their advantage the fathers and mothers of each house shall have humble access to the King and Queen in the fear of God and observance of the Rule.[12]

The emphasis on prayers for the royal family was extremely marked. Each day special psalms and prayers were said for the king and queen on ten different occasions, and, on top of the usual psalms of the Office, an additional eighteen psalms and twenty-three 'collects' or specific prayers were chanted for England's rulers.[13] The *Regularis Concordia* made it clear that it was the job of the monks of reformed houses such as Malmesbury to bombard Heaven with requests for divine assistance for their royal patrons.

The library of the re-founded monastery

The monks who were introduced by Edgar appear to have inherited a library and archive that contained at least some material that had survived the Viking onslaughts. The library was also enriched with new manuscripts. Of course, almost all of this was lost at the Dissolution, but it is possible to identify three important acquisitions from this period which survive. These give a sense of the interests and resources available

---

11 Ibid.
12 *Regularis Concordia; The Monastic Agreement of the Monks and Nuns of the English Nation*, ed. and trans. T. Symons (Oxford, 1953), 7.
13 *Regularis Concordia*, 14.

Malmesbury and the late Anglo-Saxon Benedictine reform movement

to the monks in the century before the Conquest. By far the greatest extant treasure of the late Anglo-Saxon library is a manuscript now in the Parker Library at Corpus Christi College Cambridge.[14] This is an illustrated copy of the long poem *Psychomachia* by the fourth-century Christian writer, Prudentius. It tells the allegorical story of the battle between the virtues and the vices. The illustrations, which date from the late tenth century, are magnificent, and it constitutes one of the most lavishly illustrated books that have survived from Anglo-Saxon England. On stylistic grounds it is judged to have been produced at Canterbury in the late tenth or early eleventh century, before being acquired by an abbot of Malmesbury called Æthelweard.[15] We know that it found its way to the library at Malmesbury because Æthelweard condemned in verse any potential thief, placing a curse prominently at the beginning of the manuscript. The curse makes clear that the book was the property of 'Aldhelm's monastery' in Malmesbury.

> Whoever you are who has stolen this book from holy Aldhelm, may
>   you remain damned for ever, suffering the lot of the evil.
> Let him be without pity from God who either takes this book of
>   Aldhelm away from this monastery or tries to sell it.
> You who read the verses written here, remember to beseech Christ,
>   and to say: May Æthelweard live for ever in peace, who gave this
>   volume to Aldhelm, for whose sake may bountiful Christ bring him
>   bountiful gifts, mitigating his crimes.[16]

It is difficult to date this acquisition precisely. According to William of Malmesbury there were two pre-Conquest abbots called Æthelweard, one active in the 980s and the other in the 1030s. A short version of the same 'Aldhelm curse' used in CCCC 23 appears in another surviving manuscript which is today held at the Bodleian Library in Oxford.[17] This is a copy of a Latin glossary of Hebrew words, *Interpretatio nominum Hebraicorum*, a text which drew upon the work of the first-century Jewish writer, Philo Judaeus, and was revised and finalised by St Jerome. The Malmesbury manuscript was originally produced in the late ninth century in France and was used for biblical study. The third extant manuscript from late Anglo-Saxon Malmesbury is a gospel book written in Old English and held by the British Library.[18] The tenth-century Benedictine reform campaign promoted the reading by monks

---

14   Corpus Christi College Cambridge MS 23.
15   Andy Orchard, 'Prudentius, Psychomachia', in *Anglo-Saxon Kingdoms*, ed. Claire Breay and Joanna Story (London, 2018), 258–9.
16   Corpus Christi College Cambridge MS 23.
17   Bodleian MS Marshall 19.
18   BL Cotton MS Otho C I/1. This manuscript also contains the Old English version of the 'privilege' of Sergius mentioned on pp. XX.

Malmesbury Abbey 670–1539

of the gospels both in Latin and in a new English translation, and the Malmesbury gospel book is one of the earliest surviving copies of this Old English rendering of the gospels.[19]

These three surviving works from the late Anglo-Saxon library at Malmesbury hint at a lively intellectual and religious life. The monks used the *Interpretatio nominum Hebraicorum* to elucidate obscure Hebrew names in the Latin Bible. They enjoyed the allegorical Christian poetry of Prudentius in a beautifully illustrated deluxe edition, and they read the gospel stories both in Latin and English, and were involved in a pioneering campaign to promote the circulation of the gospels in English. The two Aldhelm curses are a reminder that the late Anglo-Saxon monks were proud of their patron saint. Around three hundred years after his death they saw the saint as a real presence capable of striking down those who dared to steal from his monastery.

The patronage of Queen Ælfthryth

Edgar's wife, Ælfthryth, actively supported the monastic reform move-ment while her husband was alive.[20] She was on good terms with Bishop Æthelwold. They were both witnesses to the will of Ealdorman Ælfheah which restored land to Malmesbury. Ælfthryth has achieved notoriety because of her possible role in the murder of her stepson, King Edward the Martyr, and debate continues about the likelihood of her guilt. After Edward's death and the accession of her young son, Æthelred the Unready, Ælfthryth became one of the dominant figures in England's politics during the years of regency (978–84). It seems that Ælfthryth, with the encouragement of Dunstan and Æthelwold, continued to provide patronage to Malmesbury during the regency. An apparently trust-worthy charter from the year 982 grants ten hides at Rodbourne to the Malmesbury monks, and although issued under the name of Æthelred the witness list is consistent with the idea that it was Ælfthryth, Æthelwold and Dunstan who were the driving force behind the grant.[21] Significantly, Rodbourne was one of the 'lost' estates listed in the forged section of charter of Æthelwulf, and it was supposedly part of Aldhelm's original endowment. It seems likely that the Malmesbury monks were able to persuade Ælfthryth (together with Dunstan and Æthelwold) of the need to put right the perceived injustice of the alienation of this property which had been given to Aldhelm as a perpetual gift.

William of Malmesbury was perhaps troubled by this evidence of patronage from Ælfthryth. He included the text of the grant of Rodbourne in his *Gesta Pontificum* but made no reference to any involvement

[19]   Ursula Lenker, 'The West Saxon Gospels', *Anglo-Saxon England*, 28 (1999): 175.
[20]   *Regularis Concordia*, xxiv.
[21]   Kelly, *Charters*, 237–40.

Malmesbury and the late Anglo-Saxon Benedictine reform movement

of Queen Ælfthryth. In the *Gesta Regum* William portrayed Ælfthryth in highly negative terms, and contributed greatly to her reputation for wickedness. For William, not only was Ælfthryth complicit in her stepson's murder, but many years earlier, she had seduced Edgar and incited him to kill her first husband. She was represented as an archetype of female wickedness.[22]

In 984 Æthelwold died. This powerful ecclesiastic had, with Queen Ælfthryth, dominated the regency council and, almost certainly, encouraged young Æthelred to 'restore' Rodbourne to the monastery. His death prompted Æthelred to end the period of regency and assert his independence by adopting an aggressive and exploitative attitude towards the reformed Benedictine monasteries that had been favoured by Æthelwold and Ælfthryth.[23] His mother disappeared for a while from the public record and had, it seems, been banished from court. We do not know precisely how Malmesbury fared during these years but other monasteries, such as Abingdon and the Old Minster at Winchester, were plundered by Æthelred and members of his new circle of advisers, and Malmesbury may have befallen the same fate. One of Æthelred's associates was Bishop Wulfgar of Ramsbury, and he was later accused of abusing the resources of Abingdon Abbey.[24] As the diocesan bishop for Wiltshire, Wulfgar may also have been involved in the despoliation of the resources of Malmesbury.

The period of the king's hostility towards the Benedictine houses lasted from 984 until 993, by which time Æthelred concluded that he had made a terrible mistake: there had been a renewal of Viking aggression during these years, and Æthelred decided that this was God's punishment for his mistreatment of the Church and the monasteries. At Pentecost 993 Æthelred summoned a council to Winchester where he publicly admitted that he had been misguided, and he symbolised his repentance by restoring the resources taken from Abingdon. This act of contrition and restitution was documented in an elaborate and detailed charter which was witnessed by Abbot Ælfric II of Malmesbury.[25] Often there is some ambiguity about the identity of charter witnesses but, on this occasion, there is no doubt. One attestation reads 'Ego ælfric meal' abbas' ('I Ælfric abbot of Malmesbury'), where *meal'* is a contraction for Meal[dubiensis]. There is no evidence of any abbot from Malmesbury attesting to a charter of Æthelred in the years 984–93, and the presence of Ælfric II of Malmesbury at the council of 993 suggests that the leaders of the major

---

22 *GR* I II 157.1–2 (ed. Mynors, Thomson & Winterbottom 257–9).
23 Levi Roach, *Æthelred the Unready* (New Haven, 2016), 100–7.
24 Ibid.
25 BL Cotton MS Augustus II 38. A digitised image is available at: http://www.bl.uk/manuscripts/Viewer.aspx?ref=cotton_ms_augustus_ii_38_f001r.

Malmesbury Abbey 670–1539

monasteries with royal associations, such as Malmesbury, were being welcomed back to the witan of Æthelred.

After 993 Æthelred's rule was increasingly disrupted by Danish aggression, and a wealthy monastery, such as Malmesbury, was an obvious target for Danish depredations. The later tradition in the monastery was that the place was subject to Viking attack, and there is no obvious reason to doubt this. Faricius of Arezzo writing in the 1090s recounted how, during the 980s, Dunstan personally supervised the reburial of Aldhelm in a discreet place to protect the sacred relics from Danish invaders. He went on to describe how Danish raiders, at an unspecified date after Dunstan's death, did indeed come to Malmesbury searching for loot. They were thwarted both by Dunstan's foresight in hiding away the relics and by the direct intervention of the saint who struck blind one of the Danish attackers.

> But God, guardian of the faithful, brought a reproach on the sinful race, through the merit of His servant, our father, Aldhelm. When the army of wicked men was ranging hither and thither through the whole area of England, it finally came to *Meldunum* monastery, where they had been told that the native people had brought a quantity of gold, confident that the great bishop would protect it. The band was like a lion which goes ravening across the desert, not fearing anything that comes in its way: blinded by its burning desire for food, it seeks only what it may devour. The troop burst into the church, and in its madness approached the holy of holies. The instant one of them got hold of the forbidden object in his desire to take precious stones from the shrine, he was punished by God: he lost his sight and straightway fell on the paved floor. The rest of the crazed enemies made sure, willy-nilly, that all the other contents of the monastery were left behind, with the exception of what had already come into the hands of the wandering troop in the monks' quarters, and eagerly took to their heels.[26]

We do not know the precise date of this Danish attack on Malmesbury. There are several possibilities. The Anglo-Saxon Chronicle reports, for example, how Danish forces ravaged Wiltshire in 1010.[27] The abbot at this time was named Brihtwold and he witnessed several royal diplomas, indicating that he was often present at Æthelred's court. William of Malmesbury preserved a credible tradition that Brihtwold was forced to sell off some of the estates of the monastery to meet demands for Danegeld.

> Brihtwold, as I observe in English records, caused much trouble to the house, by selling off land altogether or mortgaging it for too low a sum. His excuse is that he was a victim of the great geld that was paid to

---

26 Faricius, *Vita*, XV.4 (ed. Winterbottom 16).
27 ASC s.a. 1010 (ed. Swanton 141).

Malmesbury and the late Anglo-Saxon Benedictine reform movement

the Danes at that time, and had no other way of solving his problems; without a thought for the future, he failed to see that this would cause difficulty later. Wulfsige brought back up to its old standard of energy the monastic life that had become much enfeebled because of the arrival of the Danes.[28]

The flight of Eilmer

In his *Gesta Regum* William told the strange story of Eilmer, 'the flying monk'. In the context of his account of events leading to the Norman Conquest, William explained that a monk called Eilmer had successfully prophesied the invasion of 1066 on the basis of his interpretation of the meaning of Halley's Comet, which appeared over England in April of that year.

> Not long after, a comet, portending (they say) a change in govern-
> ments, appeared, trailing its long flaming hair through the empty sky:
> concerning which there was a fine saying of a monk of our monastery
> called Æthelmær. Crouching in terror at the sight of the gleaming star,
> 'You've come, have you?', he said. 'You've come, you source of tears to
> many mothers. It is a long since I saw you; but as I see you now you
> are much more terrible, for I see you brandishing the downfall of my
> mother-country'.[29]

Eilmer's words, as recounted by William, appear to suggest that he had seen the comet as a child, and the previous appearance of Halley's Comet over England took place in August–September 989. Observing the comet twice was, just about, possible. It is conceivable that Eilmer was a boy oblate in 989, say seven or eight years old, when the Comet was pointed out to him by older members of the community. By 1066 he was an old man, in his eighties, but he remembered his childhood experience. Having explained that Eilmer predicted the Conquest, William proceeded, almost as an afterthought, to explain how the monk had experimented in an attempt at flight as a young monk.

> By the standards of those days he was a good scholar, advanced in years
> by now, though in his first youth he had taken a terrible risk: by some
> art, I know not what, he had fixed wings to his hands and feet, hoping
> to fly like Daedalus, whose fable he took to be true. Catching the breeze
> from the top of a tower, he flew for the space of a 'stadium' and more;
> but what with the violence of the wind and the eddies, and at the same
> time his consciousness of the temerity of his attempt, he faltered and
> fell, and ever thereafter he was an invalid and his legs were crippled.

28 *GP* I V 258.1–2 (ed. Winterbottom 615).
29 *GR* I II 225.5–6 (ed. Mynors, Thomson & Winterbottom 413–15).

He himself used to give as a reason for his fall, that he forgot to fit a tail on his hinder parts.[30]

William gave no date for this event but it must relate to the early eleventh century, and there are grounds for taking the tale seriously. If William entered the monastery as an oblate in the mid-1080s he would have encountered older monks who had known Eilmer personally and could retell his story and vouch for the reliability of his testimony. It is also not obvious why William might want to indulge in fiction at this point in his history. William's main purpose in this section of the *Gesta Regum* was to show how the cataclysm of the Norman Conquest was predicted and was God's wish. Interposing a questionable tale about a flying monk did not serve this grand purpose. Perhaps he included the story because he thought it true as well as entertaining.

The royal wedding at Malmesbury (1015)

After three decades of intermittent Danish raiding, Swein Forkbeard, king of Denmark, invaded England in August 1013 intent on the conquest of the country. During the ensuing campaign Swein's army probably came close to Malmesbury. The Anglo-Saxon Chronicle recorded how Swein went west from Wallingford and received the submission of the West Saxon people at Bath before marching back east towards London, when Swein effectively took control of all of England. Æthelred was forced into exile in Normandy but Swein died in 1014, creating an opportunity for Æthelred to return. His attempts to reassert his authority were far from successful; not only did the Danish threat remain but there was also conflict within the English elite. In early 1015 Æthelred's adviser, Ealdorman Eadric 'Streona', organised the assassination at Oxford of two powerful Mercian noblemen, the brothers Morcar and Sigeferth. Æthelred was complicit in the killing and subsequently he imprisoned Sigeferth's widow in Malmesbury, presumably inside the monastery precinct. The chronicler John of Worcester identified the widowed noblewoman as one 'Ealdgyth', but there is some debate about whether this was her actual name.[31] Æthelred's son, Edmund Ironside, responded to the murder of the Mercian thegns by staging a rebellion against his father and his adviser, Eadric, and his first act of defiance was to march to Malmesbury where he released and married 'Ealdgyth'. These events were recorded in the Anglo-Saxon Chronicle.

> 1015. In this year was the great assembly at Oxford and there Ealdorman Eadric betrayed Siferth and Morcar, the foremost thegns in the Seven

---

30 Ibid.
31 A. Williams, *Æthelred the Unready: The Ill-Counselled King* (London, 2003), 132.

Malmesbury and the late Anglo-Saxon Benedictine reform movement

Boroughs: lured them into his chamber, and in there they were killed dishonourably. And the king then seized all their property, and ordered Siferth's widow to be taken inside Malmesbury. Then after a short while the Ætheling Edmund travelled and took the woman against the king's will and had her for wife.[32]

This is the only instance of Malmesbury being mentioned by name throughout the Anglo-Saxon Chronicle. The choice of the monastery as the place of confinement for 'Ealdgyth' suggests that Æthelred saw it as a secure place that was loyal to him. Abbot Brihtwold attested charters issued by Æthelred from 1004 onwards, and was perhaps a trusted member of the king's witan.[33] It is entirely possible that Abbot Brihtwold was in Oxford for the great council meeting and that 'Ealdgyth' was personally given over to his custody. By marrying the widow of a leading Mercian thegn Edmund was seeking to strengthen support for himself in Mercia, and having demonstrated his disregard for his father's authority, Edmund marched north to Mercia to consolidate his new power base. William of Malmesbury recounted this story in his *Gesta Regum*, adding some colourful detail about the courtship and the deceit of Edmund.

> Sigeferth's wife, a lady of distinguished lineage, was removed to imprisonment at Malmesbury. This caused the king's son Edmund, concealing his intentions, to pay a hasty visit to that part of the world; he saw her, desired her, and got what he desired, having of course avoided telling his father, who was taken no more seriously by his own family than by outsiders.[34]

Malmesbury remained close to the centre of the struggle for control of England after the wedding. In 1015, Swein's son, Cnut, invaded, and with Edmund in Mercia, the Danish king was free to ravage Wiltshire and the other shires of Wessex. Eadric 'Streona' abandoned Æthelred, defected to Cnut's side, and before the end of the year the people of Wessex had formally submitted to Cnut. There was some form of reconciliation between Æthelred and his son, Edmund, during the winter of 1015–16, and the two men were together in London in April 1016 when Æthelred died. Edmund then attempted to assert his authority as the new king of England. During the summer of 1016 he waged war against Cnut. Towards the end of June 1016 their armies met in battle at Sherston, just five miles from Malmesbury. The result, according to the Anglo-Saxon Chronicle, was 'a great slaughter', but neither side secured a conclusive victory.[35] Edmund clashed again at the Battle of *Assandun* in Essex in

---

32 ASC s.a. 1015 (ed. Swanton 145–6).
33 Kelly, *Charters*, 111–12.
34 *GR I* II 179.4–5 (ed. Mynors, Thomson & Winterbottom 311–13).
35 ASC s.a. 1016 (ed. Swanton 151).

October 1016. After *Assandun* Edmund and Cnut agreed to partition England, with Edmund taking Wessex. However, there was no time for this plan to be put into effect because Edmund died on 30 November 1016 giving Cnut complete control over England.

There is a link between the events of 1015–16 and post-Conquest patronage of Malmesbury. Edmund and 'Ealdgyth' had two sons who were taken out of the country after their father's death, and went on an extraordinary European journey, reaching Hungary via Sweden. After many years in Hungary, one of the boys, Edward 'the Exile', returned to England towards the end of his life, and his daughter, Margaret married Malcolm Canmore, king of Scotland. Margaret was the mother of Matilda of Scotland, wife of Henry I, who, as we shall see, was given some level of control over the monastery. Matilda was, therefore, the great-granddaughter of Edmund and 'Ealdgyth', the couple who married in Malmesbury in 1015 in unusual circumstances.

From Cnut to the Confessor: the collapse of royal patronage

The Danish conquest of 1016 was doubtless a blow to a community that was proud of its associations with the house of Wessex. The Malmesbury monks had no alternative but to recognise Cnut as king. Abbot Brihtwold of Malmesbury attended the court of Cnut, and acted as a witness to one of Cnut's charters in 1019.[36] Malmesbury was not particularly favoured by Cnut and the other rulers of England who succeeded him in the years before the Conquest. There were no new royal gifts of land to the monastery between 982 and 1066. At the same time, abbots of Malmesbury continued to attend royal councils where they were not entirely without influence, and William of Malmesbury told a somewhat confused story of how the monastery was able to win the support of the powerful aristocrats, Godwine, earl of Wessex and his son, the future king, Harold Godwineson, in a dispute with the Bishop of Ramsbury.[37]

We are largely dependent on William of Malmesbury for our understanding of the history of the monastery in the final decades of the Anglo-Saxon period, but unfortunately the chronology of William's account is confused. He produced brief pen portraits of the pre-Conquest abbots based presumably on his archival studies and his conversations with older monks. These contained some colourful details. He recounted, for example, the story of a disreputable abbot called Brihtwold (the second abbot who bore that name) who lived in the 1040s, and whose ghost supposedly haunted the church of St Andrew before it was reburied in a distant bog.

---

[36] Kelly, *Charters*, 111–12.
[37] *GP I* II 83.6–7; *GP I* V 264.1 (ed. Winterbottom 629).

Malmesbury and the late Anglo-Saxon Benedictine reform movement

Brihtwold displayed sloth in good causes and energy in bad; and the old story is that he died a pitiful death, cut off in the town amid the trappings of a drinking bout, and was buried with his predecessors in the church of St Andrew, which was adjacent to the big church. It is known for a fact that the guardians of the place were troubled by hallucinatory apparitions until the body was dug up and plunged in a deep swamp a long way from the monastery; from there, from time to time, rises a foul smell that breathes a noisome miasma over the locals.[38]

The Malmesbury cartulary included a charter that was supposedly issued by Edward the Confessor, but its authenticity is questionable, and it is anyway a summary of the monastery's holdings rather than a new grant of property.[39] It was probably confected by the monks at the beginning of the Conqueror's reign as a means of protecting the community's landed endowment. As with the Danish takeover earlier in the century, the Norman Conquest constituted a challenge to a religious community that identified closely with the royal family of Wessex.

---

[38] *GP* I V 258.3–4 (ed. Winterbottom 615).
[39] *RM* I 321–4.

5

Responding to the Conquest (1066–1100)

The years immediately after 1066 were traumatic for the Malmesbury monks, and the prospects did not look promising for an institution that was closely associated with the former royal house of Wessex and the cult of an Anglo-Saxon saint unknown to most Normans. Despite these challenges the monastery managed to weather the storm, and by the end of the reign of the Conqueror the cult of Aldhelm had been endorsed by leading members of the new Norman elite. When seeking to understand this story we are fortunate to have the testimony of the great historian, William of Malmesbury (c. 1086– c. 1143), who devoted considerable attention to the history of the monastery in the decades after 1066 in his *Gesta Pontificum*. The last Anglo-Saxon abbot, Brihtric, was dismissed and left Malmesbury, later receiving the abbacy of Burton-on-Trent as some sort of compensation.[1] William wrote positively about Brihtric describing how 'he ruled the house with high distinction for seven years'. He had much less time for the first Norman, Turold, the first Norman abbot, recruited from the Norman monastery of Fécamp, who was high-handed and acted 'like a tyrant'. Turold's tenure at Malmesbury was extremely brief, and by 1070 he had been replaced by Warin of Lire, who was abbot until around 1091.[2]

William of Malmesbury provided a curiously partisan account of Warin's rule at Malmesbury.[3] He acknowledged that Warin introduced a good level of monastic observance, but he was also highly critical of other aspects of his behaviour, denouncing him as a man whose selfish misuse of the monastery's resources harmed the monks.

> Turold's successor was a monk, Warin of Lire, a man of achievement, especially in accustoming the monks to the Rule. But in other respects he was of little use to the church, because he was the helpless puppet of his own hopes of a higher position. That made him adept at emptying the monks' pockets and raising cash from any and every source. Still, he did not hide away the profits of his greed; instead, he wasted the church's resources on both sides of the Channel, to increase his

---

1   *GP* I V 264.1 (ed. Winterbottom 629).
2   *Heads of Houses I*, 55. *GP* I V 264.2 (ed. Winterbottom 629).
3   *GP* I V 265.1–4 (ed. Winterbottom 629–31).

Malmesbury Abbey 670–1539

influence with the great, and to cut a dash in the eyes of those who had known him as a poor man in the past.[4]

On arrival in Malmesbury Warin, at least according to William, treated many of the monastery's pre-Conquest relics with great disrespect.

> When he first became abbot, he looked with scorn on what his predecessors had achieved, and was governed by a proud distaste for the bodies of the saints. For example, the bones of Meildulf of holy memory, together with those of others, once abbots of Malmesbury and later bishops in various sees, who had had themselves buried there out of respect for their patron Aldhelm, the respectful ancients had placed reverently in two stone bowls, one on each side of the altar, keeping the bones of each man separate by means of wooden partitions. All these Warin piled up like a heap of rubble, or the remains of worthless hirelings, and threw them out of the church door. And to cap his impudence, he even removed St John the Scot, whom the monks worshipped almost as fervently as St Aldhelm. All these saints, then, he without due consideration ordered to be hidden away and blocked off with stones in a far corner of St Michael's church, which he himself had had extended and made higher. His offence was aggravated by a merry taunt: 'Now', he said, 'let the most powerful of them come to the rescue of the rest'![5]

As William wrote these words he was, apparently, overwhelmed with indignation at Warin's outrageous actions.

> What times, what behaviour! Who could find words harsh enough to do justice to such audacity? The impudence of the man![6]

Writing in 1940, the pioneering historian of monasticism, David Knowles, accepted the veracity of William's account of Warin's behaviour and saw this as symptomatic of a prevalent Norman hostility towards Anglo-Saxon saints. Using William as his source, Knowles adduced the events at Malmesbury in support of a general proposition that antagonism towards English saints was widespread after the Conquest.

> The Norman abbots, it seems, frequently outraged the feelings of their monks by their disrespectful attitude towards the old English saints [...] At Malmesbury Abbot Warin was so surfeited with the relics of English saints that he turned a number out with a jest [...][7]

---

4   *GP* I V 265.1 (ed. Winterbottom 629).
5   *GP* I V 265.2–3 (ed. Winterbottom 629–31).
6   *GP* I V 265.3 (ed. Winterbottom 631).
7   David Knowles, *The Monastic Order in England* (Cambridge, 1963), 118–19.

Responding to the Conquest (1066–1100)

Since the 1980s historians have challenged this view and have seen a much greater degree of continuity in the veneration of English saints during the early decades of Norman rule. Susan Ridyard has discussed the 'myth' of Norman hostility towards Anglo-Saxon saints, and concluded that William's account of the treatment of the Malmesbury relics was of questionable reliability.

> William's whole account of this incident may be untrustworthy [...] we are justified in wondering both whether Warin's ejection of the 'holy bodies' actually took place and whether if it did so, the indignation of contemporaries was perhaps less than the indignation of William.[8]

Was Ridyard right to mistrust William? It is possible that there was some grain of truth in William's accusations, but there are also grounds for thinking that he was deliberately selective and omitted information that might weaken his campaign to tarnish the reputation of Warin. Fortunately, other independent sources exist that can help us to test the reliability of William's portrayal. Taken together, these sources indicate that William's account of Warin was far from balanced.

The views of Faricius

In the late 1090s Faricius of Arezzo (who died in 1118) wrote his *Vita S. Aldhelmi*, a hagiographical study of Aldhelm's life and posthumous miracles, and he included an account of the translation of the saint's relics during the abbacy of Warin. Unlike William, who belonged to a later generation of Malmesbury monks, Faricius was an eyewitness to these events and was subject to Warin's authority as abbot. A skilled physician, Faricius arrived in England as a layman after the Conquest and became a monk at Malmesbury. Unlike William, who was sent to Malmesbury as a boy, Faricius chose the monastic career as a mature adult and he selected Malmesbury as the community he wished to join. There is no apparent reason to question the truthfulness of Faricius' portrait of Warin which was written after the abbot's death when there was no obvious pressure to present him in a favourable light. The testimony of Faricius provides a markedly different picture of Warin to that given by William. There is no reference at all in Faricius to the disrespectful treatment of Malmesbury relics by Warin or to his misuse of the monastery's resources. There is simply a suggestion that Warin needed initially to be persuaded of the authenticity of the particular relics that were traditionally identified as those of Aldhelm.

---

8   Susan Ridyard, 'Post-Conquest Attitudes to the Saints of the Anglo-Saxons', in *Proceedings of the Battle Conference 1986*, ed. R. Allen Brown (1987): 194.

Malmesbury Abbey 670–1539

For some while he had had doubts about the holy body, and this led him to decree a three-day fast for his faithful congregation; they were to sing psalms devoutly at appropriate places, and to humble themselves in every way in the sight of divine clemency, so that by the mercy of almighty God they might discover the relics of the great bishop.[9]

Faricius summed up Warin's career in a way that contained no hint of criticism.

Warin was the first [abbot of *Meldunum*] since the French took control of the English who had shown the monks there the example of habitual good behaviour, religious way of life, and knowledge of the monastic Rule.[10]

One event, recounted by Faricius concerned a vision of Aldhelm which he experienced personally in a dream as he slept in the monastery dormitory. In this dream Faricius was standing by Aldhelm's tomb when he saw him awakening, symbolising perhaps the renewal of the saint's spiritual power that he believed was taking place at that time. Faricius recounted how, having woken from his dream, he sought out Warin to discuss the meaning of what he had seen while asleep, 'I recounted my vision to Warin, father of the monks'.[11] Here, Faricius presented Warin in respectful terms as his trusted spiritual father and a man with whom he could share his innermost spiritual experiences in keeping with the Rule. There was, therefore, a significant difference between William's negative and Faricius' positive portrayal of Abbot Warin.

The royal charter of 1081

Who was right about the character of Warin, Faricius or William? Evidence from another source, the Abbey cartulary, proves that Abbot Warin was successful in winning royal patronage from Matilda of Flanders, the Conqueror's wife. She issued a charter in February 1081, which recorded her decision to grant land in the village of Garsdon to the monastery of Malmesbury.[12] William of Malmesbury would, without doubt, have seen the Garsdon charter in the monastery archive but he made no reference to it in his account of Malmesbury after the Conquest. Perhaps William ignored this charter because it showed Warin in an extremely good light and did not support the case against him which William wanted to make. The wording of the Garsdon charter suggests that Warin was on good

---

9   Faricius, *Vita*, XXII.4 (ed. Winterbottom 21–2).
10 Faricius, *Vita*, XXIII.1 (ed. Winterbottom 22).
11 Faricius, *Vita*, XXIII.10 (ed. Winterbottom 23).
12 *RM* I 326–7.

Responding to the Conquest (1066–1100)

terms with the queen in 1081, and Matilda characterised her gift as a response to the urgent petitioning 'of the reverend abbot Warin'.

> Wherefore I, Matilda, by God's grace queen and legal wife of William the most energetic king of the English, very powerful ruler over the other peoples roundabout, and most noble duke of the Normans, at the wish and with the sincere consent of that same most distinguished man, and at the pressing request of the reverend abbot Warin, I have given to Mary, holy mother of God, virgin most chaste, and to St Aldhelm in the monastery of *Meldunum*, some land called Garsdon, as I had it for my own, with all that is due to it, to be held in perpetuity by hereditary right, for the benefit of the monks who take part in God's work there, and who pour forth tears before the gaze of God's mercy for the remission of my sins and those of my husband and sons.[13]

Matilda's unusual use of the term 'queen and legal wife' was possibly a response to English gossip that she was the concubine rather than the properly married wife of the Conqueror. Edith, the widow of Edward the Confessor, issued a charter in Old English in 1072 in which she insultingly called the queen 'Mathyld his gebedde', that is 'Matilda his bed-fellow'.[14] While the Garsdon charter was indisputably a record of the queen's decision, the grant was ratified by the Conqueror himself, and was issued in his presence: 'I, William king of the English, confirmed this gift and signed it with my own hand'.[15] For Warin, obtaining this charter, endorsed personally by William the Conqueror, was a moment of triumph. Queen Matilda described with admiration the religious life 'of the monks who do God's work' at Malmesbury. She valued the intercessory power of the prayers of the community and expected, in return for the gift of the land at Garsdon, that the monks of Malmesbury would use their influence with God on behalf of herself, the Conqueror and their sons. The witness list indicates that one son, the future Henry I, who was aged about thirteen at the time, was present and attested to the grant.[16]

Matilda's gift signalled a resumption of royal patronage for Malmesbury after a break of almost exactly one hundred years. Prior to 1081, the most recent royal grant to Malmesbury had taken place in 982 when Æthelred the Unready granted lands at Rodbourne to the monastery.[17] Although separated in time by a century there are important connections between the grant of Rodbourne in 982 and the gift of Garsdon in 1081. Both were acts of restitution of lands supposedly given to Aldhelm by

---

13 Ibid.
14 David Bates, 'William the Conqueror and Wessex', in *The Land of the English Kin*, ed. A. Langlands and R. Lavelle (Leiden, 2020), 517–37.
15 *RM* I 326–7.
16 Ibid.
17 Kelly, *Charters*, 237–8.

King Ine of Wessex in 701 but, in the eyes of the monks, subsequently stolen from the monastery and its patron saint.[18] The community saw Rodbourne and Garsdon as part of the original royal endowment of Aldhelm's Malmesbury. Warin's request drew upon the pre-Conquest institutional memory of the monastery, and the gift of Garsdon in 1081 constituted a further stage in the restoration of Ine's gift to the Aldhelm and his community begun in 982. Matilda's grant in February 1081 also indicated that the monastery, under Warin, was viewed favourably by Lanfranc, archbishop of Canterbury. The Garsdon charter concluded with an anathema, personally issued by Lanfranc, which threatened dire spiritual penalties for anyone who attempted to take the land away from the monks in the future.

> I, Archbishop Lanfranc, with the authority of almighty God and his clerics, and with the power I have, excommunicate those who by plan or deed cause the separation of Garsdon from the proper use of the monks of *Meldunum*.[19]

It seems that Lanfranc had become convinced by the merits of the argument, made by Warin, that Garsdon, a royal gift to Aldhelm, had been wickedly alienated from the Abbey's estate and that there should be no repetition of this sinful act. The text of the Garsdon charter indicates that Abbot Warin had direct access to the royal court and was respected by both the royal family and the influential figure of Lanfranc.

The magnitude of Warin's achievement in winning patronage from the queen becomes clear when the gift of Garsdon is considered in the context of her overall approach to patronage. The Garsdon charter is, in at least one important respect, unique and has been described as 'Matilda's one surviving English diploma' because it is the only known example of a patronage charter issued by Queen Matilda during her occasional visits to England.[20] Although Matilda had a reputation for piety, the focus for her generosity towards the Church was overwhelmingly directed towards religious institutions in Normandy and not England. Elizabeth van Houts describes how, after 1066, she made gifts to only two churches in England: Malmesbury and Wells Cathedral.[21] In fact, the benefaction to Wells was not a gift; Matilda simply encouraged the bishop of Exeter to hand over disputed property in Somerset to the bishop of Wells.[22] Matilda's gift of Garsdon to the monks of Malmesbury stands alone.

---

[18] For the grant of Garsdon and Rodbourne in 701, see Kelly, *Charters*, 150–1.
[19] *RM* I 327–8.
[20] David Bates, 'Queenship in Anglo-Norman Charters', in *Frankland: The Franks and the World of the Early Middle Ages*, ed. Paul Fouracre and David Ganz (Manchester, 2020), 291.
[21] Elizabeth van Houts, *Matilda of Flanders*, ODNB (2004).
[22] Bates, 'William the Conqueror and Wessex', 517–37.

Responding to the Conquest (1066–1100)

Royal patronage and the sanctity of Aldhelm

After the Conquest Matilda was richly endowed with dower lands in England but, as a rule, she chose not to patronise English monastic institutions. Why did she make an exception when she responded favourably to Warin's 'pressing request'? There was almost certainly a strong causal connection between Matilda's decision in 1081 and Warin's successful campaign to convince the ecclesiastical authorities of Norman England to accept the sanctity of Aldhelm. It cannot be a coincidence that Matilda's unusual act of generosity took place soon after the formal recognition of Aldhelm's sainthood. Despite differences in the way they portrayed Warin, both William and Faricius agreed that, after some sort of initial hesitation, Warin set out to establish Aldhelm's credentials as a major saint. He won endorsement of Aldhelm's saintly status from Bishop Osmund of Salisbury who was appointed to the see following the death of the previous bishop, Hermann, on 20 February 1078.[23] Osmund had previously been William the Conqueror's Chancellor, and he was held in high regard by the royal family. At some point during the years 1078–80 Osmund publicly proclaimed Aldhelm's sanctity and, as a result, Queen Matilda was prepared in 1081 to issue a charter in favour of the monastery, restoring lands that were considered to be part of the historic patrimony of St Aldhelm. The recognition of Aldhelm's sanctity created the preconditions for the renewal of royal patronage after a break of a century.

Warin had the good fortune to win support for the renewed cult of Aldhelm from several senior ecclesiastics working in the region. In addition to Bishop Osmund, Warin's allies included Hubald, archdeacon of Salisbury and Serlo, the energetic and reforming abbot of Gloucester, and these men became enthusiastic advocates of the cult of Aldhelm. Osmund's origins are not known but he was, it seems, in Normandy before the Conquest. Hubald was Italian and a friend of Faricius. Osmund, assisted by Warin and Serlo, officiated at the key event which signalled recognition of the authenticity of Aldhelm's sanctity. This was the 'translation' of Aldhelm: the solemn exhumation and reburial of relics which took place in 1078 (according to William) or 1080 (according to Faricius). Faricius called the translation a moment of 'revelation': the act of translation *revealed* the indisputable sanctity of Aldhelm to the world. This account is in keeping with practice elsewhere in Latin Europe at the time. One authority on the recognition of sanctity before the development of the papal monopoly of canonisation in the twelfth century identified the act of translation by the diocesan bishop as 'the principal outward sign of recognition of a saint'.[24]

---

23 Julia Barrow, *Hermann*, ODNB (2004).
24 E. W. Kemp, 'Pope Alexander III and the Canonization of Saints', *Transactions*

David Knowles used events at Malmesbury as evidence of Norman hostility towards Anglo-Saxon saints, but the success of the campaign to promote the cult of Aldhelm suggests a rather different narrative. Five foreign clerics – Warin, Serlo, Faricius, Hubald and Osmund – embraced belief in the supernatural power of the Anglo-Saxon saint, Aldhelm, and enthusiastically promoted his veneration. Why were these foreign-born clerics devoted to Aldhelm? It is impossible to know now how far Warin was personally committed to Aldhelm's cult. He had a vested interest in the flourishing of the cult of Aldhelm because his community benefitted directly from the resulting patronage and pilgrimage, and perhaps this led him to conclude, for practical rather than spiritual reasons, that the sanctity of Aldhelm should be endorsed. While this is possible, there is no obvious reason to doubt that religious zeal inspired Serlo, Osmund and Hubald, and the hagiography of the saint written by Faricius suggests that he was driven by an intense personal devotion to Aldhelm. He maintained his reverence for Aldhelm after he left Malmesbury and became abbot of Abingdon; remarkably, he obtained a substantial portion of the bones of Aldhelm for his new community.[25]

The elite of Norman England – both secular and ecclesiastical – eventually decided to venerate certain Anglo-Saxon saints such as Aldhelm because they were convinced that these saints had strong miracle-working abilities. The defining characteristic of an important saint was the ability to intercede with God and thereby bring about miraculous cures of medical conditions. This was why Faricius and later William of Malmesbury placed great emphasis on documenting credible miraculous cures. Faricius tried to be systematic and sought to arrange his miracle tales in chronological order.[26] He dated one important miracle to the abbacy of Warin: this concerned the curing the blindness of a fisherman from the Isle of Wight who had come to Malmesbury to pray for the assistance of Aldhelm. Faricius described the miracle of the fisherman just before his account of the translation ceremony and William of Malmesbury recounted the same story, explicitly dating it to the period immediately before the translation event. It was, according to William, the cure of the fisherman that finally persuaded Warin of the need to venerate Aldhelm as a saint.

> Seeing this, the abbot had no excuse for further delay, and he put his mind to honouring the precious confessor.[27]

---

of the Royal Historical Society, 27 (1945): 13–28.
25 Historia Ecclesie Abbendonensis II 55 (ed. Hudson 67).
26 Faricius, Vita, XVII.2 (ed. Winterbottom 17).
27 GP I V 267.1 (ed. Winterbottom 633).

Responding to the Conquest (1066–1100)

Another miracle, which took place a year or two after the translation, concerned a boy with a profound disability. William claimed that this provided the crucial evidence that convinced Archbishop Lanfranc of the need to venerate Aldhelm.

> This event was so miraculous that the monks brought it post-haste to the attention of the abbot, who was away at the king's court. The abbot thought fit to show the letter to Lanfranc, and that learned man, judging the confessor's merits from this wonderful happening, proclaimed a law throughout all England ordering him to be regarded and worshipped as a saint forthwith. A yearly market was at once set up to coincide with his feast day, so that anyone who failed to be attracted by the confessor's holiness would at least be drawn by greed for goods.[28]

The story of how Lanfranc proclaimed the sanctity of Aldhelm is not found in Faricius. It seems highly surprising that Faricius failed to mention such an important event if it actually took place, and William's claim is not supported by any other sources.[29] Although there are some authentic elements in William's account, such as the fact that a fair was permitted on the saint's feast, it seems unlikely that it was news of this miracle that convinced Lanfranc that Aldhelm was worthy of veneration. As we shall see there are strong grounds for thinking that Lanfranc had given prior approval for the translation ceremony and by this act had effectively accepted Aldhelm's sanctity.

William proposed a date of 3 June 1078 for the translation event but there are technical problems with this date.[30] The chronology of Faricius is much more plausible, according to which the translation took place on 25 May 1080, since by then Osmund had been bishop for about two years, giving him plenty of time to familiarise himself with the case, consult with his superior, Archbishop Lanfranc, and conclude that Aldhelm was an authentic and powerful saint worthy of translation. Faricius' date of 1080 for the translation event makes possible an active role for Lanfranc. Osmund was not a free agent: he was Lanfranc's man. When, at some point in 1078, Osmund became bishop of Salisbury, he subscribed to a strongly worded profession of obedience to Lanfranc.[31] It seems therefore improbable that the translation took place without the archbishop's approval, and we know from other places that Lanfranc took an active interest in establishing the legitimacy of Anglo-Saxon saints.[32] The chronicle of Evesham Abbey, for example, recounted how

---

28 *GP I* V 269.7–8 (ed. Winterbottom 641).
29 *GP II* 318.
30 See Thomson's commentary in *GP II* 315–16.
31 M. Richter, *Canterbury Professions* XL (Torquay, 1973), 30.
32 See H. E. J. Cowdrey, *Lanfranc: Scholar, Monk, Archbishop* (Oxford, 2003), 184. Lanfranc's biographer, Cowdrey, discussed his 'behind the scenes'

Malmesbury Abbey 670–1539

the authenticity of Anglo-Saxon relics there was assessed and eventually approved, at about this time 'at the instruction of the venerable archbishop Lord Lanfranc'.[33]

If we accept that it was unlikely that Osmund would officiate at the translation of the relics of Aldhelm without Lanfranc's prior permission, then William's chronology surely becomes untenable. Hermann died on 20 February 1078, and William said that the translation took place on 3 June of the same year. It is impossible that in this period of just fifteen weeks the following events could have transpired: the vacancy was noted, discussed and options reviewed; Osmund emerged as a candidate as new bishop; Osmund's candidature was approved by both king and archbishop; the new bishop was formally consecrated by Lanfranc; Osmund began work in Old Sarum; among many other initial priorities Osmund established a relationship with Warin, familiarised himself with the Aldhelm case, decided in favour of Aldhelm's sanctity, and won approval from Lanfranc for the ceremony of translation; Osmund officiated at the translation ceremony in the presence of a congregation of lay and ecclesiastical dignitaries who had been formally summoned in advance. This sequence of events could not possibly be completed in the space of less than four months.

There are, therefore, compelling reasons for rejecting William's chronology. The date provided by Faricius for the translation, 25 May 1080, is much more convincing. The itinerary of Queen Matilda provided Warin with opportunities to lobby her and secure the charter in the immediate aftermath of the successful translation ceremony conducted in line with the account of Faricius in May 1080. Although Matilda spent the majority of her time after 1066 in Normandy, she arrived in England in the late summer of 1080 and was with her husband and Archbishop Lanfranc in Gloucester for the Christmas feast in late December 1080 and early January 1081.[34] The Gloucester Christmas court was the occasion for a major Church council presided over by Lanfranc in the presence of the royal family. Warin as the abbot of a major religious house probably attended. Charters in favour of other beneficiaries indicate that, on leaving Gloucester, the Conqueror and his queen were in Salisbury in February 1081. Although the place where the Garsdon charter was issued is not stated, it seems likely that it was granted in Salisbury. Warin had ample opportunity during the previous weeks to petition the queen in person and to do so in the presence of Lanfranc and Osmund, who

---

involvement in similar public demonstrations of the sanctity of Anglo-Saxon saints.

33 Jay Rubenstein, 'Liturgy against History: The Competing Visions of Lanfranc and Eadmer of Canterbury', *Speculum*, 74 (1999): 296.

34 Tracy Borman, *Queen of the Conqueror: The Life of Matilda, Wife of William I* (London, 2012), 201.

Responding to the Conquest (1066–1100)

doubtless spoke in his favour and helped him to win an exceptional gift from the queen.

There is further evidence of the results of Warin's campaign to promote the veneration of Aldhelm to the royal family. The Abbey cartulary contains a charter, issued by William the Conqueror, which gave the monastery permission to organise an annual fair around the feast of Aldhelm and to keep the resulting tolls and profits. The text shows that the king and his advisers believed in the palpable presence and spiritual power of the saint, and the beneficiary of the grant was named not as the monastery but as Aldhelm himself.

> William king of the English to his archbishops, bishops, earls, sheriffs, and all his loyal people, French and English, of the kingdom of England, greetings. Know that I have given St Aldhelm a fair every year.[35]

The Domesday Book indicates that Warin was successful in his engagement with William the Conqueror, as well as his wife. Among the Domesday entries for Gloucestershire is a description of a fishery on the River Wye, at a place called *Modesgate*, together with an associated half a hide of land, which was held by the abbot of Malmesbury in 1086. Local people said that this was a result of the king's gift ('dono regis'), that is to say the gift of the Conqueror.[36] Domesday also records that this property was part of a collection of fisheries and land held in 1066 by one Beorhtric. Property taken from the family of the former English owner had been granted to Malmesbury by King William.

The cartulary contains additional evidence that Warin was energetic and successful in promoting the economic well-being of the house. One charter purports to date from 1065 and ostensibly provides royal confirmation by Edward the Confessor of the Malmesbury estates.[37] It seems likely that the document in its final form was produced during Warin's abbacy as a way of providing legal protection for the community's estate, and there is a probable post-Conquest echo of Warin's propaganda campaign in favour of Aldhelm's cult in this document. The charter claimed that Edward's decision to issue the charter was motivated by 'reverence for Saint Aldhelm [...] whose glorious body rests venerably in the same church and shines with many miracles that have been wrought'.[38] The reference to the miracle-working powers of Aldhelm's relics is consistent with the idea that this part of the text was a forgery, sanctioned by Warin, and dating from the years when Warin was using Aldhelm's miracles as evidence of his sanctity.

---

[35] *RM* I 329.

[36] *Exchequer Domesday Book*, ed. and trans. Robin Fleming in *Domesday Book and the Law* (Cambridge, 1998), 145.

[37] Kelly, *Charters*, 244–6; *RM* I 321–5.

[38] Kelly, *Charters*, 244–6, *RM* I 321–5.

Gifts from non-royal donors

The charter evidence also indicates that Warin had some success in attracting non-royal patronage immediately after the proclamation of Aldhelm's sanctity. Faricius recounted how 'a host of noblemen and troops of knights' attended the translation, indicating that Warin was interested in winning support and patronage from elite members of the laity as well as royalty. The Malmesbury cartulary contains a charter documenting a gift by a wealthy couple of ownership of a church and a group of houses in London.[39] This charter was probably kept, despite a general policy of sifting out non-royal benefactions from the archive, because it proved the legitimacy of the monastery's title to valuable property in London. In 1084 Godwin and his wife, Turgund, gave 'reverend Abbot Warin' their proprietary church of St Nicholas Acon in the city of London, together with several houses. Warin's success in obtaining royal patronage had perhaps made the monastery in Wiltshire well known and fashionable nationally and as a result Warin was able to win a benefaction from a pious lay couple. There is further evidence that Abbot Warin was able to attract patronage from English people. In the cartulary there is the record of a gift in the late eleventh century of an estate of three hides in Newbold Comyn in Warwickshire by an English landowner called 'Wolwynus' or Wulfwine who granted the land and also became a monk of Malmesbury.[40] Wulfwine held the land before the Conquest and had retained ownership after the Norman takeover before deciding to give his worldly goods to the monastery and join the community as a monk.

The impact of Warin's activities on the wealth of the community can be seen in the Domesday Book. The net annual value of the property of the monastery rose from £119 10s in 1066 to £140 10s in 1086, an increase of 17%.[41] This figure under-represents the growth in income as it does not include greater revenue from the donations of pilgrims visiting Aldhelm's shrine of Aldhelm or the tolls and charges generated by the new trade fair granted to the monastery by William the Conqueror.

It is impossible to avoid the conclusion that Warin of Lire, although maligned by William of Malmesbury for his stewardship, was responsible for improving the monastery's fortunes after the Conquest. During his abbacy individuals as diverse as the Italian doctor Faricius of Arezzo and Wulfwine, the English landowner from Warwickshire, journeyed to Malmesbury and became monks of the house. Warin relaunched the cult of Aldhelm and thereby established Malmesbury as an important sacred place in the eyes of the Norman rulers of England.

[39] *RM* I 328.
[40] *RM* I 251–2.
[41] Berry I 48.

Responding to the Conquest (1066–1100)

Winning the support of William Rufus

The precise date of Abbot Warin's death is not known but by 1091 he had been replaced by Godfrey, a monk of Ely, who had come to England from the abbey of Jumièges in Normandy.[42] By the time of the arrival of Godfrey, the Conqueror had died and William Rufus was on the throne. While William of Malmesbury spoke warmly of Abbot Godfrey, he was highly critical of the new king and his rapacity. His only criticism of Godfrey was that, in response to exorbitant royal demands for money, the abbot was forced to sell some of the monastery's treasures.

> When the younger King William imposed an insupportable tribute on England with a view to spending the proceeds on buying Normandy from his brother Robert, Godfrey, anxious to raise his share with no trouble, disgracefully sold off the church treasures, accumulated by careful abbots of old.[43]

Again, it is interesting to compare William of Malmesbury's views with evidence from other sources. The cartulary indicates that some degree of royal benevolence towards Malmesbury continued during the reign of William Rufus. Perhaps Godfrey's willingness to comply with the king's demands bought goodwill in a way that was of practical value to the community. The cartulary contains two documents issued by Rufus in favour of the monastery. Both were made in response to successful petitioning of the king by Abbot Godfrey. In one charter the king instructed his huntsmen and foresters to respect the property rights of the monks of Malmesbury in Bradon Forest to north-east of Malmesbury. The monastery possessed private woodland in close proximity to the royal forest, and the implication of the grant was that the king's foresters and huntsmen had unlawfully entered the monks' woods to the annoyance of the abbot and his men. Royal foresters were forbidden in future to go into these woods, and a royal huntsman named Croco was ordered to drop a legal claim against the abbot.[44] The second directive issued by Rufus instructed a man named in the cartulary version as William 'de Carcario' to restore to the monastery land that had been granted to the community by his brother, Malger.[45] It is possible that the cartulary copy of the charter contains a transcription error and that the brothers' family name was 'de Cartario', a toponymic derived from Carteret, a coastal settlement in Normandy. No one with the name 'de Carcario' is listed in the Domesday Book, but one 'Malger de Cartrai' is given as holding land in Somerset.[46]

---

42 *Heads of Houses I*, 55.
43 *GP I* V 271.5 (ed. Winterbottom 647).
44 *RM I* 330
45 Ibid.
46 K. S. B. Keats-Rohan, *Domesday People* (Woodbridge, 1999); 'Text of the

Malmesbury Abbey 670–1539

According to the Norman chronicler, Wace, one 'Maugier de Cartrai' fought at Hastings.[47] It seems likely that this was the man who had given land to Malmesbury, and whose brother William subsequently interfered in the transfer of ownership. The 'de Carcario' charter is evidence both of Abbot Godfrey's ability to get William Rufus to interfere in legal disputes on behalf of the Malmesbury community and proof that the monastery was successful in winning non-royal patronage in the last decades of the eleventh century, in this case from lay members of the new Norman elite.

Somerset Domesday: Part 2', in *A History of the County of Somerset: Volume 1*, ed. William Page (London, 1906), 479–526.

[47] Wace, *Le roman de Rou et des ducs de Normandie*, ed. Frédéric Pluquet (Paris, 1827), 241–2.

6

William of Malmesbury and Queen Matilda

During the late eleventh and early twelfth centuries Malmesbury was home to a remarkable scholar known to posterity as William of Malmesbury. He was one of the great historians of the Middle Ages, and accounts by modern historians of political events in England during the eleventh and early twelfth centuries still rely heavily on information provided by William's major historical works: *Gesta Pontificum, Gesta Regum* and *Historia Novella*. In addition to these well-known surveys of national history, William wrote many other works on a range of topics such as biblical commentary, the miracles of the Virgin Mary, the lives of saints and the history of Glastonbury. William broke off from writing his last work, *Historia Novella*, at the end of 1142, and it is generally assumed that he died shortly afterwards.

In recounting the story of the Norman Conquest in the *Gesta Regum* William explained that he was of mixed parentage, both English and Norman. This, he felt, positioned him ideally as an objective and fair commentator on the career of William the Conqueror.

> The Normans in their enthusiasm have overpraised him [William the Conqueror], and his good and bad deeds alike have been lauded to the skies; the English, inspired by national enmities, have savaged their lord with foul calumnies. For my part, having the blood of both nations in my veins, I propose in my narrative to keep a middle path [...][1]

William joined the community at Malmesbury as a boy and remained a monk of Malmesbury for the rest of his life. He was, by his own account, a studious child and recalled in *Gesta Regum* how he acquired a love of learning from both his parents.

> It is many years since I formed the habit of reading thanks to my parents' encouragement and my own bent for study. It has been a source of pleasure for me ever since I was a boy, and its charm grew as I grew. Indeed I had been brought up by my father to regard is as damaging to my soul and good repute if I turned my attention in any other direction.[2]

---

1 *GR I* III Preface (ed. Mynors, Thomson & Winterbottom 207–9).
2 *GR I* II Preface (ed. Mynors, Thomson & Winterbottom 151).

Malmesbury Abbey 670–1539

Establishing when William of Malmesbury was born, and when he joined the Malmesbury community, is not straightforward. In his commentary on the Lamentations of Jeremiah, *Liber super Explanationem Lamentationum*, usually dated to 1135–6, William appeared to describe himself as being exactly forty years old as he finished the work, which has been interpreted as indicating a birth date of about 1095–6.

> I am forty today; I have come to the mid-point of the course that the divine psalmist appoints for the life of man, when he says: The days of our years in them are threescore and ten years. But if in the strong they be fourscore years: and what is more of them is labour and sorrow (Ps. 89, 10)[3]

Curiously, the reason why this text is usually dated to the period immediately after the death of Henry I concerns a reference in this work to an ostrich in the king's menagerie. William proudly told how he had seen the bird in Henry's personal zoo.

> The ostrich is a large-limbed bird, winged but flightless. We saw a such a one in England in the time of King Henry, that keen collector of prodigious exotica.[4]

The phrase 'in the time of King Henry' seems to imply that it was written after Henry's death in 1135. While Michael Winterbottom printed this rendering, he also observed that the Latin could possibly be interpreted differently as, 'in the time of the [present] king, Henry'.[5] Another important source suggests that this alternative reading of the account of Henry's ostrich must be right, making possible a significantly earlier date of birth for William. In the *Gesta Pontificum* William stated emphatically that he had personally witnessed certain miracles at Malmesbury as a boy. One of these can be dated without doubt to 1096 or earlier, and it concerns the miraculous cure of a prominent nobleman called Ernulf de Hesdin. Before recounting the story of Hesdin, William explained that his complete certainty of the authenticity of this and other miracles was based on the evidence of his own eyes: he was there.

> But it is one thing to record what one has *heard*; my pen must also strive to put down what God has granted me to *see*. [6]

The account of Hesdin's cure is full of plausible detail.[7] Hesdin had some sort of ulcerous skin condition on his hands and went to Malmesbury,

---

3   Michael Winterbottom, trans., *William of Malmesbury on Lamentations* (Turnhout, 2013), 35.
4   *Lamentations*, 276
5   *Lamentations*, 10.
6   GP I V 273.6 (ed. Winterbottom 653).
7   GP I V 274.1 (ed. Winterbottom 655).

William of Malmesbury and Queen Matilda

not looking for a miraculous cure but to consult a doctor based at the monastery called Gregory (presumably a monk who, like Faricius, was a medical specialist). Gregory's medical treatment failed, but Abbot Godfrey suggested that 'balsam' found in the tomb of Aldhelm could be applied to Hesdin's hands.[8] The result was a miracle and a complete cure; afterwards Hesdin's faith was strengthened, and 'he set off for Jerusalem with no prospect of returning'.[9] Aspects of this story can be corroborated from other sources. Hesdin was not a shadowy figure and William was correct in stating that Ernulf went on crusade and did not return. The Warenne chronicle (also known as the Hyde chronicle) recounted how Ernulf fell out with William Rufus in 1096 and journeyed to the Holy Land where he was killed at the siege of Antioch between late 1096 and June 1097. William's account of Hesdin's visit to Malmesbury is, therefore, entirely consistent with evidence derived from other sources. William claimed unequivocally that he saw Ernulf of Hesdin at Malmesbury and implied that this was not long before Ernulf went on crusade, so the likely date for the event in the monastery is around 1095–6, possibly earlier but definitely not later. Unless William had curiously misremembered or invented the whole story, this renders impossible a date of birth for William of 1095–6. If William was present at Hesdin's visit, he must have been a boy oblate, aged say between eight and ten years old, and this gives us a likely birth date in the range 1086–8. Such a date is consistent with other evidence. As we shall see, William met Queen Matilda, wife of Henry II, and was researching her family history and the wider story of the kings and queens of England at the time of her death in 1118. If we assume that his first encounter with Matilda took place a little earlier, say 1115, it seems inconceivable that the queen would commission an important work from a monk who was barely twenty years old. It is much more plausible to assume that William was in his late twenties when he began to work for the queen.

William's education

William's presence in the monastery during the visit of Ernulf of Hesdin in 1096 or earlier means that he must have known personally Faricius of Arezzo, who was a monk of Malmesbury until he became abbot of Abingdon in 1100. Faricius made no reference in his hagiographical study of Aldhelm to the miracle of Ernulf of Hesdin, but both Faricius and William claimed that they were personally present at another miracle which concerned a partially paralysed woman who came to Malmesbury hoping for a cure. Both men, in their accounts of Aldhelm's miracles, claimed that they were in the conventual church one Easter Monday, and

8   *GP* I V 274.4 (ed. Winterbottom 655).
9   Ibid.

77

Malmesbury Abbey 670–1539

had witnessed the 'ludus peregrini', the liturgical drama during which monks acted out the story of the risen Christ encountering two disciples on the road to Emmaus.[10] Each man provided different details about what happened. William recalled that he was part of the choir chanting a particular verse from the antiphon 'Christus Resurgens' when the woman 'crashed to the stone floor' to the alarm of those present.[11] Faricius explained that he was 'nearby in a group' when the woman fell to the ground and that he 'thought, wrongly, that she had had an epileptic fit'.[12] All was in fact well: the woman stood up and announced that she had been cured. While William observed this as a junior chorister, Faricius, as a senior member of the community, was called upon to investigate the matter which he did the following day, providing the interesting detail that, since he spoke no English, he needed access to interpreters in order to interview the woman.

William's accounts of the miracles wrought by Aldhelm during his own boyhood and youth give a lively sense of daily life in and around the monastery on great feast days. Members of the public had access to the conventual church, and the monks interacted with the public outside the church during solemn processions and the display of relics. At times the results were chaotic.

> Mingling with the throng of pious people who came to the festival can be found a fair number of rascals who pick up an easy living by making their audience guffaw with jokes prepared in advance. When I was a boy, one of this type had arrived; his wit was sharper than that of others, and he was also good at making obscene gestures if words did not do the trick. When the shrine of the saint was carried out of doors – it is improper even to tell the story – this man brazenly confronted it. He first polluted the air by baring his private parts, then went on to foul it by farting. This made fools laugh but the monks were aggrieved that a scoundrel's babble should go unpunished.[13]

William had joined the monastery of Malmesbury as a boy before the departure of Ernulf of Hesdin on crusade in late 1096. The abbot of Malmesbury during these years was Godfrey of Jumièges, who ruled over Malmesbury from around 1091 until his death in around 1106.[14] William had fond memories of Abbot Godfrey, praising him for promoting good monastic observance and enriching the library.

> In his time and thanks to his energy the church gained greatly in prestige, and its religious life was much enriched. He put in hand

---

10 *GP I* V 276.3 (ed. Winterbottom 659).
11 Ibid.
12 Faricius, *Vita*, XXX.9 (ed. Winterbottom 30).
13 *GP I* V 275.1–2 (ed. Winterbottom 657).
14 *Heads of Houses I*, 55.

78

William of Malmesbury and Queen Matilda

many embellishments, so far as he could at such busy period and when resources were so meagre.[15]

With the abbot's support William undertook an extensive programme of higher study with an emphasis on history, and it is possible that he undertook his studies outside Malmesbury at a better equipped monastery such as Glastonbury or Canterbury. William recalled this education in the Prologue to Book II of the *Gesta Regum*.

> I studied many kinds of literature, though in different degrees. To logic, the armourer of speech, I no more than lent an ear. Physic, which cures the sick body, I went deeper into. As for ethics, I explored parts in depth, revering its high status as a subject inherently accessible to the student and able to form good character; in particular I studied history, which adds flavour to moral instruction by imparting a pleasurable knowledge of past events, spurring the reader by the accumulation of examples to follow the good and shun the bad.[16]

William appears to have had access to family money which enabled him to buy his own books. At some point he decided that he would like to go beyond reading the works of others and embark upon a writing career.

> After I had spent a good deal of my own money on getting together a library of foreign historians, I proceeded in my leisure moments to inquire if anything could be discovered concerning England worth the attention of posterity. Not content with ancient works, I began to get the itch to write myself, not to show off my more or less non-existent erudition but in order to bring forcibly into the light things lost in the rubbish-heap of the past. Feeling an aversion to fleeting opinion, I collected chronicles from far and wide – almost, I confess, to no purpose: for when I had gone through them all I remained ignorant, not finding anything to read before I ceased to feel the urge to read it.[17]

From a young age William developed both a love of history and a deep sense of personal identification with Malmesbury and devotion to St Aldhelm. In the Prologue to Book V of *Gesta Pontificum* he described how he, 'as a monk of Malmesbury', was particularly well placed to write the authoritative biography of Aldhelm. William was unusually well-travelled for a monk, with first-hand knowledge of many other places. Hinting perhaps at experience of homesickness when on his travels, he stated that the prospect of writing about Aldhelm made him feel 'as though after a long period of foreign travel, I am coming home'.[18]

---

15 *GP I* V 271.1 (ed. Winterbottom 645).
16 *GR I* II Preface (ed. Mynors, Thomson & Winterbottom 151).
17 Ibid.
18 GP *I* V Prologue 1 (ed. Mynors, Thomson & Winterbottom 500).

Malmesbury Abbey 670–1539

Malmesbury was both his home and a sacred place because of its association with Aldhelm. As a gift to his brethren and a homage to Aldhelm, William created a special edition of his *Gesta Pontificum* that culminated in the addition of Book V, which combined the biography of Aldhelm, an account of his miracles and a general history of the monastery. In writing this final section of the work William considered that he was repaying a debt that he owed to the saint.

> Would it be fair for me to refuse to use my voice in praise of one who, second only to God, conferred on me what small ability I have? Should I not give the services of my tongue to one for whom if necessary I would give my life?[19]

The power of Queen Matilda

Assuming that William was born around 1086–8, he became a professed monk after 1100, and by the time that he took his solemn vows Queen Matilda, wife of Henry I, was the dominant figure in the life of the monastery. As part of her marriage settlement Matilda was given the Crown rents and other income from the borough of Malmesbury and some level of control over the monastery itself and its revenues.[20] Matilda's subsequent actions are consistent with the idea that Henry I saw Malmesbury as a royal 'Eigenkloster' or proprietary church and granted his rights as owner to his wife as part of her dower, and as a result the queen exercised 'formal jurisdiction over the abbey'.[21] The clearest evidence for this is a surviving letter from Matilda to Archbishop Anselm. The context for the letter was the need to appoint a new abbot following the death of Godfrey of Jumièges. Writing in the summer of 1106 the queen informed Anselm that she had decided to fill the vacancy at Malmesbury with a monk from Winchester called Aedulf.

> Relying on the favour of your Holiness I have committed the Abbey of Malmesbury, in those things which are under my jurisdiction, to Dom Aedulf, a monk and once sacristan of Winchester, who I believe is known to you.[22]

There was no question in Matilda's mind that the monks should have a free election. The decision was hers because she believed that 'the Abbey of Malmesbury' was her property. Writing two decades later to Matilda's

19 GP *I* V Prologue 1–2 (ed. Mynors, Thomson & Winterbottom 500).
20 For the dower of Queen Matilda, see Lois L. Huneycutt, *Matilda of Scotland: A Study in Medieval Queenship* (Woodbridge, 2003), 65.
21 Ibid.
22 *The Letters of Saint Anselm of Canterbury*, trans. Walter Fröhlich (Kalamazoo, 1994), 139–40.

80

William of Malmesbury and Queen Matilda

daughter, the Empress Matilda, and after the death of her mother, William of Malmesbury confirmed that Queen Matilda controlled the monastery under the terms of her dower.

> [...] because by royal gift she possessed our church, we enjoyed her compassion more fully than other men. Under her rule the light of religion shone abundantly in the place where her charity in its fullness was pre-eminent.[23]

In this same letter William recalled how the queen personally encouraged him to undertake a history of the English royal family in a way that would be linked to her own family history.

> Thus on one occasion we were engaged in conversation with her on the subject of St Aldhelm, whose kinswoman she claimed with proper pride to be, and she asked for information about his family. When told in reply that his lineage was the same as that of the kings of the West Saxons, she asked us to set out his whole family history in a short essay for her benefit, claiming that she was unworthy to receive the tribute of a volume on traditional lines on the history of the English kings. In our humble position we could not refuse a request backed by such imperious authority.[24]

Matilda was right, as William knew, to consider that she was related to Aldhelm. As the great-granddaughter of Edmund Ironside, Matilda was descended from the royal house of Wessex to which Aldhelm had also belonged. William complied with the queen's request and produced a summary account of the names and dates of English kings.

> We therefore arranged for the drawing up of a brief list of the English kings, both names and dates.[25]

They met again, and at this point Matilda changed her instructions, instructing him to go further and produce a comprehensive history of the kings of England.

> She was then attracted by the project of a somewhat fuller narrative, and with that charm which was one of her strong points she easily induced us to contemplate a full history of her predecessors. So we came 'to set on foot a greater enterprise' about our kings, one that would (as she put it) make them better known, bring her credit and be both useful and honourable to our foundation.[26]

---

23 *GR I* Ep. II.2.
24 *GR I* Ep. II.4–5.
25 *GR I* Ep. II.5.
26 Ibid.

Malmesbury Abbey 670–1539

This conversation was a pivotal moment in William's career. It was the genesis of one of the greatest historical works produced in England during the Middle Ages. William understood just how momentous this encounter was for him as a writer, and in describing how the queen initiated 'a greater enterprise' William was alluding to a passage in Virgil's *Aeneid* where the poet described the epic historical scope of the second half of the work:

A greater history opens before my eyes,
A greater task awaits me.[27]

Virgil summoned the Muse to help him to 'call up the kings, the early times [...] for I must tell of wars to chill the blood, ranked men in battle, kings by their own valour driven to death'.[28] By using this literary allusion William was comparing himself with Virgil. The historical sweep of the *Gesta Regum* was similar, he implied, to that of the *Aeneid*.

In order to gather archival material for this grand historical project, William somehow obtained permission and funds to go on an astonishing journey, or sequence of journeys, across England and Wales and perhaps beyond. There are references in his work to visits made to a bewildering variety of places: Carlisle and Hexham in the far north of England, St David's and Bangor in different parts of Wales, Canterbury and Lewes in the south-east, Bury St Edmunds and Ely in East Anglia, Tavistock and Exeter in the south-west. He studied Roman ruins at Bath, Chester, Gloucester and York.[29] It was almost certainly the fact that he was originally undertaking a royal commission that allowed William to be freed from monastic discipline and provided with the resources needed for these journeys.

Queen Matilda's correspondence provides further detail about the precise degree of authority that she claimed over Malmesbury. Here the date of her letter proposing Aedulf as abbot is significant. She wrote to Anselm in 1106 at precisely the time when the so-called 'investiture controversy' was being resolved. Anselm had been in dispute with Henry I since the beginning of his reign in 1100 concerning his right, and that of any other lay person, to 'invest' or formally appoint someone to a high ecclesiastical office. This dispute caused Anselm to go into exile in 1103. In July 1105 Anselm met King Henry at L'Aigle in Normandy and negotiated the basis of a compromise: the king agreed that he had no right to give the symbols of spiritual authority to a bishop or abbot, but he was entitled to demand homage before a prelate could be granted the temporal resources that belonged to the relevant ecclesiastical office. This compromise was accepted by Pope Paschal II in March 1106, shortly before Queen Matilda wrote to Anselm about the

---

[27] Virgil, *The Aeneid*, trans. Robert Fitzgerald (London, 1983), 196.
[28] Ibid.
[29] For William's travels, see Thomson in *GP II*, xxxix–xliv.

82

William of Malmesbury and Queen Matilda

Malmesbury vacancy. Matilda's proposal for Malmesbury echoed the L'Aigle compromise, although in a way that was favourable to her as the lay patron of Malmesbury. The queen told the archbishop that she had granted Aedulf authority in areas that pertained to her jurisdiction but that 'the bestowal of the crozier and [responsibility for] for pastoral care' were wholly matters for 'the judgement of your discretion'.[30] In fact, this was a form of legal fiction because the appointment of Aedulf was clearly viewed by the queen as a *fait accompli*. Anselm was simply being invited to ratify in a technical way a decision that she had already made. The archbishop wanted the investiture controversy to be resolved and had no problem with the formulation proposed by the queen; he wrote back to Matilda telling her that 'in what pertains to you, you have acted well and according to the will of God'. However, Anselm objected to this particular appointment on other grounds, claiming that Aedulf had disqualified himself through simony, having improperly sent the archbishop a goblet to win his approval.

> For, by the same messengers who brought me the letters from you and from others about this case, he [Aedulf] sent me a goblet. This goblet I did not wish to keep under any circumstances, but I was very sorry because I do not see how he can be excused from guilt in this matter.[31]

Despite Anselm's objections concerning the charge of simony, Matilda's will prevailed and the appointment of Aedulf stood; he remained abbot until 1118 when he was deposed, after Matilda's death, by Bishop Roger of Salisbury. Aedulf was, therefore, William of Malmesbury's abbot for about twelve years (1106–18). Curiously, William made no reference to him in any of his extant writings, perhaps because he disapproved of the way that Aedulf had been foisted upon the community by Queen Matilda.

William's criticism of the queen

Matilda gave William his big opportunity to produce a great work of history, and it may, therefore, seem surprising that William used this same work to make critical remarks about the character of the queen. In a coded and ironic way, William suggested that Matilda was complicit in her husband's many extra-marital relationships. Henry was notorious for his uncontrolled libido: he had more known illegitimate children than any other king in the history of England. In the *Gesta Regum* William implied that, after the birth of her two children, Matilda was grateful that Henry left her alone in London and respected her wish to refrain

---

30   *The Letters of Saint Anselm*, 139–40.
31   *The Letters of Saint Anselm*, 141.

Malmesbury Abbey 670–1539

from sex. In return, she turned a blind eye to the many sexual adventures Henry pursued in the setting of the peripatetic royal court.

> The bearing of two children, one of either sex, left her content, and for the future she ceased either to have offspring or to desire them, satisfied, when the king was busy elsewhere, to bid the court goodbye herself, and spend many years at Westminster.[32]

This criticism was veiled but the meaning would be clear to those of his readers who had heard the gossip about the king's behaviour. In another section of the *Gesta Regum* William, in ironic and surely comic mode, praised Henry I for his selfless commitment to extra-marital sex which, he claimed, was motivated not by lust but by a sense of duty.

> All his life he was completely free from fleshly lusts, indulging in the embraces of the female sex (as I have heard from those who know) from love of begetting children; for he thought it beneath his dignity to comply with extraneous gratification, unless the royal seed could fulfil its natural purpose.[33]

These curious observations did not reflect well on Matilda: William was perhaps suggesting that Henry had a royal duty to make children but his wife's distaste for sex and babies forced him to fulfil this responsibility outside marriage. *Gesta Regum* contained a summary view of Matilda's character in which William praised her for her piety but was highly critical of her tendency to favour foreigners over the English and her predatory behaviour towards 'her own people'.

> Her bounty went to all sorts of men, especially to foreigners, who might accept her presents, and then advertise her fame in other countries [...] our lady was beguiled into sweetening with presents all the foreigners she could [...][34]

> Thus it came about that she did not escape the vice of prodigality, laid all kinds of claims against her tenantry, used them despitefully and took their livelihood, winning the name of a generous giver but ignoring the wrongs of her own people. But a right judgement of her conduct will attribute it to the cunning of her servants, who like harpies seized with their talons all they could [...][35]

William felt aggrieved: his community received relatively little patronage compared to foreign clerics and Matilda's business managers were

32 *GR I* V 418.2.
33 *GR I* V 412.1–2.
34 *GR I* V 418.4.
35 *GR I* V 418.5.

William of Malmesbury and Queen Matilda

grasping in their treatment of her dower property, which included the monastery and borough of Malmesbury. There is some independent evidence that indicates that William was justified in holding these views about the queen. No charters record any acts of substantial generosity on Matilda's part towards the Abbey; she did extend the time allowed for St Aldhelm's Fair from three to five days, but this cost her nothing.[36] While Matilda gave little of value to the monastery, she was extremely generous to two French cathedrals: Chartres and Tours. Substantial portions of Matilda's correspondence have survived, and in one letter Ivo, bishop of Chartres thanked Matilda for a magnificent gift of new bells for his cathedral.[37] The archbishop of Tours, Hildebert of Lavardin, also wrote a letter of thanks to Matilda, expressing gratitude for her gift of a splendid golden candlestick. He congratulated Matilda for her generosity, praising the purity of the gold and the exquisite artistry of the work.[38] This was the generosity to 'foreigners' that so much annoyed William.

William's second charge was that Matilda was predatory towards 'her own people'. Her agents were greedy and 'like harpies seized with their talons all they could'. While in exile in France, Archbishop Anselm sent a letter of reproof to Matilda that is consistent with William's accusation. Although there was no explicit mention of Malmesbury, Matilda was reprimanded for her treatment of 'the churches in your hands'.

> After I left England, I heard that you were dealing with the churches in your hands otherwise than is expedient for them or for your own soul. I beseech you as my lady, advise you as my queen and admonish you as my daughter – as I have done before – that the churches of God which are in your power should know you as mother, as nurse, as kind lady and queen.[39]

There was, perhaps, another reason why William had serious reservations about Matilda. It seems highly likely that he resented the favour she showed towards the former Malmesbury monk, Faricius, who was well known for his medical expertise. Soon after his accession to the throne Henry I retained the services of Faricius as his personal physician, ensuring that he was appointed to the abbacy of Abingdon on 1 November 1100.[40] The Abingdon chronicler recorded his role as the royal physician and his high standing in the eyes both of Henry I and his wife, Queen Matilda.

---

36 *RM* I 333.
37 Ivo of Chartres, Ep. 142, *Patrologia Latina 162*.
38 Hildebert of Lavardin, Ep. 9, *Patrologia Latina 171*.
39 *The Letters of Saint Anselm*, 142.
40 Richard Sharpe, *Charters of William II and Henry I Project*. Available online at https://actswilliam2henry1.files.wordpress.com/2013/09/h1-abingdon-2013-1.pdf.

Malmesbury Abbey 670–1539

This man, then, was a Tuscan by birth, a citizen of the town of Arezzo, a most esteemed physician by practice, to the extent that the king often believed himself only curable by the compounds of his antidotes. He was very circumspect in worldly prudence, which at this time was essential for the governing of churches, and especially outstandingly learned in the knowledge of letters. The queen too entrusted herself to him before other physicians, as also did the more highly born men of all England.[41]

Henry proceeded to shower Faricius and Abingdon with gifts. On the very day of his wedding to Matilda – 11 November 1100 – King Henry issued three different charters in favour of Faricius and Abingdon Abbey.[42]

Faricius was not remembered with great fondness by William of Malmesbury. In his introduction to the fifth book of his *Gesta Pontificum* William made disparaging remarks about the hagiographical study of Aldhelm written by Faricius, criticising the quality of the research undertaken by the Italian and suggesting that his own work was much superior. He commented, somewhat tetchily, that fair-minded readers who compared the two works would judge in his favour, even though Faricius, as an abbot, might have more worldly status. Quoting Virgil, he claimed that he, just as much as Faricius, was worthy of respect for his achievements.

> I ask my readers to think well of me and to judge me fairly, so that my lack of distinction is not effaced by the prestige of an abbot. Yet if you look at honours attained, 'I too have won some name and glory'.[43]

William also provided an ambivalent account of Faricius in another part of *Gesta Pontificum* which recorded his career as abbot of Abingdon. The depiction of the achievements of Faricius at Abingdon took the form of a poem written by another monk of Malmesbury identified as Brother Peter.[44] Writing, surely ironically, William explained that Peter's poem sought to highlight 'the virtue of a praiseworthy abbot'. True, Peter's poem began by describing Faricius as 'upright' and 'wise' but the main thrust of the poem was that the extraordinary medical skill of Faricius gave him a degree of power over others, including the greatest in the land, that he used ruthlessly to promote the interests of Abingdon Abbey and humble his enemies.

> [...] he made even kings beholden to him by his cures.
> You might have seen kings and magnates bow down before him in obedience,

---

[41] *Historia Ecclesie Abbendonensis*, II 55 (ed. Hudson 65).
[42] Sharpe, *Charters of William II and Henry I Project*.
[43] *GP* I V Prologue.5 (ed. Winterbottom 501).
[44] *GP* I II 88.4–5 (ed. Winterbottom 301–5).

William of Malmesbury and Queen Matilda

Believing it the safe course to live by his precepts.
Court favour thus so emboldened him
That he dared to vie as of right with the powerful.
Them he so broke to his will, reduced to such a pass.
That he lorded over lords, pressing them beneath him.[45]

This is not the straightforward celebration of the career of a distinguished Malmesbury alumnus by the admiring brethren he had left behind. Why was there antagonism between the Malmesbury monks and their former colleague, Faricius? One reason, perhaps, was the way that Faricius used his influence with Matilda to obtain for Abingdon large chunks of the most precious treasure held by the Malmesbury monks: the physical remains of St Aldhelm. The twelfth-century chronicle of Abingdon itemised the relics of the house, highlighting how Faricius had obtained several pieces of the skeleton of Aldhelm.

He also acquired the whole thigh-bone, with part of the head, one tooth, and part of the shoulder-blade, of St Aldhelm, bishop of Malmesbury [sic] [...][46]

The Abingdon chronicle gave a completely unconvincing account of how the gift of part of the head of Aldhelm, and other substantial parts of his skeletal remains, were a consequence of the gratitude of Malmesbury monks towards their former cellarer, the officer of the monastery responsible for their food and drink.

Nor is it any wonder that the abbot acquired such great relics of this saint because he shed his worldly garb in the monastery where Aldhelm fell asleep, and he provided many benefits for the brethren living there during his monastic life with them.[47]

It is inconceivable that the monks of Malmesbury dismembered the sacred remains of Aldhelm to thank Faricius for the quality of the catering during his time as cellarer. A much more likely explanation is that the dismemberment was the result of a request by Faricius, authorised by Matilda. This could not be challenged because of the degree of control that Matilda exercised over Malmesbury Abbey. Another clue suggesting Matilda's involvement in the removal of Aldhelm's bones can be found in the Abingdon chronicle, which recorded how Malmesbury was compensated with 'part of the arm of St John Chrysostom'.[48] The chronicle explained that the Byzantine Emperor, Alexius I Comnenus, had recently sent this relic from Constantinople as a gift to Henry I and

---

45 *GP I* II 88.5–6 (ed. Winterbottom 303).
46 *Historia Ecclesie Abbendonensis*, II 55 (ed. Hudson 67).
47 *Historia Ecclesie Abbendonensis*, II 55 (ed. Hudson 68).
48 *Historia Ecclesie Abbendonensis*, II 55 (ed Hudson 69).

Malmesbury Abbey 670–1539

his wife, Queen Matilda. It seems likely that Matilda was instrumental in arranging a swap: Malmesbury was obliged to surrender part of Aldhelm but was granted the bone of John Chrysostom.

We know from other sources that Faricius was acquisitive as abbot and used his standing at the royal court to impose his will on others and enrich Abingdon. Faricius obtained seventy-six royal writs from Henry I during his abbacy providing royal backing for him in legal disputes. Far more writs were issued by Henry in favour of Abingdon than any other religious house.[49] By contrast, only three writs were granted to Malmesbury during the reign of Henry.[50] Faricius could rely on royal backing in almost any dispute he had with another prelate or magnate.[51] The Abingdon chronicle confirmed that Faricius had considerable influence over the royal family.

> [...] it was not difficult for that abbot to obtain what he was seeking [...] so agreeable to the king was everything which the abbot did.[52]

In addition to obtaining some of Aldhelm's bones from Malmesbury, Faricius received a shoulder blade and arm bone severed from the skeleton of St Æthelwold which was held at Winchester. As at Malmesbury Faricius probably benefitted from the powerful intervention of Queen Matilda. The remains of Æthelwold were ceremonially moved or 'translated' at Winchester in the presence of the queen in 1111.[53] At this ceremony the bishop of Winchester, William Giffard, formally agreed to the dismemberment of the skeleton and the granting of large fragments to Abbot Faricius. It seems likely that he was obliged to consent to the transfer of part of the saint's remains because this had been requested by the queen.

In his poem 'in praise' of Faricius, Brother Peter of Malmesbury commented obliquely and mysteriously on the success enjoyed by Faricius in a struggle with Bishop William Giffard.[54] This has puzzled scholars, but perhaps it was a reference to the way Faricius forced the bishop to give him a large piece of Æthelwold, just as he had obliged Malmesbury Abbey to hand over a chunk of the skeleton of Aldhelm.

---

[49] Sharpe, *Charters of William II and Henry I Project.*
[50] Kevin Shirley, *The Secular Jurisdiction of Monasteries in Anglo-Norman and Angevin England* (Woodbridge, 2001), 67.
[51] Shirley, *Secular Jurisdiction,* 66.
[52] *Historia Ecclesie Abbendonensis,* II 55 (ed. Hudson 66).
[53] *Annales Monasterii de Wintonia,* ed. H. R. Luard, in *Annales Monastici II* (London, 1865), 43–4.
[54] *GP I* II 88.6 (ed. Winterbottom 303).

7

The ascendancy of Bishop Roger of Salisbury

William of Malmesbury made no reference in his surviving works to one of the most dramatic events in the history of the Abbey that he personally witnessed: the deposition by Bishop Roger of Salisbury of Abbot Aedulf in 1118. We only know that this happened because it was recorded in the chronicle known as *Annales de Wintonia*, which stated that in the immediate aftermath of Queen Matilda's death Aedulf was dismissed 'without good cause' from the abbacy of Malmesbury.[1] It is no coincidence that this act was recorded in a Winchester chronicle because Aedulf was a Winchester monk prior to his promotion to Malmesbury. To the profound annoyance of the Malmesbury community, Bishop Roger then became titular abbot and treated the institution as an episcopal priory rather than an autonomous abbey. In the years that followed William of Malmesbury played a central role in a protracted but discreet campaign to question the correctness of Roger's takeover. He began work almost immediately on this project: in around 1119 William produced an edition of the papal history known as *Liber Pontificalis*, in which he included the full text of the 'privilege' of Sergius, the document granting the monastery perpetual exemption from episcopal interference.[2]

During the early 1120s William was working on his major historical works: *Gesta Regum* and *Gesta Pontificum*.[3] He used both works to indicate, in a veiled way, that the Malmesbury community rejected the legitimacy of Roger's power over them. In *Gesta Pontificum* William incorporated the full text of three ancient documents, all of which appeared to indicate that the independence of Malmesbury from episcopal control had been solemnly endorsed in charters granted to Aldhelm. The first was the 'privilege' of Sergius.[4] The second was Bishop Leuthere's 'foundation charter', which purported to date from 675 and declared that no future bishop should 'exercise a tyrant's power' over the monastery.[5] The third document was a charter supposedly issued by Aldhelm himself in 705, which included a directive forbidding future episcopal interference.[6]

---

1   *Annales de Wintonia*, 45.
2   Thomson, *William*, 119–36.
3   *GP II* xix–xxiii.
4   *GP I* V 221.1–11 (ed. Winterbottom 555–9).
5   *GP I* V 199.1–6 (ed. Winterbottom 525–7).
6   *GP I* V 225.1–9 (ed. Winterbottom 567).

Malmesbury Abbey 670–1539

The 'privilege' of Sergius may contain authentic elements, but the other two charters are generally seen as twelfth-century forgeries designed, probably with the collusion of William, to invalidate the claims of Bishop Roger. The Leuthere charter contains a highly suspicious clause forbidding future bishops or kings from meddling in the monastery's liberties.

> But lest any occasion for contention arise in future, I attach this condition to my declaration, that no succeeding bishop or king exercise a tyrant's power violently to assault this our charter of donation, obstinately pressing the claim that it might seem to have been taken from the rightful control of the bishopric.[7]

Similarly, Aldhelm's charter includes clearly fabricated text in the form of a concocted dialogue between Aldhelm's monks and the abbot himself in which he is persuaded that his community should never, after his death, be ruled over by an 'overweening bishop' or another tyrannical outsider.

> […] But this we all beg you as suppliants, that, on Holy Writ, and with the clear consent of well-regarded men, you should lay down firmly that no one after your death, whether reckless king or overweening bishop or any man of rank church or lay, is to claim for himself rule over us without our willing consent. To this very proper request on the part of those who are my monks but who are also, most importantly, servants of God, I willingly agreed […][8]

William made oblique references to the oppression of Roger in his *Gesta Regum*. In his account, for example, of the relics given by Æthelstan to the monastery, the historian mentioned that the community had, in his time, lost 'its liberty'.

> […] the pieces of the Cross and the crown he entrusted to Malmesbury, and their support still, I believe, gives that place fresh life, after the shipwreck of its liberty and all the unjust claims it has to meet.[9]

The most detailed allusion to the oppression of Bishop Roger in William's historical work of the 1120s is evident in his treatment of the career of Bishop Ealhstan of Sherborne (died 867). In both *Gesta Regum* and *Gesta Pontificum* William described how Ealhstan asserted some degree of control over the Malmesbury community and its resources, and he compared this to the monastery's difficulties in 'our own time'.

> […] I would gladly praise him [Ealhstan], had he not been carried away by human greed to lay hands on what was not his, in subjecting to his

[7] *GP* I V 199.5 (ed. Winterbottom 525–7).
[8] *GP* I V 225.5–6 (ed. Winterbottom 569).
[9] *GR* I II 135.6 (ed. Mynors, Thomson & Winterbottom 221).

The ascendancy of Bishop Roger of Salisbury

own purposes the abbey of Malmesbury [...] although on his death the monastery at once recovered completely from his violence, and so remained until our own time, when it has again undergone the same ordeal. Thus does Avarice 'with her curst appetite gnaw mortal hearts', thus are men great and illustrious in other respects plunged by her into the pit.[10]

It was daring of William to imply, even in a heavily coded way, that Bishop Roger deserved to be thrown into the infernal abyss because of his aggression towards Malmesbury. William made similar points in *Gesta Pontificum*, where he stated that, as in Ealhstan's time, the monks of the 1120s were sighing for lost liberties and subject to the violence of episcopal robbers.

> I should be glad to sing his praises were it not that, overcome by a mortal man's greed, he seized what was not his due when he subjected our own monastery to his private purposes [...] the place has managed to fight off all violence inflicted by bishops right up to our own time when the same problems have recurred [...] It was less to their shame that the monks of those days sighed for the liberty they had been deprived of than to ours that we have lost it, especially considering that *they* won it back at once [...] Eahlstan was outstandingly generous, as well as ardent in his greed, whereas *our* plunderers oppress as well as rob us, leaving us no chance to give free expression to our woes.[11]

Seeking the patronage of the Empress Matilda

The succession crisis in England following the White Ship disaster of 1120 eventually provided an opportunity for the Malmesbury monks to act and seek a new patron even more powerful than Bishop Roger. Following the death of her husband, the Emperor Henry V, in May 1125 the Empress Matilda emerged as a potential heir to the throne of England. At some point in 1125 or 1126 the community decided to attempt to win the favour of the Empress, by recognising the legitimacy of her claim to sovereign rule in England while, at the same time, calling upon her to become the patron of a restored abbey. We know this because of a remarkable discovery made in the early 1950s by Roger Mynors at the Bibliothèque Municipale in Troyes which houses the medieval library of the great Cistercian monastery of Clairvaux. Mynors examined a Clairvaux manuscript of *Gesta Regum* and discovered two previously unknown prefatory letters addressed to the Empress and to her uncle, King David of Scotland. Mynors transcribed the letters and sent them to Richard Southern in 1953 as part of an abortive collaboration on a new

10 *GR* I II 108.3 (ed. Mynors, Thomson & Winterbottom 157).
11 *GP* I II 79.4–6 (ed. Winterbottom 277–9).

Malmesbury Abbey 670–1539

edition of the *Gesta Regum*. The letters were finally printed for the first time in 1975.[12]

Although the letters were formally written on behalf of the Malmesbury Abbey community, the author was clearly William of Malmesbury. In the letter to King David William asked him to facilitate the transmission of a request for patronage to the Empress. He assumed that David – the brother of Queen Matilda – was not only familiar with Malmesbury but was attached to it because of his family connection to Aldhelm. The letter appealed to David to act because of 'your love for the monastery of St Aldhelm your kinsman'.[13] William thought that the chances of the second letter to the Empress herself reaching her and being received favourably could be greatly increased with David's endorsement and assistance.

> [...] we seek your Majesty's authorization in offering to your niece our lady the Empress Matilda this *History of the English Kings*, the writing of which we arranged with the encouragement of our lady your sister Queen Matilda, O illustrious and most glorious king and justly our honoured lord. We therefore beg your Majesty, best of kings, to accept from your poor desolate convent this offering which is yours by inheritance, to add your own authorization, and to arrange for the gift, together with our messenger, to be sent forward to our lady the empress.[14]

In his letter to the Empress William explained that the *Gesta Regum* justified her claim to the future crown of England.

> So now this book, which deals entirely with your forebears, and with what power the Creator has advanced your imperial house down to yourself, cannot be offered to any living person with more justice than to you. In it you can also discover that none of those chronicled in this present book, whether king or queen, has more royal or more glorious claim to the hereditary crown of England than yourself. May your imperial Majesty therefore deign to accept our humble gift, and by our gift the right to rule over us.[15]

The *Gesta Regum* explored the lineage of the Empress and demonstrated that she had a better claim to the English throne than any other candidate. In return for this declaration of commitment to her cause, the Malmesbury monks asked her to take an interest in their plight.

---

[12] E. Könsgen, 'Zwei unbekannte Briefe zu den Gesta Regum Anglorum des Wilhelm von Malmesbury', *Deutsches Archiv*, 31 (1975): 204–14.
[13] *GR I* Ep. I.2 (ed. Mynors, Thomson & Winterbottom 3).
[14] *GR I* Ep. I.3 (ed. Mynors, Thomson & Winterbottom 3–5).
[15] *GR I* Ep. II.7 (ed. Mynors, Thomson & Winterbottom 9).

The ascendancy of Bishop Roger of Salisbury

Lend your imperial ear, furthermore, for the sake of the souls of your mother and all your predecessors, to the requests which we make by the bearer of the book, and do not forget to show us compassion.[16]

It was brave of the monks to seek to overturn the rule of Bishop Roger over the monastery in this way. Aware perhaps of the need to minimise the provocation, neither letter mentioned Roger or his power over Malmesbury explicitly. Indeed, the letters went beyond this, and effectively blamed Queen Matilda for the monastery's predicament. The letter to David makes an oblique reference to the way the community was without a 'shepherd' or abbot in the aftermath of Queen Matilda's death. There was no mention of the fact that the previous 'shepherd' had been deposed by Roger and not replaced.

[...] she left our church a flock without a shepherd. As a result, the sheep whom our lady gathered into the fold are, we must tell you, unjustly scattered.[17]

William made the same point in his letter to the Empress.

[...] no exception can be taken to anything else in her life except that she left our church without a head, it is the height of justice that the wisdom of so powerful a daughter should set right the one point in which a truly blessed mother has so far by her ignorance laid herself open to criticism.[18]

We do not know if Matilda ever received the letter, and if so, what she made of it. In any event, the attempt by the monastery to escape from the control of Bishop Roger failed, and no new abbot was appointed. Roger proceeded to strengthen his grip over Malmesbury by obtaining further papal and royal ratification of his authority. On 1 January 1126 the bishop secured a bull from Pope Honorius II confirming that the monastery at Malmesbury was episcopal property and not an autonomous abbey.[19] In 1131 Henry I issued a charter granting the monastery for all time to the bishops of Salisbury and confirming the status of the community as a mere priory under the direct, personal control of Bishop Roger and his successors.

Be it known to all, now and in the future, that it has been acknowledged, through the claim of Roger bishop of Salisbury and his predecessors, that the church of Malmesbury was in past time [within] the episcopal see of Wiltshire during the passage of many years. Wherefore know

---

16 Ibid.
17 *GR I* Ep. I.7 (ed. Mynors, Thomson & Winterbottom 5).
18 *GR I* Ep. II.3 (ed. Mynors, Thomson & Winterbottom 7).
19 *Papsturkunden in England II*, ed. W. Holtzmann (Berlin, 1952), 141–2.

Malmesbury Abbey 670–1539

that I have given and granted as alms, to God and to the church of St Mary's Salisbury and to the said Roger and all his successors, the said church of Malmesbury, with all its appurtenances, as his demesne and personal seat: this after consulting the archbishops and bishops of my realm and in their hearing: for the souls of my fathers and kin, and for the remission of my sins, and for the state and safety of my kingdom: in such a way, however, that in the same church of Malmesbury the order of monks be preserved in perpetuity under their prior, and ever remain in the personal control, lordship and protection of the bishop.[20]

The complete failure of the attempt to escape from the control of Bishop Roger must have been hugely disappointing for William and his brethren.

William, Roger and the great rebuilding of the conventual church

One of the many puzzles concerning the life of William of Malmesbury concerns the great rebuilding of the main monastic church which took place during the twelfth century. Did William witness this? He said nothing specific about the erection of the new church, and some architectural experts have concluded that the work began after his death. More recently a different view has emerged: Bishop Roger of Salisbury is now seen by several scholars as the probable patron of the rebuilding, and William would, therefore, have seen the start of the building campaign.

The extant Romanesque architectural remains include the lower storeys of the twelfth- century nave, the magnificent south porch with its rich sculptural ornamentation together with the ruins of the west end, the crossing and transepts. Nothing survives of the eastern half of the Romanesque church beyond the piers of the crossing. The design of the nave, and presumably the rest of the church, involved the classic three-storey elevation found in major Norman churches: on the ground level the main arcade, above that a triforium gallery, and a clerestory between the triforium and the roof. At Malmesbury the Romanesque arcade and triforium survive, while the twelfth-century clerestory was rebuilt and raised during the fourteenth century, when a new stone roof replaced the earlier wooden structure. The design of the twelfth-century church was ambitious. The Anglo-Saxon church was completely swept away. The new work was extensive and of the highest craftsmanship: the sequence of biblical sculpture on the south porch is generally seen as one of the masterpieces of Romanesque art in England. The pointed arches of the main arcade are innovative and prefigure later Gothic design. Since the years 1139–54 were a time of great disruption when the Abbey and its

[20] *Charters and Documents Illustrating the History of the Cathedral, City, and Diocese of Salisbury, in the Twelfth and Thirteenth Centuries*, ed. R. W. Dunn McRay (London, 1891), 6.

The ascendancy of Bishop Roger of Salisbury

estates were devastated by war, the rebuilding must surely have been conceived either before or after the period of the so-called Anarchy. The ambition and cost of the work is consistent with the idea that Bishop Roger commissioned the rebuilding as part of his plan to transform the place, for all time, into an episcopal priory.

William of Malmesbury's own testimony on the rebuilding of the conventual church is enigmatic but not inconsistent with the possibility that Bishop Roger began the extensive remodelling of the building. In the *Gesta Regum* William provided a brief pen portrait of Roger, and stressed his love of buildings, highlighting Malmesbury as a place where he was active.

> As a bishop he was liberal, and never spared expense provided he could accomplish what he had in mind to do, especially his buildings. This can be seen above all at Salisbury and Malmesbury, for there he erected buildings large in scale, expensive, and very beautiful to look at, the courses of stone being laid so exactly that the joints defy inspection and give the whole wall the appearance of a single rock face.[21]

Some commentators have suggested that this is inconclusive because William's account of buildings at Malmesbury could refer to his castle. This is possible. But the context of the passage appears to be an account of the ecclesiastical buildings he was responsible for 'as a bishop'. In the lines that followed this passage William proceeded to describe the cathedral at Old Sarum, and made no reference to the castle there. The account of the fine masonry at Salisbury and Malmesbury which resembled a natural rock face could easily have been a reference to the walls and piers of the Romanesque church at Malmesbury. William wrote about Roger's work building work in the *Gesta Regum* while the bishop was still alive. He returned to the theme in his *Historia Novella* written after Roger's disgrace and death in 1139 and again emphasised how important both secular and religious buildings were to the bishop. William reflected on Roger's obsession with architectural schemes which were 'unsurpassed within the recollection of our age',[22] explicitly making reference to Roger's church building campaign across the diocese of Salisbury.

> His own see he glorified beyond measure by wondrous ornaments and buildings, without any sparing of expense.[23]

While William's own comments are inconclusive, an active role for Roger is suggested by stylistic evidence. Malcolm Thurlby has dated the start of the work to the 1120s and has identified a range of detailed similarities

---

21 *GR* I V 408.3 (ed. Mynors, Thomson & Winterbottom 739).
22 *Historia Novella* II 33 (ed. King 67).
23 Ibid.

Malmesbury Abbey 670–1539

between Malmesbury and other buildings associated with the patronage of Bishop Roger, including Old Sarum cathedral, Sherborne Abbey, Abbotsbury Abbey and the parish church of St John's Devizes. Many distinctive features can be seen both at Malmesbury and these other sites with connections to Bishop Roger, such as carved 'beaks' at the base of columns, column capitals in the form of monstrous masks, cats' heads and stylised palm leaves. It seems highly likely that the same masons who designed and built the cathedral at Old Sarum and the church next to Roger's castle at Devizes were working at Malmesbury.[24]

The fall of Bishop Roger

Immediately after the death of Henry I in 1135 Bishop Roger supported the seizure of the crown by Stephen of Blois. Roger became a key adviser to Stephen as king, and his son, Roger le Poer, was made Chancellor. The situation changed in 1139 when Stephen began to believe that Roger could not be trusted and was potentially dangerous because he controlled a network of strong castles including Malmesbury. The king decided to destroy Roger and take his castles. In June 1139 Stephen summoned Roger to a council meeting in Oxford where he planned to arrest him. The *Historia Novella* recounts how William was present when Roger got the summons to Oxford, presumably at Malmesbury.

> The bishop of Salisbury was most unwilling to set out. I heard him speaking to this effect: 'By my blessed lady Mary, somehow I am disinclined to this journey, I know not why! This I do know, that I shall be as useful at court as a colt in battle.' Thus did his mind forebode the evil to come.[25]

Roger was of course right to be worried about the summons. His nephews, Bishops Nigel and Alexander, were also ordered to go to Oxford, and Bishop Roger was accompanied by his son, Roger le Poer. Once there Roger and his family fell into a trap: a fight was provoked between their men and some other soldiers in the retinue of Stephen's barons. Roger, his son and one nephew, Bishop Alexander of Lincoln, were arrested on a trumped-up charge of disturbing the peace of the court, but Bishop Nigel of Ely managed to escape, much to Stephen's displeasure, and fled to the castle of Devizes. Stephen demanded the surrender of Roger's castles and the castles of his nephews. William of Malmesbury in his *Historia*

---

[24] S. E. Rigold, 'Romanesque Bases', in *Ancient Monuments and their Interpretation*, ed. M. R. Apted, R. Gilyard-Beer and A. D. Saunders (Chichester 1977); Malcolm Thurlby, 'The Romanesque Abbey Church of Malmesbury: Patronage and Date', *WANHM*, 112 (2019): 230–64.

[25] *Historia Novella* II 23 (ed. King 47).

The ascendancy of Bishop Roger of Salisbury

Novella described how Bishop Roger and his son were taken as captives to Devizes where Bishop Nigel was persuaded to surrender.

> Then he brought Bishop Roger, without chaining him, and the chancellor, who was said to be the nephew or an even closer relation of the same bishop, in chains, to Devizes, which castle had been built at great, almost immeasurable expense, not, as the bishop kept on saying himself, for the adornment but, as is in fact the case, for the injury of the Church.[26]

William thought it was scandalous that the bishop had a son and primly called him a 'nephew or an even closer relation'. He then proceeded to record how all the castles of Roger were taken by the king.

> In the course of siege-warfare the castles of Salisbury, Sherborne and Malmesbury were delivered up to the king. Devizes itself was surrendered after three days, when the bishop had imposed on himself a voluntary fast, so that by undergoing this suffering he might weaken the resolve of the bishop of Ely, who had taken possession of the place.[27]

Following the disgrace and death of Roger in 1139, William of Malmesbury was finally free to express his true feelings of unhappiness at the way that Roger had acted. The references to the current situation in the *Gesta Regum* and the *Gesta Pontificum* were discreet. By contrast, in *Historia Novella*, written after Roger's death, William discussed, openly and triumphantly, the restoration of the Abbey's independence, explicitly stating that the renewed freedom of the house was in keeping with the privilege of Pope Sergius I.

> In the eleven hundred and fortieth year of the Incarnate Word the monks of the abbeys that Bishop Roger had unlawfully seized approached the king and obtained the restoration of their ancient privileges and their abbots. In accordance with the terms of the privilege that the blessed Aldhelm had gained from Pope Sergius four hundred and sixty-six years before and got ratified by Ina King of Wessex and Ethelred King of Mercia, the monks elected as abbot of Malmesbury a monk of the same place named John, a man especially distinguished by his kindly nature and noble mind.[28]

William was full of praise for Abbot John, who was freely chosen by the monks in 1140: he was a hero who had encouraged the monks to assert themselves after the period of 'slavery' under Bishop Roger.

---

26 *Historia Novella* II 23 (ed. King 49).
27 Ibid.
28 *Historia Novella* II 35 (ed. King 71).

Malmesbury Abbey 670–1539

[...] for no monk of that place. I frankly confess, would have taken part in so spirited an act had not John given a lead. Then let his successors be praised if they maintain the freedom of the church but it was he beyond doubt who rescued it from slavery.[29]

A community of scholarship

William of Malmesbury greatly resented the way in which Roger of Salisbury controlled the monastery for over twenty years. But there is no evidence that the bishop interfered much in the day-to-day life of the monks and, paradoxically, the period of the 'slavery' of the monks under Roger coincided with a phase of intellectual and spiritual renewal at Malmesbury led by William. Rodney Thomson has suggested that in the 1120s and 1130s William sought to develop 'a community of Christian scholarship' at Malmesbury.[30] William had an opportunity to attempt the transformation of life at Malmesbury because he held the post of precentor, with responsibility for the library and the liturgy in the conventual church, and there is no evidence that Bishop Roger got in the way of his plans. The monastery library at Malmesbury mattered a lot to William: in the Prologue to *Historia Novella* he introduced himself to readers as 'William the librarian of Malmesbury'.[31] In the *Gesta Pontificum* William explained how he radically improved the book stock, building upon the achievements of Abbot Godfrey of Jumièges.

> If I single out this activity, I think I have every right to do so, for in this area especially I have been inferior to none of those who went before; indeed (if I can say this without boasting) I have easily surpassed them all. May there be someone to look after the present stock! I have collected much material for reading, approaching the prowess of my excellent predecessor at least in this respect; I have followed up his laudable start as best I could. Let us hope there may be someone to cherish the fruits of our labours![32]

William considered that the use of the enhanced library led to much improved standards in scholarship and religious observance in the monastery.

> The monks, who had been mere stutterers in common or garden learning, were now given a proper education. The service of God was liberally endowed and put into effect as a matter of urgency, with the

---

29 Ibid.
30 Thomson, *William*, 36.
31 *Historia Novella* Prologue (2–3).
32 GP I 271 3–4 (646–7).

The ascendancy of Bishop Roger of Salisbury

result that no monastery in all England excelled Malmesbury, and many yielded precedence to it.[33]

As librarian William supervised the production of new manuscripts in the monastic scriptorium. A surprising number of these works have survived in autograph form. William's nineteenth-century editors knew that his handwriting could be seen in the manuscript of Anselm's works held by Lambeth Palace,[34] and in 1870 Nicholas Hamilton published his discovery that the manuscript of the *Gesta Pontificum* in Magdalen College Oxford[35] was the author's working copy.[36] Armed with knowledge of the characteristics of his hand, it has been possible to identify twelve manuscripts in which the transcription was, at least in part, the work of William.[37] Ten of these manuscripts contain, in addition to evidence of William's hand, transcriptions by other monks, and in all these manuscripts provide evidence of fifty-two different monks at work in William's scriptorium.[38] The skill levels of these men varied considerably, indicating that William was, at times, obliged to call upon any available member of the community to assist him in the scriptorium. One document, now in the Bodleian, was produced by a team of fourteen, and Thomson said of this manuscript: 'Here is an extraordinary repertoire of hands, mostly individualized and startlingly differentiated from each other, mostly unskilled although two or three really fine hands appear for short sections.'[39] While many monks took turns in the scriptorium, William drew upon the support of a smaller group of trusted assistants whose hands can be seen in more than one manuscript. The scribal collaborators of William are anonymous with one exception: one scribe whose work can be seen in three manuscripts identified himself, with a flourish, as being named Richard.[40] If we assume that many, perhaps all, of these manuscripts were produced at Malmesbury, they provide important clues about practice in the scriptorium in the 1120s and 1130s. William was in charge of the complete process of manuscript production, from the identification of suitable works for copying to the correction and approval of finished texts.[41] He was well placed to instruct others because his use of the pen was the most polished of all the contributors. For the guidance of

---

33 Ibid.
34 Lambeth Palace Library MS 224.
35 Magdalen College Oxford MS lat. 172.
36 William of Malmesbury, *Gesta Pontificum*, ed. N. Hamilton (London, 1870), xi.
37 Thomson, *William*, 76–96.
38 Thomson, *William*, 77.
39 Thomson, *William*, 84
40 Thomson, *William*, 89.
41 Samu Niskanen, 'William of Malmesbury as Librarian: The Evidence of his Autographs', in *Discovering William of Malmesbury*, ed. Rodney M. Thomson, Emily Dolman and Emily Winkler (Woodbridge, 2017), 117–28.

Malmesbury Abbey 670–1539

members of his mixed ability scriptorium William collected together five treatises on grammar and orthography – spelling conventions – written by classical and pre-Conquest English authors. This collection does not survive in autograph form but exists in a fourteenth-century copy.[42]

The Malmesbury scriptorium manuscripts were varied in format but for the most part were neat and plain in appearance with minimal decoration, intended for use rather than display. The contents of the manuscripts give some indication of William's priorities for the edification of the brethren. He wanted members of the Malmesbury community to understand the pre-Christian Roman world; however, life in the past and present needed to be seen through the lens of orthodox Christian teaching. Surviving products from the scriptorium include a collection of extracts relating to the history of Rome,[43] a set of classical texts about military strategy[44] and works by Roman writers such as Cicero,[45] together with Christian material including biblical commentary,[46] extracts from the oeuvre of Gregory the Great,[47] and a collection of canon law documents.[48] The scriptorium produced a copy of *De Divisione Naturae* or *Periphyseon*, a philosophical treatise by the ninth-century writer, John Scotus Eriugena. This was an important work in its own right but William's interest in Eriugena was doubtless heightened by his erroneous belief that Eriugena had retired from the Frankish court to Malmesbury where he was murdered by his students. One of the most important surviving manuscripts produced by William and his team was a collection of letters and philosophical treatises by Anselm, the archbishop of Canterbury who died in 1109. For William, Anselm was the greatest contemporary theologian and promoter of the primacy of monastic life. He visited Canterbury for research purposes and may have taken the originals of some of Anselm's letters away from Canterbury to Malmesbury for transcription.[49]

William wanted the monks of Malmesbury to be well educated and not 'mere stutterers in common or garden learning'. He saw himself as their teacher and 'collected much material for reading' by the brethren. We know that these instructional materials included challenging unabridged texts such as his edition of the letters and works of Anselm, but he also edited anthologies and digests intended to be 'more accessible to less

---

[42] BL Harley 3969.

[43] Bodleian MS Arch, Seld. B. 16.

[44] Lincoln College MS lat. 100.

[45] Bodleian MS Rawlinson G. 139. This contains works by Cicero, pseudo-Quintilian and Aulus Gellius.

[46] Oxford Merton College MS 181.

[47] Cambridge University Library MS Ii. 3. 20.

[48] Oxford Oriel College MS 42.

[49] Richard Southern, *St Anselm: A Portrait in a Landscape* (Cambridge, 1990), 400–1.

The ascendancy of Bishop Roger of Salisbury

gifted monks'[50] such as his anthology of extracts drawn from the work of St Gregory. Unsurprisingly, William as the monastery precentor believed that it was important for his fellow monks to understand the principles of correct church ritual. He created a shortened version of the ninth-century liturgical treatise of Amalarius of Metz,[51] a work which provided detailed guidance on the prayers, ceremonies and vestments suitable for different occasions. William abridged Amalarius but also sought to bring the guidance up to date.

By about 1125 William had completed the first editions of his two great historical works. In the years that followed he had some sort of crisis of conscience concerning his love of history and secular literature and felt a need to concern himself more with religion. With the spiritual needs of his Malmesbury community in mind, William wrote a commentary on the biblical book of Lamentations of Jeremiah and a treatise in praise of the Virgin Mary, and in introductory remarks to his work on Lamentations William described his new direction.

> For in the past, when I amused myself with histories, the charm of the subject suited my greener years and happy lot. Now advancing age and worsening circumstances demand a different kind of work. The ideal will be something able to warn me off the world and set me on fire towards God.[52]

William's treatise on the Virgin Mary had two distinct parts, hinting again at his sense of the variable capacity of his brethren: the work began with a serious introductory theological essay on the intercessory role of Mary, and this was followed by a much more accessible and entertaining collection of miracle stories. His interest in the Virgin Mary was part of a wider upsurge in Marian devotion among the monks of early twelfth-century England, which was inspired in part by the teachings of Anselm. William's Marian miracle stories were probably intended to be read in the Malmesbury refectory on feast days related to Mary,[53] and as precentor William had responsibility for selecting such readings. In this work, as elsewhere, William demonstrated a marked sensitivity to his audience, explaining mid-way through the text his doubts about whether the stories were sufficiently interesting, and commenting that he was anxious 'not to bore any readers I may have'.[54]

---

50 Rodney M. Thomson, *William of Malmesbury*, ODNB (2004).
51 The *Abbreviatio* survives in five medieval manuscripts. See Thomson, *William*, 44.
52 *Lamentations* Prologue (ed. Winterbottom 32).
53 Kati Ihnat, *Mother of Mercy, Bane of the Jews: Devotion to the Virgin Mary in Anglo-Norman England* (Princeton, 2016), 131.
54 William of Malmesbury, Miracles *of the Blessed Virgin* Mary: *An English*

Astronomy, astrology and the dangers of the dark arts

William and the Malmesbury monks studied the stars, and they subscribed to the received wisdom that astronomy, together with arithmetic, geometry and music, constituted the 'quadrivium', the higher curriculum suitable for those who had completed the study of the basic 'trivium' of grammar, logic and rhetoric. William demonstrated his awareness of the concept of the quadrivium in his account of the career of Gerbert of Aurillac when he made reference to 'the permitted arts, arithmetic, music, astronomy, and geometry'.[55] Astronomical knowledge was important both as one of the liberal arts and as a precondition for the correct calculation of the date of Easter and other moveable feasts. William's positive attitude towards astronomy is evident in his characterisation of Bishop Robert Losinga of Hereford (died in 1095) as a man who was 'highly skilled in all the liberal arts, and in particular had gone into the abacus, the reckoning of time by the moon, and the course of the stars in the sky'.[56]

There was, therefore, a need to provide astronomical texts for the monastery library. By William's time, Malmesbury possessed a copy of *De nuptiis Philologiae et Mercurii* by the fifth-century writer Martianus Capella, an encyclopaedic work that included a treatise devoted to astronomy. This manuscript survives at Corpus Christi College Cambridge and contains annotations in the hand of William.[57] The Malmesbury scriptorium, under William's direction, also produced a collection of computus and astronomical texts, including works by Bede and Isidore of Seville, which is extant and is held by the Bodleian Library.[58]

Interest in celestial phenomena was made manifest architecturally at Malmesbury in the 1120s or 1130s when the Romanesque west front of the new conventual church was ornamented with sculptures depicting the signs of the Zodiac and the Labours of the Months. While much of the western façade was ruined after the Dissolution, badly eroded fragments remain today of carvings representing Gemini – two boys wrestling – and Sagittarius – a centaur archer.[59] The carvings are similar stylistically to those representations of the Zodiac, from around the same period, on the west front at Vézelay. The use of Zodiac iconography did not, by itself, indicate approval for predictive astrology because information about the

---

Translation, ed. and trans. by M. Winterbottom and R. M. Thomson (Woodbridge, 2015), 70.

[55] *GR I* II 167.3 (ed. Mynors, Thomson & Winterbottom 281).

[56] *GP I* V 162.1 (ed. Winterbottom 459).

[57] CCCC MS 330.

[58] Bodleian MS Auct. F. 3. 14.

[59] Malcolm Thurlby has recently dated the Romanesque west front of Malmesbury Abbey to the period of the ascendancy of Bishop Roger, when William was at the height of his powers. See Thurlby, 'Further Aspects of Romanesque Malmesbury Abbey', *WANHM*, 115 (2022).

The ascendancy of Bishop Roger of Salisbury

movement of the moon, sun and planets through the constellations of the Zodiac was part of the body of conventional non-predictive astronomical knowledge established in antiquity and endorsed by Christian writers such as Isidore and Bede. William of Malmesbury showed off his knowledge of the Zodiac at key moments in the *Gesta Pontificum*: thus, when writing about the death of his hero, Aldhelm, he broke into verse, and used the technicalities of the Zodiac to date and emphasise the solemnity of the event. According to tradition Aldhelm died on 25 May when the dominant Zodiac sign was Gemini, and William's poem explained how the saint 'freed himself from the ties of this world' 'twice five dawns' after the sun had entered Gemini.[60] In a similar way, William used the Zodiac calendar to describe and commemorate the momentous death of Æthelstan on 27 October 939 when Scorpio was the dominant, again turning to a combination of verse and the language of the Zodiac to give appropriate gravity to his account of this tragic event.

> The sun had lit up Scorpio with its twelfth dawn
> When he struck down the king with his tail.[61]

William was, in all probability, intrigued by the possibility of predictive astrology but concerned about the risk of encouraging his fellow monks to stray into the forbidden and dangerous realms of black magic. He was familiar with key texts by Augustine, Bede and Isidore which condemned astrology, and his own works contained cautionary tales about those who engaged in black magic. In the *Gesta Regum* he told the story of a woman from Berkeley in Gloucestershire who was 'versed in the ancient arts of soothsaying'.[62] Her powers derived from a pact with the Devil who, after her death, carried her off from the local church to Hell on the back of a demonic horse. William's collection of Marian miracle stories also contained accounts of the perils of necromancy. He included the proto-Faustian tale of Theophilus, seduced into Devil worship by a Jew 'skilled in the dark arts, and with command over spells'.[63] In the same work William told how a studious clerk, having mastered 'the permissible arts [...] turned, out of normal human curiosity, to illicit ones too'. In the *Gesta Regum* William devoted several pages to an essay on the necromancy of Gerbert of Aurillac, later Pope Silvester II, who died in

---

60 *GP* I V 227.2 (ed. Winterbottom 573). See Winterbottom, 'Versificus', 118
61 *GP* I V 246.5 (ed. Winterbottom 595). See Winterbottom, 'Versificus', 119. William's Zodiac calendar references contained some discrepancies when compared with other Zodiac tables such as the *Enchiridion* of Byrthferth of Ramsey. Byrthferth gave 18 May for the commencement of Gemini and 18 October for Scorpio. The table that William was using gave him in both cases a date three days earlier.
62 GR II 204.1–6 (ed. Mynors, Thomson & Winterbottom 377–9)
63 *Miracles of the Blessed Virgin Mary*, 16.

Malmesbury Abbey 670–1539

1003. He recounted how Gerbert travelled to Spain 'to learn astrology, and other such arts, from the Saracens'. In Spain Gerbert studied the use of the Arab abacus, the astrolabe and the astrological works of the Roman writer, Julius Firmicus. William explained how Gerbert entered into a pact with the Devil which enabled him to have a glittering ecclesiastical career back in France and Italy, culminating in his appointment to the papacy, but eventually Gerbert's luck ran out, and he suffered a terrible death brought about by his own sorcery.

Gerbert lived a century before William's time. In his first edition of the *Gesta Pontificum*, completed around 1125, William included a much more recent story of alleged necromancy. [64] He recounted how Archbishop Gerard of York, who died in 1108, had a reputation for black magic, stating that Gerard was an enthusiastic reader of the astrological works of Julius Firmicus, the same writer about astrology that Gerbert had studied in Spain.

> He is also said to have been a devotee of the black arts, on the grounds that he used to make a practice of reading Julius Firmicus secretly in the afternoon.

William explained how Gerard died suddenly and near his body was found 'a book of curious arts on his pillow'. The implication was clear: Gerard, like Gerbert before him, had stepped over the line and indulged in diabolical witchcraft, probably leading to his damnation.

These stories constituted a warning from William to any of his readers in Malmesbury or beyond who were tempted to dabble in illicit magic, but there was also some ambivalence in William's position. He did not emphatically reject all forms of astrology and spoke, for example, with apparent approval about the way that Eilmer, the 'flying monk', correctly predicted the Norman Conquest as a result of his study of Halley's Comet. His account of Gerbert of Aurillac was hostile but he suggested that some of Gerbert's remarkable achievements might be attributable to forms of legitimate science. William did not see all aspects of Arabic science as necromancy and chose to include a treatise on the astrolabe, attributed (wrongly) to Gerbert, in his collection of computus texts. This work was, in effect, a celebration of Arabic learning and included an account of the Arabic names for several stars.[65] Curiously, William included an excerpt from the astrological work of Julius Firmicus, in his work known as *Polyhistor*, an anthology of excerpts from pagan and Christian authors selected for the edification and entertainment of the Malmesbury monks.[66] This was the same text that William had associated

[64] *GP* I III 118.2–3 (ed. Winterbottom 393–5).
[65] Bodleian MS Auct. F. 3.
[66] Thomson, *William*, 60.

The ascendancy of Bishop Roger of Salisbury

with black magic in his accounts of both Gerbert (in the *Gesta Regum*) and Archbishop Gerard of York (in the *Gesta Pontificum*). Here the dates are important. The accounts of the black magic of Gerbert and Gerard were completed by around 1125. Julius Firmicus on astrology was a relatively rare work, and it is possible that William was aware of it but had not actually read it when he initially made reference to its black magic contents. Perhaps William obtained a copy for the first time after 1125 and decided that the astrology of Julius Firmicus was, on close examination, not morally dangerous after all and should be made available to his Malmesbury brethren. When William revised the narrative of Archbishop Gerard's death in a new edition of the *Gesta Pontificum* in the 1130s, he removed the accusation that the reading of Julius Firmicus demonstrated the archbishop's interest in 'the black arts'.

'Those whom I love with the deepest affection'

It is clear from his work that William greatly valued friendship with other Malmesbury monks. He stated many times that particular works were undertaken in response to conversations with friends of the cloister. He made, for example, reference to the importance of his friendship circle in the *Gesta Regum* when explaining his decision to complete the work and extend the narrative into more recent times despite the challenges that this would create.

> Besides, there was the incitement of my friends, with whose slightest hints it was my duty to comply; and they for their part gently urged me, eager as I already was, to continue what I had begun. Quickened therefore by the encouragement of those whom I love with the deepest affection, I set to work, that they may receive from my heart's treasure-house an enduring pledge of friendship.

Having completed the *Gesta Regum* and taken a break from writing, William's decision to compose his commentary on the Lamentations of Jeremiah was prompted by an unnamed friend – a 'beloved brother' – as he recounted in the Prologue to the work.

> You have often urged me to draw from the sheath of sloth a pen that has long been on holiday, and to employ it on writing things that are all-important. My beloved brother, I obey your commands, only asking pardon for the shortness of the work: brevity, as you well know, is something that has always been my friend and familiar. Yes, I obey, and the more readily because what you advise is in accord with your character and at the same time consonant with my own intention.

On occasion William named his friends of the cloister, highlighting how he was seeking to meet their intellectual or spiritual needs. The

Malmesbury Abbey 670–1539

production of the anthology known as *Polyhistor*, for example, was prompted by a request from a monk called Guthlac.

> William to his friend Guthlac. Since you have thought proper to consult me as to what books of the heathen that we have ought to be read [...] Here then you have a book of varied content, to strengthen your purpose and delight your mind.[67]

Similarly, William explained that the *Abbreviatio Amalarii* was produced for a monk and friend called Robert: in the Preface William described how the idea for the work arose when the two men were together 'in our library' reading and discussing books. Robert confessed that he found the work of Amalarius too taxing, and asked William to help by abridging the work: William was happy to oblige.[68]

Perhaps the most intriguing cloister friendship hinted at in William's works was that between him and a Malmesbury monk called Peter. William wrote a letter to one 'Peter' by way of a Preface to his edition of the *Periphyseon* of John Scotus Eriugena.[69] The tone was extremely warm: Peter was addressed as a 'most beloved brother' to whom William was bound both by ties of fraternal affection and a shared commitment to the study of philosophy. Michael Lapidge has identified Peter as, in all probability, Peter Moraunt, who later became abbot of Malmesbury (1141 – c. 1158/9).[70] Peter and William, and probably other Malmesbury monks, shared an interest in the composition of Latin verse.[71] 'Brother Peter' was the author of a poem about Faricius included in the *Gesta Pontificum*. William called Peter 'a supreme craftsman in verse', adding that the verses relating to Faricius were 'but a slight instance of Peter's eloquence; he has in other works attained higher fame on a wider front'.[72] Moraunt was a former monk of Cluny. It seems highly likely that Moraunt introduced William to contemporary Latin verse from France including the work of Hildebert of Lavardin, and as a result William became a huge admirer of Hildebert. The metre used in Peter's poem about Faricius

---

67 M. R. James, *Two Ancient English Scholars: St Aldhelm and William of Malmesbury* (Glasgow, 1931).

68 R. W. Pfaff, 'The "Abbreviatio Amalarii" of William of Malmesbury', *Recherches de théologie ancienne et médiévale*, 47 (1980): 77–113.

69 The letter was printed by William Stubbs, *Gesta Regum I* (London, 1887), cxliii–cxlvi.

70 M. Lapidge, 'Some Latin Poems as Evidence for the Reign of Athelstan', *Anglo-Saxon England, 9* (1981): 71.

71 There are several instances of William's verse in his writing. See Winterbottom, 'Versificus', 117–27. We may have lost other poetic works by William. Following his visit to Malmesbury John Leland claimed to have seen a collection of poems by William concerning the four evangelists: see J. Leland, *Commentarii de scriptoribus Britannicis II*, ed. A. Hall (London, 1709), 195–6.

72 *GP I* II 88 4 (ed. Winterbottom 303).

The ascendancy of Bishop Roger of Salisbury

was similar to that used in verses probably written by William which were included in the *Gesta Pontificum,* and Michael Winterbottom has suggested that William and Peter wrote verse following the rules of a common 'Malmesbury house style'.[73]

William and the prejudices of the cloister

William had many opinions which he presumably held in common with his fellow monks. Social status mattered, and for most people rank in society was determined for life at birth by the position of parents. William was interested in subtle gradations of relative gentility or baseness as determined by birth, describing for example, a local woman who was 'not so low-born as to be quite plebeian nor so well-born as to aspire too high; her middling birth gave her a middling competence'.[74] The Malmesbury monks were not cut off from the local community. Liturgical processions took them outside the monastic precinct and into the town, and lay people were permitted in the conventual church and parts of the monastery campus: as a result the monks regularly encountered people of different backgrounds including some desperately poor and troubled people. William recalled how as a boy he was frightened by an aggressive, disturbed man who sat close to Aldhelm's shrine, and spat at him and the other choristers.[75] William's prejudices reflected his own privileged social background, and he displayed little sympathy for the local poor. He recounted, with approval, the way a local beggar who claimed to be dumb was tortured by the authorities in order to establish that he was not faking his disability.

> [...] such rigour was unavoidable, because a number of unfortunate creatures mock God and men by simulating any disease you care, so as to beg small change on the basis of the fiction and fill their empty bellies.[76]

There is no evidence that William had much respect for more prosperous Malmesbury townsfolk who were engaged in trade. He made disparaging remarks about the mercantile class in his collection of Marian miracles, describing as exceptional a character who was an honest businessman.

> [...] he made his living by a means that especially seduces men into sullying the truth. He was in fact a trader: you can see almost no one in this line who is afraid to expose his sworn word to perjury if he can

---

73 Winterbottom, 'Versificus', 124.
74 *GP* I V 272.1 (ed. Winterbottom 649).
75 *GP* I V 275.5 (ed. Winterbottom 657).
76 *GP* I V 277.1–2 (ed. Winterbottom 659).

Malmesbury Abbey 670–1539

turn a penny or two. What is more, when open cheating does not serve, they take advantage of the unwary by craft.[77]

William admired French culture while taking great pride in his own Englishness. He had little time for those he saw as members of marginal national groups. William's account of the European response to the First Crusade revealed his highly stereotypical views of ethnic identity and expressed in contemptuous and comic terms his characterisation of some of the more 'barbarous' peoples of western Europe.

> The time had come for the Welshman to give up hunting in his forests, the Scotsman forsook his familiar fleas, the Dane broke off his long drawn-out potations, and the Norwegian left his diet of raw fish.[78]

William's prejudices included violent antisemitism, and strident anti-Jewish sentiment is evident in several of his religious works. William was troubled by the beliefs of the Jewish people and their denial of the virgin birth and the divinity of Christ. Many of the miracle stories in William's Marian treatise featured Jews as villainous blasphemers and enemies of the Virgin. In one tale William discussed with approval the murder of a Jew who had mocked Christian beliefs.

> The Christian was incensed (a noble wrath befits a noble man); he punched the Jew and left him dead at his feet. What prowess to be able to lay down a rascal with the blow of a bare hand![79]

William's commentary on the Lamentations of Jeremiah is replete with hostile remarks about Jews both of ancient and more recent times. Michael Winterbottom suggested that William may have chosen to undertake this work because 'it gave ample scope for the expression of his prejudice'.[80] Antisemitism can also be found throughout the *Abbreviatio Amalarii*, where William systematically heightened the negativity of all the major references he found to Jewish practices when abridging the work of Amalarius.[81]

---

[77] *Miracles of the Blessed Virgin Mary*, 92.
[78] *GR* I V 348.2 (ed. Mynors, Thomson & Winterbottom 607).
[79] *Miracles of the Blessed Virgin Mary*, 28.
[80] *Lamentations* (ed. Winterbottom 16).
[81] Pfaff, '"Abbreviatio"', 100–1.

8

The Abbey and the Anarchy

The succession crisis that followed the death of Henry I in 1135 led to protracted political turmoil and conflict in England. Civil war broke out in 1139, and the monks of Malmesbury witnessed several episodes of conflict in the years that followed. We are blessed with exceptional sources for the study of Malmesbury during Stephen's turbulent reign. William of Malmesbury provided commentary on the early stages of the conflict between Stephen and Matilda in his *Historia Novella*. William was not an objective witness because the work was commissioned by Robert of Gloucester, Matilda's half-brother and general, who was one of the main actors in the events of the period.[1] Despite his partisan perspective the *Historia Novella* was carefully written and well-informed, and it remains a source of immense value to historians today. William's testimony breaks off towards the end of 1142 but the anonymous chronicle, the *Gesta Stephani*, provides a narrative guide to the whole conflict. *Gesta Stephani* was written by someone with in-depth knowledge of the Malmesbury area: over a quarter of all the places mentioned in it lie within a 25-mile radius of Malmesbury.[2] On the basis of substantial circumstantial evidence the author has been identified as Robert of Lewes, Bishop of Bath.[3] In addition to the *Historia Novella* and the *Gesta Stephani*, other chroniclers such as Henry of Huntingdon and John of Worcester provided detailed accounts of events at Malmesbury during the Anarchy.

It is clear from these contemporary sources that both sides in the war between Stephen and Matilda were anxious to control Malmesbury because of the strategic importance of its castle. The precise location of the castle is not known but it was undoubtedly very close to the conventual church. In his *Historia Novella* William of Malmesbury stated that Bishop Roger had established the castle 'in the churchyard itself, hardly a stone's throw from the abbey'.[4] No trace remains above ground of the structure because the monks, who greatly resented the castle's existence, completely

---

1 Robert Patterson, *The Earl, the Kings, and the Chronicler: Robert Earl of Gloucester and the Reigns of Henry I and Stephen* (Oxford, 2019), 178.
2 Introduction to *Gesta Stephani*, ed. Potter & Davis, xxiii.
3 For the evidence supporting this identification see *Gesta Stephani*, ed. Potter & Davis, xxxiv–xxxviii.
4 *Historia Novella* II.22 (ed. King 45).

Malmesbury Abbey 670–1539

destroyed all traces of the fabric following their acquisition of the site in 1216. However, we can surmise that the castle was substantial and built to a high specification because it was besieged in 1144 and 1153 but on both occasions the attackers were unable to take it by force. The chroniclers alluded briefly to its strength: Henry of Huntingdon described it as a 'very high keep [...] reducible only by starvation';[5] the author of the *Gesta Stephani* called the building 'an impregnable work of skill'.[6]

Following the fall of Bishop Roger, Malmesbury Castle was garrisoned by soldiers loyal to Stephen. This was not especially good news for the monks of Malmesbury: they had hated Bishop Roger, but in the context of the succession crisis they supported the Empress Matilda and her half-brother, Robert Earl of Gloucester. So, while the monks were happy to see the back of Roger, they were not at all pleased by the arrival of a military force in Malmesbury that was controlled by their political enemy, King Stephen.

The brigand, Robert Fitz Hubert

Soon after Bishop Roger's fall a Flemish mercenary captain named Robert Fitz Hubert appeared in Malmesbury and seized control of the castle through trickery, burning down much of the town. William of Malmesbury described how Stephen, alarmed by this, came in person to regain control of the castle.

> On 7 October a certain Robert Fitz Hubert, a cruel and savage man, stealthily entered by night the castle of Malmesbury, which Bishop Roger had begun under an evil star, and after burning the town boasted of it as though it were a great victory. However, within fifteen days he was cast down from his rejoicing, being put to flight by the king. The king gave orders for the castle to be guarded for a time until, with the coming of peace, it could be demolished.[7]

John of Worcester gave a fuller account of the episode. After Robert had tricked his way into the castle the king's knights took refuge in the Abbey church, but the mercenary captain barged into a meeting of the monks in their chapter house and demanded that they should hand over the knights. The monks refused to comply but did agree to give up the horses of the royalist forces.

> A certain knight called Robert was the son of Hubert, a noble man. He feared neither God nor man, but trusted completely in his own strength.

---

5 Henry of Huntingdon, *Historia Anglorum* X.34. See *Historia Anglorum: The History of the English People*, ed. and trans. Diana Greenaway (Oxford, 1996), 763.
6 *Gesta Stephani* I.43 (ed. Potter & Davis 93).
7 *Historia Novella* II.31 (ed. King 63).

110

The Abbey and the Anarchy

He attacked the castle of Malmesbury by a cunning ploy. Some of the royal knights in the castle took refuge in the church of the holy bishop Aldhelm for sanctuary. Robert pursued them, and one day broke into the Chapter House of the monks at the head of armed men. With terrifying threats, he ordered the brethren to hand over the mighty king's soldiers and their horses if they valued their property. The monks were horrified at the breaking of the peace of God and of their blessed patron, Aldhelm, and refused to do as he asked. In the end, and, unwillingly, they handed the horses over, to appease his wrath.[8]

The Worcester chronicler explained how King Stephen was unable to take the castle by storm but negotiated the surrender of the castle in return for Robert's freedom and a promise of safe passage out of the area.

After Robert had remained in the castle for some time and had devastated the surrounding countryside, the king arrived with his army and besieged the castle for almost eight days. William of Ypres, who was said to be a kinsman of the same Robert, was the go-between for the surrender of the castle, and at last gained the king's agreement to a peace settlement and the surrender of the castle with a total submission to the king.[9]

This reign of terror only lasted a couple of traumatic weeks. But about six months later, in March 1140, Robert Fitz Hubert and his gang reappeared in Wiltshire, this time at Devizes Castle. Once again Fitz Hubert managed, through trickery, to seize control. The mercenary captain made the mistake of going out from Devizes to negotiate with John Marshal, the constable of Marlborough Castle. Fitz Hubert was double-crossed, captured, taken back to Devizes and hanged in front of his men.[10]

Following the departure of Fitz Hubert, Malmesbury Castle was held by King Stephen's adherents until 1153, and during these years the garrison behaved extremely badly towards both monks and local people. Influenced by what he saw around him, William of Malmesbury gave a grim summary of the way castle garrisons terrorised nearby neighbourhoods.

There were many castles all over England, each defending its own district or, to be more truthful, plundering it. The knights from the castles carried off both herds and flocks, sparing neither churches nor graveyards.[11]

---

8 *Chronicle of John of Worcester* s.a 1139. See *The Chronicle of John of Worcester: Volume III: The annals from 1067 to 1140*, ed. P. McGurk (Oxford, 1998), 286–7.
9 Ibid.
10 *Historia Novella* II.3 (ed. King 75).
11 *Historia Novella* II.36 (ed. King 71).

Malmesbury Abbey 670–1539

The Abbey's fortunes in 1140 were mixed: while the Abbey lands and property were pillaged by an aggressive castle garrison, the monks were finally free of the control of Bishop Roger. The status of the Abbey as an autonomous institution subject only to papal authority was recognised both by the king and his brother, the powerful papal legate, Henry of Blois. John, the first abbot of the liberated Abbey, died in August 1140 after only a few months in office, and he was replaced by Peter Moraunt, who remained abbot for much of the next two decades. The Worcester chronicler spoke highly of Peter, ascribing his appointment to the influence of the legate, Henry of Blois who was the bishop of Winchester.

> Peter the monk, who was of great learning and knowledge, was made abbot of Malmesbury by Henry, bishop of Winchester, legate of the holy Roman see. He had been a monk at Cluny, and for some time had been prior of La Charité. Thence he became abbot of the monastery of the holy pope Urban in the diocese of Châlons-sur-Marne. When troubles arose and threatened him, he was forced to leave that house, and, at the prompting of the bishop of Winchester, he came to England, and took over the rule of Malmesbury in this year.[12]

The dominance of Walter of Pinkney

In the early 1140s the castellan or commander of the castle of Malmesbury was Walter of Pinkney or Picquigny, a man with a reputation for violence and extortion. Gilbert Foliot, the abbot of Gloucester, was unhappy with the predatory behaviour of Pinkney and the castellan of Marlborough, John Marshal. After Jocelin of Bohun became bishop of Salisbury in 1142, Foliot wrote to him calling for him to take firm action against these two brigands.

> [...] Beloved father, we bewail our troubles into the ears of your sanctity, begging humbly that your admonition should restrain and your discipline check those who are wronging us. The fact is that John of Marlborough and Walter of Picquigny are continually harassing us, your humble friends, and feel no shame in laying violent hands on things that comfort us in our pilgrimage through life and expending them for wicked purposes [...] We ask, in the confidence we do well to place in you, that the pastoral rod you wield may lay low those whom sacred admonition has no power to restrain. For your sanctity must be aware that the two I have mentioned have stolen from us more than 200 marks in coin and in what coin buys and have reduced to almost nothing the possessions we have in their vicinity.[13]

---

12 *Chronicle of John of Worcester* s.a 1139 (ed. P. McGurk 293).
13 *The Letters and Charters of Gilbert Foliot*, ed. Adrian Morey and C. N. L. Brooke (Cambridge, 1967), 71–4.

The Abbey and the Anarchy

There is no evidence that Bishop Jocelin took any effective action against the Malmesbury garrison in response to this request, and Walter of Pinkney continued to terrorise the region, much to the irritation of the Empress Matilda and her general, Robert of Gloucester. Most of the west country was loyal to Matilda; Robert's great stronghold was Bristol Castle, and from 1142 the Empress based herself nearby in Bishop Roger's former castle in Devizes, just twenty miles south of Malmesbury. With its commitment to Stephen, Malmesbury Castle was an outlier in a region that Matilda and Robert saw as their home territory. According to the *Gesta Stephani* Matilda became preoccupied with the need to deal, once and for all, with Walter of Pinkney, characterised by the chronicler as 'the man whom she hated more unrelentingly than any of her enemies'.[14] In 1144 Matilda attempted to end Pinkney's control of Malmesbury Castle. Robert of Gloucester took personal charge of the operation, and knowing that taking the strong keep of Malmesbury by storm would be difficult, he decided instead to starve the castle garrison into submission. Robert built three temporary 'siege castles' around the town in order to enforce the blockade. From these fortifications it would be possible to observe the town and castle and make sure that no food was allowed to enter and that none of Stephen's soldiers were permitted to leave. The chronicle recorded the rapid construction of the siege castles, and how the blockade stopped Walter of Pinkney from sending out raiding parties. The siege lasted long enough for the garrison to be 'in extremity of hunger'. The chronicle focused on the military story, but the consequence of the blockade was that the monks and townsfolk, as well as the soldiers of the castle, faced starvation.

> The Earl of Gloucester quickly built three [temporary siege] castles close to Malmesbury, while the king was occupied elsewhere in calming the disturbances of the kingdom, and not only carefully checked the garrison's wonted raids through the country but continually and firmly shut them in until they were in extremity of hunger.[15]

Stephen was concerned to hear of this blockade and personally led a large force to end the siege of Malmesbury. Stephen's army dispersed Robert of Gloucester's forces and having replenished the garrison's food supplies, they went on the offensive, ravaging the lands in areas loyal to Robert and Matilda. Doubtless ordinary villagers suffered the most as Stephen's men sought to demonstrate their power.

> When the king learnt the truth about his men's grievous plight he at once called a vast army together. He arrived at Malmesbury suddenly and unexpectedly. After putting in supplies to last for a very long time

14 *Gesta Stephani* II.93 (ed. Potter & Davis 179).
15 *Gesta Stephani* II.87 (ed. Potter & Davis 171).

Malmesbury Abbey 670–1539

he used his strength in a most terrible way, with pillaging, fire and sword, everywhere round the castles that the Earl had built.[16]

The Malmesbury garrison had withstood the siege of 1144, and Walter of Pinkney remained castellan. The conditions for the Abbey were becoming increasingly desperate, and once again Abbot Gilbert Foliot of Gloucester attempted to act as advocate. When Eugenius III became pope in February 1145, Foliot wrote to him to request the appointment of a new papal legate to deal with problems of the Church in England, of which the most critical was the state of Malmesbury Abbey. Since the powers of the previous legate in England, Henry of Blois, had lapsed in 1143, Gilbert called for a man of action to be given legatine powers so that he could deal robustly with those who were making life impossible for the monks of Malmesbury.

> If, in the words of the prophet, the sword of the Lord 'is sharpened, furbished that it may glitter', we wish that it may stand in the hand of the god of Israel, striking and avenging the insults to his flock. Your charity could show us nothing more merciful than to send to these parts one capable of handling God's affairs and yours with proper zeal.[17]

Gilbert gave the pope background information about the calamities facing Malmesbury Abbey. This, he explained, was the single most troubled monastic community in England, and the cause of the problem was the castle, situated within the Abbey precincts.

> Though, beloved father, the face of the churches of all England, sorely bereft as it is, sighs to you, yet the church of Malmesbury is the one that, unless help comes quickly, now has no remaining consolation except that worst feature of adversity, the thought that it was happy in the past. For just as the lamb caught in the wolf's jaws can find no way to escape, so she, straitened by the walls, and afflicted by the denizens, of the castle that is sited in its enclosure and churchyard, must deeply groan at the disappearance of all the earthly wealth it boasted and all the religion and order it cherished in her bosom. There is scarce room now for any possible addition to its calamity, when its site has been given over to extreme desolation and its sons to be scattered.[18]

The letter laid the blame for the Abbey's predicament squarely on the castle garrison. Foliot claimed that without papal intervention, Abbot Peter Moraunt might have to consider abandoning Malmesbury altogether.

> For in the place where, since the time of the holy father Aldhelm, the praise of God has resounded, today ravens an armed throng of

---

[16] *Gesta Stephani* II.88 (ed. Potter & Davis 173).
[17] *The Letters and Charters of Gilbert Foliot*, 74–4.
[18] Ibid.

The Abbey and the Anarchy

hirelings, a troop of knights all too ready to commit any impiety into which it is led. It remains then for our beloved brother Lord Peter, abbot of the church, either to be rescued from these harassments forthwith, or not to be able to return to it at all.[19]

It is not known precisely how the pope responded to this letter. But there is no evidence that he took effective action, and we do know that he did not appoint a legate for England until 1149. The critical situation facing the monks did not fundamentally change. Although the forces loyal to Empress Matilda had failed to take Malmesbury by siege, they did win a small victory against the castle garrison later in 1145 when the constable of Malmesbury Castle, Walter of Pinkney, the bane of the monks of Malmesbury, was captured through some form of subterfuge and handed over to the Empress Matilda who imprisoned and tortured him. King Stephen responded, yet again, by coming to Malmesbury in person to stabilise the situation and to ensure that, despite the loss of their commander, the soldiers of Malmesbury Castle remained loyal to him.

And the king arrived at once on hearing of Walter's capture, put in reinforcements and a large supply of food. The countess [Empress Matilda] [...] burnt with one emotion towards the man [Pinkney], that of cruelty, and after fettering him tightly delivered him to torment in a filthy dungeon.[20]

Henry Plantagenet comes to Malmesbury

There was a significant reduction in the level of conflict in the late 1140s following the death of Robert of Gloucester in 1147. A year later the Empress Matilda retired to Normandy, and the leadership of the struggle against Stephen passed to Henry Plantagenet, the son of the Empress; while Robert of Gloucester had been a commanding figure, Henry was extremely young and inexperienced. Despite the reduced level of fighting, the presence of the royalist garrison continued to be highly disruptive for the Abbey. At some point in the years 1150–1 complaints were sent again to Pope Eugenius about the behaviour of the men of the castle. In March

19 Ibid.
20 *Gesta Stephani* II.93 (ed. Potter & Davis 179). Things did not turn out well for Walter of Pinkney. After two years in Matilda's dungeon Pinkney was released in 1147. He immediately began fighting again for King Stephen. Walter did not return to Malmesbury which now had a new constable. Instead he and some companions seized control of the castle at Christchurch in Dorset and began terrorising the local area. Shortly afterwards he was ambushed at the church in Christchurch by a gang of local townsfolk and villagers who were tired of his oppressive acts. One of the Dorset men killed Walter with an axe blow to his head. See *Gesta Stephani* II.111 (ed. Potter & Davis 213).

Malmesbury Abbey 670–1539

1151 the pope issued a bull instructing the senior clergy of England to take action to discipline the garrison, emphasising the special relationship between the papacy and Malmesbury Abbey.

> Bishop Eugenius, servant of the servants of God, to his venerable brothers T[heobald] archbishop of Canterbury, legate of the apostolic see, and bishops J[ocelin] of Salisbury, J[ohn] of Worcester, R[obert] of Lincoln, and R[obert] of Bath, greetings and the apostolic blessing. Places that are worthy of veneration and dedicated to God should not be buffeted by any troubles or wearied by any vexations or oppressions. It has come to our notice that the castellans quartered around the monastery of Malmesbury are disturbing our beloved sons, Abbot P[eter] and the brothers of the place, by many exactions and every kind of vexatious troubles. Therefore, because this monastery is under the jurisdiction of the blessed Peter and is protected and defended by the apostolic see, we neither can nor should be found wanting in what concerns its justice. Accordingly, by this present document we order that you strictly instruct the castellans who are known to be oppressing and vexing the place to refrain altogether from harassing the monastery, and to leave him [Abbot Peter] in peace. If they neglect to obey your instructions, you are to do strict justice by them.
>
> Given at Ferentino, 30 March.[21]

There is no evidence that these instructions led to any change in the circumstances at Malmesbury. Meanwhile, the power of Henry Plantagenet was on the rise. In 1150 Henry became the Duke of Normandy, and in 1152 he married the recently divorced queen of France, Eleanor of Aquitaine, thus acquiring a huge block of territory in western and southern France. By January 1153 he felt strong enough to try to seize the crown of England. The weather was terrible; despite this, Henry crossed the Channel and landed in Dorset. The chronicler, Henry of Huntingdon, emphasised how daring and unusual it was to make such a journey in mid-winter and explained that Henry's plan on reaching England was first to wrest control of Malmesbury Castle from the forces of his enemy, King Stephen.

> That he should have embarked on a stormy sea in the very middle of winter his supporters considered to be heroic, while others thought it rash. But the valiant young man, hating to delay, gathered his men and laid siege to the castle of Malmesbury.[22]

Henry marched north from the Dorset coast and proceeded to overrun the town of Malmesbury with great ease; but he was unable to dislodge Stephen's garrison from the castle. The bare bones of this story have long been known. However, in the early 1950s an important discovery was

---

21 *RM* I 381–2.
22 *Historia Anglorum*, X.34 (ed. Greenaway 763).

made that greatly added to our knowledge of these events. The chronicle, the *Gesta Stephani*, provides much rich detail about events in Malmesbury and Wiltshire during the reign of Stephen but the final section of the text describing events from 1147 onwards was thought to be lost. In the 1950s the British scholar, Roger Mynors, found a copy of the chronicle containing the lost ending in the municipal library in Valenciennes in France. The rediscovered conclusion to *Gesta Stephani* provides much more information about what happened when Henry and his troops stormed the town of Malmesbury in early 1153.

The massacre in Malmesbury Abbey

The final section of the *Gesta Stephani* recounted in detail the chaotic and bloody events that took place when Henry Duke of Normandy, the future King Henry II, took the town of Malmesbury by storm in the early weeks of 1153. When Henry's army appeared outside the town the people of the town rushed to the walls. Young Henry had brought with him specialist infantrymen who soon overwhelmed the town militia. The defenders fled for sanctuary to the Abbey church, but Henry's troops did not respect the sanctity of the Abbey, and they pursued the Malmesbury militia into the church where they massacred both monks and those people of the town who had tried to take refuge.

> So the Duke, collecting his forces, and with the barons flocking in eagerly to join him, made without delay for the castle of Malmesbury, which was subject to the king. A crowd of common people flew to the wall surrounding the town in order to defend it. The Duke ordered his infantry, men of the greatest cruelty, whom he had brought with him, to assail the defenders with arrows and missiles, while others devoted all their efforts to demolishing the wall. And they being chosen and equipped for this task, very quickly carried ladders and other gear to the wall and scaled the wall itself with the greatest enthusiasm. When the defenders, unable to bear their fierce assault any longer, fled to the church, containing a convent of monks living According to monastic rule, the attackers burst into the church with them and, after plundering and murdering monks all over it, did not shrink from laying hands on the very altar.[23]

The soldiers who carried out the massacre at the Abbey church were Breton or Flemish mercenaries, and after the fall of Malmesbury, they went on the rampage in the town and the surrounding villages. Meanwhile the castle garrison, safe in the keep, was immune from the carnage.[24] The

---

23 *Gesta Stephani* II.118 (ed. Potter & Davis 231).
24 *Gesta Stephani* II.118 (ed. Potter & Davis 233).

Malmesbury Abbey 670–1539

bloodshed was so extreme that Henry eventually relented, on the advice of his barons, and ordered a halt to the indiscriminate violence.

> So savagely and brutally did their reckless and unblushing presumption rage without any pity against all, and especially the possessions of the churches, that the barons of England shuddered in utter loathing of their company, and being unable to endure their bestial and brutal acts any longer, suggested to the Duke that he should allow them to go home. So the Duke hearing what dreadful and abominable things they had done in a short time, moved with pity ordered most of them to cross the Channel in haste.[25]

Some of the dismissed mercenaries were drowned in a shipwreck when crossing the Channel; the chronicler saw this as divine retribution.[26] Following the massacre in the Abbey church, Henry proceeded to lay siege to the castle. The constable at Malmesbury Castle, one Jordan, managed to escape and inform Stephen about the turn of events. The king responded by moving rapidly towards Malmesbury with a substantial army, intending to break the siege of the castle, just as he had done in 1144. This dramatic turn of events was recounted by Henry of Huntingdon.

> Distressed by these evil tidings, the king's face changed from grandeur to wrinkled grief, but he lost no time in gathering all his forces and pitching his tents not far from Malmesbury. On the day after his arrival, he drew up his battle lines in handsome style, filling them with select horsemen and disposing them according to military precepts. It was indeed a huge army, densely packed with numerous nobles, gleaming with golden banners, both very terrible and beautiful, but God, in whom alone is perfect safety, had retired far away from them.[27]

With the castle still untaken, two armies faced each other across the River Avon just outside the town. Conditions were not good for battle: the weather was terrible and the Avon was in flood. It seems that Stephen ordered his troops to advance and try to find a way to ford the river but, in the middle of a wild storm, this manoeuvre disintegrated into chaos. Henry of Huntingdon explained that the full force of the storm was in the face of Stephen's men. The king relented and gave up on his attempt to engage Henry in battle at Malmesbury. The rediscovered ending to the *Gesta Stephani* recounted how Henry and Stephen then agreed to negotiate.

> It was arranged between them and carefully settled that they should demolish the castle, both because they could not join battle on account

---

[25] *Gesta Stephani* II.87 (ed. Potter & Davis 171).
[26] *Gesta Stephani* II.119 (ed. Potter & Davis 233).
[27] *Historia Anglorum* X.34 (ed. Greenaway 765).

The Abbey and the Anarchy

of the river and its very deep valley intervening and because it was a bitter winter with a severe famine in those parts.[28]

They compromised and agreed that neither side should be allowed to control the castle: instead, it should be demolished. This looked like a good outcome for the monks who hated the castle; unfortunately for them the demolition did not happen, and instead Henry seized the castle by subterfuge. Stephen's castellan, Jordan, secretly agreed to change sides and support Henry. Entering Malmesbury Castle with Stephen's approval, supposedly to begin organising the demolition, Jordan announced that he was holding the castle for Henry. So Malmesbury Castle had been finally taken by the enemies of King Stephen, not through siege warfare but through treachery.

The triumph of Henry Plantagenet

The fall of Malmesbury Castle was a big blow to Stephen. We know that he visited Malmesbury at least four times to ensure that the castle remained under his control. After the taking of Malmesbury in 1153 inconclusive manoeuvres by the two sides took place over the following months. The armies of Stephen and Henry came face to face again at Wallingford in August 1153. As at Malmesbury earlier in the year, the two sides failed to engage in a pitched battle, and serious peace talks finally began. These negotiations led to the Treaty of Winchester in November 1153, through which Stephen recognised Henry as his heir. A year later Stephen died, and Henry became king. The period of armed conflict, 1139–53, had been disastrous for Malmesbury Abbey. The religious life of the monks was seriously disrupted. Their lands were ravaged. The ambitious rebuilding of the conventual church begun by Bishop Roger was almost certainly halted. One major benefit arising from the end of hostilities following the triumph of Henry II was that it was now possible to resume the rebuilding of the Abbey church.

Despite the massacre of 1153 Abbot Peter Moraunt appears to have had a largely amicable relationship with Henry Plantagenet. One charter issued not long after the massacre hints at some degree of guilt and remorse on Henry's part. It has a regal tone, but Henry carefully avoided any suggestion that he was as yet king. Instead, he styled himself Duke of Normandy and Aquitaine, which dates the charter to the early months of 1153 when Henry began to use this title in other charters. Although not king, Henry acted as if he had sovereign authority over the Malmesbury area, and he confirmed that the monks were entitled to all the rights granted by his grandfather, King Henry and his great-uncle, William Rufus. This was a friendly act.

28 *Gesta Stephani* II.118 (ed. Potter & Davis 233).

Malmesbury Abbey 670–1539

Henry duke of Normandy and Aquitaine, count of Anjou, to all archbishops, bishops, earls, barons, justiciars, sheriffs and all his loyal people, French and English, greetings. You must know that I have granted and confirmed to the church of St Aldhelm of Malmesbury, and the abbot and monks serving God there, all their liberties and immunities which they had in the time of my predecessors as kings of England, and in particular immunity from toll throughout England, as granted them by King Henry. And I grant them the custody of their forests as granted them by King William, in such a way that no royal forester is to interfere in them. I also wish and irrevocably order that the aforesaid church should hold all its possessions and everything pertaining to the church well and in peace, freely and quietly and honourably, in woodland, in plains, meadows, pastures, waters, lakes, ways and paths, with soke and sake, toll and team, and *infangthief*; together with all other things and dignities and immunities and liberties pertaining to that abbey, as it held them best and most freely in the time of my predecessors.[29]

At some point between 1155 and 1158 Henry II came back to Malmesbury with a retinue that included his chancellor and future archbishop, Thomas Becket. Henry issued a charter in favour of the Abbey granting a valuable financial benefit to the Abbey.

You must know that I have granted to the abbot and monks of St Aldhelm of Malmesbury that they may have and hold all their holdings in lands and churches, tithes and other things well and in peace, freely and quietly. Besides, I give and grant them for perpetual alms 6 pounds and 10 shillings which they used by custom to give as quittance for shires and hundreds, which they are usually call *hundredsilver*: in such a way however that they are quit throughout England of shires, hundreds, pleas, plaints, and all royal custom, excepting murder-fines and Danegelds. Wherefore I wish and irrevocably order that they should have and hold all their holdings, and specifically £6 10s. in good, in peace, freely, honourably, quietly and fully, in woodland, in plains, meadows, pastures, lakes, fishponds, in waters and mills, in ways and paths, in borough and outside, and in all places, with soke and sake, toll and team, and *infangthief*; and with all the liberties and free customs belonging to the church. I also give them immunity from toll through all England, which King Henry my grandfather gave them, and the custody of their forests which King William II granted them, in such a way that no royal forester is to interfere in them.

> Witnessed by Thomas the chancellor and others,
> at Malmesbury.[30]

[29] *RM* I 320–1.
[30] *RM* I 321–2.

The Abbey and the Anarchy

The charter constituted a significant act of patronage. The monastery was no longer required to pay £6 10s each year to the Crown as 'hundred-silver' in order to obtain exemption from the authority of the hundred courts. From a modern perspective one sinister element in this grant and restatement of previous privileges was the confirmation that the Abbey had the rights known by the legal term *'infangthief'*. The term was derived from the Anglo-Saxon *'infangenþēof'* meaning literally 'thief seized within'. Manorial lords with rights of *'infangthief'* were permitted to try and execute thieves caught red-handed on their lands, taking the goods of the criminal which were forfeited.

9

The dispute with the bishops of Salisbury (1142–1217)

Bishop Roger of Salisbury seized control of Malmesbury Abbey in 1118, ensuring that there was no abbot for over twenty years. In 1140, following Roger's disgrace and death, the abbacy was restored, and a Malmesbury monk called John was elected to the post. The powerful papal legate, Henry of Blois, disapproved of this particular candidate because, as William of Malmesbury recounted, he accused the abbot-elect of simony.

> The legate approved their claim to elect but disapproved of the person elected, for in no way could he be convinced that the king had agreed to the election without a bribe. And it is a fact that a certain amount of money had been promised, but it was to secure the freedom of the Church, not the election of a person.[1]

Perhaps it was because of the legate's attitude that John felt immediately obliged to go to Rome to seek blessing directly from Pope Innocent II. William of Malmesbury wrote an account, unfortunately now lost, of the journey to Rome.[2] Abbot John died soon after his return from Rome and was replaced by Peter Moraunt, the close friend of William of Malmesbury, and a second Malmesbury delegation went to Rome in the early months of 1142 hoping to obtain formal endorsement from the pope of the validity of Malmesbury's status as a community that was exempt from episcopal control. Abbot Peter was politically astute and had had obtained prior approval for his mission from both King Stephen and Henry of Blois. The embassy to Rome proved successful: on 23 May 1142 Pope Innocent II issued a detailed charter to Malmesbury Abbey confirming the grant of exemption made by Pope Sergius to Aldhelm.[3] The papal diploma made it clear that the pope welcomed the fact that the petition from Malmesbury was endorsed by King Stephen. The charter of Innocent II also required the Abbey to make an annual payment – a so-called 'census' – of an ounce of gold. While the value of the payment was relatively small, the giving of 'census' was a visible sign of a special relationship with Rome.

---

1   *Historia Novella* II.35 (ed. King 71).
2   Leland, *Commentarii de scriptoribus Britannicis II*, 195.
3   *RM* I 346–8.

123

Malmesbury Abbey 670–1539

Roger's successor as bishop of Salisbury, Jocelin de Bohun, enjoyed an extremely lengthy episcopal career, from 1142 to 1184. During his first two decades in post he was in no position to challenge the Abbey's claims to independence, and his power to act was reduced after 1154 because of his initially poor relationship with the new king, Henry II. Bishop Roger had established a grand episcopal castle in Devizes, which Jocelin considered his property as Roger's successor, but the Empress Matilda had ignored the bishop's claims and used Devizes Castle as her personal base during her time in England between 1142 and 1147. Henry, her son, knew the castle as a boy; as king he took Devizes for himself, and was deeply offended by Jocelin's temerity when the bishop attempted to challenge the royal seizure of the castle.[4]

As soon as the Abbey emerged from the chaos of the Anarchy, Abbot Peter took steps to reassert once more exemption from the oversight of the bishop of Salisbury. Within weeks of the massacre of 1153, the abbot sought and obtained permission from Henry Plantagenet for Abbey representatives to travel to Rome. At the Lateran palace on 23 July 1153, Pope Anastasius IV granted representatives from Malmesbury confirmation of the independent status of the monastery.[5] Henry remained well disposed towards Malmesbury Abbey once crowned as king. Following the accession of Pope Adrian IV, Malmesbury monks were again permitted to travel to Rome and obtain confirmation of the Abbey's exempt status in 1156.

The Becket controversy

Bishop Jocelin of Salisbury could do nothing in the 1140s and 1150s to assert his authority over Malmesbury Abbey. The situation began to change in the 1160s because of the crisis in the relationship between the king and Archbishop Thomas Becket. Bishop Jocelin won favour by taking the king's side in the dispute. The bishop had a son – Reginald – probably born in Italy when Jocelin was there as a student in the 1130s. As a young man Reginald was a member of the household of Thomas Becket but, to Becket's disgust, he switched sides during the conflict with the king and became a clerk of the royal household, active in the campaign against Becket. Bishop Jocelin also demonstrated, at an early stage in the dispute, that he stood with the king and not Becket. In 1166 the bishop appointed John of Oxford, a clerk of the royal court and loyal servant to the king, to the post of dean of Salisbury against the wishes of Becket: Jocelin did this at the direct bidding of the king. Becket, by this time in exile at Vézelay, was incensed and responded by suspending Jocelin

---

4   David Knowles, *The Episcopal Colleagues of Archbishop Thomas Becket* (Oxford, 1951), 21–2.
5   *RM* I 366.

The dispute with the bishops of Salisbury (1142–1217)

from episcopal office. Undeterred Jocelin continued to support Henry's defiance of Becket, and in April 1169 the bishop was one of a group of royalist supporters excommunicated by Becket.

The attitude of the Malmesbury monks towards the Becket crisis is not clear, but we do know that a key member of Becket's entourage considered that Malmesbury Abbey was a potential ally and a possible source of spiritual comfort. In 1166, Herbert of Bosham, Becket's close adviser, sent a letter to Abbot Gregory of Malmesbury, seeking his support in the conflict. Herbert was with Becket in exile in France when he wrote, using language suggesting that he saw Gregory as a special friend. We know little about Gregory, who was abbot from 1159 to 1168, having previously been a monk of Lire in Normandy,[6] but Herbert's letter implied that Malmesbury, under Gregory's stewardship, had a reputation as an important, disciplined centre of religious observance. Herbert requested prayers rather than practical action in support of Becket and used the letter to express his hopes for spiritual assistance from the wider community of monks and nuns in England.

> [...] all the holy convents in the church of the English, who day and night zealously sing psalms and hymns and spiritual canticles, who to defend our (or rather the Saviour's) house often spend the whole night in tears and prayers. In these we place our hope: a renowned source of comfort in our troubles. We are not submerged in sadness, rather, to tell the truth, my soul rejoices and exults. It rejoices and exults, to be sure, because we have help in our land [...][7]

Herbert's style was oblique, but he appeared to be suggesting that, with Gregory as its ruler, Malmesbury was a distinguished centre of spirituality: one of 'the holy convents in the church of the English, who [...] spend the whole night in tears and prayers'. He assumed that Malmesbury Abbey was a serious place where the Daily Office was recited with care and zeal. Herbert used a military metaphor: in his battle with Henry II, Becket needed 'arms', including the spiritual firepower of a place like Gregory's Malmesbury. The prayers of the Malmesbury monks and others had the potential to be 'a renowned source of comfort in our troubles'. He implied that Becket, in a way that was foreshadowed by his Anglo-Saxon predecessor, Ælheah, was on track for martyrdom and would need to be sustained during the crisis by the prayers of supporters such as the Malmesbury community.

Although we do not know how Abbot Gregory responded to Herbert's letter, the Abbey had a practical interest in the Becket cause because of the exemption claim. One of the main areas of disagreement between

---

6 *Heads of Houses* I, 55–6.
7 Herbert of Bosham, 'Epistola XIX- Epistola Herberti ad Gregorium Abbatem de Malmesberia', in *Patrologia Latina 190*.

Malmesbury Abbey 670–1539

Becket and the king concerned the right of the clergy to appeal beyond the Church authorities in England to the papal curia. Becket himself accepted the validity of Malmesbury's claims to exemption from diocesan control. We know this because Becket wrote to the monks of Malmesbury on two occasions, in November–December 1169 and May 1170, asking for their support. Identical letters were addressed to the communities of Malmesbury, Bury St Edmunds, St Albans, St Augustine's Canterbury and Westminster. All these Benedictine monasteries claimed episcopal exemption and a direct line of accountability to the papacy. Protocol required that Becket should communicate directly with these monasteries because, as exempt houses, they could not be instructed via their diocesan bishops. Beyond protocol, Becket also hoped that these communities would have a special loyalty towards him because he was fighting for their rights, and the two letters sent to Malmesbury and the other exempt houses in 1169–70 indicate that Becket expected support because of their privileged relationship with the papacy.

> The greater your friendship with the holy Roman Church, the more manfully should you rise up to repel and punish her wrongs and prove by the evidence of your actions how loyally you are bound to her.[8]

> The more richly the holy Roman Church has endowed your monastery with favours, the more diligently are you bound to obey its mandates.[9]

In one way Becket's martyrdom proved useful to Malmesbury because afterwards, as a result of the Treaty of Avranches (1172), Henry II was obliged to concede the right of appeal to the papacy. This agreement made possible several appeals by Malmesbury Abbey to the papal curia in the years that followed. In another way the martyrdom was problematic for Malmesbury because it strengthened Bishop Jocelin's hand, emboldening him, after three decades of acquiescence, to challenge the autonomy of Malmesbury.

Bishop Jocelin's attack on Malmesbury's independence

The royal Pipe Rolls indicate that a new abbot called Robert Venys took charge of Malmesbury Abbey in the eighteenth regnal year of Henry II (1171–2).[10] Robert was both a monk and medical doctor, and had

---

8 The text is taken from the letters to St Augustine's Canterbury and the other exempt monasteries including Malmesbury in Ann Duggan, ed. and trans., *The Correspondence of Thomas Becket, Archbishop of Canterbury, 1162–1170*, Volume 2 (Oxford, 2000), 1107.
9 Duggan, *Becket Correspondence*, 1243.
10 *The Great Roll of the Pipe for the Eighteenth Years of the Reign of King Henry the Second* (London, 1894), 128.

The dispute with the bishops of Salisbury (1142–1217)

previously been physician to Henry II.[11] The accession of Abbot Robert appears to have prompted Bishop Jocelin to question Malmesbury's claims to independence. Jocelin had never accepted the monastery's claim to exemption from episcopal control. He had tolerated the situation for three decades but, in the aftermath of the Becket crisis, he felt able to act. The bishop's standing at the royal court was greatly increased because of the loyalty he and his son, Reginald, had displayed during the dispute. In 1173 the king rewarded Reginald, by choosing him as the bishop of Bath, while at the same time appointing Richard of Dover as archbishop of Canterbury to replace his murdered predecessor. Both Reginald and Richard were obliged to go to Rome to have their appointments ratified, and they returned together to England in September 1174. It seems likely that Reginald and Richard discussed the Malmesbury case while they were in Italy and on their journey home.

During the autumn of 1174 Archbishop Richard of Dover, newly back in England, undertook a formal visitation of his archdiocese. He had the power of a papal legate, allowing him to inspect monasteries that claimed local exemption, and we know that he toured the west of England, challenging at least one other claim to episcopal exemption during the visitation. The archbishop went to Gloucester, where the canons at the St Oswald's Priory claimed that they had papal privileges exempting them from the authority of the bishop of Worcester and placing them instead under the supervision of the archbishop of York.[12] Richard rejected these claims and excommunicated the Gloucester canons, who proceeded to appeal to Pope Alexander III. On 24 November 1174 Archbishop Richard was not far from Malmesbury when he officiated at the grand enthronement of his friend, Reginald, as bishop of Bath.[13] It was probably around this time that the archbishop was told that Abbot Robert of Malmesbury had refused to give an oath of obedience to Bishop Jocelin, and had instead received a benediction from Nicholas ap Gwrgan, the bishop of Llandaff. The archbishop investigated, and ap Gwrgan was duly suspended. Greatly alarmed by this, the bishop wrote a grovelling letter of submission and apology, not to the archbishop but to Jocelin, asking for help in having his suspension lifted, and presenting himself as a man who was desperate to make his peace.

> In accordance with the debt that human nature owes, my weakness increases daily. As I await the days assigned by fate, I recall, to my sorrow, the faults of my youth, and with constant penitence deplore the errors of my old age. For my conscience is accused and sorely burned

11 *Heads of Houses I*, 55.
12 'Houses of Augustinian Canons: The Priory of St Oswald, Gloucester', in *A History of the County of Gloucester II*, ed. William Page (London, 1907), 84–7.
13 *Radulfi de Diceto decani Lundoniensis Opera Historica: Volume 1*, ed. William Stubbs (London, 1876), 398.

Malmesbury Abbey 670–1539

by the fact that at my very end strange children, halting from their paths,[14] so tricked me that, to the loss of brotherly honour and at the cost of your church, I was so rashly presumptuous as to disregard your appeal and grant the gift of blessing to the [abbot] elect of Malmesbury, though it was illicit [...][15]

This letter indicates that on hearing of the possibility of a benediction by ap Gwrgan, Jocelin had requested that he delay the ceremony subject to a hearing in front of the new archbishop of Canterbury. The Welsh bishop had ignored this and had gone ahead with the blessing. Bishop Nicholas accepted that, on reflection, his actions were wrong, and he apologised profusely for acting arbitrarily.

I should not have ventured on this action, refusing even an appeal, though a suit on that matter was pending between you and the monastery of Malmesbury, in the presence of our lord of Canterbury, and the time for its hearing had been fixed. Deservedly then was it that at your urging punishment followed on this blameworthy action; for by the authority of our lord of Canterbury the power of my order and office was removed from me. But though every time of life is prone and liable to lapse, it is the sign of an obstinate and impenitent mind to refuse to recognise or admit a wrong. I did sin, I fell into the snare I myself made,[16] and I beg with deep groans that where sin abounded so also may grace more abound.[17]

Bishop Nicholas was writing to Jocelin, hoping that he would intercede with the archbishop, who was the person with the power to absolve him.

Therefore concerning this fault I am and shall be prepared to stand by your judgement and that of our lord of Canterbury. May you too, for my sake, feel fraternal pity for a converted sinner, and see fit to work diligently to ensure that the rigour of the sentence passed on me may be relaxed.[18]

While Bishop Nicholas made an abject apology, Abbot Robert responded in a markedly different way. Using the freedom provided by the Treaty of Avranches, he rejected the archbishop's ruling and appealed to the papal curia. Aware that the new abbot had petitioned the pope, the archbishop of Canterbury sent a letter about the Malmesbury case to the curia. This letter was, in fact, drafted by his secretary, Peter of Blois, and was highly critical of the behaviour of Abbot Robert, demonstrating a wider antagonism towards the monastic communities of England.

14 cf. Ps. 17: 46.
15 *Charters and Documents*, 41–2.
16 cf. Ps. 7: 16 and Ps. 34: 8.
17 *Charters and Documents*, 41–2.
18 Ibid.

The dispute with the bishops of Salisbury (1142–1217)

The monastery of Malmesbury, which lies within the diocese of Salisbury, had recently chosen an abbot for itself. When the bishop of Salisbury had lodged an appeal and had constantly on your behalf forbidden the elect to receive the gift of blessing from anyone but him, he nonetheless betook himself privily to Wales, obtained for himself a clandestine and furtive blessing, and wrongfully took over the office of abbot.[19]

Archbishop Richard's letter explained how he summoned the two sides to a formal hearing where he asked to see the documents that justified the Abbey's claims to independence.

The parties were accordingly brought into our presence, and the privileges of the churches were publicly produced; but we found no reason why the monastery of Malmesbury should not be subject to the bishop of Salisbury and humbly obey him.[20]

The archbishop and his advisers were unconvinced by the documents that were produced by the Abbey: the seals on the papal charters looked suspect, and the documents 'in no way smelt of the style of the Roman curia'. Richard's letter stated that he convened a second hearing where he attempted to bring about a reconciliation, but the abbot rejected his attempts to help, insisting that he was only answerable to the pope.

But the abbot, on the advice of some advocate, took refuge in the crafty trickeries of the law, and would not acquiesce in the judgment or admit the word of peace, averring that in future he would not answer as to profession or obedience to any bishop or archbishop, but only to the pope. He left the room with a show of contumacy, saying: 'Abbots are cheap and wretched creatures if they do not completely rid themselves of the power of bishops, when for an ounce of gold a year they can win full freedom thanks to the see of Rome'.[21]

Archbishop Richard used the letter to Pope Alexander as an opportunity to express more general concern about the arrogance and indiscipline of monks and their abbots.

The mischief is spreading far and wide. Abbots are puffing themselves up against primates and bishops, and no one reverences or honours his superiors. The yoke of obedience has been nullified, though in it lay the one hope of salvation, the remedy for long-standing transgression. Abbots loathe having anyone to correct their outrages; they embrace

19 Letter of Richard of Dover to Pope Alexander III as drafted by Peter of Blois, in ed. J. A. Giles, *Petri Blesensis Bathoniensis archidiaconi opera omnia* (London, 1847), 201–5.
20 Ibid.
21 Ibid.

Malmesbury Abbey 670–1539

an unlimited licence of impunity, and relax the yoke of service in the cloister to make themselves free to do anything they like. This is why the resources of almost all monasteries have been given over to plunder and pillage: abbots outwardly make provision for the flesh in its concupiscences,[22] having not a care in the world so long as they make an elegant show and there is peace in their days,[23] while the cloister monks are free to enjoy leisure and idle talk [...][24]

The letter concluded with a full-blown attack on the integrity of Abbot Robert of Malmesbury and an accusation that Malmesbury and many other monasteries were guilty of forgery when claiming exemption from episcopal control.

> If then the abbot of Malmesbury, who is in my estimation a barren tree, a foolish fig and a useless trunk, comes to you or sends to you, you should weigh his life and his opinion in the scales of justice, and not admit his privileges until it is absolutely clear, by comparison of the script and the seals, at what time and by what fathers they were granted. For the deceitful malice of forgers has so armed itself to the despite of bishops that falsehood prevails in the exemption of almost all monasteries [...][25]

The archbishop and his advisers had some grounds for being suspicious of the documents produced by the Abbey. As we have seen key documents in the archive had almost certainly been altered to strengthen the Abbey's claims to autonomy during Bishop Roger's ascendancy.[26]

The counter-offensive of Malmesbury Abbey

The attack on the reputation and independence of Malmesbury Abbey failed. Pope Alexander III sided with the Abbey and ruled against Bishop Jocelin and the new archbishop of Canterbury. In a letter calling for advice from the bishops of London and Worcester (dating from either December 1174 or December 1175) Pope Alexander made it clear that he did not accept that the bishop of Llandaff had acted improperly and did not consider that Bishop Jocelin had legitimate authority in this matter.

> [...] if it becomes clear to you that [Abbot] Robert [of Malmesbury], fortified as he is with the privilege of the church of Rome, has had

---

22 cf. Rom. 13: 14.
23 cf. Is. 39: 8.
24 Letter of Richard of Dover to Pope Alexander III as drafted by Peter of Blois, in ed. J. A. Giles, *Petri Blesensis Bathoniensis archidiaconi opera omnia* (London, 1847), 201–5.
25 Ibid.
26 Kelly, *Charters*, 128–9.

The dispute with the bishops of Salisbury (1142–1217)

himself blessed by another person, you should not permit him or the bishop who blessed him to be held to account by the said bishop of Salisbury in any inquiry concerning this matter, but rather entirely absolve them both from his proceedings, no appeal being allowable [...][27]

A second papal letter also confirms that the pope was unimpressed by Bishop Jocelin's claims. On 22 May 1175 Pope Alexander wrote that he was unhappy to learn from Malmesbury Abbey about the way that Bishop Jocelin had been harassing the community.

On behalf of our dear sons, the abbot and brothers of the monastery of Malmesbury, which is known to pay *census*[28] to us, you must know that it has come to our hearing that our venerable brother, J[ocelin] bishop of Salisbury, is continually harassing them in manifold ways, demanding obedience and subjection from them, though the said monastery is said to be exempt from his jurisdiction, by privileges issued by the Roman church.[29]

The pope requested more information about the case but, manifestly, his working assumption was that Bishop Jocelin was in the wrong.

But because we do not wish to, and ought not, tolerate the said bishop causing any trouble or harassment to the monastery, which pays *census* to us, we by our apostolic letter order and prescribe to you in your wisdom to have the privileges of the monastery presented to you [...][30]

Once the documentation had been checked, and unless something surprising came to light, the pope instructed the judges delegate to be firm and act to defend the Abbey.

[...] and if you find that the monastery is exempt from the jurisdiction of the said bishop, you are on our behalf strictly to restrain him from causing trouble or harassment, in person or through others, to the abbot and brothers of the said monastery [...][31]

Further evidence that Jocelin failed in his attempt to constrain the independence of Malmesbury comes from the work of Gerald of Wales. In his book, *Gemma Ecclesiastica*, Gerald recounted how, at some point in the 1170s, the monks of Malmesbury became unhappy with Abbot

---

27 *RM I* 371–2.
28 The census was the annual payment to the papacy made by exempt monasteries.
29 *RM I* 371.
30 Ibid.
31 Ibid.

Malmesbury Abbey 670–1539

Robert because he was so badly educated.[32] Circumventing Jocelin, the monks had gone straight to Pope Alexander with their complaint, and the pope responded by asking the bishops of Exeter and Worcester to investigate.[33] The bishops tested Robert's ability to read Latin by asking him to translate a passage from the *Acts of the Apostles*: the abbot failed the test, translating the Latin word 'repente', meaning 'suddenly', as 'he repented'. While his inability to understand rudimentary Latin was proven, the investigating bishops decided not to recommend Robert's dismissal, on the grounds that he was a diligent and effective manager of the monastery's affairs.

> [...] because he was good at business, at ruling his house and at administering things secular, he won his case against the monks; but the prior and subprior were enjoined to make up for his deficiencies in spiritual matters.[34]

This story proves that the Malmesbury community was able to send representatives to the papal curia independently and without the permission of the abbot. The deployment of papal 'judges delegate' to investigate allegations of incompetence against Abbot Robert was a consequence of the community communicating concerns to the curia, presumably against the abbot's wishes. This evidence of collective action by the monks, without the endorsement of the abbot, is consistent with what David Knowles called, 'the democratic movement among the black monks of the time, by which the chapters, isolated from the abbot, were claiming to act as a body with definite rights'.[35]

The direct complaint of Malmesbury monks to Pope Alexander III about Abbot Robert is alluded to in another document in the Abbey's cartulary.[36] The bishop of Worcester confirmed in writing a settlement that he and the bishop of Exeter had negotiated 'for the restoration of peace between Robert abbot of Malmesbury and some of his brothers,

---

[32] Gerald of Wales, *Gemma Ecclesiastica*, ed. J. S. Brewer (London, 1862), 346.

[33] The *Registrum* text describes the second of the judges delegate as 'Bartholomeo Oxoniensis'. This was a transcription error by a Malmesbury scribe. Bartholomew, bishop of Exeter (1161–84) [Exoniensis], was often called upon by Pope Alexander III to act as his agent. There were no bishops of Oxford at this time.

[34] Gerald of Wales, *Gemma Ecclesiastica*, 346. We see, perhaps, evidence of Abbot Robert's business acumen in a contract for the running of a fulling mill that survives in the Abbey cartulary. The contract between 'Abbot Robert' and Walter Handsex has been identified as one of the earliest known examples of a fulling mill in operation in England. See *RM* I 435 and Reginald Lennard, 'Early English Fulling Mills: Additional Examples', *The Economic History Review*, 33 (1951): 342–3.

[35] Knowles, *Monastic Order*, 475.

[36] *RM* II 15.

The dispute with the bishops of Salisbury (1142–1217)

as mandated by the lord pope Alexander'. As part of the agreement the abbot agreed to make available for the benefit of the community additional income that the abbot received from the church of Shipton.

The dedication of the new monastic church in 1177

Although Pope Alexander took the side of the Abbey, the community remained wary of Bishop Jocelin's aggressive intentions. In 1177, after a building campaign that had probably started in the 1120s, the monks officially celebrated the completion of the magnificent new monastic church with a service of dedication. It was considered that an episcopal blessing should be a central feature of the dedication, and that a presiding bishop was therefore required. The monks were concerned that if they asked Jocelin to officiate he would use this as an opportunity to demand a promise of obedience, and the pope was petitioned on this matter. On 11 February 1177 Pope Alexander III asked the bishops of London and Worcester to investigate the issues surrounding the episcopal blessing of the new building, instructing these 'judges delegate' to convene a meeting with Bishop Jocelin and Abbey representatives. The pope directed his agents to check the documents relating to exemption and then, unless something surprising came to light, to direct Bishop Jocelin to respect the exempt status of the Abbey and to provide a blessing for the new building without imposing any conditions. If Jocelin refused to comply on these terms, either the bishop of London or Worcester should officiate instead.

> [...] you are on our behalf strictly to order the bishop not to presume rashly to usurp anything for himself in the monastery or to dare improperly to disturb the abbot or his brothers, or their rights; but when he is requested by the same, he must dedicate [the monastery] freely and without any malpractice and without exacting obedience. Otherwise *you* are to dedicate the said monastery by our authority, without any appeal getting in the way.[37]

The Malmesbury delegation in Italy during the early weeks of 1177 petitioned Pope Alexander on plans to dedicate the new Abbey church and also sought papal support on other matters. Bishop Jocelin was, it seems, proving troublesome when he was asked to approve those parochial clergy who served churches where the Abbey was the patron. The pope granted the Abbey permission to choose and formally present clergy to parishes without any power of veto on the part of the diocesan bishop. The pope also allowed the monks to take or 'impropriate' revenues from the parish churches of St Mary's Westport in Malmesbury and Purton for the use of the Abbey. Ordinarily impropriation would

---

37 *RM* I 370.

Malmesbury Abbey 670–1539

require episcopal dispensation but, in this case, the Abbey wanted to avoid any dependency on the goodwill of Bishop Jocelin. The visitors to the papal curia from Malmesbury in 1177 had a further request: they wanted the pope to cancel the debts incurred by Malmesbury monks during a previous visit to Italy. It seems that Italian moneylenders were pursuing these debts in England, and on 25 February 1177 the bishops of London and Worcester were directed to look into the matter. This was two weeks after the same 'judges delegate' had been issued with directions to investigate arrangements for the dedication of the new church at Malmesbury. Alexander's letter summarised the case:

> A complaint of the abbot and brothers of Malmesbury monastery has been sent to us, that the merchants who frequent our curia repeatedly harass them by calling in debts, asserting that they had lent money to certain of their brothers in the past. The abbot and brothers stoutly assert that those of their brothers who have, according to the merchants, borrowed money from them did not have letters from them and did not borrow the money with their agreement.[38]

Delegations to the curia often had to spend months in Italy, and there was a well-established credit system on the margins of the papal court so that supplicants from different countries could borrow money to meet their subsistence needs. The complaint from the Abbey seems to have been that Malmesbury monks, while in Italy, had exceeded a previously agreed credit limit and had, therefore, no authority to borrow the amount of money in question. For reasons that are not clear the pope sided with the Abbey and against the merchants, instructing his agents to sanction the cancellation of the debts if it could be proved that the money had been borrowed without official authorisation.

> Therefore we instruct and order you, our brothers, by this apostolic document, altogether to absolve, on our authority, with no excuse or appeal, the said abbot and brothers from paying the debts which the merchants are demanding, if it is your lawful conviction that these merchants lent money to any of the brothers of the monastery without the assent of the abbot and chapter or the greater and sounder part of it.[39]

[38] *RM* I 374.
[39] Ibid.

The dispute with the bishops of Salisbury (1142–1217)

The conflict continues under Bishop Hubert Walter

Bishop Jocelin retired in 1184, after an episcopate of over forty years. During Jocelin's final years in office Malmesbury was ruled by Abbot Osbert Foliot (1180–2), previously prior of Gloucester,[40] and Abbot Nicholas (1183–7) who had been a monk of St Albans.[41] Henry II kept the see of Salisbury vacant from 1184 until 1189, and during the episcopal vacancy Abbot Nicholas was deposed by the king for running up heavy debts and refusing to put this right.[42] Thus, when Henry II died in 1189 both the abbacy of Malmesbury and the see of Salisbury were vacant. The new king, Richard the Lionheart, permitted the filling of both posts. The successor to Abbot Nicholas was Robert of Melun (1189/90–1205), formerly a Winchester monk. King Richard issued a charter in favour of Robert, calling him 'our beloved and special clerk' and implying some sort of royal service before his promotion to the abbacy.[43] The royal adviser Hubert Walter was appointed bishop of Salisbury in 1189 by the new king, and he immediately revived the campaign to assert control over Malmesbury Abbey. According to the chronicler, Richard of Devizes, the renewal of the dispute was the Devil's work.

> The King of Darkness, that old Incendiary, having added fresh fuel, fanned the ancient spark between the church of Salisbury and the monastery of Malmesbury into renewed flames.[44]

Richard of Devizes recounted how the abbot was summoned by the bishop and instructed that he would have to give up his crozier, symbol of his equality with bishops. Hubert intended, just like Bishop Roger earlier in the century, to reduce Malmesbury to a priory under episcopal control. The bishop, who was influential at court, obtained letters from the king confirming that he had been granted authority over the monastery. Although King Richard had departed for the Crusades, and was travelling across Europe, Abbot Robert was able to get a messenger to him, and obtain letters putting at least a temporary stop to the takeover. Bishop Hubert decided to wait until Richard's return to England before he attempted to settle the matter, and the abbot used this pause in hostilities as an opportunity to petition the pope of the time, Celestine III. The appeal to the curia was successful, and the Abbey obtained confirmation of exemption in 1191.[45] At the same time the Malmesbury delegation to the curia obtained a dispensation for irregularities committed by the

40 Ibid.
41 Ibid.
42 BL Cotton MS. Faustina B. I.
43 *RM* I 337.
44 *The Chronicle of Richard of Devizes*, ed. James Bohn (London, 1841), 14.
45 *RM* I 359.

135

Malmesbury Abbey 670–1539

former abbot, Nicholas, before his deposition,[46] and papal confirmation of the use by the Abbey of revenues from the churches of St Mary's Westport, Crudwell, Kemble, Purton and Bremhill.[47]

The final phase of the conflict

In 1208 Walter Loring became abbot of Malmesbury, and in the same year Pope Innocent III placed England under Interdict because of his dispute with King John. The Interdict made it impossible in practical terms for 'exempt' monasteries such as Malmesbury to make appeals to Rome, but when it ended in 1214 Abbot Walter was finally able to make contact with the pope and sent messengers to Rome. It is possible that Abbot Walter personally attended the Fourth Lateran Council in November 1215 and stayed on in Rome afterwards. The Council was well attended, with hundreds of bishops and abbots gathering from across Europe. We can deduce that there was a Malmesbury delegation in Rome in the months following the Council because Innocent III issued a bull confirming exempt status in March 1216.[48] Curiously, Pope Innocent issued, at around the same time, documents both confirming the exemption of Malmesbury from episcopal control and reprimanding the Abbey for allowing immoral, poorly educated candidates to become monks in return for cash payments. Although showing the monastery in a bad light, the cartulary preserved a directive from the pope ordering the Abbot Walter Loring to change his corrupt admissions policy, and this was issued just a few days before Pope Innocent confirmed exemption status. Clearly someone had complained to the pope about poor quality of monastic observance at Malmesbury. The obvious explanation is that both the bishop of Salisbury and the abbot of Malmesbury were in Rome to attend the Council and, while the bishop denounced the standard of religious and intellectual life in Malmesbury, the abbot sought confirmation of Malmesbury's exempt status. Innocent's response was even-handed: condemning the malpractices while confirming exemption based on his view of the precedent set by his predecessors.

A renewal of the conflict with the bishop of Salisbury took place in 1217 when a new bishop, Richard Poore, was appointed and took steps, for what was to be the final time, to end the exempt status of Malmesbury Abbey. The bishop wrote to Honorius III, who had recently succeeded Innocent III, complaining about the disrespectful attitude of Malmesbury Abbey towards him. On 15 July 1217, Honorius appointed Abbot Adam of Waverley and Abbot Jordan of Durford to examine the matter.[49] The

---

[46] *RM* I 375.
[47] *RM* I 374.
[48] *RM* I 377.
[49] *RM* I 401–4.

The dispute with the bishops of Salisbury (1142–1217)

instructions from Pope Honorius were curt: he required the matter to be resolved for good, with no appeal allowed.

> Our revered brother the bishop of Salisbury has complained to us, relating how the abbot and convent of Malmesbury in the diocese of Salisbury are injuring him in respect of the dignities, liberties and other things regarding his church; and so we are ordering your Discretion by apostolic writings to summon the parties, hear the case, and with no appeal granted bring it to a due end [...][50]

A tribunal was held, presided over by the two investigating abbots. Pandulf (Pandolfo Verraccio), the powerful papal legate to England, was also present together with representatives of the boy king, Henry III. Pandulf was a force to be reckoned with, having played a crucial role a few years earlier in the ending of the Interdict imposed upon England by Pope Innocent. At the hearing each side was asked to present its case. While the bishop spoke in person, the Abbey was represented by a senior monk, John Walsh, who later became abbot. The bishop showed no initial mood for compromise and rejected the legitimacy of the Abbey's claims to exemption. He sought a return to the situation that had applied under Bishop Roger when, of course, Malmesbury was treated as a priory dependent on Salisbury Cathedral.

> The said bishop, on his own behalf and that of his church, established his charge in the hearing before us as follows, bringing merely a possessory action, and saying that the abbot and monks ought to be fully subject [to him] as abbot and bishop, in both temporal and spiritual matters; and he sought for himself the putting right of the aforesaid things, back to the state in which the bishop said that the church of Sarum was in the time of bishop Roger of good memory, his predecessor, not only by common right but also by the authority of the apostolic see [...][51]

An argument ensued. The Malmesbury cartulary account suggests that the discussion was heated, and that it was the papal delegate, Pandulf, who effectively curtailed the debate, making a ruling which both parties were obliged to accept.

> And when there had been for some while dispute about these things in our presence, after many propositions from both sides, finally on the advice and command of the revered father Pandulf, [bishop] elect of Norwich and legate of the apostolic see, and also the illustrious king of England, Henry son of King John, we brought the parties to make peace.[52]

50 Ibid.
51 Ibid.
52 Ibid.

Malmesbury Abbey 670–1539

Pandulf and the king's representatives, in essence, accepted the validity of the Abbey's claim to exemption, and following instruction from them, the presiding judges, Abbots Adam and Jordan, ruled that the 'privilege' of Sergius and the charters of his successors were valid. The Abbey precinct was therefore to be seen as an autonomous area where the bishop had no authority.

> [...] the monastery of Malmesbury should be exempt from all subjection to the said bishop and his successors, according to the content of its privileges granted by Sergius, Innocent II and Alexander III, in both temporal and spiritual matters, within the bounds of the graveyard and the said monastery, as it is well known to us to be, by inspection of its privileges, namely those granted by the popes of Rome written above.[53]

Bishop Richard was given some tangible compensation for agreement to the terms of the arbitration in the form of property rights in Wiltshire: the Abbey was forced to hand over to the bishop the manor of Highway and the revenues from the churches at Bremhill and Highway. Complex arrangements were made for the keeping of the key documents related to the compromise.[54] The monks were careful to preserve the bishop's acceptance of the agreement in the Abbey's archive,[55] and Pope Honorius III confirmed the compromise agreement in 1222.[56] After over a century of bitter dispute the matter was settled. The monks made sure that the agreement imposed by Pandulf explicitly precluded for all time the possibility that the bishops might abandon the inhospitable surroundings of Old Sarum and establish Malmesbury as a new diocesan cathedral. The ruling was clear:

> [...] no bishop may set up his seat in the monastery [...][57]

Richard Poore, the bishop of Salisbury, proceeded to pursue an alternative plan. He abandoned Old Sarum and moved to New Sarum, laying the foundation stones for a splendid new cathedral on 28 April 1220.[58]

Pilton and the bishops of Exeter

While the Abbey won its war of independence against the bishops of Salisbury, some Malmesbury monks were subject to episcopal oversight during the later Middle Ages. Pilton Priory near Barnstaple was a

53 Ibid.
54 *RM* I 404–6.
55 *RM* I 395–8.
56 *RM* I 378.
57 *RM* I 401–4.
58 Matthew M. Reeve, *Thirteenth Century Wall Painting of Salisbury Cathedral* (Woodbridge, 2008), 33.

The dispute with the bishops of Salisbury (1142–1217)

dependency of the Abbey, and from the twelfth century onwards two or three Malmesbury monks lived there under the supervision of a prior. The priory was not covered by the 'privilege' of Sergius, and, as a result, the bishops of Exeter had authority over Malmesbury monks when they resided in Devon. The origins of Pilton Priory are obscure, and although the tradition in the Middle Ages was that the institution was founded by Æthelstan, the earliest documentary reference to the existence of the priory dates from the 1180s.[59] The bishops of Exeter had a technical power of veto over the choice of priors of Pilton. Thus in 1260, when Abbot William of Colerne nominated Adam de Beteslegh, a monk of Malmesbury, as prior of Pilton, he acknowledged that he needed approval from Bishop Walter Branscombe, to whom he sent a courteous letter recommending Beteslegh.[60] Several future abbots of Malmesbury served first as prior of Pilton, including Simon of Aumeney (1349), John Andever (1446–57) and Thomas Olveston (1472–80). In each case their appointment required confirmation by the bishop.[61] For the most part the bishops of Exeter appear to have had an amicable relationship with the Malmesbury monks. We know, for example, that in 1332 Bishop Grandisson borrowed a manuscript from Malmesbury Abbey which he returned a year later to Pilton.[62]

---

59   RM II 32. A fine fifteenth-century seal survives from Pilton showing the king with sceptre and orb. See Julian M. Luxford, 'The Seals of Malmesbury Abbey and Pilton Priory', *WANHM*, 115 (2022): 75–86.

60   RM II 79.

61   See *Heads of Houses II*, 124 and *Heads of Houses III*, 143.

62   Martin Heale, *The Abbots and Priors of Late Medieval and Reformation England* (Oxford, 2016), 85.

10

A self-confident age:
the Abbey in the thirteenth century

After the high drama of the previous century, the period from 1208 until 1296 was a time of comparative tranquillity and institutional consolidation. During these years the Abbey was ruled over by just four abbots. The first of these, Walter Loring (1208–22), responded astutely to the political crisis that played out during the final years of King John's reign and greatly increased the Abbey's resources without resort to external patronage. Loring was opportunistic and skilfully exploited the weakness of John's position during the baronial rebellion of 1215–16. On 18 July 1215 the king was in Oxford.[1] He had agreed to Magna Carta just one month earlier, but this had not brought an end to his troubles. When John reached Oxford, he was preparing for war and needed money and supporters. Shortly after arriving the king agreed to sell the castle and borough of Malmesbury, together with control of the three local hundred courts, to Loring.[2] In return for these assets, the abbot made an immediate payment of 60 marks, pledging an annual contribution of £20 to the Crown as a so-called 'fee farm'.

This was an extremely good deal for the Abbey which obtained, for the first time, ownership of most of the houses in the town, profits from local justice, control of the castle and the right to levy a range of additional fees on townsfolk – such as 'landgable' and 'churchscot' – that were previously due to the Crown. The clauses relating to the castle were explicitly advantageous to the Abbey: the king, not the abbot, was responsible for the cost of garrisoning the place 'should there be war in England'. Arguably, the property rights in Malmesbury were not John's to sell because ever since his accession he had been involved in a bitter dispute with the dowager queen, Berengaria, widow of his brother, Richard the Lionheart.[3] Berengaria claimed the profits from Crown holdings in Malmesbury and much else besides, as part of her dower income: in effect, her widow's pension. To compound this problem further, John had also granted the income from Malmesbury to his wife, Isabella of

---

1   J. C. Holt, *Magna Carta* (Cambridge, 2015), 304–5.
2   *RM* I 339–40. See also TNA C53/14.
3   Nicholas Vincent, 'Isabella of Angoulême: John's Jezebel', in *King John: New Interpretations*, ed. S. D. Church (Woodbridge, 2003), 186–7.

Malmesbury Abbey 670–1539

Angoulême, following their marriage in 1200. It seems that John sold the borough of Malmesbury while ignoring the claims of his sister-in-law and without seeking the agreement of his wife.

The destruction of Malmesbury Castle

Things went badly for John in the year that followed the grant of 1215. On 21 May 1216 the heir to the French throne, Prince Louis, invaded England and proceeded to take London. King John fled west. By 9 June he was in Devizes in Wiltshire and, desperate for money, he sold the right to Abbot Loring to demolish the castle in return for an additional payment of 100 marks and a palfrey. John insisted that the site should be demilitarised so that it would not fall into the hands of his enemies.

> Know you that we have granted, handed over and quitclaimed, from us and our heirs forever, to God and the church of the Blessed Mary and to St Aldhelm of Malmesbury, and to the monks serving God there, for the salvation of our soul and the souls of our ancestors and successors, the site of the castle of Malmesbury, as the rightful property of that church: namely, in such a way that the monks pull down the aforesaid castle according to their wish, and convert the place to their own uses, by erecting buildings there, or constructing other things necessary for their house, or, by disposing of it in any other manner they wish: in such a way that henceforward the aforesaid monks are not in any way taken to law by us or our heirs at any time on account of the destruction of the same castle or the site of the place, provided, however, that no fortification is built by them there in the future.[4]

King John died in October 1216, just a few months after granting permission for the demolition of the castle. Perhaps alarmed by the king's demise, Abbot Walter took steps to establish beyond question that the Abbey had a good title to the castle site and to the borough. By the early months of 1217, the abbot had obtained confirmation from John's widow, Queen Isabella, that she had relinquished her dower rights to property in Malmesbury in return for an immediate fee of thirty-seven marks and agreement that she, as queen dowager, would be the beneficiary of the annual fee farm payment of £20.

> We have also granted to the same abbot and monks in perpetuity the site of the castle in the actual court of the church of Malmesbury, which they have converted to their own purposes in order to extend their buildings. They are to possess the place in peace with no problems as being the rightful property of their church, and will not be troubled in any respect at any future time by us or our people.[5]

4   *RM* I 340.
5   *RM* I 430.

142

A self-confident age: the Abbey in the thirteenth century

The monks wasted no time in ensuring the destruction of the hated castle, and by the time that Queen Isabella issued her charter, which was at the latest during the early months of 1217, the building had already been destroyed. Having won Isabella's agreement to the transfer of property, the monks immediately sent a representative to Rome to obtain papal ratification of the transaction. Pope Honorius III issued a bull 'at Rome at St Peter's' on 11 May 1217 confirming that the borough of Malmesbury and the site of the castle had been granted to the monks by King John and his wife, and the pope threatened with dire spiritual consequences anyone who dared to challenge the Abbey's claim to the property.[6] The monks had triumphed, thanks to their energetic abbot, Walter Loring, who was lauded as a heroic figure by the community long after his death. Towards the end of the thirteenth century Abbot Walter of Colerne celebrated the achievements of his predecessor.

> [...] special prayers should always be offered first for Abbot Walter Loring [...] for he acquired at fee-farm for our church the town of Malmesbury with the adjacent hundreds, obtaining at the same time charters of King John and Queen Isabella, and procured the pulling down of the castle which was situated in the churchyard of our monastery, to its grave disgrace and unspeakable harm, King John being given 160 marks and the queen 37 [marks].[7]

In the 1360s, almost 150 years after the demolition of the castle, a monk of Malmesbury wrote the world history known as *Eulogium Historiarum*, within which he noted as an important event Loring's demolition of the castle, including a charming little doodle of the castle in the margin of his autograph manuscript.[8]

The energetic rule of Abbot John Walsh

Loring was succeeded by John Walsh, who proved to be another highly effective manager, dedicated to the defence and expansion of the Abbey's resources. Building on Loring's work, Abbot John extended further the Abbey's property holdings in the town.[9] The later Abbey cartulary celebrated his enterprise, recording how the new properties were 'acquired as a result of the industry of Abbot John'.[10] He used rents from four new town properties to fund the candles used on 'the great candle-sticks in the main church of Saint Aldhelm'.[11] While Abbot John expanded

---

6   *RM* I 379.
7   *RM* II 80–1.
8   Trinity College Cambridge, MS R.7.2.
9   *RM* II 71.
10   Ibid.
11   *RM* II 68–9.

the Abbey's urban property portfolio, he was forced to alienate one rural property to a powerful magnate with north Wiltshire interests. In 1231 he surrendered the Abbey's claim to a 'park' near Wootton Bassett to Alan de Basset, who was busy establishing a grand hunting lodge in the area which became known as Vastern.[12] In return for the land, Alan and his wife promised to give eleven pounds of wax each year for candles in the Abbey. This was not a symmetrical deal although records indicate that the payment of wax continued for many years and was still being made by the owners of Vastern as late as 1399.[13]

Abbot John was assiduous in his protection of the economic interests of the Abbey and was prepared to use the power of the papacy when defending the revenues of the house. We see this, for example, in the way he handled a dispute with the rector of Yatton Keynell concerning the Abbey's claim to be exempt from the payment of tithes for crops grown on the demesne farm at Yatton. Abbot John's response to the rector's demand for payment was to send a representative to Italy to obtain a papal ruling about this dispute between Wiltshire neighbours. Pope Gregory IX received the request at his palace in Perugia and, on 12 March 1230, instructed the abbot of Eynsham and the dean of Oxford to investigate the matter. These papal delegates duly took depositions in England, and judged in favour of the Abbey on 28 June 1230, absolving the Abbey from any requirement to pay tithes.[14]

After the demolition of the castle, the royal family looked to the Abbey to provide occasional accommodation within the Abbey precinct. Abbot John offered hospitality to Henry III on at least two occasions. On 4 August 1235 Henry spent the night at Malmesbury: he had been at Bath Abbey the day before, and on 5 August left for Bradenstoke Priory.[15] On 16 July 1241 Henry arrived again, having spent the previous night at Marlborough;[16] by 18 July he had moved on to Cirencester. The *Liberate Rolls* indicate that four tuns of wine were sent from Bristol to Malmesbury for consumption during this visit.[17]

John Walsh was prepared to be assertive and combative. He was one of the most prominent of those monastic leaders who challenged the exorbitant demands of the papal representative, Master Martin, who arrived in England in 1244 intent on raising as much money as possible from the English Church. The chronicler, Matthew Paris, monk of St Albans, described the arrogance of Martin, identifying Abbot John of Malmesbury as one of the few prelates who were prepared to take a stand

12   *RM* II 520–53.
13   Berry I 242.
14   *RM* II 58–60.
15   Cal. Pat. 1232–47, 86–122
16   Ibid..
17   *Calendar of Liberate Rolls* II 1240–1245 (London, 1930), 65.

A self-confident age: the Abbey in the thirteenth century

against the pope's agent. In response to this challenge Master Martin temporarily suspended the abbot from office.[18]

The 'sun and moon of Malmesbury'

While much of the surviving evidence from the thirteenth century relates to estate management and administration there are some other sources that shed light on the intellectual life of the Abbey. A surviving manuscript from Malmesbury, held today by the Bodleian and produced in the first half of the thirteenth century, includes a life of Thomas Becket by John of Salisbury and a biblical commentary on Genesis by Alcuin.[19] The Malmesbury monks had an opportunity to reflect on Alcuin's views on some thorny questions that readers of Genesis might raise such as:

- Why was Abraham not guilty of adultery when he slept with his servant while still lawfully married?
- How was it possible that representatives of all the animals of the world were able to fit inside Noah's Ark?

There was, during the thirteenth century, a long-standing scholarly partnership between the Malmesbury monks and the Augustinian canons of Cirencester Abbey.[20] Some sort of fraternal relationship was established between the two communities while William of Malmesbury was alive,[21] and the Cirencester canon, Robert of Cricklade, was an enthusiastic reader of William's religious works. A century later a prior of Malmesbury returned the compliment, expressing profound admiration for the work of Alexander Neckam who had been the abbot of Cirencester. Neckam was a prolific and important writer, and following his death in 1217 a canon of Cirencester called Walter de Melida sought to perpetuate his memory and promote the circulation of his works. Walter corresponded on the subject of Neckam with a senior monk of Malmesbury: a letter to Walter survives that was written by the Malmesbury man, who styled himself as 'Prior S', and was full of praise

---

18 Translation in *Mathaei Parisiensi monachi Sancti Albani Chronica Majora IV*, ed. H. R. Luard (London, 1877), 284–5.
19 MS Wood Empt 5.
20 Andrew Dunning has uncovered and documented the story of this relationship. See Andrew Dunning, 'Alexander Neckam's Manuscripts and the Augustinian Canons of Oxford and Cirencester', unpublished doctoral thesis, University of Toronto (2016).
21 The Cirencester canon, Robert of Cricklade, was a contemporary and admirer of the religious works of William of Malmesbury. Writing in the years 1135–40, Robert praised William of Malmesbury's *Defloratio Gregorii, De Miraculis Beatae Virginis Mariae*, and *Liber super Explanationem Lamentationum* and ensured that Cirencester Abbey had copies of these works. See Dunning, 'Alexander Neckam'.

Malmesbury Abbey 670–1539

for Neckam.[22] 'Prior S' described at length the many splendid qualities of one particular work by Neckam, *Corrogationes Promethei*, which provided a commentary on the meaning of difficult biblical passages. The Malmesbury prior implied that he had known Neckam personally and now had a duty to honour him for 'it is the part of his friends to extol the titles of master Alexander, a praiseworthy man and a great friend'. The letter of 'Prior S', written perhaps around 1220, provides a window into the intellectual and educational culture of the time in Malmesbury Abbey. For the prior, Neckam's work was a valuable resource for boys studying within the Abbey but useful also for more mature members of the community, and the letter hints at the existence of a serious milieu, within which the enhancement of biblical understanding among all members of the community was a priority.

'Prior S' presented himself as a learned man with a serious commitment to both friendship and scholarship. Not only was Neckam his 'great friend', the prior also addressed Walter de Melida in similarly affectionate terms, calling him 'a most dear friend and brother in Christ'. Walter was portrayed as a generous man who was incapable of malice. Interestingly, 'Prior S' also suggested that astrological forces had been kind to Walter, helping to shape his virtuous character: 'for the benevolent zodiac so gazed on your birth [...]'. The prior was well read and peppered his letter with biblical references: he compared, for example, the experience of reading Neckam's *Corrogationes Promethei* with a visit to the Temple of Solomon. The letter also included references to pagan classical works, such as a self-deprecatory allusion to the poet Horace and his account in *Ars Poetica* of the tale of the mountain who went into labour only to give birth to a mouse. 'Prior S' artfully fused together imagery derived from the Song of Solomon and from Virgil when he compared Neckam's *Corrogationes* to a well-stocked larder of good things maintained by a diligent wife and mother.

> This is also the faithful bride who keeps every new and old fruit for the beloved, so that she can say to anyone with restrained cheerfulness, as if on behalf of her family: *We have ripe apples, tender chestnuts, and plenty of pressed cheeses.*[23]

---

[22] Two manuscript witnesses for the letter exist: Paris Bibliothèque Nationale, MS lat. 11867 and British Library, Royal MS 5 C. v. For the text of this letter and a translation, see Andrew Dunning, 'The Correspondence of Walter of Mileto at Cirencester Abbey, c. 1217', *Library of Digital Latin Texts* (2019).

[23] Translation from Dunning, 'Walter of Mileto'. The first part of this sentence is a clear echo of the Song of Solomon: 'at our gates are all manner of pleasant fruits, new and old, which I have laid up for thee, O my beloved' (Song of Solomon 7.13 King James Version). The quotation at the end of the sentence is taken from Virgil, *Eclogues* 1.80–1.

A self-confident age: the Abbey in the thirteenth century

The partnership between Malmesbury and Cirencester, which began in the 1130s, reached its climax during the abbacy of Geoffrey (1246–60). Abbot Geoffrey was much less successful as a steward of Abbey resources than his immediate predecessors, and on his death in 1260 the Abbey was encumbered with a debt totalling £147, some of which was owed to Jewish bankers.[24] Geoffrey was, it seems, a poor manager but was highly regarded for his religious observance. At some point during his abbacy a manuscript containing an anthology of Alexander Neckam's work was compiled by Geoffrey Brito, canon of Cirencester and Neckam's nephew. The miscellany was dedicated to Abbot Geoffrey of Malmesbury and contained a prefatory poem that praised him in fulsome terms.

> O sun and moon of Malmesbury, light of the monks,
> May your honour accept, I ask, a new song
> Which the devotion of simple Geoffrey offers you.[25]

Geoffrey Brito expressed enormous admiration for the Malmesbury abbot, whose scholarship was highly esteemed. He was an exemplary figure: the sun and moon of Malmesbury. Later in the text there was a further reference to the exceptional virtues of Abbot Geoffrey.

> [...] Geoffrey, pious father, father of all wisdom [...] O man of honesty
> [...] good Geoffrey, whose praise resounds everywhere [...][26]

The first draft of this collaborative manuscript was produced in Cirencester. The monks of Malmesbury proceeded to augment the text with additional material, and in this way an unusual collaborative document was produced as an expression of the fraternity between the two communities. The initial Cirencester text was a collection of extracts from Alexander Neckam's work, and the subsequent Malmesbury contribution was a substantial extract from Geoffrey of Monmouth's prophecies of Merlin. The Merlin material was written by two Malmesbury scribes in distinctive hands and was illustrated with drawings of the Welsh and English dragons of Merlin's prophecies. The manuscript also included fine drawings portraying the mendicant saints, Francis and Dominic, and their followers; it is possible that these drawings were also produced at Malmesbury. The black monks of Malmesbury and the regular canons of Cirencester had, it seems, no problem expressing admiration for the new friars, and these representations of the mendicants have been described as 'amongst the earliest depictions of their subjects in English art'.[27]

---

24 *RM* II 81.
25 Dunning, 'Alexander Neckam's Manuscripts', 76.
26 Dunning, 'Alexander Neckam's Manuscripts', 80.
27 Patrick Zutshi, 'Images of Franciscans and Dominicans in a Manuscript of Alexander Nequam's Florilegium', in The Franciscan Order in the Medieval

Malmesbury Abbey 670–1539

The businesslike abbacy of William of Colerne

Between 1260 and 1296 the Abbey was ruled over by William of Colerne, a man of astonishing entrepreneurial ability. Colerne was able to expand considerably the Abbey's resources, and he used the resulting profits to improve both the productivity of the estate and to enhance the domestic buildings and amenities of the Abbey. We know little about his background but he presumably came from the Wiltshire village of Colerne. Much more is known about his approach to the stewardship of the Abbey estate because, in about 1290, he ordered the creation of a cartulary which survives as the National Archives manuscript, E164/24. It was this text that was published in the nineteenth century in two volumes as the *Registrum Malmesburiense*. The cartulary was intended to celebrate and memorialise Colerne's achievements, and through a study of the document it is possible to track the way the abbot set about increasing the size and profitability of the Abbey's landed estate, acquiring three new manors to the south-west of Malmesbury: Blackland near Calne, Thickwood near Colerne and Fowlswick near Chippenham. The purchase of these new estates cost a total of £753 13s. 4d. This was a good deal with an excellent return on investment because the yearly income from the new estates was £183 5s, and the acquisitions contributed greatly to the long-term profitability of the Abbey estate.[28]

Colerne obtained little by way of external patronage. Although he was on good terms with Henry III and later Edward I, he received hardly any royal largesse. In the immediate aftermath of the decisive Battle of Evesham in 1265, Abbot William entertained the victorious Henry III and his son, the future Edward I, at Malmesbury. He calculated that the cost of entertaining the king and prince was the large sum of 100 marks. Crown records indicate that, in return for this costly hospitality, the Abbey was granted a modest gift of six deer and four oak trees from the nearby Forest of Bradon.[29] Perhaps Henry III, who was known for his piety, was impressed by the Abbey's relics during this visit because in the following year he made a relatively small gift of twenty marks for the enhancement of one of the abbey shrines.[30] Overall, the Crown took far more from the Abbey than it gave, and Colerne's cartulary records many costs associated with royal impositions. The wars of Edward I were a drain on the Abbey resources. Colerne's accounts contain several references to the cost of paying for the service of three knights for the royal

---

English Province and Beyond, ed. Michael Robson and Patrick Zutshi (Amsterdam, 2018), 51–6.

[28] A. Watkin, 'Abbey of Malmesbury', *History of the County of Wiltshire III* (London, 1956), 210–31.

[29] Cal. Pat. 1258–66, 446; Cal. Close, 1264–8, 70.

[30] Henry Summerson, *William of Colerne*, ODNB (2015).

A self-confident age: the Abbey in the thirteenth century

army, and they recorded that the abbot had spent 115 marks supporting Edward I's campaigns against the Welsh prince, Llewelyn.[31]

In the absence of royal or aristocratic patronage, Colerne relied on his business acumen to increase the wealth of the Abbey. He was opportunistic. Blackland was purchased at a bargain price from the previous owner, Christina de Haddon, who was keen to sell following a bruising legal encounter concerning her right to the property.[32] During the 1260s John Long granted the substantial vill of Thickwood, including all tenants 'both free and servile', to Malmesbury Abbey.[33] This was not an act of piety but rather another example of skilful opportunism on the part of Colerne. John Long was seriously indebted to three Jewish moneylenders: Samson of Wilton, Abraham fitz Isaac of Caerleon and Isaac fitz James. In 1268 Colerne agreed to settle these debts and to provide for Long and his wife for the rest of their lives, in return for the transfer of the Thickwood property to the Abbey. The arrangement with Long was that, as compensation for the perpetual alienation of the family property, he and his wife would be given accommodation, clothing and food for the rest of their lives. The abbot would also take some responsibility for their daughter's dowry and promised to make provision for their sons' well-being.[34]

The abbot's enterprise can also be seen in the way he created a new vill and demesne farm at Fowlswick, near Chippenham. Master Nicholas of Malmesbury, rector of Christian Malford, owned the core of the estate and granted it to the Abbey in 1265–6.[35] In return it was agreed that Nicholas could retain the land for life and that the Abbey would employ a chaplain to say regular prayers on behalf of Nicholas and his relatives after his death. By 1281 Master Nicholas had died, and the Abbey was in full control of the land, burdened only with the modest cost of employing and housing a chaplain. Abbot William then began to expand the holding by a land exchange with the prior of Monkton Farleigh, proceeding to drain and enclose much of the newly consolidated Fowlswick estate. Colerne built a substantial new demesne grange at Fowlswick, which was commemorated in the cartulary.

> At Thickwood he built all the houses, and had the whole courtyard walled.[36] [...] At Fowlswick he built a hall and a chamber in between two other chambers at the gable of the hall, a byre and a kitchen, and he built two stables faced in stone, and he had the courtyard enclosed with a stone wall, and had the whole area lying on each side of Fowlswick

---

31 *RM* II 362.
32 Berry I 135.
33 *RM* II 89–90.
34 Berry I 137–8.
35 *RM* II 127–9, 213–14.
36 *RM* II 366.

149

Malmesbury Abbey 670–1539

Wood enclosed by a ditch and a quickset hedge, together with the land called Rowemarsh, and this too he had enclosed by a quickset hedge.[37]

William's management was also characterised by extremely close supervision of his urban and rural tenants and careful book-keeping. Within the cartulary a rent roll is preserved of the abbot's property in the town from the 1280s, together with a list of the rents due from those manors held by him as abbot for the year 1284.[38] The abbot's urban tenants were listed by name and street and, similarly, in each manor every tenant was named with their rents itemised and a record of the substantial additional payments that were due both in cash and in kind. In the large manor of Crudwell, for example, William's clerks recorded that in addition to the basic rent payments totalling £18 6s 1d annually, an almost identical cash revenue of £17 8s 0d was generated by a range of additional charges and manorial fines. The in-kind contributions were documented precisely: the tenants of Crudwell were required to hand over a render of 86 hens each Christmas and 1645 eggs at Easter. Abbot William and his officers carried out a formal inspection of each manor annually in late September. The cartulary recorded the 'articles' or questions that were used during the inspection:

- How well were the demesne lands being cultivated?
- How well were the woods, meadows and pasture lands being maintained?
- What was the state of the barns and the accommodation for livestock?
- What quantities of different types of livestock were present?
- Were the cart horses well maintained?
- Were customary tenants providing the labour services that they owed?
- Were the 'in-kind' food renders being properly collected and sent to the Abbey?
- Were the manor buildings being well maintained?
- Was the land being marled and manured appropriately?
- Were manorial officials – including reeves, bailiffs and woodwards – performing their duties properly?
- What was the state of the manor smithy, brewery and tannery?[39]

Further light is shed on the close supervision of the estate by another document, *De modo inquirendi de statu maneriorum*, which was not in the *Registrum* manuscript but is contained in a fragmentary document held

---

[37] *RM* II 367.
[38] The rent roll can be found in *RM* I 138–201.
[39] *RM* I 201–2.

A self-confident age: the Abbey in the thirteenth century

by the British Library.[40] Although undated, *De Modo* was almost certainly issued by Colerne. The document described how the management of each demesne farm was the responsibility of a reeve, a local villein whose rent was reduced in return for his contribution to manorial administration. The reeve was responsible for all aspects of the agricultural process: marling, ploughing, sowing, harvesting, threshing. He collected the rents and the feudal charges imposed on customary tenants, supervising the fertilising of the fields and keeping a record of any related costs. Colerne expected each reeve to make sure that the payments in kind were properly collected and handed over to the Abbey officials.

In 1284 the farming practice was supervised directly by the abbot on thirteen manors: Bremhill, Blackland, Brokenborough, Charlton, Cole Park, Crudwell, Fowlswick, Kemble, Long Newnton, Norton, Purton, Sutton Benger and Thickwood. A further five manors were managed separately because they were the responsibility of obedientiaries: Brinkworth, Euridge, Garsdon, Grittenham and Whitchurch. Most tenants were unfree, with villein land held in strips across large open fields. The standard holding was either a virgate (about 40 acres) or half a virgate, with the strips contained within huge open fields, and cultivation rotated on an annual basis. Some manors (Sutton Benger for example) operated a two-field rotational system[41], while other manors (Crudwell for example) possessed three open fields.[42] By the late thirteenth century most weekly labour services for villein tenants had been commuted to cash rents, with the exception of harvest time when they were still required to provide unpaid labour on the demesne fields.[43]

The cartulary records an extraordinary programme of building work that took place on Colerne's manors. Fourteen great stone barns, tiled or thatched, were built across the estate. The following description of the enhancements at the important manor of Crudwell is characteristic of his investment in the economic fabric of the Abbey estate.

> At Crudwell he made a big grange faced in stone, and another thatched grange called Putbern. He also made another thatched grange, the one, that is, by the north gate. He also had the chancel of Crudwell chapel completely renewed. He also had the area next to the courtyard of Crudwell completely surrounded with a quickset hedge. He also had the garden enclosed by a stone wall, and the big fish pond repaired. He also built a house next to the garden, faced in stone, and another by the east gate there. He also had the old hall by the cemetery renewed.[44]

---

40 This was discovered by Nigel Berry. See British Library Add. MS. 38009.
41 Berry I 99.
42 Berry I 428.
43 Berry I 217.
44 *RM* II 366–7.

151

Malmesbury Abbey 670–1539

William of Colerne was preoccupied with the need to increase the profit-ability of the Abbey's estates, and he sought to improve the income of the house through acquisition of lands, investment in the capital and direct management of the demesne manors. He was not alone in making estate management his priority; Colerne was one of several businesslike abbots of larger Benedictine houses at this period who spent much of their time carefully managing their lands. David Knowles said nothing about Colerne in his magisterial study of medieval monasticism but did describe the careers of several of his contemporaries who were similarly preoccupied with high productivity farming. The best-known of these farming prelates was Henry of Eastry, prior of Christ Church, Canterbury but Knowles also outlined the work of a series of farming abbots at Glastonbury. Since Glastonbury owned several manors close to Malmesbury, it is possible that Colerne was influenced by pioneering practice on nearby Glastonbury manors such as Christian Malford.[45]

The *Registrum* portrays Colerne as a man who was relentless and fearless in his defence of the Abbey's economic rights. Disputes with prominent members of the aristocracy were carefully recorded. One document in French recorded how the abbot defended his rights to fatten demesne pigs on the mast – the acorns and other forest nuts – in Flisteridge Wood which stood between the Abbey's manor at Crudwell and the lands of the earl of Hereford at Oaksey. In 1278 the earl was present at Oaksey and ordered his villeins to break into the wood, enabling their pigs to eat the mast.[46] Abbot William's tenants, presumably with his blessing, responded by entering the wood and seizing the Oaksey pigs. The earl of Hereford retaliated by sending the Oaksey men to retrieve their pigs, using great violence against the inhabitants of Crudwell, before letting the pigs loose again in Flisteridge Wood.

> [...] then came the Abbot's people and impounded the Earl's hogs and the hogs of his men, at his manor of Crudwell. Soon after came the demesne people of the Earl and the people of the manor with great force and broke down the gates and forcibly took out the hogs, and wounded the Abbot's people, even to the death, so that the coroner was sent for to look into this great affray. The hogs they forcibly drove back to the wood of Flisteridge and kept there for fifteen days and upwards with great force of people, so that no one of those who were with the Abbot dared to come near the wood.[47]

Abbot William had lost this first round in his dispute with the earl of Hereford, but he was dogged in his pursuit of the Abbey's rights and engaged in litigation against the earl, spending forty marks on legal

[45] David Knowles, *The Religious Orders in England I* (Cambridge, 1974), 32–52.
[46] *RM* II 423.
[47] Ibid.

A self-confident age: the Abbey in the thirteenth century

fees.[48] The abbot ultimately won the case, and an undated document in the cartulary records the earl of Hereford's official retraction of his claim to any rights of pannage in Flisteridge Wood.[49]

The compilers of his cartulary were keen to document Abbot William's successful pursuit of wardship rights relating to the marriage of heirs to the Abbey's military fees. Three opportunities arose during his career to obtain a windfall payment from wardship.[50] The Abbey made a modest profit of fifteen marks from the wardship of John le Bret, who held a fee in Long Newton. A far more spectacular profit arose from the Abbey's assertion of its right to determine the marriage of the heir to the manor of Dauntsey: in around 1275 the property was inherited by a minor called Richard of Dauntsey, and Abbot William sold his marriage to Matilda Countess of Gloucester for the enormous sum of 800 marks.[51] The profit on this transaction was, however, considerably reduced by the costs of legal challenges, which amounted to 300 marks.[52]

In June 1277, John Comyn, one of the Abbey's wealthier tenants, was murdered in Ireland by a lay brother of the Cistercian abbey of St Mary's, Dublin,[53] Comyn held land from Malmesbury in Warwickshire and Wiltshire, and he was also the lord of the manor of Kinsealy near Dublin. He left a widow, Mabel, and a young son and heir, also called John. Abbot William believed that Malmesbury Abbey owned the rights to revenues arising from the wardship of this John Comyn the Younger. Mabel Comyn challenged the abbot's claims and took legal action against him in a dispute which centred on the question as to whether the Comyn lands were held from Malmesbury Abbey as a knight's fee or as a non-military tenancy. Wardship rights belonged to the lord in the case of military tenure, but to the family if the land was held as a non-military tenancy known as 'socage'. The litigation between Mabel Comyn and Abbot William was protracted and was not finally resolved until 1288, eleven years after the murder of Comyn the Elder. The Abbey was ultimately successful: Margaret Comyn was finally forced to accept defeat and to purchase from the Abbot the right to determine the future wife of her own son for a price of 80 marks.[54] This was, however, a pyrrhic

48 *RM* II 363.
49 *RM* II 345–6.
50 Berry I 222–3.
51 A. P. Baggs, Jane Freeman and Janet H. Stevenson, 'Parishes: Dauntsey', in *History of the County of Wiltshire: Volume 14, Malmesbury Hundred*, ed. D. A. Crowley (London, 1991), 65–75. British History Online http://www.british-history.ac.uk/vch/wilts/vol14/pp65-75 [accessed 7 April 2022].
52 *RM* II 361.
53 Geoffrey J. Hand, 'The Common Law in Ireland in the Thirteenth and Fourteenth Centuries: Two Cases Involving Christ Church, Dublin', *The Journal of the Royal Society of Antiquaries of Ireland*, 97.2 (1967): 97–111.
54 Berry I 222–3.

victory for Abbot William because he had spent 201 marks on legal costs connected with the case.[55]

Enhancing the Abbey buildings

Colerne engaged in a major rebuilding programme at the Abbey, where his focus was not on the conventual church but on the domestic amenities of the community. Most of his extensive building work was swept away at the Dissolution but one substantial fragment survives in the form of the undercroft which constitutes the basement of Abbey House. Colerne greatly improved several of the main monastic buildings: the infirmary, the dormitory, the chapter house and the guest house. An appendix to his cartulary provided a detailed and fulsome account of these building activities.

> He also had the infirmary repaired with beams and forked timbers and to some extent renewed in its wall and faced in stone. After that he had the dormitory demolished right up to the walls, and walk-ways constructed on the walls on both sides, and rebuilt with new wood as well as the beams previously there, and faced in stone. He also had the chapter house demolished right up to the walls, and completely rebuilt with new wood and faced in stone, and [he made] walk-ways right round the chapter house. After that he had three windows made in the guest hall.[56]

The dormitory and chapter house were virtually rebuilt. The text is confusing about the infirmary: at one point suggesting that it was 'repaired', while elsewhere indicating that 'an infirmary was built from scratch'. Walter built two new halls and a new kitchen. Presumably the kitchen was for his own use and that of his personal guests, since there was a separate conventual kitchen. The roof of the abbot's own chamber was completely rebuilt.

> Next to the abbot's garden, he built a large and handsome hall, together with a second smaller one at its gable, faced in stone. And from the house that had previously been the hall, he had a chamber laid out. Next to the hall he had a kitchen built. And he had the larder renewed in its walls and enlarged with beams, and faced in stone.[57]

Colerne was a keen gardener; he expanded the Abbey precinct by purchasing neighbouring properties and he used the additional land to lay out a vineyard and herb garden. Vines and other fruits were also planted extensively in the abbot's garden.

[55] *RM* II 362.
[56] *RM* II 365.
[57] Ibid.

A self-confident age: the Abbey in the thirteenth century

And when the abbot had bought from Randulph de la Porte and from the former wife of Thurstan le Brasur their messuages and curtilages lying next to the abbot's garden, the abbot had a vineyard planted in that area and surrounded by a stone wall. Next to this vineyard he made a herb garden in the direction of the king's wall. He also had vines and apple trees planted everywhere in the abbot's garden. He also had a piece of land bought for a carpenter's shop, which he had enclosed by a stone wall. He also erected two houses next to the carpentry.[58]

A new brewery, granary and mill were built, and the convent kitchen was enhanced with the addition of three new ovens. The monastery was obviously self-sufficient in all aspects of the baking of bread and the brewing of beer.

Later, he had a granary built next to the bakery, and the building that was once the granary he added to the cellar. He also had the old brew-house razed to the ground, and had it built and re-constructed with new walls and new wood.[59]

Horses were of course everywhere in the precincts of a large monastery. Abbot Walter's building campaign led to the construction of at least three new stables, and one was designed, curiously, as a joint dwelling for horses and for the local poor.

On the west side of the brew-house he built a house for keeping cart horses. He also built a new workshop and had it faced in stone. Also, between the prison and the sacrist's stable he erected a house, assigning one half to the poor, the other to be a stable for horses.[60]

One of Colerne's most ambitious projects was his plan to bring fresh water to the community through some sort of aqueduct. His cartulary proudly recorded how, after the expenditure of £100 on the construction of the pipe, fresh water flowed into the Abbey on the feast of St Martin, 1284.[61]

Colerne was a man of action. We know little about his religious or cultural interests, although he spent some money enhancing the ornamentation of the Abbey church.[62] In addition a chapel dedicated to St Aldhelm was built in the main convent garden. In 1274 Colerne went to the general council held by Pope Gregory X at Lyons. Characteristically, the cartulary records the large cost of his trip – £100 – but says nothing

---

58 Ibid.
59 Ibid.
60 *RM* II 365–6.
61 *RM* II 361.
62 Berry I 235. During the years 1290–6 the ornamentation of the abbey church cost £47 13s 4d.

Malmesbury Abbey 670–1539

about any contribution that Colerne might have made to the proceedings. Some hints at the extent to which, under him, the Abbey was a place of serious study comes from a list of the bequests made by one of William's monks, a man called William Favel, who served as almoner.[63] Favel gave several books including works by Augustine and Ambrose, and a biological treatise by Aristotle. This monk had been personally active in the creation of new manuscripts. He gave two psalters, one of which was described as 'a great psalter which the said William had written'. The inclusion of a work on biology by Aristotle hints at a lively intellectual environment at Malmesbury and a wish to keep up to date with the academically fashionable Aristotelianism of the period.

The regulations for the misericord

Colerne wanted a harmonious community, and in 1293, towards the end of his abbacy, he acted decisively to resolve a serious dispute that had broken out among the monks regarding the unfairness of the arrangements for eating meat. In the refectory meat was forbidden but, as in other Benedictine houses, there was another dining room, known as the misericord, where meat could be eaten. Several monks had complained that the prior and sub-priors who determined invitations to dine in the misericord were guilty of favouritism, and they called for a fairer system.

> The diet of certain of our brothers, whom the grace of lesser favour attended rarely or coolly, is normally restricted and scanty so far as being restorative goes, while that of other brothers, blessed with the good fortune of special status, is usually pretty rich and sumptuous, as happens in many monasteries. Some look liberally enough on those they wish, but are slow to invite others from the cloister to dine, with scant regard to the indulgence of the decretal that says that 'now these, now those are to be asked to the grace of a restorative meal by those who preside'. Hence some of our brothers were humbly asking us that they might, in the unity of charity and peace, follow the Psalmist's precept in this respect, through whom it is said: 'Blessed is he who maketh men of one manner to dwell in a house'.[64] Accordingly, we, to bring a complete end in God to the reproach resulting from murmuring on the part of the Lord's flock, grant gracious assent to their requests.[65]

William's direction was, in essence, that the monks should take turns dining in the misericord on alternate days as long as a minimum of thirteen monks were always present in the refectory.

---

[63] RM II 379–80.
[64] Ps. 67: 7.
[65] *RM* II 382–3.

A self-confident age: the Abbey in the thirteenth century

> [...] at all times of the year when it is allowed to eat meat, half the convent should eat one day in the misericord, and the next day the other half in the refectory, apart from those who are to be summoned to the abbot's table and those who are by reason of illness or weakness living in the infirmary: with this proviso, that always at all meal times at least thirteen monks are to be in the refectory for lunch, and that no monk should eat meat in the misericord with the prior or the sub-prior or anyone else on two consecutive days.[66]

The record of this dispute sheds light on domestic arrangements in the Abbey. The misericord diet involved a substantial lunch before midday and a much lighter supper.

> Those who eat in the misericord shall be served three courses at lunch and one at supper.[67]

It seems that during the winter months the monks dining in the misericord were not only permitted to eat meat, but they were also released from the liturgical duties immediately after lunch and supper.

> From Easter until the feast of the Exaltation of the Holy Cross [14 September] those who eat in the misericord are all to be in the convent at midday, as the Rule lays down. But at other times of the year, when they have eaten and drunk enough, they should devoutly give thanks to God together for what they have received, and return decently to the cloister, at the latest when the convent's servants have processed into the church with a *miserere* when lunch is over, busying themselves with divine readings or at least, if they wish, praying privately; and let the same be rigorously observed by each and all after supper.[68]

While most monks could relax after dining in the misericord, an exception was made for the junior monks, who were expected to be present for the service of compline.

> But the junior monks who have eaten in the misericord should be duly present with the convent at compline, unless he who presides in the convent wishes to give them special indulgence on this point.[69]

Monks were exempt from the dietary regulations regarding meat if they were staying temporarily in the infirmary. Colerne's dietary regulations addressed meat eating in the infirmary and indicate the significance of the custom of bloodletting for the monks. Every few weeks choir monks were released from liturgical discipline and were bled, in principle for

---

66 *RM* II 383.
67 Ibid.
68 *RM* II 384.
69 Ibid.

health reasons, but also to give them a holiday. William of Colerne's regulations indicate that monks were given three days in the infirmary to recuperate, during which time they did not participate in the Divine Office and were allowed to eat meat.

The dietary regulations were approved with great solemnity in the chapter house on 30 March 1293. William's regulations concluded with a warning of spiritual peril for any brother, no matter what his status, who sought to breach the rules.

> But if any of the brothers, of whatever status or dignity, tries to impede this our ordinance, or in some way secretly or openly goes against it, so as to prevent the observance of the articles of this our ordinance, let him be subject to the sentence of excommunication, and after the end of his days go without the vision of God and incur the curse of the glorious Virgin and the apostles Peter and Paul and all God's saints, and after his temporal death let him be placed with the angels of Satan to be incessantly punished with eternal pains, unless he is worthily penitent and gives satisfaction for so heinous a crime. We promulgated this sentence of condemnation and excommunication in our Chapter House wearing stoles and with lit candles in our hands, on 30 March 1293, with the approval of the same by all the brothers, who unanimously replied: 'So be it. So be it. Amen'.[70]

William expected these arrangements to persist for all time. In fact, the requirement for a quorum of monks in the meat-free refectory was still considered as a tradition of the house as late as 1527. The abbot also sought to achieve a form of immortality within the community by the creation of his cartulary, and he took other steps to ensure that he was remembered for all time, ordering that the date of his death should be commemorated by a solemn mass and a special allowance for the monks of 'clear and most pure wine'.[71]

[70] *RM* II 385.
[71] *RM* II 380.

11

The Despenser years and the criminal career of Abbot John of Tintern

Abbot William of Badminton (1296–1324) had a long and distinguished public career, and David Knowles considered that he was 'the only abbot of note' produced by Malmesbury after 1216.[1] Towards the end of his abbacy he became entangled in the bitter conflict that broke out between Edward II's advisers, the Despensers, and the king's baronial opponents; but prior to this he had been a successful and respected prelate. In 1298, soon after becoming abbot, Badminton was chosen as one of the 'presidents' who organised the provincial chapter or conference of all Benedictine abbots in those parts of southern England subject to the archbishop of Canterbury. He continued to act as president until 1310 or 1311, visiting Rome twice, in around 1301–2 and also at some point between 1309 and 1314.[2] Badminton played a central role in the campaign to ensure that the most talented Benedictine monks from English monasteries received a university education. In 1283 a small dependent cell of monks from Gloucester was established at Oxford, and in the 1290s the provincial chapter decided to expand Gloucester College, as it was known, and to make it a college for Benedictine monks from all over the Canterbury archdiocese. In 1298 Malmesbury Abbey was given a major stake in the governance of the institution. By this time a pious nobleman, Sir John Gifford, who owned the college's site, was living in retirement at Malmesbury Abbey, and he granted formal ownership of the premises to Malmesbury: the abbots of Malmesbury became the landlords of the college. William of Badminton appointed the first prior of the newly constituted college, and Malmesbury monks remained involved in the management of the institution throughout the fourteenth century. The site of the college is today part of Worcester College, and a late medieval sculptural shield bearing a griffin, the heraldic device of Malmesbury Abbey, can still be seen on the doorway of one set of rooms.

There is no reason to doubt that the Divine Office was taken seriously under the rule of William of Badminton. A beautiful psalter and hymnal survives from early fourteenth-century Malmesbury, which is held today in the library of Sankt Gallen in Switzerland.[3] The manuscript contains

---

1   Knowles, *Religious Orders I*, 315.
2   Watkin, 'Abbey of Malmesbury', 176–8.
3   St Gallen MS Cod. Sang. 26. See also Nigel J. Morgan, *English Monastic Litanies*

Malmesbury Abbey 670–1539

a calendar of feasts celebrated by the Malmesbury monks and the text of the version of the Litany of Saints used by the Abbey. Malmesbury traditions were carefully observed including the veneration of Aldhelm, some six hundred years after his death, which features prominently both in the calendar and the Litany. Another distinctive feature of the Litany is the prayer to St Ursinus of Bourges, which is found in no other English Litany. The cult of Ursinus must have been introduced by Abbot Peter Moraunt, the special friend of William of Malmesbury, in the twelfth century.[4]

The Despenser connection

William of Badminton was active in Church affairs, committed to the education at university of Benedictine monks, and concerned about monastic observance. It is therefore surprising that he took part in a mass brawl in the Gloucestershire town of Lechlade in 1318. Humphrey de Bohun, earl of Hereford, complained about the abbot's behaviour to Edward II.

> [...] William, abbot of Malmesbury, and John of Tynterne, his fellow monk [...] Roger Hasard and John his son, and William brother of the same John [... and 37 other named men ...] by force and arms, took and carried away the goods and chattels of the same earl to the value of £200 at Lechlade, and made an assault upon his men and servants there, and beat, wounded and mistreated them [...][5]

The allegation was that William of Badminton went to Lechlade with forty supporters, each named in the complaint, and intent on trouble. Their surnames indicate that Badminton's accomplices were men from Malmesbury and the surrounding villages. They included some prominent burgesses such as Roger Hasard and his two sons; Hasard had represented the borough in Parliament of 1295. The events at Lechlade were the result of Badminton's decision to align the Abbey with the faction of Hugh Despenser and his son, Hugh Despenser the Younger, who were the enemies of Humphrey de Bohun. Although de Bohun made no reference to the Despensers in his complaint, the fight can only be understood as part of an ongoing feud between him and the Despensers, two families who were both vying for regional and national ascendancy.[6] Earlier in 1318 Despenser the Elder, to the annoyance of

---

    of the Saints after 1100 I (London, 2012), 31.
4   Morgan, *Litanies*, 31
5   TNA C 66/150; Cal. Pat., 1317–1321, 294–5. Two years earlier in 1316 three Malmesbury monks were excommunicated for assaulting a clerk of Rodborough in Gloucestershire: see Watkin, 'Abbey of Malmesbury', 178.
6   'Lechlade', in *A History of the County of Gloucester: Volume 7*, ed. N. M. Herbert

The Despenser years and the criminal career of Abbot John of Tintern

de Bohun, had been granted the borough of Lechlade by the monks of Hailes Abbey.

Following the death of Piers Gaveston in 1312, the Despensers became the leading advisers to Edward II, to the great annoyance of many other barons. The estates of the older Despenser included land in north Wiltshire, and he developed the manor of Vastern, near Wootton Bassett, as a grand park and hunting lodge. This property bordered the estates of Malmesbury Abbey, and it became one of Despenser's principal residences. The exact nature of the relationship between Abbot William of Badminton and Hugh Despenser the Elder is not clear, but the abbot was in some sense a 'client' of Despenser, who offered the Abbey protection (and perhaps patronage) in return for financial and military support. Despenser had a similar relationship with another local monastery, the Cistercian house of Stanley near Chippenham. Badminton and the Malmesbury monks may have felt that they had no choice other than to follow directions from their powerful neighbour. In 1320 the abbeys of both Malmesbury and Stanley each ceded 300 acres of land in Brinkworth to Despenser so that he could greatly enlarge his park at Vastern.[7]

> Licence for the abbot and convent of Stanley to grant to Hugh le Despenser, the elder, 300 acres of wood in Braden, which are of the appurtenances of the manor of Midgehall adjacent to his park of la Fasterne, and for the abbot of Malmesbury to grant 300 acres of waste in their manor of Brynkeworth adjacent to the said park, also held in chief, to the said Hugh, to hold to him and his heirs for the enlargement of his park; licence also for the said Hugh to empark the same [..]

This looks like an act of coercion with the two monasteries forced under duress to accept the transfer of huge amounts of land. There is no indication that they received any compensation.

In May 1321 Humphrey de Bohun and other baronial opponents of the Despensers staged a rebellion that is known today as the Despenser War. After initial attacks on the lands of Despenser the Younger in south Wales, the rebel army swept across southern Gloucestershire and northern Wiltshire in June and ravaged the estates of Hugh Despenser the Elder. We do not know whether they damaged the Abbey's property but this is certainly possible since the monks were allied to Despenser the Elder. The baronial force definitely came close to Malmesbury and the rebel leaders broke into Despenser's house at Vastern where they vandalised the property. The rebels also despoiled Stanley Abbey, where Despenser the Elder kept some of his treasure.[8] This baronial revolt was initially successful, and by late July the rebels had encircled London. In August

---

(Oxford, 1981), 106–21.

7   Cal. Pat., 1317–1321, 432.

8   Cal. Close, 1318–23, 540–59.

161

Malmesbury Abbey 670–1539

Edward was forced to admit defeat and to send both Despensers into exile while issuing pardons for the rebels.

The Despenser War must have been a shocking experience for the Malmesbury monks; however, there is no evidence that the Abbey wavered in its loyalty to the Despenser cause. Later in 1321, the pendulum swung against the baronial rebels when Edward II launched a counter-offensive and at Christmas 1321, he called on those loyal to him to muster at Cirencester. We know that representatives of Malmesbury Abbey responded to the call and were present at the royal court in Cirencester, and in the midst of his plans for war, the king found the time to ratify the sale of lands between certain Malmesbury burgesses and the Abbey. The land transactions were relatively minor and concerned the transfer of a handful of small properties in the Malmesbury area.[9] The fact that Edward II considered that it was a priority to ratify these modest land transfers at a time of high political tension showed that the Abbey, with its close association with Despenser the Elder, was viewed favourably at court. The royal army that gathered at Cirencester probably included forces supplied by or paid for by Malmesbury Abbey. From Cirencester this army marched west, and then north, during the early weeks of 1322 in a successful campaign against the rebels. The counter-offensive culminated in victory at the Battle of Boroughbridge on 16 March 1322, where Humphrey de Bohun, earl of Hereford, was killed.

During the early 1320s a highly ambitious and expensive building campaign began which ultimately remodelled much of the Abbey church. While the twelfth-century work was preserved at the arcade and gallery level, the old church was dismantled from the gallery upwards and the twelfth-century wooden roof was replaced. New clerestory windows and a vaulted roof for the church were installed, to designs that have been tentatively assigned to Thomas of Witney, one of the finest architects of the age.[10] It is possible that Hugh Despenser the Elder was somehow involved in the initial plans to rebuild the Abbey. During the eighteenth and nineteenth centuries medieval tiles were discovered in the cloister area at Malmesbury, and one section of pavement prominently displayed the coat of arms of Isabella de Beauchamp, Hugh Despenser the Elder's wife. Another set of tiles incorporated a version of the arms of Despenser himself as part of an elaborate design, combined with decorative leaf-work and comic depictions of monkeys and squirrels.[11]

---

9   Cal. Pat., 1321–1324, 30–53.

10   John Harvey, 'Thomas of Witney', in *The Grove Encyclopedia of Medieval Art and Architecture*, Volume 2, ed. Colum Hourihane (Oxford, 2012), 79. John Harvey, *English Medieval Architects: A Biographical Dictionary Down to 1550* (Gloucester, 1987), 338–41.

11   Harold Brakspear, 'Malmesbury Abbey', *Archaeologia*, 64 (1913): 399–436.

The Despenser years and the criminal career of Abbot John of Tintern

The rebuilding of the Abbey church was a massive undertaking, and, although we have no documentary evidence relating to the cost, the work must have placed considerable strain on the Abbey's finances over several decades. There is nothing to indicate that, after the fall of the Despensers, the community benefitted from any significant royal or aristocratic patronage. The cost of remodelling the church was, therefore, borne by the Abbey itself, and it is possible that the resulting financial pressures contributed to the aggressive actions of some monks in the 1330s, which were motivated by a wish to protect the economic interests of the community.

John of Tintern

These turbulent years marked the beginnings of the controversial public career of John of Tintern. He was the abbot of Malmesbury from 1340 to 1349, but many years earlier as a young monk he had accompanied William of Badminton to the fight at Lechlade. Tintern clearly achieved some seniority at an early age and when William of Badminton died in 1324, it was Tintern who took the news of the abbot's death to the royal court.[12] The monks proceeded to elect one of their own, Adam de la Hok, as the new abbot, and the events of the next few years indicate that Abbot Adam saw John of Tintern as his man of business and chief lieutenant. The election of la Hok did not change the Malmesbury affiliation with the Despenser faction, but the power of the Despensers came to a violent end in 1326. Edward's wife, Isabella went on a diplomatic mission to France in 1325. Once there, she repudiated her husband, joined forces with Roger Mortimer, who was in exile, and began to organise the invasion of England. Isabella and Mortimer landed in Suffolk on 24 September 1326, and support for the king rapidly ebbed away. On 2 October the king and both the Despensers abandoned London and fled west, pursued by Isabella and Mortimer. Hugh Despenser the Elder tried to shelter at Bristol Castle, but on 27 October he was captured and was immediately executed. Despenser the Younger was taken in Wales a few days later and executed in Hereford on 24 November.

The fall of the Despensers was extremely bad news for Malmesbury Abbey because of its close association with Despenser the Elder. It is not clear what role Malmesbury Abbey played during the last days of Despenser power. However, there is compelling evidence indicating that the Despensers attempted to store much of their war chest in Malmesbury as they fled from London. Over a decade after the execution of the Despensers, an extraordinary discovery was made. John of Tintern was arrested in August 1337, following claims that he (and his abbot, Adam

---

12   Cal. Pat., 1317–1321, 416.

Malmesbury Abbey 670–1539

de la Hok) had been found to be in possession of a store of Despenser treasure worth a staggering £10,000. The accusations were made by unnamed people in the presence of Edward III at a meeting of the royal court held at the palace of Clarendon, near Salisbury. The precise allegations were not initially made public, and the court records described opaquely how John of Tintern was detained following allegations of 'certain misdeeds'. After spending much of August in the custody of the sheriff of Wiltshire, John was granted bail and released.[13] The matter was resolved the following year at a meeting of the court on 26 April 1338, and at this point the magnitude of the charges became clear.

> By an inquisition taken before the king at Clarendon on Sunday after the feast of St Peter ad Vincula last it was found that the abbot of Malmesbury and John de Tynterne, his fellow-monk, had in their possession £10,000 of the moneys of Hugh le Despenser the elder and Hugh le Despenser the younger, which should have come to the king by their forfeiture; and the same John and abbot were afterwards accused by divers bills exhibited before the king of the concealment of some larger sums [...][14]

The charge was that John of Tintern, in collusion with his superior, Abbot Adam, had failed to declare possession of the Despenser treasure. £10,000 had now come to light and there was talk of 'the concealment of some larger sums'. These were astonishing amounts of money; by way of comparison, in the regnal year 1330–1 the total revenue of the government of Edward III from all sources was less than £40,000.[15] The discovery of the concealed treasure looks like a clear-cut case of manifest guilt because it is difficult to see how evidence for such a charge could be fabricated. It is perhaps surprising, therefore, that on 26 April 1338 the government dismissed the charges on the grounds that the allegations were groundless and the result of the malice of others.

> [...] on careful examination of the inquisition and bills before the king and council it appears by trustworthy testimony that these charges were laid upon them by malice and that they are wholly innocent hereof [...][16]

This is a puzzling outcome. There seems no obvious reason to doubt that the Malmesbury monks had indeed been found to be in possession of the money and that it was originally Despenser property. These facts were not disputed by the monks, and it is impossible to imagine that anyone seeking to defame the monks could obtain and hide such an amount in

[13] Cal. Close, 1337–1339, 251–62.
[14] Cal. Pat., 1338–1340, 31–63.
[15] James Ramsay, *A History of the Revenues of the Kings of England, 1066–1399* (Oxford, 1925), 292.
[16] Cal. Pat., 1338–1340, 50.

The Despenser years and the criminal career of Abbot John of Tintern

the Abbey for the purpose of falsely incriminating them. For reasons that are not clear, it suited the Crown to accept the enormous cash windfall while officially exonerating the monks. The most likely explanation is that the monks obtained pardon in return for a substantial payment of cash, and it is important to remember that in the years, 1337–8, the king's overwhelming priority was the need to raise large sums to fund his war in France. It is also highly likely that the monks were also protected from justice because of a corrupt relationship with Gilbert of Berwick, the sheriff of Wiltshire. On 26 April, the same day that the Malmesbury monks secured a pardon, Berwick was also cleared of wrongdoing in the affair of the Despenser cash. The terms of his pardon suggest that, in addition to the £10,000 found in the possession of the monks, a further £1000 was discovered in Berwick's hands.[17] It seems likely that the monks had asked him to look after a portion of the Despenser hoard. As we shall see Gilbert of Berwick had strong business links with John of Tintern and was later accused by a local jury of being his accomplice to murder.

What was the truth about the Despenser hoard?

When Edward and the two Despensers fled London and headed west in October 1326, their plan was to go to Wales in order to re-group, raise an army and launch a counterattack against Isabella and Mortimer. They would need money to pay for troops. It seems likely that the £10,000 which surfaced in Malmesbury was one component of their war chest. Hugh Despenser the Younger kept much of his ready cash with Italian bankers in London. On 16 September 1326, days before he fled from London, he emptied his account with the Peruzzi bank, withdrawing £2000 in cash,[18] Hugh Despenser the Elder was known to keep cash in the hands of friendly monastic houses.[19] In 1321, for example, he had placed £1000 for safekeeping with the Cistercian monks of Stanley Abbey.[20] At the time of his fall, Despenser had cash and treasure in East Midlands monasteries close to his estates.[21] It makes perfect sense, therefore, to imagine that, as they fled westwards, the Despensers left a substantial part of their cash with their allies at Malmesbury Abbey.

For Malmesbury Abbey, making public the existence of the hoard was highly problematic in the immediate aftermath of the coup of 1326. The safekeeping of cash intended to fund an army was, in effect, an act of war against Isabella and Mortimer, who were known to be vengeful towards their enemies. Instead of handing over the treasure to the new

---

17 Cal. Pat., 1338–1340, 51.
18 E. B. Fryde, *Studies in Medieval Trade and Finance* (London, 1983), III 362.
19 Fryde, *Studies*, III 258.
20 Cal. Close, 1318–1323, 540–59.
21 Fryde, *Studies*, III 258.

165

government, John of Tintern and Abbot Adam simply kept quiet until their secret was revealed by some Wiltshire enemies over ten years later. By this time the keeping of the Despenser treasure was a much less dangerous political act because Edward III had overthrown and executed Mortimer in 1330, and he was seeking to rehabilitate the memory of his father. In the aftermath of the fall of Edward II and the Despensers, the Malmesbury monks were probably in a state of some trepidation and appear to have pursued a policy of discretion. The elaborate cloister pavement decorated with the arms of Despenser's wife was ultimately defaced and the arms were removed. Other tiles representing the arms of the triumphant Mortimer family have been discovered in the area of the cloisters: the Abbey was almost certainly keen to demonstrate loyalty to the new regime.[22]

In January 1327 Edward II was forced to abdicate in favour of his young son, and in September he died mysteriously at Berkeley Castle, twenty miles from Malmesbury. The chronicle of Gloucester Abbey recorded how the body of the dead king was offered to three neighbouring monastic houses, including Malmesbury Abbey. All three communities refused to accept the body for fear of antagonising Queen Isabella and Roger Mortimer.

> After his death certain nearby monasteries feared to accept his venerable body, namely St Augustine's Bristol, St Mary of Kingswood and St Aldhelm of Malmesbury, for terror of Roger de Mortimer and Queen Isabella and their other accomplices.[23]

Can this account be trusted? The chronicle that tells this story is traditionally attributed to Abbot Walter Frocester of Gloucester (1381–1412) who was writing long after the event. Nevertheless, the tradition that the monks of Malmesbury were terrified about accepting the dead body of the king is quite plausible and consistent with their wish to distance themselves from their recent involvement with the disgraced Despenser faction.

The gangsterism of John of Tintern

John of Tintern was, for many years, the 'right hand man' of Abbot Adam de la Hok. In 1330, for example, John was a 'proctor' who represented Malmesbury Abbey at a meeting of Parliament instead of the abbot.[24] In December 1338 Abbot Adam was given royal permission to go

---

22 Brakspear, 'Malmesbury Abbey', 399–436.
23 *Historia et cartularium monasterii Sancti Petri Gloucestriae I*, ed. W. H. Hart (London, 1863), 44.
24 Phil Bradford and Alison McHardy, *Proctors for Parliament: 1248–1539* (Woodbridge, 2017), 83.

The Despenser years and the criminal career of Abbot John of Tintern

to the papal curia; unsurprisingly, the abbot granted power of attorney over the Abbey, for a period of one year, to John of Tintern,[25] authorising him to run the Abbey in the absence of the abbot. By early 1340 Abbot Adam was back from Avignon. On 1 March 1340 the royal court received a complaint from him about the harshness of the way government taxes were being collected in the Malmesbury area. This was not an altruistic complaint: the abbot's main concern was that because the taxes levied from some were exorbitant, the Abbey was unable to collect rents from impoverished tenants.

> […] his petition setting forth that the collectors of tenths, fifteenths and other quota granted to the king […] in assessing the town of Malmesbury and the three hundred adjoining […] have levied such contributions on the poor and mean men sparing the wealthy and the powerful, whereby many of the former are so impoverished that they cannot render their rents and services […][26]

This complaint is the last known act of Abbot Adam; within days he was dead, and on 29 March messengers from Malmesbury informed the royal court of his death, seeking permission to elect his successor. This was granted and the monks of Malmesbury immediately chose John of Tintern as abbot; on 10 April 1340 the king granted his assent.[27] There is no evidence that the government had any particular reservations about the appointment of John, and he was considered sufficiently trustworthy to be appointed in August 1340 as the 'receiver' or tax collector for the subsidy of the ninth and fifteenth for the county of Wiltshire.[28] Some aspects of institutional life carried on as before. The royal family continued to use Malmesbury, like other monasteries, as a retirement home for senior servants and their spouses through the system of corrodies. The monks may have been surprised when on 27 April 1341 a woman was sent to live at the Abbey.

> Ellen de Wyght, late the wife of William de Wyght, for William's good service to Queen Philippa and the king, is sent to the abbot and convent of Malmesbury to receive such maintenance from that house for life as Richard le Keu of Swynesford, deceased, had there at the request of the king.[29]

As a new abbot John acted vigorously to defend the interests of the house. On 12 July 1342, for example, he complained to the king about an attack

---

25 Cal. Pat. 1338–40, 161. We know nothing more about Adam de la Hok's trip to Avignon. He was certainly back in England by early 1340.
26 Cal. Pat. 1338–40, 435.
27 Cal. Pat. 1338–40, 452.
28 Cal. Close, 1339–1341, 612–23.
29 Cal. Close, 1341–1343, 130–44.

167

Malmesbury Abbey 670–1539

on the Abbey's property at Bremhill near the town of Calne.[30] John's situation changed dramatically in 1343 when he fell foul of a special government investigation into crime in Wiltshire and Hampshire. On 4 March Edward III appointed Robert Parvying, one of his senior justices, to investigate law and order in these counties. Parvyng took rapid action and held hearings with local juries in Wiltshire for eighteen days (17 March–7 April). The accusations made by the Wiltshire juries survive unpublished in the records of the Court of the King's Bench.[31] This source has received little previous attention. The jurors in 1343 accused John of Tintern personally of involvement in no fewer than four different murders carried out in the years 1332–6 before he became abbot. In three cases the actual killing was carried out a man named by the jurors as Henry of Badminton. These were contract killings: the juries claimed that John of Tintern ordered the murders but was not personally present when they were carried out. The first case was the murder of William of Trowbridge which took place in the village of Monkton Farleigh near Bradford-on-Avon in May 1332. Afterwards Henry of Badminton and his companions were sheltered in the Malmesbury Abbey country house at Cowfold, known today as Cole Park.

> [...] they say that the same John of Tintern, Henry of Badminton and certain others feloniously killed William de Trowbridge in the field of Farleigh on Monday next after the feast of the apostles Philip and James in the sixth year of the reign of the now king, together with the help of others, and the said abbot harboured the aforesaid felons after the aforesaid felony at Cowfold, knowing that they had committed that felony.[32]

The next murder took place, according to the local jurors, in March 1333. The setting was the village of Yatton Keynell, ten miles to the north of Monkton Farleigh, and the jurors recounted a similar pattern of behaviour. Badminton and others were instructed by Tintern to kill one Walter of Coumbe, and afterwards the killers sheltered at Cowfold. On this occasion the jurors identified another conspirator: William Caynel, a member of the local landowning family after whom the village of Yatton Keynell is named.

> The jurors of the first inquisition say upon their oath that John of Tintern, abbot of Malmesbury, William Caynel and certain others, by conspiracy made between them, at Malmesbury, procured and arranged the death of Walter de Cumbe, who by their assent was feloniously killed at Yatton on Saturday next after the feast of the Annunciation of the Blessed Mary

---

30 Cal. Pat., 1340–1343, 545.
31 TNA KB27/352.
32 Ibid.

The Despenser years and the criminal career of Abbot John of Tintern

in the seventh year of the now king, by Henry of Badminton and others, who were harboured at Malmesbury by the said abbot before the felony and after the felony had been done, the same abbot knowing that they had committed the aforesaid felony.[33]

The third murder, ordered by Tintern and carried out by Badminton, occurred in the summer of 1336. The location was the north Wiltshire town of Calne, and the victim was Robert Phelips, who held land from the Abbey in the village of Brinkworth. John of Tintern was also implicated in the account of a fourth murder in 1336, although on this occasion he was not identified as the person who had ordered the killing. He provided shelter to Thomas Kaylewaye after he had murdered Walter Benedicite at Purton, north of Malmesbury.

> The jurors of another inquisition say that Thomas Kaylewaye, son of John Kaylewaye, around the feast of the decollation of St John the Baptist in the tenth year of the reign of the now King Edward, feloniously killed Walter Benedicite at Rachesthorp in the parish of Purton, and that John of Tintern, abbot of Malmesbury, harboured the said Thomas, knowing that he was a felon.

'And all these things were done for the desire of lands'

The Wiltshire jurors accused John of Tintern of involvement in several murders, but said little about his motives. One case is different: the killing of Robert Phelips of Brinkworth was described in the King's Bench documents in some detail, revealing that the crime was linked to Tintern's wish to deprive one of the Abbey's tenants of land which he wished to give to his associate, Gilbert of Berwick, who was the sheriff of Wiltshire at the time. As we have seen Berwick was involved in the case of the Despenser hoard and had been accused of hiding £1000 of the contraband money. The King's Bench records contain statements about this crime made by two juries of local men. One produced no more than a terse statement of allegations.

> Item, they say that Henry of Badminton and certain others came to Calne on the feast of St Mary Magdalen in the tenth year of the now king and there by the order of the said John the abbot beat and wounded a certain Robert Phelips of Brenkeworth against the peace, by which he died.

A much more detailed account of this crime was provided by the other jury, and this implicated not only Tintern but two other prominent members of Wiltshire society: a landowner called Sir John of Bradenstoke

---

33 Ibid.

Malmesbury Abbey 670–1539

and Gilbert of Berwick. The jurors explained that the background to the crime was a long-standing conspiracy to take land held in Brinkworth by Robert Phelips. Tintern, Bradenstoke and Berwick first acted against Phelips in September 1331, when they seized his land and procured his imprisonment. Following his release, the same group of men attempted to kill Phelips in December 1332.

> Item, the jurors of a certain other inquisition say upon their oath that the aforesaid John of Tintern, Gilbert of Berwick and John of Bradenstoke, knight, together conspired at Malmesbury and elsewhere in the county at the feast of St Michael in the fifth year of the reign of the now lord king, by which Robert Phelips was disinherited of his lands and tenements in Brinkworth, and they caused the same Robert to be indicted, and they detained him for a long time in prison. And the aforesaid John de Bradenstoke, knight, together with others unknown, came by force and arms to the house of the same Robert [Phelips] of Brinkworth during the night of the Saturday next after the feast of St Nicholas in the sixth year of the now king to kill the said Robert.[34]

Phelips managed to bar the door against his enemies, whereupon, according to the jurors, his attackers attempted to burn down his house with him inside. Somehow, he managed to escape and fled from Brinkworth, but two years later Henry of Badminton and others tracked Phelips down to Calne where they assaulted him so violently that he later died of his wounds.

> Which same Robert was in his chamber, by which [reason] they could not reach him, and therefore they set fire to his said chamber. Whereupon the said Robert scarcely escaped and afterwards two years later there came Henry of Badminton and certain others in the field of Calne on Monday next before the feast of the Nativity of St John the Baptist, and there they beat and wounded the said Robert, broke his arms and legs and mistreated him, by which the said Robert, on Sunday next after the feast of St Bartholomew in the aforesaid year, died.[35]

The death of Robert Phelips allowed Tintern to give the land in Brinkworth to Berwick. This was, it seems, the intention all along.

> After whose death the said John of Tintern by reason of his lordship entered the tenement of the aforesaid Robert and enfeoffed the aforesaid Gilbert de Berewyk thereof, who is still the tenant. And all these things were done by conspiracy and by the order of the above-said men for the desire of lands.[36]

[34] Ibid.
[35] Ibid.
[36] Ibid.

John of Rodbourne: Tintern's partner in crime

John of Tintern was not the only monk accused in 1343 of murder by the Wiltshire jurors. They identified as his chief lieutenant another monk, John of Rodbourne, who held office as the monastic steward of the Abbey. Like Tintern, Rodbourne was denounced for ordering a contract killing. While Tintern used Henry of Badminton as his hired killer, Rodbourne called upon the services of Richard Talbot.

> Item, the jurors of another inquisition say that John of Rodbourne, monk of Malmesbury and steward there, appropriated to himself Richard Talebot, who is a common disturber of the peace of the lord king and a common manslayer, and the said John bought lands at Notton in the county of Wiltshire, and gave them to the said Richard, so that he could have a harbouring in the said county, and so that he was nearby to maintain and carry out the mandates of the said John and the foolish acts of the said John.[37]

The jury accused John of Rodbourne and Richard Talbot of killing John atte Orchard of Brokenborough in the manor of Thickwood near Colerne. No specific date was given for this crime.

> And they say that the said John harboured the said Richard on several occasions, after he feloniously killed John atte Orchard of Brokenborough in the manors of the abbot of Malmesbury, *viz* at Thickwood, with him knowing about the said felony. And they say that all men of the county of peaceful and good condition are in trepidation and are fearful, because the said Richard is thus living in the said county.[38]

The arson attack at the manor house of Lea

One of Tintern's most bitter disputes concerned him and a member of the Wiltshire gentry called Ralph of Coumbe, lord of the manor of Lea, a village little more than a mile outside Malmesbury. Ralph held Lea as a tenant of the Abbey. The jurors of 1343 alleged that John of Tintern burnt down the manor house at Lea and then abducted, perhaps with her consent, Ralph's wife, Margaret. Subsequently, the jurors claimed that Tintern and Margaret of Coumbe lived together openly in Malmesbury for several years. The feud between the abbot and Ralph was a topic that was widely discussed among the people of the area: three different juries in 1343 told a version of the story. All agreed that Abbot John had sanctioned an arson attack on the manor house at Lea and had seized

---

37 Ibid.
38 Ibid.

Malmesbury Abbey 670–1539

Ralph's wife. There was, however, a serious discrepancy in dating. One jury dated the attack to February 1335.

> The jurors of another inquisition say upon their oath that John of Tintern, abbot of Malmesbury, feloniously broke and set fire, on Monday after the feast of the Purification of the Blessed Mary in the ninth year of the now king, to the house of Ralph of Combe at Lee, and seized and abducted Margaret, wife of the said Ralph.[39]

Another jury recalled the date of the arson attack at Lea as January 1337, and this account highlighted the role of Henry of Badminton in the crime.

> Item, they say that Henry of Badminton and certain others with the assent and by the order of the said John of Tintern came to Lea and beat and wounded there Ralph [de Coumbe] atte Lee and Boeges of Combe at the house of the same Ralph, and seized and carried away Margaret, wife of the said Ralph, together with the goods and chattels of the same Ralph to the value of 100 marks, on Thursday next after the feast of the Epiphany of the lord in the eleventh year of the now king, and he is a common wrongdoer.[40]

A third jury account of these same events gave no date but provided an important additional detail: these jurors reported that it was widely thought that Margaret had colluded in the burning down of her husband's house. In their view she consented to the arrangement whereby she deserted her husband and went to live with Tintern. Ralph had long feared the attack and had fortified the manor house to repel any attack from the forces of his feudal lord and neighbour, the abbot of Malmesbury.

> The jurors of another inquisition say upon their oath that Ralph de Combe constructed a certain house in the manner of a fort to keep his wife from John de Tynterne, abbot of Malmesbury, who wanted to have seized her, and they say that the said John and Margaret, wife of the said Ralph, jointly conspired to set fire to the said house, and they say that Henry de Badmyntone and certain others feloniously set fire to the said house by the order of the said John of Tynterne, abbot, and the said Margaret freely rejected her husband and lived continuously with the said abbot at Malmesbury, knowing that the same abbot was a felon and of bad condition.[41]

Tintern was abbot at the time of this jury deposition but not at the time of the crime. It seems therefore that Abbot Adam de la Hok was complicit in Tintern's wrongdoing and permitted him to live openly with mistress.

---

39 Ibid.
40 Ibid.
41 Ibid.

The Despenser years and the criminal career of Abbot John of Tintern

The arrest of John of Tintern and his gang

The jurors of Wiltshire accused John of Tintern and his associate Brother John of Rodbourne of five specific murders and two arson attacks. One jury casually alluded to other murders, stating that, in addition to using Henry of Badminton as a killer, Tintern also called upon the services of one George Selyman 'to beat and kill divers men in the aforesaid county'. The government enquiry into crime in Wiltshire began on 17 March 1343. The senior judge, Robert Parvyng, had soon heard enough and concluded that there was a strong *prima facie* case against John of Tintern. Following advice from Parvyng, on 28 March the king ordered the arrest of the abbot, but Tintern, alarmed by news of the jury testimony, had gone on the run with members of his entourage.[42] The warrant ordered that sheriff of Wiltshire should arrest Abbot John and a further thirty-seven named suspects associated with his criminal acts, including the abbot's mistress, Margaret and her maid, Joan Chausy.

> Appointment of John Mauduyt, sheriff of Wiltshire [...] to arrest John of Tintern, abbot of Malmesbury, John of Rodbourne, his fellow monk, Margaret wife of Ralph of Coumbe, Joan Chausy, her handmaid [... and 34 other named persons] who are indicted of divers felonies and misdoings before Robert Parvyng and his fellows, justices of oyer and terminer in the county of Wilts, and are now vagabond in divers counties perpetrating very many damages and crimes [...][43]

The three individuals who had been identified by local juries as the Abbey's hired killers – Henry of Badminton, Richard Talbot and George Selyman – were named as wanted men. Several clerics were also listed as part of John of Tintern's gang, including William Balsham, a renegade monk who had been formerly prior of the Cluniac monastery at Monkton Farleigh.[44] The former sheriff of Wiltshire, Gilbert of Berwick, who was accused of colluding in the murder of Robert Phelips of Brinkworth, was also listed as a renegade suspect.

Abbot John of Tintern, Brother John of Rodbourne and Henry of Badminton surrendered to the sheriff of Wiltshire soon after the issuing of the warrant, and they were all granted bail. The case against them was disrupted by the death of the chief investigating justice, Robert Parvyng, on 26 August 1343. The king appointed another justice, William Trussell, to take charge of the case. The selection of Trussell as the presiding investigator was, perhaps, good news for Tintern. The two men probably

---

42 Cal. Pat., 1343–1345, 78–9.
43 TNA KB27/352
44 For Balsham, see 'House of Cluniac Monks: Priory of Monkton Farleigh', in *History of the County of Wiltshire III*, ed. R. B. Pugh and Elizabeth Crittall (London, 1956), 262–8.

Malmesbury Abbey 670–1539

knew each other: Trussell was a trusted courtier and served on occasion as the Speaker of the House of Commons, while Tintern was a regular participant in meetings of Parliament during the 1330s, as proctor of the abbot of Malmesbury. It seems likely that, in September 1343, a deal was done between Trussell and Tintern: a pardon would be issued in return for a massive fine. On 1 October 1343 the three principal accused men appeared at the court of the King's Bench. The records suggest that Abbot John behaved confidently, claiming that he and his two companions were exempt from prosecution under the terms of the charter of pardon granted to him on 26 April 1338 in the aftermath of the investigation into the concealment of the Despenser treasure. He had the document with him and showed it to the court.

> And now before the lord king there comes the aforesaid abbot and he spoke about how he wished to be acquitted concerning the premises, saying that the lord king by his charter [of 1338] pardoned them of all kinds of felonies, transgressions, oppressions, extortions, damages, grievances, confederations, conspiracies, falsities, the taking of fees from both sides, alliances, concealments and contempts made by them, just as is more fully contained in the aforesaid charter of the king. And he produces here the aforesaid charter of the king, which bears witness to this.[45]

This pardon not only covered any charges relating to the hiding of the £10,000. It also provided immunity for any other crimes performed before its issue, and the court record noted the relevant contents.

> And, in addition, out of our special grace we pardoned the aforesaid abbot and John the suit of our peace, which pertained to us, for every kind of felony and transgression perpetrated by them in our said kingdom of England against our peace.[46]

On the basis of this evidence, William Trussell and the court of King's Bench accepted Tintern's defence and refused to even consider the multiple accusations of murder made by Wiltshire juries. The court did, however, conclude that there was a high level of likely culpability, imposing a huge fine of £500 which the abbot agreed to pay. Tintern was doubtless relieved at this outcome. He was, it seems, particularly anxious about those accusations of arson which had not been explicitly covered by the pardon of 1338, and the royal justices formally accepted that John was exempt from future prosecution for arson as part of the earlier agreement.

> In addition, we have pardoned, out of our special grace, the aforesaid John the abbot, brother John of Rodbourne and Henry [of Badminton]

[45] TNA KB27/352.
[46] Ibid.

The Despenser years and the criminal career of Abbot John of Tintern

for the greater security of the same men and for the greater declaration of our pardon of the aforesaid felonies, the suit of our peace, which pertains to us, concerning the setting fire to houses and any other felonies, whereof they are indicted, accused or appealed [...][47]

Over the next few months, the focus shifted entirely from the question of John's guilt with regard to allegations of murder to his ability to pay in instalments the large fine of £500. The first payment of £250 was paid by 31 October 1343.[48] During the early months of 1344 the abbot paid a further £150 but by the autumn he was reminded that he still owed the final £100.[49] When this was handed over on 21 October 1344 Abbot John of Tintern was formally discharged, and the case was closed.[50]

Tintern's most persistent enemies were, it seems, the victims of his arson attacks. In 1343 he was particularly keen to get explicit recognition that any accusations of arson were void because of the general immunity granted to him against prosecution. In 1347 the abbot anxiously returned to the same issue and sent representatives to Edward III, who was then at Calais, to seek further confirmation that the pardon of 1338 applied also to charges of arson. Royal endorsement was duly provided John of Tintern's immunity from prosecution for historic instances of arson.

Whereas by letters patent dated 26 April, in his twelfth year, the king pardoned the then abbot of Malmesbury; and brother John of Tintern, his fellow monk, for all felonies and trespasses done by them; the said John, now abbot of the said place, fearing that by the procurement of his enemies he may hereafter be disturbed for the burning of houses, has made petition to the king for a special pardon of such burning, and the king has granted the pardon prayed for all burning of houses by him before the said date [...][51]

'May God have mercy on his soul'

John of Tintern and his companions escaped severe punishment for any crimes they had committed. But John's conscience may have troubled him because in late 1344, he applied to Pope Clement VI, who was then in Avignon, requesting a plenary indulgence providing forgiveness for all of his sins at the hour of his death. The application was registered and accepted on 27 December 1344.[52]

---

47 Ibid.
48 Cal. Close, 1343–1346, 190–4.
49 Cal. Close, 1343–1346, 418–28.
50 Ibid.
51 Cal. Pat., 1345–1348, 51.
52 Cal. Papal Registers, 1342–1362, 172–82.

Malmesbury Abbey 670–1539

The Black Death reached England in 1348. Tintern died in August 1349 and there is a very good chance that he was a victim of the plague.[53] He died over thirty eventful years after his appearance in the historical record as a participant in the mass brawl at Lechlade in 1318. The Malmesbury chronicle, known as the *Eulogium Historiarum*, was written in the early 1360s by a monk of Malmesbury who must have been familiar with some of this extraordinary story. The author joined the community in about 1349, while the plague was still raging and around the time of the death of John of Tintern. The *Eulogium* contains an account of the Black Death and immediately afterwards notes the death of Tintern, dating this precisely to 8 August 1349. The chronicle made no reference to Tintern's life and the serious allegations that were made against him, simply noting his death and stating, 'May God have mercy on his soul'.[54]

By the standards of any age John of Tintern was an incorrigible criminal.[55] He was also energetic, resourceful and resilient, and he avoided serious punishment. Tintern's charmed life was probably the consequence of his court connections and the fact that the government of Edward III, and justices such as William Trussell, were more concerned with raising money for war with France than punishing wrongdoers such as the abbot of Malmesbury.

---

[53] *Heads of Houses II*, 51.
[54] *Eulogium III* V CLXXXIV(ed. Haydon 214).
[55] There are parallels between the careers of John of Tintern and Thomas de Lisle, bishop of Ely, 1345 to 1361 who, like Tintern, was accused of arson and murder. See John Aberth, *Criminal Churchmen in the Age of Edward III: The Case of Thomas de Lisle* (Pennsylvania, 1996).

12

Thomas of Bromham
and the *Eulogium Historiarum*

Around the year 1360 a monk of Malmesbury called Thomas of Bromham set out to write a history of the world, from the Creation to the present day. Bromham's book is generally known today as *Eulogium Historiarum* although the author called it simply *Eulogium*. A first draft of the work was completed by 1362, but the author continued to revise the book, adding extra material until late 1366, at which point the chronicle breaks off abruptly. The author's autograph manuscript has survived and is held by Trinity College, Cambridge.[1] While Bromham was not a writer of the calibre of Aldhelm or William of Malmesbury, his work sheds light on the intellectual life and interests of the Abbey in the immediate aftermath of the Black Death.

The writer of the *Eulogium* was, without doubt, a monk of Malmesbury Abbey. Although the work was a universal history that attempted to summarise in encyclopaedic fashion the totality of human experience, significant prominence was also given to events and personalities relating to Malmesbury. There are frequent references to Malmesbury throughout the text, and the chronicle often juxtaposes events of national or international significance with information about the history of Malmesbury. We are told, for example, that in 637 the Prophet Muhammad died, and that 'in the same year the monastery of Malmesbury was founded'.[2] Similarly, for 675 the key events considered worthy of record were the devastation of Sicily by Muslim Arabs and Aldhelm's success in moving the Malmesbury community to a site provided by the local bishop.[3] This pattern of juxtaposing local and much wider history can be seen throughout the work. The summary entry for 1215, for example, relates how in that year the baronial enemies of King John seized control of London and Abbot Walter Loring obtained control of Malmesbury Castle.

The Malmesbury provenance of the chronicle is thus patent, but the authorship is less clear. The work is presented as an anonymous text, but the Victorian editor of the *Eulogium*, Frank Scott Haydon, skilfully

---

1   Trinity College Cambridge, MS R.7.2.
2   *Eulogium* III 279. In fact the author was mistaken and the Prophet Muhammad died in 632.
3   *Eulogium* I LXXXV (ed. Haydon 221–2).

177

Malmesbury Abbey 670–1539

worked out that the author's first name was manifestly Thomas.[4] In an account of a miraculous vision towards the end of Book III of the work, the writer refers to St Thomas of Canterbury as 'nostro patrono' meaning 'our patronal saint'. Since Becket was not Malmesbury Abbey's patron saint, Haydon deduced that this was a reference to the saint after whom the author was named and concluded that he was either baptised as Thomas or adopted this name when he became a monk.

The *Eulogium* contains two chronicles: the full history and an abbreviated version, the *Chronicon Brevius*. The shorter chronicle is laconic, with brief annalistic references for some years and many years in which nothing was noted at all; for the years 1341–50, for example, there are entries for only four out of ten years. The author was highly selective in his choice of events worthy of inclusion in the *Chronicon Brevius*, and yet, curiously, for 1350 there is an entry stating that this was the year when a man called Thomas of Bromham became a monk.[5] The monastic career of Thomas of Bromham was for some reason of interest to the writer, and the obvious explanation is that Bromham was the author. The autograph manuscript in Trinity College Cambridge reveals that having written about how Thomas of Bromham took monastic vows in 1350, the writer proceeded to blot out this entry. Haydon, undaunted, successfully deciphered the writing beneath the ink of the attempted erasure, but it seems that Bromham, having proudly included personal information in his first draft of the work, had second thoughts and attempted to remove this reference to himself.

The ennui of Thomas of Bromham

The *Eulogium* begins with an unusual personal Preface which combines both derivative and original elements. Some of the text was heavily dependent on Ranulf Higden's Preface to his *Polychronicon* with many sentences taken verbatim from Higden, but in addition Bromham added some highly personal revelations about his own state of mind that owed nothing to Higden. While Ranulf Higden had begun his work by expressing the conventional medieval view that the study of history was morally beneficial because understanding the past reinforced the case for virtuous living, Bromham proposed a distinctly different position, explaining that his reflections on the rules of virtuous living did 'not supply any savour to my dullness, for I am unsuited and inadequate'.[6] Bromham used the Preface to emphasise his unhappiness and feelings of

---

4   *Eulogium* I xxv–xxviii; the relevant passage is in *Eulogium* I CXV (ed. Haydon 406).
5   *Eulogium* III (ed. Haydon 309). Bromham is a village about twenty miles south of Malmesbury.
6   *Eulogium* I Preface (ed. Haydon 1).

Thomas of Bromham and the Eulogium Historiarum

unworthiness, and in an extraordinary passage he discussed the tedium of monastic life at Malmesbury and the deep sense of spiritual malaise that he experienced before he began work on the *Eulogium*.

> So sitting in the cloister, often tired out, my consciousness blunted, disappointed in [my search for] virtues, often wounded by the worst possible thoughts, because of the lengthy readings and the wearisome prayers, because of [my] empty boastings and the evil actions [I] once performed when in the world, the pleasure [I] took in them and [my] complicity in them, and, worst of all, their great number – pondering therefore how I could somehow extinguish such assaults, such fiery javelins, sent by him [i.e. the Devil] who endeavours to wound the conscience of a cloister monk with manifold scars [...][7]

If we can take this passage at face value, it seems that Bromham was extremely badly suited to monastic life. His comments on his 'evil actions once performed when in the world' suggest that he had probably joined the community as a mature adult rather than a youth. Bromham proceeded to explain that the prior of the monastery was aware of his troubled state of mind and invited him to write the *Eulogium* as a form of therapy.

> For I was often asked by the prior of my cloister to put in hand something in chronicle form concerning the feats of the ancients, places near and far, wonders, wars, the antique deeds of Christians and pagans, in such a way that I might effortlessly rid myself of other quite profitless leisure-time activities. I favoured his request and putting my wishes at the service of his desires, adhering to the manner and subject matter he had ofttimes intimated to me in the past [...][8]

If his novitiate lasted about a year, which was the norm at the time, it is possible that Bromham joined the community in 1348–9, and he did this as some sort of personal response to the crisis of the Black Death which was raging at this time. Bromham certainly had a strong sense of the scale and horror of the event, and one passage in the *Eulogium* gives a graphic account of the course of the plague.

> In 1348, at about the feast of the Translation of St Thomas the martyr [7 July], the cruel pestilence, hateful to all future ages, arrived from countries across the sea on the south coast of England at the port called Melcombe in Dorset. Travelling all over the south country it wretchedly killed innumerable people in Dorset, Devon and Somerset [...] Next it came to Bristol, where very few were left alive, and then travelled northwards, leaving not a city, a town, a village, or even, except rarely, a house, without killing most or all of the people there. So that over

7   *Eulogium* I Preface (ed. Haydon 2).
8   Ibid.

179

Malmesbury Abbey 670–1539

England as a whole a fifth of the men, women and children were carried to burial. As a result there was such a shortage of people that there were hardly enough living to look after the sick and bury the dead. Most of the women who survived remained barren for many years. If any did conceive they generally died, along with the baby, in giving birth. [...] And this pestilence raged in England for two years and more before it was purged. By the time the plague ceased at divine command it had caused such a shortage of servants that men could not be found to work the land, and women and children had to be used to drive ploughs and carts, something unheard of.[9]

Bromham and the foundation narrative of the Abbey

Thomas of Bromham was an enthusiastic local historian, and he wrote a detailed account of the establishment the Abbey by the Irish monk, Meildulf. His narrative was a considerably expanded version of the briefer version of the same events found in the *Gesta Pontificum* of William of Malmesbury.[10] Bromham took William's succinct account and enlarged it considerably, making the exposition three times longer than that of William of Malmesbury.

> There was in the region of *Scotia* a monk called Meildulf, who was so harassed by plunderers and robbers in his own land that he was hardly able to go on living. Realising he could not last for long there, he took to flight, made a hasty journey, and came as far as England. Here he went around the country pondering where God would provide for him, and finally came to a pause beneath Bladon Castle, which was called *Ingelbourne Castel* in Saxon. The castle had been built in 642 BC by a British king called Dunwallo Molmuncius, eighteenth in line from Brutus.[11] There had been a city there once, but it had been altogether destroyed by foreigners. The castle, safe behind its fortifications, stood for a long time after the Incarnation with no one living nearby. The king's dwelling and his manor (pagans as well as Christians) were at *Kairdureburgh*, now called *Brukeburgh* or alternatively *Brokenbern*. Our dweller in the wild named Meildulf chose a place for his hermitage under the castle, requesting and obtaining a spot from the castle keepers: for no large number of people lived there. Here, finding himself short of essentials, he collected schoolboys to teach, meaning to make good his slender means by their generosity [...][12]

While making use of William's text, Bromham added significant detail. It is not clear how he obtained the additional information, and there is no

---

9   Translation from R. Horrox, *The Black Death* (Manchester, 2013), 63–4 slightly adapted.
10   *GP I* V. 189.1–3 (ed. Winterbottom 501–3).
11   Geoffrey of Monmouth, *Historia Regum Britanniae* II c.34.
12   *Eulogium* I XCII (ed. Haydon 224–5).

180

Thomas of Bromham and the Eulogium Historiarum

independent evidence to support any of the claims that Bromham made in his fuller account of the career of Meildulf. Perhaps he had access to sources now lost; more likely, he invented the expanded account, using superficial details found in a range of sources to add a patina of credibility to a fabricated account. Bromham claimed that the fortress at Malmesbury was founded by a British king called Dunwallo in 642 BC. He repeated a version of this claim about Dunwallo elsewhere in the book, which contains a detailed account of the reign and achievements of Dunwallo in Book V Chapter XIII. Here it was stated that King Dunwallo founded 'three cities with three forts' namely, Malmesbury and the nearby settlements of Tetbury and Lacock.[13] His main source for assertions about Dunwallo's career was Geoffrey of Monmouth's *Historia Regum Britanniae* but, while Monmouth wrote at length about Dunwallo, he made no reference to any role in the foundation of Malmesbury.[14] The *Eulogium* text implied that the fortress at Malmesbury, first built by Dunwallo many centuries before the birth of Christ, was still, in some measure, intact over a thousand years later in the centuries following the departure of the Romans. In Book V Chapter CVIII Bromham indicated that the fortress was not destroyed until the time of a barbarian king called Gurmundus.[15] This, again, is a reference to a character found in the *Historia* of Geoffrey of Monmouth, which outlined the career in the sixth century AD of one Gormundus, an African king who mysteriously turned up in Ireland with an army prior to an invasion of Britain.[16] Geoffrey's tale of the deeds of Gormundus makes no reference to the destruction of Malmesbury, though it does describe how he devastated Cirencester and other cities.

Again going beyond the account of William of Malmesbury, Bromham claimed that there was an ancient British fort or castle at Malmesbury before the arrival of Meildulf, and that the British name for the fort was Bladon Castle. He suggested that the conquering Saxons renamed the place Ingelbourne Castle, and here the most probable basis of the proposed ancient place name was Bromham's imagination, stimulated by details found in the work of William of Malmesbury and documents in the Abbey's cartulary. The Abbey archive contained a charter purporting to date from 675, by which Bishop Leuthere confirmed a grant of land to Aldhelm. William of Malmesbury included the charter in both the *Gesta Regum* and the *Gesta Pontificum*.[17] Leuthere's charter also survives in

---

13 *Eulogium* II XIII (ed. Haydon 236).
14 See Geoffrey of Monmouth, *Historia*, Book XI c.8 and c.10.
15 *Eulogium* III CVIII (ed. Haydon 61).
16 Geoffrey of Monmouth, *Historia*, Book XI c.8 and c.10.
17 *GR I I* 30 (ed. Mynors, Thomson & Winterbottom 45); *GP I* 199.1–6 (ed. Winterbottom 525–7); Kelly, *Charters*, 125.

Malmesbury Abbey 670–1539

several pre-1300 manuscript versions of the cartulary.[18] The charter ends with a statement that it was signed 'in public at the River Bladon' on 26 August 675. Bromham apparently assumed that the charter was signed at Malmesbury and concluded that the old name for the River Avon at Malmesbury was, therefore, Bladon. Based on this 'fact' Bromham, it seems, decided that Bladon would be a credible name for the original British fortress that predated the monastery.

In a similar way, Bromham appears to have used information from the cartulary as inspiration for his assertion that the place was given the name Ingelbourne Castle by the Saxons. The name, Ingelbourne, meaning 'the stream of the English', features in a document setting out the boundaries of the Malmesbury estate of Brokenborough. This survives in three thirteenth-century cartulary documents that would have been available to Bromham.[19] In the Brokenborough boundary clauses 'Ingelbourne' refers to the branch of the Avon that flows into Malmesbury from Long Newnton and Tetbury. Again, Bromham seems to have invented a name for the fortress based on what he thought was the name of a local river. He developed the notion that just as the ancient Britons called the place Bladon, because it stood on the River Bladon, the Saxons named the stronghold after their name for the river, Ingelbourne.

The charter of 675, supposedly signed by the River Bladon, is for the most part an early twelfth-century forgery, designed to assist the Abbey to free itself from the control of Bishop Roger of Salisbury. Some elements of a genuine seventh-century charter from another place may have been reused; but even if the reference to an event at 'Bladon' has some degree of authenticity, it is almost certainly a reference to the river now known as the Evenlode in Oxfordshire.[20] Bromham explained that while the former city of Bladon was deserted when Meildulf arrived there was a royal settlement nearby at the place that later became known as *Brukeburgh* or *Brokenbern*. The modern village of Brokenborough is about a mile outside Malmesbury. In the Middle Ages the word Brokenborough was used to describe both the village and other components of the landed estate of the Abbey.[21] In the *Eulogium* it was stated that the pre-Saxon British inhabitants called Brokenborough *Kairdureburgh*. It is not possible to ascertain Bromham's source for this name. However, he was clearly using the Old Welsh place name prefix *Kair-* or *Caer-* meaning a fortress or settlement. Bromham was almost certainly influenced in his approach to place names by Geoffrey of Monmouth, who made extensive use of names

18 Kelly, *Charters*, 125.
19 Kelly, *Charters*, 251.
20 Kelly, *Charters*, 130.
21 Kelly, *Charters*, 254–5.

182

Thomas of Bromham and the Eulogium Historiarum

prefixed with *Kaer-* in his *Historia*.[22] Perhaps he invented the place name *Kairdureburgh*, on the model of names he found in Monmouth.

Belief in Bladon as an ancient place name was promoted by the Tudor antiquary, John Leland, who visited Malmesbury to examine its library in 1533. His own papers, published in the eighteenth century as *Collectanea*, included a substantial transcription of extracts from the *Eulogium* including the story of Meildulf.[23] Leland also drew upon his reading of the *Eulogium* in his topographical study of England known as his *Itinerary*.

> It was for some time a castle of great fame, wherein the town hath since been built: for in the beginning of the Saxons' reign, as far as I can learn, Malmesbury was no town. This castle was named by the Britons Cair-Bladun. The Saxons first called it Ingelburne.[24]

Leland converted Bromham's *Castellum de Bladon* into the British or Old Welsh style place name *Cair-Bladun*. Since Leland's time other antiquarian writers have repeated his claim that this was the ancient name of the place, and it is a version of this name 'Caer Bladon' that still has some currency today as the supposedly 'original' name of Malmesbury.[25]

The purpose of the *Eulogium*

The Preface to the *Eulogium* is understated in its claims for the work: Thomas described himself in modest terms and highlighted his own limitations as a writer.

> I have with my own hand shaped this brief account in a manner that is not fitting or ornate but turgid and close-packed, with a structure of no elegance [...][26]

> I do not presume [to compose] this [work] on the strength of my own abilities, for they are non-existent. So I ask you, reader, to be kind to me and not to bite me with a poisoned tongue.[27]

22 Monmouth had made use of the list of British cities, all prefixed with the element *Caer*, found in *Historia Brittonum*, a ninth-century work that was traditionally ascribed to Nennius.

23 Leland, *Collectanea*, II 302–3.

24 Leland, *Itinerary*, I 131. The original version was as follows: It was sum tyme a castelle of greate fame, wher yn the toun hath syns be buildid: for in the beginning of the Saxons reigne, as far as I can lerne, Malmesbyri was no toun. This castelle was named of the Britons Cair-Bladun. The Saxons first caullid it Ingelburne.

25 See for example: http://www.gatehouse-gazetteer.info/English%20sites/3642.html.

26 *Eulogium* I Preface (ed. Haydon 2).

27 *Eulogium* I Preface (ed. Haydon 4).

Malmesbury Abbey 670–1539

The *Eulogium* was intended, among other things, to be a collection of entertaining marvels drawn from different times and places. The author claimed that he saw his role as involving both searching for accounts of suitably curious wonders and checking on their veracity because his readers would be understandably sceptical of unsubstantiated 'wonderful or unheard-of prodigies'.

> Whatever I have brought together in these books, I hope that Truth will not be put to shame by it. As a matter of fact, if some wonderful or unheard-of prodigies are read or narrated, credence is rarely afforded them, because those who always live in their native country will rarely see the wonders they could have seen if they had travelled in foreign parts.[28]

Thomas portrayed himself as little more than the organiser of an anthology of well-chosen 'juicy pieces' taken from other authors and presented the *Eulogium* as a work that could provide harmless diversion to monks during moments of leisure.

> [...] it will produce the utmost refreshment to those who study and pray when they wish to rest from their labours, both to avoid sloth and to root out evil thoughts; if some fruitful occupation should be available, the heart of one who studies or prays is much gladdened, especially if something unheard of is heard or something not seen before is seen.[29]

The author was perhaps being rather disingenuous with his modest claims regarding his purpose because there is evidence in the text that Bromham had a much grander intent than the entertainment of monks during their free time. In the view of some modern scholars his hope was that his more discerning readers would see that the *Eulogium* had a startling apocalyptic message: people living in the 1360s were witnessing the climax of world history, and a king of England was about to play an important role in defeating Antichrist and making possible the Second Coming of Christ.

One unusual feature of the *Eulogium* is the author's preoccupation with prophecy and scattered across the work are three substantial sections devoted to prophecies that Thomas apparently considered to be significant:

- Chapter CXX of Book III is an anthology of short prophecies relating to the future role of a powerful, reforming king.[30]
- In the middle of Chapter CLXXXIV of Book IV Thomas broke off from his narrative, and, with no warning, inserted the complete text

---

28 *Eulogium* I Preface (ed. Haydon 3–4).
29 *Eulogium* I Preface (ed. Haydon 4).
30 *Eulogium* I CXX (ed. Haydon 417–20).

Thomas of Bromham and the Eulogium Historiarum

of *Vade Mecum in Tribulacione,* an extraordinary millenarian treatise written in 1356 by the French Franciscan writer, John of Rupescissa, who predicted that the world was about to be convulsed by a series of catastrophic events ending in 1370, when Christ would reappear and begin a 1000-year period of peace and spiritual fulfilment. There is no obvious connection between the treatise and the sections of the chronicle that come immediately before and after it.

- The third major prophetic component can be found in Book V where Thomas devoted four whole chapters (XLII–XLV) to a transcription of the *Prophecies of Merlin* from the *Historia* of Geoffrey of Monmouth.[31]

Are these prophecies relevant to the overall purpose of the work? The Harvard scholar, Morton Bloomfield, thought so, and he was the first to suggest that the *Eulogium* should be read as the work of an author whose message was that the Second Coming of Christ was imminent.[32] In 1961 he called the work 'an excellent representative of the apocalyptic monastic view of history', and in his view the *Eulogium* author believed that prophecies collected in Book III were coming to pass in the account of contemporary events recorded at the end of Book V. Extreme storms, strange astronomical phenomena and political upheavals itemised in the *Eulogium* were divine signs that the Second Coming was about to happen, leading to a millennium of spiritual bliss.

> History is moving towards a renewal, and the social and natural orders give all the evidence needed to the perceptive man. The whole world is agonizing towards a new birth.[33]

Building on the work of Bloomfield, other scholars have endorsed his view that the *Eulogium* needs to be read as an apocalyptic text.[34] It is, however, difficult to be sure about its exact meaning because Bromham

---

31 *Eulogium* II XLII-XLV (ed. Haydon 284–301).
32 Morton Bloomfield, *Piers Plowman as a Fourteenth-Century Apocalypse* (New Brunswick, 1961), 87.
33 Ibid.
34 See K. Kerby-Fulton, *Reformist Apocalypticism and Piers Plowman* (Cambridge, 1990), 187–8. Lesley Ann Coote, *Prophecy and Public Affairs in Later Medieval England* (Woodbridge, 2000), 136–8; Ruth Nisse, 'Prophetic Nations', in *New Medieval Literatures IV* (Oxford, 2001), 9. Kerby-Fulton saw the *Eulogium* as an example of 'reformist apocalypticism' which operated within the framework of millenarian ideas established by Joachim of Fiore and was 'reformist' because the prophecies in Book III predicted that the reform or return of the Church to its pristine state would be necessary before the Second Coming. Coote and Nisse placed particular stress on the significance of the inclusion in Book IV of the prophetic treatise, Vade Mecum. They independently reached the same conclusion: the account of contemporary English history given in Book V was meant to illustrate that Rupescissa's prophecies were coming to pass and that his millenarian predictions would, in turn, come true.

Malmesbury Abbey 670–1539

did not explain his views with any detail or clarity and Book V of the work has a chaotic, unfinished quality. What does seem certain is that Bromham envisaged a special future role for Edward, the Black Prince, and expected that Edward when king would fulfil some of the prophecies that he collected.

Thomas of Bromham wrote at a time of war with France. His stance was patriotic, and he rejoiced at the victories of the English recalling, for example, how as a result of the personal courage of Edward III and God's assistance the English had triumphed at the Battle of Crécy in 1346. He listed with satisfaction the distinguished casualties on the French side, including two kings, two dukes, six counts, together with two thousand knights and countless common foot-soldiers.[35] Bromham admired Edward III but held his son, the Black Prince, in even higher esteem. It seems likely that he began the *Eulogium* thinking that Edward III, who had been on the throne for over three decades by 1360, would soon die, and in several of his entries Thomas prematurely described the Black Prince as Edward IV. The *Eulogium* devotes many pages to the campaign of the Black Prince in 1356, and it is clear that Bromham had access to an eyewitness record of the itinerary followed by the prince as his army moved across France.[36] This account of the events of 1356 is one of the most detailed of all contemporary chronicles.[37] The culmination of the itinerary was the devastating blow the Black Prince dealt to the French at Poitiers, which Bromham duly emphasised.

> In this year on 19 September Edward the fourth since the Conquest, prince of England and not yet king, near the town of Poitiers seized in mortal combat John the said king of France with his son Philip, and imprisoned many great men, counts and barons and killed many, and took John the king to Bordeaux and detained him in custody there for some time.[38]

The autograph manuscript has an index compiled by Thomas which indicates that Book III of the work contained a prophecy concerning the career of 'Edward the fourth king since the Conquest'. This is a reference to Chapter CXX of Book III which contains the text of three prophecies that Thomas saw, apparently, as credible predictions of the future career of the Black Prince. These prophecies were not composed by the *Eulogium* author, and they can be found in other fourteenth-century manuscripts. All three prophecies appeared, for example, in a manuscript held by British Library which was written in the first half of the fourteenth century and predates the autograph manuscript of the

---

[35] *Eulogium* III CLXXXII (ed. Haydon 210–11).
[36] *Eulogium* III CLXXXV–CLXXXVI (ed. Haydon 215–16).
[37] Peter Hoskins, *In the Steps of the Black Prince* (Woodbridge, 2011), 4.
[38] *Eulogium* III Chronicon Brevius (ed. Haydon 309–10).

Thomas of Bromham and the Eulogium Historiarum

Eulogium.[39] One of these three texts is a poem known from its opening words as *Ter Tria Lustra,* concerning a mysterious, heroic ruler known as Sextus. Bromham provided a commentary on this poem, claiming that he had access to special information which enabled him to interpret the prophecy correctly:

> An ancient metrical prophecy concerning Edward king of England, [numeral missing] since the Conquest, which is somewhat obscure and mysterious unless it is more fully explained. An exposition of it has been taken from a book of King Edgar which he left at Winchester, and especially from the books of the Ancient Britons.[40]

In the autograph manuscript the numeral has been erased, but it seems certain that it originally was 'the fourth', since the author's index clearly indicates that Book III of the *Eulogium* would contain a prophecy about 'Edward IIII'. One manuscript of the *Eulogium* held by Trinity College, Dublin, has no erasure and refers here to the 'Edward king of England, fourth since the Conquest' as the subject of the prophecy.[41]

Bromham claimed that his exposition was based on what he had read in an Old English text linked to King Edgar, who ruled 959–75, together with information from 'the books of the Ancient Britons'.[42] This claim cannot possibly be true because the *Ter Tria Lustra* prophecy dates from the fourteenth century.[43] There cannot, therefore, have been any analysis of the poem dating from before the Norman Conquest. Perhaps Bromham himself composed the explanation of the meaning of the prophecy which proposed that the Black Prince as king would become the ruler of the world and would reform the international Church.

> He will turn the world upside down [...] and will bring the clergy back to their previous state.[44]

Bromham provided no commentary on the other two short prophecies – known as *Illius Imperium* and *Anglia Transmittet* – but they also concerned a great ruler and, presumably, were seen by Bromham as foretelling aspects of the glorious forthcoming career of the Black Prince. *Illius*

---

39 Cotton Claudius B. VII.
40 *Eulogium* I CXX (ed. Haydon 417–18).
41 Trinity College Dublin, MS E. 2.26.
42 In the early sixteenth century John Leland read the *Eulogium* manuscript carefully and was impressed by the claim that the commentary was based on ancient works dating from the time of King Edgar. See Leland, *Collectanea,* II 304.
43 For example, Victoria Flood, *Prophecy, Politics and Place in Medieval England* (Woodbridge, 2016), 146, states that 'Ter Tria Lustra' was 'a composition of the reign of Edward III'.
44 *Eulogium* I CXX (ed. Haydon 418–19).

Imperium comprised just four lines and predicted a powerful monarch who would be granted rule over Rome and would bring great lustre to his role as Roman emperor. *Anglia Transmittet* recounted the deeds of an English warrior king known as the Leopard who would crush the French 'Lilies', and reform the Church

> The Leopard's claws will tear apart the kingdoms of Gaul [...]
> The Lilies will wither, the power of the Leopard will be vigorous,
> And under him the pristine liberty of the Church will return.[45]

Bromham provided no commentary on the other two substantial bodies of prophetic material that he included in the *Eulogium*: the prophecies of Merlin from the work of Geoffrey of Monmouth and the treatise, *Vade Mecum in Tribulacione* by John of Rupescissa. In both cases the prophecies envisaged powerful future rulers who would reform the Church. The inclusion of the work of Rupescissa is perhaps the most surprising. In the middle of a chapter describing events leading up to the Norman Conquest, the author interrupted his narrative, copied out *Vade Mecum in Tribulacione* in full and then resumed the story of the Conquest. Twenty-five pages of the autograph manuscript were devoted to this insertion. Rupescissa wrote *Vade Mecum* as a prisoner, held in the dungeon of the papal palace of Avignon on account of his unorthodox views. He had been imprisoned as a suspected heretic by different Church authorities more or less continuously since 1344. It is striking that Thomas of Bromham, a monk of the conservative Benedictine order, promoted the ideas of this controversial writer relatively soon after the writing of the treatise. Bromham cannot have found the transcription of the *Vade Mecum* a comfortable experience: the work prophesied that 'rich religious orders' such as the Benedictines would 'without a single exception [...] be severely afflicted' by catastrophic events during the 1360s.[46] Despite this disturbing prospect Bromham was probably impressed by Rupescissa's view that the English victory at Poitiers represented 'the terrible fall of the power of the Gallic empire' and could be explained 'through a most certain demonstration from Divine Scripture'. This is likely to have resonated well with Bromham, who also saw Poitiers as an event of world historical significance.

The final section of Book V of the *Eulogium* is confusing and somewhat disorderly. Some of the annalistic entries are in the wrong chronological order. It reads like a work in progress that was interrupted and never properly finished. This makes it difficult to be sure about the author's intended message. There are, however, suggestions that Bromham saw

---

45 *Eulogium* I CXX (ed. Haydon 420).

46 The translations here are taken from *John of Rupescissa's Vade Mecum in Tribulacione*, ed. and trans. Matthias Kaup (London, 2017). Kaup used the *Eulogium* autograph at Trinity College Cambridge as one of 27 textual witnesses on which he based his edition.

Thomas of Bromham and the Eulogium Historiarum

himself living in a decadent age, and that the signs of decay and disorder were consistent with the prediction of John of Rupescissa that the period 1360–5 would be characterised by 'terrible misfortunes beyond all human imagination, storms from the heavens, that have never been seen elsewhere'.[47] Bromham proceeded to document such events in detail; for example, in this account of a great storm:

> This year, on January 15 [...] in the evening, an unprecedented wind blew up from the south and west, choking men and uprooting trees; it laid low houses, towers, monasteries, belfries and steeples, orchards and woods, and brought many other ills on human kind. Hence some believe it was a dreadful punishment from God.[48]

Rupsecissa identified 'horrible future earthquakes' as a sign of the End Times. Bromham took a great interest in reports of a devastating earthquake that took place on the island of Rhodes in 1364. He was keen to establish the veracity of this account and claimed that one of his fellow monks had received eyewitness testimony of the earthquake from a returning crusader called Richard Chastellayn.[49] The *Vade Mecum* outlined the titanic struggles that would soon take place between Christian forces and pagan 'Tartars, Saracens and Turks'. The world emperor would ultimately utterly destroy the Muslim forces. In the *Eulogium* Bromham recorded in some detail a battle that took place in 1364 'on the plains of Turkey' between a Christian army and a huge 'pagan' force commanded by 'the Sultan of Babylon, Baldak king of Turkey and Belmarinus, the king of the Tartars'. At least 40,000 men of the 'pagan' army were slain, while over 5000 Christian soldiers were killed, and some taken prisoner.[50]

Other events recounted by Bromham were consistent with his reading of Rupescissa's prediction that the 1360s would be a time of extraordinary tumult. The *Eulogium* outlined the terrifying anarchy in France resulting from the aggression of the 'Free Companies' – roving gangs of unemployed mercenaries and English soldiers who were demobilised after the Treaty of Brétigny (1360) but refused to return home. Bromham called them 'the races without heads' because they were 'headless' or lordless men who rejected legitimate authority.[51] The actions of 'the

---

47 Kaup, *Vade Mecum*, 171
48 *Eulogium* III CLXXXVI (ed. Haydon 229). This was one of the greatest storms ever experienced in Britain, and is recorded in many chronicles.
49 *Eulogium* III CLXXXVI (ed. Haydon 237–8).
50 *Eulogium* III CLXXXVI (ed. Haydon 238).
51 *Eulogium* III 229. This is a reference to the Battle of Brignais that was fought in April 1362 between an army loyal to the French king and a force of Free Companies. The French royal army was heavily defeated. Bromham was mistaken in locating the battle to neighbourhood of Montpellier. Brignais is in eastern France near Lyon.

Malmesbury Abbey 670–1539

people without a head' represented an unnatural overthrowing of the right order of things. Bromham saw the same pattern of unnatural behaviour in more trivial matters such as costume. By the early 1360s, men's fashions had, he claimed, become outrageously effeminate. In a reversal of nature men were dressing like women.

> [...] some are long, reaching to the ankles, not opening in the front, as is proper for men, but laced up the side to the armhole in the style of women's clothes, so that from the back the wearers are taken to be women rather than men [...] They also have little hoods, tightly buttoned under the chin in the fashion of women [...][52]

Bromham saw the effeminate male fashions of the day as a manifestation of great decadence, and in the same passage he highlighted several other ways in which the baronial elite demonstrated catastrophic moral decline. He predicted a terrible reckoning.

> In the hall they are lions, on the battlefield hares [...] Hence it is believed that because God gives them too much, the people lust after savagery, pride, lechery and greed and the rest of the deadly sins; hence it is to be feared that a fearful punishment from God may be on the way.[53]

The *Eulogium* ends abruptly following entries describing events in late 1366. Perhaps death or incapacity brought Bromham's work to a sudden end. Nothing is known of his life beyond the text of his chronicle, and so we do not know what befell him after he stopped work on the manuscript. In his final entries Bromham demonstrated his continuing interest in both his own community and in the Black Prince's career. He reported the election in 1362 of Walter of Camme as abbot of Malmesbury, and he gushed enthusiastically about the celebrations that surrounded the baptism of the Black Prince's first son, Edward, in March 1365 at the castle of Angoulême, in the presence of an enormous and distinguished assembly.[54]

To the end, Bromham continued to report extreme weather events, eclipses and other strange phenomena. One of the last entries in the work concerned an astonishing celestial display reported to Bromham by two Malmesbury monks on returning from a journey in October 1366. The brothers had seen multiple beams of fire in the sky issuing from the moon and coming down to earth like the flames of enormous torches. This extraordinary sight continued for two hours.[55] In his

---

52 *Eulogium* III CLXXXVI (ed. Haydon 230). Such criticisms of fashion were of course a commonplace in the Middle Ages and were not necessarily linked to millenarian views.

53 *Eulogium* III CLXXXVI (ed. Haydon 231).

54 *Eulogium* III CLXXXVI (ed. Haydon 236).

55 *Eulogium* III CLXXXVI (ed. Haydon 241).

Thomas of Bromham and the Eulogium Historiarum

Preface Bromham presented his work as a harmless anthology of tales from the past intended to amuse monks when they were not working or praying; but perhaps perceptive readers were being invited to see a much deeper message. The *Eulogium* told the complete story of human experience from Creation and that universal history was about to reach its final dramatic climax.

13

After the Black Death

The Black Death had, of course, a devastating impact on Malmesbury Abbey, just as it did on every community in England. Victims probably included Abbot John of Tintern, and the prior of the dependent cell at Pilton, John of Lokyngham, both of whom died in 1349.[1] There were doubtless many other victims in the monastery and the neighbourhood of the Abbey. There is no documentary evidence relating specifically to the death rate among the monks of Malmesbury Abbey but data from other Benedictine communities suggests that the mortality level was often extremely high. At Durham Cathedral Priory about half of the community died during the Black Death.[2] Although we do not know how many monks died, it is possible to estimate quite precisely the rate of mortality among some of the rural poor in the Malmesbury area using the records of Glastonbury Abbey which owned property extremely close to Malmesbury Abbey in north Wiltshire.[3] Four Glastonbury manors lay within a ten-mile radius of Malmesbury: Christian Malford, Grittleton, Kington and Nettleton. The village of Christian Malford was just six miles from Malmesbury and immediately adjacent to the manor of Sutton Benger which belonged to Malmesbury Abbey. Records survive from the Glastonbury archive which can be used to demonstrate the death rate of 'garciones', adult male villeins without land, on Glastonbury's Wiltshire estates. It is reasonable to assume that the mortality rate in the villages owned by Malmesbury Abbey resembled that on the nearby Glastonbury lands, where the death rate among this class of villeins ranged from 48% to 66%.

Glastonbury Manors in North Wiltshire	Mortality Rate of Landless Villeins: 1348–9
Christian Malford	66%
Grittleton	63%
Kington	56%
Nettleton	48%

---

1   *Heads of Houses II*, 51 (for Tintern), 124 (for Lockyngham).
2   Joan Greatrex, *The English Benedictine Cathedral Priories* (Oxford, 2011), 35.
3   Martin Ecclestone, 'Mortality of Rural Landless Men before the Black Death', *Local Population Studies*, 63 (1999): 26.

Malmesbury Abbey 670–1539

The mortality for townsfolk was doubtless high also. One indicator of the disappearance of whole households in the town is found in legal records from 1352, which state that four men from Malmesbury – Nicholas Handsex, Thomas Smyth, Richard Uphulle and Thomas Terry – were guilty of 'carrying doors and windows from empty tenements in Malmesbury'.[4]

At a national level the shortage of labour after the Black Death created problems for monastic landlords, and eventually led to the end of direct demesne farming. At Malmesbury this process was protracted: the abandonment of demesne farming took place at some point in the early fifteenth century. The 'inquisition post-mortem' for Abbot Walter of Camme, following his death in 1396, indicates that his demesnes were largely still in hand, although with dilapidated buildings and lands wasted by the pestilence.[5]

The rule of Simon of Aumeney

The tumultuous abbacy of John of Tintern ended with his death on 8 August 1349, and within days the community chose another Malmesbury monk, Simon of Aumeney, as abbot. Aumeney ruled for the following thirteen years.[6] In May 1349, just a few months before his election as abbot, Aumeney had been appointed by Tintern as prior of Pilton, the Malmesbury dependent cell in Devon. Within just a few months of moving to Devon he was recalled as the new abbot of Malmesbury. There is no evidence at all that Aumeney sought to distance himself from his disreputable predecessor. Quite the contrary, one of Aumeney's first acts was to appoint John of Rodbourne to the now vacant post of prior of Pilton. As we have seen, Rodbourne had been a close associate of Tintern and had been accused by Wiltshire juries of a range of crimes including murder. Aumeney must have been aware of these accusations and of Rodbourne's terrible reputation; he promoted him despite this. In addition, Aumeney almost certainly knew that Rodbourne was the father of an illegitimate daughter called Denise, born to an unfree woman who lived on the estates of Malmesbury Abbey. As prior of Pilton, Rodbourne attempted to arrange the marriage of his daughter to a member of the Devon gentry. The facts concerning the daughter of Prior John of Rodbourne came to light in a court case held in 1361. Having moved to Devon, Rodbourne bought the right to marry his daughter to an orphan called Richard Wolf who was the heir to property in the county. Some members of Wolf's family complained that this was illegal because

---

[4] E. M. Thompson, 'Offenders against the Statute of Labourers in Wiltshire', *WANHM*, 33 (1904): 400–1.

[5] Berry I 182.

[6] *Heads of Houses* II, 124.

After the Black Death

Denise was of 'villein blood', and that such a marriage 'disparaged' the boy. The matter reached the royal court at Westminster on 21 June 1361 when Edward III ruled that the proposed marriage was invalid because the mother of Denise was a villein.[7]

It was during Aumeney's period of office that Thomas of Bromham began to write the *Eulogium*. As we have seen, its Preface indicates that Bromham, as a Malmesbury cloister monk, was unhappy and found the liturgical round burdensome. Another apparently disaffected monk was Andrew of Tiderinton, who was absolved by papal letter in 1353, having previously abandoned the monastic life.[8] Abbot Simon was personally involved in one event reminiscent of the career of his predecessor. In April 1353 there was a dramatic clash between Malmesbury Abbey and the Augustinian canons of Llanthony Secunda Priory near Gloucester.[9] The Llanthony community owned an agricultural grange in Podsmead, on the edge of Gloucester. The prior of Llanthony complained to the king that Malmesbury Abbey had illegally seized property from Podsmead. The accusation was that Abbot Simon and his fellow monk, Walter of Camme, had gone in person with a group of their men to the grange and had carried away goods – presumably agricultural produce – worth the huge sum of £1000. The king ordered an enquiry; unfortunately, the result of the investigation is not known.

The ambitions of Walter of Camme

We know a considerable amount about the Abbey during the long rule of Abbot Walter of Camme, who succeeded Aumeney in 1361, and remained in charge until his death in 1396. Before his promotion Camme had been the 'prior loci', the senior monk with responsibility for the management of the college premises at Gloucester College, Oxford. In this role he was prepared to make himself unpopular: in 1356 he was involved in argument with Ralph of Otteforde, a student monk from St Augustine's Canterbury. Walter refused to give Brother Ralph access to his room after the monk had returned from a period of absence.[10]

Walter of Camme was extremely energetic in pursuit of the Abbey's interests, and was the last abbot of Malmesbury to make substantial additions to the institutional property portfolio. He bought houses in London and Bristol as well as Malmesbury and increased the landed estate of the Abbey through acquisitions in the villages of Bremhill, Crudwell and Hankerton. Camme used some ingenuity in order to

7   Cal. Pat., 1358–1361, 582–3.
8   Cal. Papal Letters, v, 546–7.
9   'Hempsted', in *A History of the County of Gloucester: Volume 4, the City of Gloucester*, ed. N. M. Herbert (London, 1988), 420–9.
10   *Documents Illustrating the Activities of the General and Provincial Chapters of the English Black Monks III*, ed. William Abel Pantin (London, 1937), 25–6.

Malmesbury Abbey 670–1539

obtain land. John Broun from Hankerton killed a man in 1362 and was eventually hanged for this offence in 1368. The property of a murderer would be forfeited to the Crown, but between the date of the crime and the punishment a complex series of legal moves took place that resulted in Abbot Walter taking control of the land. A jury in 1373 cleared the Abbey of collusion and confirmed the Abbey's title to Broun's land.[11]

Camme provided himself as abbot with a substantial London base. Between 1366 and 1379 he purchased properties in Holborn in London including a large building which had been the first Lincoln's Inn, the headquarters of the legal fraternity bearing that name. The lawyers moved elsewhere enabling Camme to purchase and develop the building and nearby garden as a grand London town house suitable for him as an ecclesiastical dignitary of considerable standing. In 1380 he decreed that much of the Lincoln's Inn site, including the garden and kitchen, should be reserved for his use when visiting London for parliament and other business.[12] The religious life of the Abbey was of importance to Camme, and he was particularly keen to promote the cult of the Virgin. For this reason, he greatly increased the standing of the monk official known as the Custodian of the Altar of St Mary, assigning substantial additional property to the Custodian, including rental property in the town and land in the countryside. As a result of these grants, the Custodian became a major landlord in the borough. The rent roll of the Custodian survives for 1399, which lists 73 properties that he controlled.[13]

It was probably during Walter of Camme's abbacy that an attempt was made to promote the cult of Æthelstan to pilgrims. The tomb of Æthelstan that is still extant in the Abbey church was constructed in the late fourteenth or early fifteenth century, and the figure of the king is dressed in the costume of this time. It is possible that the remodelling of the royal tomb was linked to a campaign to promote the veneration of Æthelstan as a saint. A reference to Malmesbury as the place where the body of 'sanctus Aethelstanus' rested can be found in a late medieval manuscript now in Lambeth Palace Library.[14]

There is no reason to doubt that Camme sent a regular supply of young Malmesbury monks as students to Gloucester College, and that he promoted scholarship within the community. Some insights into the intellectual interests of Malmesbury monks shortly after Abbot Walter's death are provided by a collection of manuscript fragments from the Abbey that can be dated to around 1400.[15] Just over half a Malmesbury

---

[11] Berry I 179.
[12] Berry I 177.
[13] Berry I 251.
[14] For these insights, see Julian M. Luxford, *The Art and Architecture of English Benedictine Monasteries* (Woodbridge, 2005), 135.
[15] N. R. Ker, *Medieval Manuscripts in British Libraries III* (Oxford, 1971), 331–5.

After the Black Death

manuscript of originally about 200 leaves survives from this time,[16] a close examination has revealed that this 'was probably written at Malmesbury Abbey around the turn of the fifteenth century'.[17] We know that the scribes responsible for this document were working after the coronation of Henry IV in 1399 because this event is mentioned in the document. The text was a miscellany of several works, many of which were historical in nature:

1. Latin verses on the Gospels
2. Old Testament stories from Genesis to 4 Kings in Anglo-Norman rhyming couplets
3. *Historia Troiana* by Guido de Columnis
4. *Chronica Pontificum et Imperatorum* by Martinus Polonus
5. An account of the consecration of Henry IV in 1399 and his genealogy from Adam
6. The 'short version' of the Anglo-Norman Prose *Brut*
7. A continuation of the Anglo-Norman Prose *Brut*
8. A list of the names of kings of England from Brutus to Edward III
9. A list of the casualties at the Battle of Poitiers (1356) in Anglo-Norman
10. The text of the treaty of Brétigny (1360) in Anglo-Norman
11. A constitutional text based on *Modus Tenendi Parliamentum*
12. A French version of *The Travels of Sir John Mandeville*.

The continuation of the historical work, *Brut*, in Anglo-Norman which survives uniquely in this manuscript was composed shortly after 1357, possibly in or near Malmesbury.[18] It tells the story of the conflict between France and England 1332–57. As we have seen this was a topic of great interest to Thomas of Bromham who wrote his *Eulogium* at Malmesbury at about the same time, and the author of the *Brut* continuation shared with Bromham an anti-French perspective. Overall, this collection of works suggests that the Malmesbury monks were trilingual, nationalistic and interested in history. The books of Columnis and Polonus were popular thirteenth-century continental historical works; much of the other material concerned British history, the English royal family and the recent conflict between England and France.

---

16 James Lyell (1871–1948), a collector of medieval manuscripts, acquired the fragments and bound them in three separate volumes. After his death one volume was acquired by Yale University and the other two became the property of the parish church of Malmesbury Abbey, where they remain today.

17 Trevor Russell Smith, 'The Malmesbury Continuation of the Anglo Norman Prose Brut, 1332–1357: Text and Translation', *The Medieval Chronicle*, 14 (2021): 238.

18 Smith, 'Continuation', 247.

Malmesbury Abbey 670–1539

Under the direction of Abbot Walter, the Abbey church buildings were substantially altered, and by around 1400 two massive towers had been added to the monastic church: one at the west end and the other over the central crossing to the east of the nave. The western façade was also reshaped with the addition of a large late fourteenth-century window of which slight traces still remain. The crossing tower was crowned with the addition of a tall spire, and John Aubrey preserved the tradition that this spire was almost as high as that of old St Paul's cathedral in London.[19] If Aubrey was correct, the Malmesbury spire was one of the tallest in medieval Europe. These spectacular additions to the exterior of the Abbey church were almost certainly the initiative of Abbot Walter Camme.

Abbot Walter had a marked sense of his own dignity. In 1379 he sent representatives to Pope Urban VI in Rome seeking a formal re-affirmation of Malmesbury Abbey's special position as a monastery that was exempt from episcopal control. His main concern appears to have been his own 'pontifical' status as the abbot of an important exempt monastery. The pope complied with the request and issued a statement of Malmesbury privileges on 15 February 1379.[20] He did this in the form of an extant letter of instruction to Simon Sudbury, the archbishop of Canterbury. The pope referred to a 'petition' that he had received from Abbot Walter. This document has not survived, but it is possible to reconstruct some of its contents from the papal letter of instruction. Walter wanted two things from the pope: confirmation that he had permission to wear the vestments and insignia of a bishop, thereby indicating that he was equal to a diocesan bishop, and the right to undertake ceremonial activities that were usually the preserve of bishops. Two episcopal ceremonial prerogatives were specified: the carrying out of 'the first tonsure', the act of hair cutting which signified that a layman had become a member of the clerical estate, and solemn benediction during important parts of the liturgy. Pope Urban confirmed these rights, explicitly stating that the abbot of Malmesbury was indeed entitled to wear a mitre, ring and special pontifical sandals in the same manner as a bishop. One striking detail in the letter of Pope Urban VI is his reference to the link between the status and the wealth of Malmesbury Abbey. The pope commented that the petition from Malmesbury argued that the Abbey was worthy of respect because its revenues 'are said to rise to six thousand florins of gold annually'. This sounds like the voice of Abbot Walter himself, proudly informing the pope that Malmesbury was wealthy enough to deserve special treatment and helpfully translating the sterling value of the Abbey's income into an Italian currency. Having obtained this letter

[19] John Aubrey, *The Natural History of Wiltshire,* ed. John Britton (London, 1847), 100.

[20] *Concilia Magnae Britanniae et Hiberniae III,* ed. David Wilkins (London, 1727), 142–4.

from the pope in February 1379, Abbot Walter sent a Malmesbury monk called John Welles to Lambeth Palace in September to present the papal instruction to Archbishop Sudbury, who responded by issuing a charter, which addressed Abbot Walter directly and recognised his right to wear episcopal insignia at a range of formal events.

Camme was active in the meetings of the national chapter of Benedictine monks which brought together the superiors of all the houses of the Black Monks of England. In 1363, not long after he was appointed as abbot, Walter was chosen by the chapter to be one of a select group of 'diffinitors' who were responsible for drafting the ordinances that were considered by all the superiors collectively in their chapter meetings.[21] Abbot Walter continued to act as one of the presidents in the early 1380s, and was acting in this capacity at the time of the Peasants' Revolt. On 12 May 1381 – just weeks before the uprising – he sent a letter from Malmesbury to the heads of the Benedictine houses calling on them to pay their dues which were needed to maintain Gloucester College in Oxford. In April 1383 Pope Urban VI wrote to him and the abbot of Ramsey Abbey instructing them to promote the regulations for Benedictine houses promulgated by Pope Benedict XII in his constitutions of 1336. These included recommendations to ensure that at least one in twenty monks received a university education. The papal bull was lost in transit, and Abbot Walter had to write an explanatory letter to the pope.[22]

Preaching Lollardy and free love to the tenants of Malmesbury Abbey

As a young man Abbot Walter Camme may have known the radical theologian, John Wyclif, because they were both at the University of Oxford in the late 1350s: Camme as one of the priors of Gloucester College and Wyclif as a fellow of Merton College. By the 1370s Wyclif was issuing a series of treatises in which he denounced the corruption of the Church and the religious orders. We know that leaders of the Benedictine monks of England such as Camme were alarmed by Wyclif and his followers, the Lollards, and sought papal condemnation of their views. One curious episode during the abbacy of Walter Camme involved the appearance in the Malmesbury area during the 1380s of an itinerant Lollard preacher called William Ramsbury.[23] His surname indicates that he probably came from the Wiltshire village of Ramsbury, and he was known to have preached extensively in north Wiltshire, including the Malmesbury Abbey estate villages of Sutton Benger and Brinkworth. Ramsbury was

---

21 *Chapters of the English Black Monks*, III, 1937, 33.
22 *Chapters of the English Black Monks*, III, 1937, 80–2.
23 Charles Kightly, 'The Early Lollards: A Survey of Popular Lollard Activity in England, 1382–1428', unpublished doctoral thesis, University of York (1975).

Malmesbury Abbey 670–1539

arrested and tried for heresy by the bishop of Salisbury in July 1389, and the case attracted national interest. Thomas of Walsingham, the chronicler and monk of St Albans, included an account of Ramsbury's trial in his *Chronica Maiora.*

> All who were ordained in this way by the heretics had no fear of anything, believing that they were permitted to do anything they liked, to celebrate Masses, to conduct divine services, and to administer the sacraments. This wickedness was exposed by one of those ordained by them, who, being pricked in his conscience, confessed his sin to the bishop of Salisbury at his manor of Sonning.[24]

Ramsbury confessed to preaching several heretical ideas which were in line with the teachings of Wyclif.[25] He denied the authority of the pope and rejected the idea of transubstantiation, stating that 'after the consecration there is bread on the altar, not the body of Christ'. Ramsbury preached to the tenants of Malmesbury Abbey that the monastic ideal of chastity was completely misguided: monks would be better off married and out in the world sharing the good news of the Gospel with the people.

> [...] it would be better and more meritorious for all priests and religious persons to take wives and apostacise than to live religiously and in chastity; and he held and preached the same with respect to nuns [...] Also: that it would be more meritorious for priests to go through their homeland with a Bible under their arms and preach to the people than to say Matins or celebrate masses or carry out other divine offices.[26]

Going beyond the teachings of Wyclif, Ramsbury also advocated free love and claimed that he had personally had sex with several 'virgins, wives and other women' while engaged in his missionary work.

> Also: that it is permissible for any priest or other man to know carnally any women, even nuns, virgins and wives, and this for the multiplying of the human race; and this is what the said William did, knowing virgins, wives and other women [...][27]

Ramsbury was condemned by the bishop, and was ordered to recant publicly at Salisbury Cathedral and at each of the more important churches where he had preached and to restrict himself to a diet of bread and water for the rest of his life.[28]

---

24   Thomas Walsingham, The St Albans Chronicle: The Chronica Maiora of Thomas Walsingham, I: 1376–1394, ed. John Taylor, Wendy R. Childs, and Leslie Watkiss (Oxford, 2003), s.a. 1389.
25   Kightly, *Lollards*, 315–17.
26   Ibid.
27   Ibid.
28   Kightly, *Lollards*, 327.

200

14

The abbots of the fifteenth century

The fifteenth century witnessed important developments in the management of the estates of Malmesbury Abbey. Unfortunately, the evidence is fragmentary or circumstantial, but at some point following the death of Abbot Walter Camme in 1396 the demesne manors of the Abbey were all leased out, and the supervision of agricultural work was no longer a responsibility of the abbot and obedientiaries. The exact chronology is not known but by the time of an inquisition post-mortem following the death of Abbot Thomas Bristow in 1456 only cash income from the manors was recorded, almost certainly indicating that all the demesnes had been leased out.[1]

As in the rest of England, the labour shortages after the Black Death eventually led to the collapse of serfdom on the estates of Malmesbury, and by the early Tudor period only a tiny minority of families in Wiltshire were, in the eyes of the law, villeins.[2] The late medieval estate records of Glastonbury Abbey relating to its north Wiltshire manors are much more comprehensive than any Malmesbury Abbey documents for the same period, but it is reasonable to assume that the trends in the manors held by Malmesbury were similar to those in nearby Glastonbury lands. The Glastonbury estate rental of 1518 made a careful note of any tenants who were serfs,[3] and in the four manors near Malmesbury only one family was identified as having villein status. Serfdom had almost, but not quite, disappeared from north Wiltshire. Malmesbury Abbey did not welcome the disappearance of serfdom, and as late as 1500 the abbot of Malmesbury was accused of wrongly imprisoning a prosperous farmer called Robert Carter, and seizing his livestock, on the grounds that he was the Abbey's villein.[4] Just two years before the Dissolution, in 1537, the last abbot of Malmesbury, Robert Frampton, was charged with falsely claiming that a local man was his 'bondman' or serf.[5]

---

1   Berry I 182.
2   John Hare, *A Prospering Society: Wiltshire in the Later Middle Ages* (Hatfield, 2011), 124–30.
3   Hare, *Society*, 125.
4   *Select Cases before the King's Council in the Star Chamber*, ed. I. S. Leadam (London, 1908), 118–28.
5   L. & P. Hen. VIII, xii. 443–81.

Malmesbury Abbey 670–1539

Although the Abbey leased out the demesne farmland during the fifteenth century, wooded closes were retained in several manors. At these locations the abbot had the right of 'free warren' entitling him and his guests to hunt specific birds – pheasant and partridge – and hares and rabbits. The abbot also retained the house and park of Cowfold – known today as Cole Park – which was stocked with deer; here he was able to provide hunting opportunities for his guests and perhaps, like Chaucer's monk in the *Canterbury Tales*, the abbot and other monks hunted themselves. Records from the Court of Common Pleas suggest that the abbots of fifteenth-century Malmesbury were greatly troubled by poachers and people stealing timber from the Abbey's woodland. Perhaps the abandonment of the system of manorial reeves had made it more difficult to police the countryside.

The early fifteenth century

Walter of Camme died in 1396 after a long and largely successful abbatial career. We know far less about the next two abbots: Thomas Chelworth (1396–1424) and Roger Pershore (1424–34). It seems that before Walter of Camme's death there was a rebellion by the community against his domineering ways, and that he agreed in response to change his behaviour and act in a more collegiate manner. His successor Thomas Chelworth initially honoured the understanding made between Camme and the community, but he changed his mind and in 1403 petitioned Pope Boniface IX asking to be freed from a solemn oath that limited his power as abbot. The pope granted the request, subject to an investigation by the abbot of the nearby Cistercian house of Stanley.

> To the abbot of Stanley, in the diocese of Salisbury. Mandate at the recent petition of Thomas abbot of Malmesbury – containing that before provision was made to him of that monastery, then void by the death of abbot Walter, he was induced by the convent to swear to observe, if appointed abbot, certain statutes and ordinances, donations etc. said to have been formerly made by the said abbot Walter, afterwards by that abbot and the convent renewed and approved, and read in the presence of, and well understood by, abbot Thomas, then a monk of the monastery; adding that if he, who was afterwards appointed abbot, were compelled to observe the said oath, it would be to the detriment of his abbatial dignity; and asserting that his predecessors were not wont to take such oath – if he find the above to be true, to absolve abbot Thomas, after enjoining a salutary penance, from the observance of the said oath, and to declare him and his successors not to be bound thereto or to the observance of a like oath.[6]

---

[6] Cal. Papal Registers, 1398–1404, 543–57.

The abbots of the fifteenth century

The government used Malmesbury Abbey as a convenient base for occasional legal investigations into Wiltshire matters. After the Lollard Revolt in 1414 the rebel leader, Sir John Oldcastle, was executed, and his lands were forfeited. Oldcastle had held two manors in north Wiltshire jointly with his wife, Lady Joan Oldcastle, and the authorities wanted to investigate whether this property should be seized. A tribunal was held at Malmesbury Abbey in September 1418 at which it was decided that the manors were Joan's personal property and not subject to forfeiture.[7]

Few Abbey estate documents are extant from the fifteenth century, but to some extent this lack of evidence is redressed by the survival of a considerable amount of material from many legal cases involving the Abbey. These show that throughout the century the abbots were highly litigious and assiduous in their use of the courts as a means of defending their interests. The records of the Court of Common Pleas list many cases initiated by Malmesbury abbots, which mostly concern debt or poaching. Abbot Thomas Chelworth was constantly striving to deter local poachers: in 1401, for example, he complained about the behaviour of Robert Heywey of Charlton who had broken into 'free warren' closes at Purton and Charlton, taking timber and game. The court found in favour of the abbot; however, Heyway failed to show up for the hearing, and so his neighbours – as his guarantors or 'mainpernors' – were held responsible.

> [...] by force and arms, he entered the free warren of the same abbot at Purton and Charlton and hunted in it without his licence and will, and felled his trees, lately growing there, and took and carried away those trees to the value of 100s and hares, rabbits, pheasants and partridges from the aforesaid warren, and [inflicted] other outrages, etc, to the serious damage, etc, and against the peace, etc. And he has not come. And he is distrained by chattels to the value of 10s. And he is mainprised by Richard Hilton, Henry Selk, Simon Est and Edmund West. Therefore, they are in mercy.[8]

Abbot Roger Pershore was similarly keen to preserve the Abbey's hunting rights. In one case in 1427 he asserted his claim to a monopoly over the hunting of wild boar on Abbey lands when he sued a Malmesbury butcher for killing a boar with dogs at Milbourne, just outside the town. The abbot claimed that the valuable wild animal belonged to him.

> [...] Richard Blankepayn of Malmesbury in the aforesaid county, butcher, by force and arms, hunted a certain wild boar of the same abbot, worth 40s, found at Milbourne, with certain dogs, inciting those dogs to bite the aforesaid wild boar, so that by that hunting and the bites of the aforesaid dogs that wild boar died. And he depastured,

7   Cal. Close, 1413–1419, 487–92.
8   TNA CP 40/561.

trod down and consumed his grass, lately growing there, with certain beasts, and [inflicted] other outrages, etc, to the serious damage of the same abbot and against the peace of the king, etc[9]

Those accused by the abbots of poaching in the early decades of the fifteenth century came from many different backgrounds. One repeat offender was the rector of Draycot Cerne, a village immediately adjacent to the Abbey's manor of Sutton Benger. Edward the 'Parson' was sued for trespass in 1432 for hunting in the 'free warren' of Sutton Benger.

> The abbot of Malmesbury by his attorney appeared [...] against Edward Parson, parson of the church of Draycote Cerne in the aforesaid county, concerning a plea, whereby, by force and arms, he entered the free warren of the same abbot at Sutton [Benger], and hunted in it without his licence and will, and took and carried away hares, rabbits, pheasants and partridges. And [he inflicted] other outrages, etc, to the serious damage, etc, and against the peace, etc. And he has not come. And the sheriff was ordered to take him, etc. And the sheriff now reports that he is not found [...][10]

Abbot Thomas Bristow and the remodelling of the cloisters

Thomas Bristow was chosen as abbot on 17 April 1434. His career is much better documented than those of his two immediate predecessors and a record of his election survives in the *Register* of Robert Neville, Bishop of Salisbury.[11] It seems that a genuine contest took place, with Bristow obtaining a narrow majority over another Malmesbury monk, William Aust. Twenty-six monks voted, and it was recorded that there were two named runaway or 'apostate' monks who were not entitled to vote. Assuming that some monks were away and unable to vote by proxy at the dependent cell at Pilton and others possibly absent on business or for study, the number of electors suggests a total community of about 30 monks.

During the fifteenth century the Abbey cloisters were remodelled, and fashionable fan vaulting was introduced. The cloisters were destroyed after the Dissolution, but a small fragment of the work survives above ground in the form of the porch of a processional doorway that linked the cloisters to the monastic church. In the late eighteenth century, a tile pavement was discovered in the north alley of the cloister that contained the initials of Thomas Bristow, suggesting that he was heavily involved in the improvement of the cloisters.[12] An archaeological investigation

---

9   TNA CP 40/664.
10   TNA CP 40/685.
11   Watkin, 'Abbey of Malmesbury', 210–31.
12   Walter Leedy, *Fan Vaulting: A Study of Form, Technology, and Meaning* (London, 1980), 182–3.

The abbots of the fifteenth century

in 1910 revealed that each of the four cloister alleys had eight bays for study carrells, creating a total of thirty-two study cubicles, enough to provide one for each monk. The roof of the cloisters was decorated with elaborate fan vaulting in the style of the cloisters at Gloucester, which still survive today.[13]

Abbot Thomas and the poachers

Bristow contended with poachers like his predecessors, and he was particularly litigious. In just one law term, Hilary 1442, the abbot took legal action on seven occasions against people from Malmesbury and the surrounding area either for debt or trespass for the purpose of poaching.[14] In one typical case Bristow accused two Malmesbury weavers, a father and his son both named John Chaloner, of breaking into his park at Cowfold with two other associates from the town: once inside the park they had hunted without permission and had taken away game worth, according to the abbot's deposition, the large sum of £20.[15] Cowfold was at the centre of an extraordinary outbreak of poaching in the early 1450s. While most accusations of poaching led to civil litigation in the Court of Common Pleas, these events attracted the attention of the King's Bench justices, who dealt with serious criminal matters. In the records of the court are complaints from the abbot that in January 1452 a large gang broke into Cowfold, and stole beef worth 13s 4d.[16] The robbers also took fish from the Cowfold fishponds. Two leaders of the gang were identified and were designated as 'gentlemen' in the court documents: Wybert Charlton and Walter Charlton from the village of Charlton. Their accomplices were a mix of 'yeomen' from Charlton and a group of tradesmen – weavers, tailors, sawyers – from the town of Malmesbury. A woman intriguingly identified as 'Colette Frenchwoman, servant of Malmesbury' was listed as one of the people who received the stolen goods. Colette's presence in the town was probably a consequence of the growing woollen industry in this part of Wiltshire, which had attracted other migrant workers from France and Flanders. It is not clear what happened as a result of these complaints, but we do know from another source that Abbot Thomas had little faith in the capacity of the legal process to protect him from the Charlton gang.

---

13 Our knowledge of the design of the fifteenth-century cloisters was significantly increased by the archaeological research of Harold Brakspear who excavated the cloister area in 1910 and found enough material to create a convincing reconstruction. See Brakspear, 'Malmesbury Abbey', 399–436.

14 TNA CP 40/724.

15 Ibid.

16 TNA KB 9/134 part I.

Malmesbury Abbey 670–1539

In addition to making accusations to the royal justices, the abbot also complained directly to the Chancellor of England. His petition, written in English, has survived. It was addressed 'To the most reverend Father in God John Cardinal Archbishop of York, Chancellor of England'.[17] The recipient was Cardinal John Kemp, the powerful Chancellor to King Henry VI and the petition must date to before July 1452 when Kemp was promoted to the archbishopric of Canterbury. Abbot Thomas complained about the long delays involved in getting effective action from royal justices, claiming that Wybert Charlton and his followers simply disregarded any commands of the sheriff of Wiltshire that they should keep the peace.

> [...] neither the sheriff of the said shire nor his ministers for fear of the great multitude of the said misdoers dare not take upon them to execute neither precept nor commandment of the king's against the said misdoers [...][18]

The abbot's petition alleged that the monks and their servants were under almost constant attack by the gang led by several 'gentlemen' from Charlton.

> Wibert Charleton, Robert Charleton, Walter Charleton and James Chaterton late of Charleton in the said shire, gentlemen, with many other misdoers [...] armed and arrayed [...] were proposing utterly to destroy your said beseecher and his said monastery, with force and arms daily unto this time at Malmesbury aforesaid and at other places within the said county, lying in wait to slay your seid beseecher, his commons and servants and daily assault and chase them so that they dare not go out of the said monastery and other places which they be n but in great fear of their lives.[19]

Bristow accused the Charlton poachers of placing the Abbey under siege and threatening to harm all persons who attempted to bring in food and

---

[17] TNA C 1/18/172.

[18] Ibid. The original version was as follows: [...] nor the sheryf of the seid shire ne his ministres for fere of the greet multitude of the seid misdoers dare not take upon hem to execute no p[re]cept ne comaundement of the kynges ayenst the seid mysdoers [...]

[19] Ibid. The original version was as follows: Wib[er]t Charleton Rob[er]t Charleton Walt[er] Charleton and James Chaterton late of Charleton yn the seid shire Gentilmen With many other mysdoers [...] armed and arrayed [...] Were p[ro]posyng utterly to destruye your seid besecher and his seid monast[er]ie with force and armes dayly yn to this tyme at Malmesbury aforeseid and at other places withynne the seid counte lyen yn a Wayte to slee your seid besecher his co[m]moignes and s[er]vauntes and hem dayly assauten and chacen so that they dare not go oute of the seid monast[er]ie and other places Wheche they ben yn but yn grete fere of ther lyves.

The abbots of the fifteenth century

other supplies without their permission. The result was that no person dared 'for dread of death' to disobey them. The abbot described how the gang entered his hunting grounds brazenly, both day and night, and proceeded not only to kill the abbot's deer but also to place the heads of the deer on the 'pales' or fences of the park as trophies. The outcome of 1452 complaint to the Chancellor of England is not clear. Wybert Charlton does not appear to have suffered any serious penalties, and he was clearly at liberty in 1455 when he was sued for debt in the Court of Common Pleas.[20]

A case of manumission

Serfdom was becoming increasingly rare in north Wiltshire during the first half of the fifteenth century as a result of a combination of migration and formal manumission of local families. Although the detailed estate records from Malmesbury Abbey for this period have been lost, one graphic anecdotal account of manumission on a Malmesbury manor has survived. In 1500 an elderly man called John Newman recalled in a deposition to the Star Chamber how in about 1440 he had witnessed the manumission of Thomas Carter, a villein from the manor of Long Newnton.[21] Newman was Carter's servant at the time and was aged about fifteen. The Star Chamber papers are confusing on the chronology, but this event must have taken place during the abbacy of Thomas Bristow. Although prosperous enough to be able to employ a servant, Carter's family were technically servile and subject to legal restrictions and a degree of social stigma. Newman explained that Thomas Carter, towards the end of his life, was driven by an intense wish to free himself and his family from the ignominy of villeinage.

> [...] his said master then bondman to the house of Malmesbury was very desirous to be free and to be manumitted howbeit that he was very aged and had not many years to live, yet nevertheless he had great mind that his heirs and blood after him might be free and that he might be free ere he died and if he might bring that about it would be more joyful to him than any worldly good.[22]

---

20 TNA CP40/776.
21 Leadam, *Select Cases*, 118–28.
22 Leadam, *Select Cases*, 127. The original version was as follows: [...] his said maistre then bond to the house of Malmesberie was very desirous to be free and to be manumised howbe it that he was very aged and had no many yeres to lyve, yet natheless he had great mynd that his heires and blode aftre him m.ight be free and that he might be free ere he died and if he might bring that aboute it wold be more joifull to him then any worldlie goode.

207

Newman recounted how Carter, having collected the money needed to buy his freedom, travelled with his closest friends to Malmesbury. In a great hall of the Abbey the money was carefully counted before the solemn issuing of the deed of manumission by the abbot. Newman was present, and it was his job to bring two capons from Long Newnton so that after the ceremony of manumission Carter and his friends could enjoy a celebratory meal in a nearby tavern. A few days later Carter's newly purchased freedom was promulgated formally at an assembly held in the house of the rector of Long Newnton.

> [...] on the Sunday following, at the parson's house of Newnton whose name was Sir Hugh, a northern man, in presence of the substance of the parish there and then for this cause assembled at the desire of the said Thomas Carter, the said deed was openly read and declared to the understanding of all them that were there by the same Sir Hugh and all the people there enjoyed and were glad that the said Thomas was manumitted, he and heirs and were glad thereof [...][23]

Jack Cade's rebels reach Malmesbury

There is no evidence that the tenants of Malmesbury Abbey were involved in the Peasants' Revolt of 1381. Malmesbury was, however, the setting for violent disturbances in September 1450 during the popular uprising known as Jack Cade's Rebellion which took place during the abbacy of Thomas Bristow. After the uprising the Abbey was used by government justices as a base as they sought to identify and punish Wiltshire rebels. Although the main location of Cade's rebellion was the south-east of England, there was considerable unrest in Wiltshire and the surrounding counties. The single most dramatic act in the west country occurred on 29 June 1450 when the bishop of Salisbury, William Aiscough, was dragged out of the parish church of Edington, taken up a nearby hill and hacked to death by a mob of local people. Disturbances continued across the county over the following weeks, and on 1 September a gang of about forty armed men appeared in Malmesbury intent, according to a local jury reporting the following year, on murder, robbery and revolution. Their leader was John Dyer, who was almost certainly involved in the woollen trade, and from Lacock; the authorities categorised him as a 'yeoman', which suggests that he had some social status.

---

23 Leadam, *Select Cases*, 128. The original version was as follows: [...] on the sonday folowyng, at the parsons hous of Newnton whos name was Sir Hugh a northern man in presence of the substaunce of the parissh there then for this cause assembled at the desire of the said Thomas Carter, the said dede was opinlie red and declared to the understanding of all thaim that were there bi the same Sir Hugh and all the people there enioyed and were glad that the said Thomas was manumysed he and heires and were glad therof [...]

The abbots of the fifteenth century

John Dyer of the parish of Lacock in the county of Wiltshire, yeoman, with many other wrongdoers, insurgents and disturbers of the peace of the lord king, unknown, by force and arms, and arrayed in warlike manner and riotously, to the number of 40 men, *viz* with swords, bows, arrows, hauberks, 'jakkes', 'salettes' and other defensive arms, in the manner of a new insurrection, on the first day of September in the twenty ninth year of the reign of King Henry VI after the conquest, at Malmesbury in the aforesaid county, assembled themselves in divers unlawful conventicles to kill the true subjects of the lord king, and to rob and plunder them of their goods and chattels and things.[24]

The jury stated that before reaching Malmesbury, Dyer's gang had raided the manor of Rowdon, near Chippenham, which was the property of a great nobleman, Lord Robert Hungerford of Moleyns. Hungerford happened to be at Rowdon when Dyer's gang arrived and confronted them; Hungerford was a very aggressive man, whose feud with John Paston is recorded in the *Paston Letters*. Just months earlier, on 28 January 1450, he had sent a thousand men to dispossess Paston of the manor of Gresham; Paston was absent but Hungerford's forces assaulted Paston's wife, Margaret. Perhaps Dyer considered it unwise to challenge Hungerford, who was probably well armed, and decided to move on to the easier target of Malmesbury Abbey. Before he withdrew from Rowdon, Dyer announced his willingness to overthrow the king and personally take on the role as sovereign of England.

[...] and he made known, published and declared divers unlawful and dishonourable words especially sounding against the lord king at Rowdon in the said county of Wiltshire, in the presence of Robert Hungerford of Moleyns, knight, and uttered by the said John according to the examination of the aforesaid Robert, *viz* that if the same wrongdoers and insurgents due to their injuries had wished to elect the same John Dyer as king, whether he wished to accept upon himself the royal status and rule of the aforesaid kingdom or not, and the aforesaid John Dyer said that, if he had been elected and chosen as king of England by the aforesaid wrongdoers and insurgents, he could accept upon himself the status of the aforesaid king, to the great audacity of the others offending in this case or in a worse case, unless a suitable remedy was thereupon made, etc.[25]

Knowing as they surely did of the recent murder of the diocesan bishop, the arrival of Dyer in Malmesbury must have been terrifying for the monks. We do not know the fate of Dyer, but the Abbey was the scene of a government commission into the disturbances in the following year. On 30 July 1451 the commission at Malmesbury issued arrest warrants

24 TNA KB 9/133 no. 39.
25 Ibid.

Malmesbury Abbey 670–1539

for suspected rebels from across Wiltshire and Somerset. There was a preponderance of suspects from the centres of woollen manufacture such as Bradford-on-Avon and Westbury.[26]

A scholarly abbot

Bristow's successor was John Andever who was abbot between 1457 and 1462. Although his abbacy was short-lived his career has some points of interest. As a young Malmesbury monk he was identified as suitable for university study, and in the early 1430s he was sent to Gloucester College to undertake his bachelor's degree. Andever was illegitimate, and the Abbey petitioned Rome to obtain the dispensations needed for him to hold ecclesiastical office despite being born out of wedlock. On 18 August 1437 Pope Eugenius IV granted the necessary permissions.

> To John Andevir, a Benedictine monk of St Mary's, Malmesbury, in the diocese of Salisbury. Dispensation to him, who is S[acrae] T[heologiae] B[accalaureus] and a priest, notwithstanding his illegitimacy as the son of a priest and an unmarried woman, to receive and hold any administrations, offices and benefices, and likewise dignities, even conventual and abbatial, of the said monastery and order [...][27]

Andever undertook doctoral studies at Oxford and was a fellow of Gloucester College between around 1439–41. He was one of several senior monks at Gloucester College who lodged a complaint about the claim of Thomas Knight, a monk of Glastonbury, to have been duly chosen as prior of the College. By July 1441 Andever had obtained his doctorate and was formally commended by the University. Between 1446 and 1457 he served as the prior of the Malmesbury dependency at Pilton in Devon.[28] In his guide to British writers, published in 1559, John Bale listed Andever as the author of two treatises of biblical commentary, including one on the book of Revelation.[29] These works have now been lost, but Bale implied that he had read the treatises, and that the texts made reference to Andever's study of 'profane literature' at Oxford before he decided to concentrate on theology.

As a senior prelate Andever was on occasion required to act as a judge delegate by the papacy. In 1459 he was one of the investigators called upon by Pope Pius II to investigate a case of heresy in Wiltshire. Richard Wodehill or Woodhill, a layman from Little Durnford near Salisbury, was accused of stating 'that the crime of fornication is not a mortal sin,

---

[26] TNA KB 9/134 part II.
[27] Cal. Papal Registers, 1427–1447, 637–41.
[28] *Heads of Houses*, 143.
[29] John Bale, *Scriptorum Illustrium Maioris Brytanniae Catalogus* (Basel, 1559), X.90.

The abbots of the fifteenth century

and that lambs born after the feast of St Mark the Evangelist are not titheable'.[30] Wodehill apparently recanted his heresies and was reconciled to the Church.[31] Shortly after the investigation into the heresy of Wodehill, Abbot John Andever went to Rome on business and in order to visit the pilgrimage sites of the city. He travelled in some style with a retinue of twenty-four servants.[32] However, he died not long after his return from Rome.[33]

Abbot John Ayly and Edward IV

Andever's successor, John Ayly (1462–80), was abbot during a turbulent period of English history as the houses of Lancaster and York vied for the throne. Edward IV, who came to power in violent fashion in February 1461, was known personally to the Malmesbury monks. Just a few months after seizing power and deposing Henry VI, Edward visited the Abbey. He held court in Malmesbury on 9 and 10 September 1461, issuing edicts concerning the control of castles in Wales and the steps needed to strengthen his navy.[34] In January 1466 the king granted his new wife, Elizabeth Woodville, a dower including the annual payment of £20 from the fee farm of Malmesbury.[35] The community witnessed great drama in March 1471 when George, the Duke of Clarence, brought an army to Malmesbury and demanded hospitality for his immediate entourage from the Abbey.[36] This was a pivotal moment in the Wars of the Roses because immediately after leaving Malmesbury, Clarence made public his decision to change sides, renounced his allegiance to his father-in-law, the earl of Warwick (the so-called 'kingmaker') and gave his military support to his brother, Edward IV. Without Clarence's support, Warwick was fatally weakened, and he was defeated and killed at the Battle of Barnet on 14 April 1471.

These were dangerous times. For reasons that are not clear, Abbot John Ayly briefly incurred the displeasure of Edward IV, possibly because the king suspected him of disloyalty. The sequence of events is curious. On 27 November 1476 the king suspended the abbot and gave control of the Abbey to the prior of Bath Abbey for an initial period of five years: the reason given was the blindness and financial incompetence of the abbot.

---

30 Cal. Papal Registers, 1455–1464, 525–49.
31 A. P. Baggs, Jane Freeman and Janet H. Stevenson, 'Durnford', in *History of the County of Wiltshire XV* (London, 1995), 79–93.
32 Cal. Pat. 1452–61, 529.
33 Cal. Pat. 1452–61, 210.
34 Cal. Pat. 1461–7, 40, 99.
35 Cal. Pat. 1461–1467, 481.
36 Clarence wrote to Henry Vernon from Malmesbury on 30 March 1471. See *The Manuscripts of His Grace the Duke of Rutland*, ed. H. C. Maxwell Lyte (London, 1888), 4.

Malmesbury Abbey 670–1539

Protection, for five years, for John Ayly, the abbot, and the convent of Malmesbury; and the abbey and its cells, manors, lands, rents, possessions and goods, which the king has taken into his hands because the abbey has been burdened by bad government and heavy expenses and because the abbot is blind and cannot govern, and commission of the custody of the same to the prior of Bath, so that the issues shall be expended on the sustenance of the abbot and convent and their servants, the relief of the abbey and its cells, the support of annuities, corrodies and pensions and the payment of debts.[37]

Clearly something was badly amiss. But just a month later, on 28 December, the king reversed his decision, and rescinded his mandate to the prior of Bath: Abbot John was back in charge. It seems likely that he was increasingly infirm and did have impaired sight, since in 1478 he sought permission to retire from Pope Sixtus IV. On 21 June of that year the pope agreed to his request and instructed the bishop of Salisbury and the abbot of Stanley to arrange for a transfer of power at Malmesbury.

> To the bishop of Salisbury and the abbot of Stanley in the diocese of Salisbury. Mandate to grant to John, abbot of the monastery of Malmesbury, O[rder] S[aint] B[enedict] immediately belonging to the Roman church, in the diocese of Salisbury, who on account of old age and bodily weakness, loss of sight and grave infirmities, is no longer able to rule the said monastery, etc., that in the event of his resigning, and provision being made of it to another person, he may enjoy and use for life all the *insignia* etc. which he at present enjoys and uses, and moreover to reserve and assign to him a yearly life pension of a third of the fruits etc. of the said monastery, to be paid to him by such person (provided that the latter consent) and by his successors.[38]

What is striking about Ayly's proposed 'pension' is that the abbot could expect to receive for the rest of his life, one third, a huge proportion, of all the income of Malmesbury Abbey. His insistence on the right to wear pontifical insignia has been described as 'a studied concern for the dignity of his position'.[39] Ayly's demands reveal just how grand the self-conceit of heads of houses such as Malmesbury had become by the late fifteenth century. As it happened, the proposed arrangements proved hypothetical because Ayly died before he was able to enjoy his pension.[40]

37 Cal. Pat. 1476–85, 12.
38 Cal. Papal Registers, 1471–1484, 666–9.
39 Martin Heale, 'For the Solace of their Advanced Years: The Retirement of Monastic Superiors in Late Medieval England', The Journal of Medieval Monastic Studies, 8 (2019): 143–67.
40 Cal. Pat. 1476–85, 190.

15

The Tudor Abbey

A sixteenth-century prayer book from Malmesbury Abbey survives in the Bodleian Library, containing an inscription naming its owner as 'Thomas Olston'.[1] The book almost certainly belonged to Thomas Olveston, who was the abbot of Malmesbury for three decades (1480–1510), and his prayer book suggests that he took monastic observance seriously. It included the text of the Malmesbury version of various monastic services: the Office of the Virgin, the Psalms of the Passion, the Penitential Psalms and the Office of the Dead. The book also contained the Litany of the Saints as chanted at Malmesbury and the calendar of feasts that were observed in Tudor Malmesbury, with instructions as to how particularly important feasts should be celebrated,[2] specifying how the commemoration of certain key saints required processional ritual by the community carrying thuribles for the burning of incense and wearing elaborately embroidered copes. There is evidence here of an extraordinary degree of continuity of practice from late Anglo-Saxon to Tudor times. The fragment of the Holy Cross that was the gift of Æthelstan in the tenth century was in the Tudor period still being taken in a solemn procession around the Abbey each year on 14 October. The feasts of two relatively obscure saints – Audoenus and Paternus – were celebrated with the greatest possible solemnity. In both cases these were saints whose relics had been acquired by the Abbey before the Norman Conquest. The Litany of the Saints called upon the intercessory power of many saints but singled out for a double invocation only three saints: Peter, Aldhelm and Paternus. St Paternus of Avranches was an extremely obscure individual, who had been a bishop of Avranches in the sixth century. According to William of Malmesbury, Æthelstan presented the relics of Paternus to the church of Malmesbury, and Olveston's prayer book indicates that the relics had been continuously venerated there for almost six centuries.

Enhancing the conventual church

Thomas Olveston had architectural ambitions, and he installed elaborate stone screens in the church, three of which are still visible: one made of solid stone was placed between the western piers of the crossing

---

1   Bodleian MS Rawl. Liturg. g. 12.
2   Morgan, *English Monastic Litanies of the Saints*, I, 31–2.

Malmesbury Abbey 670–1539

and, nearby, screens with openwork stone tracery were placed in each of the aisles.[3] The central screen was capped with a cornice that was decorated with the royal coat of arms and a series of heraldic emblems. It also contained a doorway, now blocked up, which acts today as a decorative reredos for the high altar. It is difficult to date these structures precisely purely on the basis of an analysis of the tracery of the open stonework of the aisle screens; however, important dating clues can be found in the iconography of the frieze of the central screen. The heraldic devices include a Tudor rose and the pomegranate, the symbol of Catherine of Aragon, indicating that the work was intended to celebrate one of Catherine's two royal weddings: either to Henry VIII (in 1509) or to Henry's older brother, Arthur (in 1501). The other heraldic devices include a ship's rudder which was the symbol used by Robert Willoughby, Steward of King Henry VII's household.[4] The rudder motif allows us to say with certainty that the frieze was erected in honour of the earlier wedding of Catherine and Prince Arthur and we know from other sources that Willoughby played a major role in the ceremonial associated with the arrival of Catherine of Aragon in England, formally welcoming her at Plymouth in October 1501 and escorting her to London prior to her wedding in November. Since both Willoughby and Prince Arthur were dead within a year of the wedding, we can date the work relatively precisely to the years 1501–2, during the abbacy of Olveston. The frieze was a demonstration of loyalty to the Tudor dynasty. The screens also indicate an interest in the monastic liturgy because they were designed to provide a grand setting for processional ritual.[5]

In addition to improving the church building, Olveston had to respond to the disastrous collapse of the huge spire that sat on top of the central tower. The fall of the spire is an important but somewhat mysterious topic that was commented upon by John Leland.

> There were in the abbey churchyard three churches: the abbey church a right magnificent thing, where were two steeples, one that had a mighty high pyramid, and fell dangerously *in hominum memoria*, and since was not reedified: it stood in the middle of the transept of the church, and was a mark to all the country about.[6]

---

3   The best account of the building programme is in D. Robinson and R. Lea, *Malmesbury Abbey: History, Archaeology, and Architecture to Illustrate the Significance of the South Aisle Screen* (London, 2002).

4   Barry Dent, 'The Royal Arms and the Frieze in Malmesbury Abbey', *WANHM*, 117 (2022): 87–92.

5   Robinson and Lea, *Malmesbury Abbey*, 83.

6   Leland, *Itinerary*, I 131. The original version was as follows: Ther were in th'abbay chirch yard 3. chirches: th'abbay chirch a right magnificent thing, wher were 2. steples, one that had a mightie high pyramis, and felle daungerusly in hominum memoria, and sins was not reedified: it stode in

The Tudor Abbey

According to Leland, the central pyramidal spire fell 'in hominum memoria', that is within living memory, and by this he presumably meant that elderly people who were still alive in the early 1540s had witnessed the event. This almost certainly dates the collapse to the period of the abbacy of Olveston (1480–1510). In the Victorian period some commentators concluded that the fall of the spire also caused the destruction of the central tower, and that this was so catastrophic that it led the monks to abandon much of the conventual church and move their choir to the nave. Subsequent scholarship has rejected this idea.[7] The spire, made of wood and lead, stood on a stone tower, and it is perfectly possible to imagine that the community patched up the damage to the tower stonework caused by the fall of the spire, allowing the whole conventual church to remain in use up to the Dissolution. There is no evidence for the relocation of Aldhelm's shrine before the Dissolution, which would have been necessary if the eastern end of the church had been abandoned. There is, therefore, no reason to think that the community abandoned the eastern end of the church either during the life of Olveston or in the years that followed his death in 1510.

Allegations in the Star Chamber against the Abbey

During Olveston's abbacy two complaints were made to the Star Chamber concerning the oppressive behaviour of monks: in 1494 John Culford from Brinkworth protested about the way that he and his family had been violently evicted from their cottage and smallholding; while in 1500 Robert Carter of Malmesbury accused the abbot of falsely imprisoning him, and seizing his goods on the grounds that he was a villein of the Abbey.[8] The cases suggest a high degree of tension between the Abbey and local people as the monks sought to generate as much income as possible from the estate. These cases also illustrate a remarkable degree of resourcefulness on the part of the plaintiffs, who were able to get a royal court in London to consider their grievances against the monks. Culford informed the Star Chamber that he had taken up a copyhold tenancy in Brinkworth on 12 April 1474, explaining that this form of tenancy gave him limited rights to pursue redress using common law processes.[9]

---

the midle of the transeptum of the chirch, and was a marke to al the countre about.

7 For an account of this debate, see Robinson and Lea, *Malmesbury Abbey*, 41.

8 Leadam, *Select Cases*, 118–28.

9 Leadam, *Select Cases*, 46. The original version was as follows: Seing that your pouer liegeman hath doon & made grete byldinges and costes upon & in the same Messuage and landes in divers weyes and hath implayed his said lands to his moost avauntage & profite more than it hath ben before by his grete labour of husbondry to his grete coste & charge […].

215

Malmesbury Abbey 670–1539

Culford paid the large sum of £4 6s 8d as an 'entry fine' following the death of his father who had held the cottage and associated land before him: he thus bought the right to hold the land for his lifetime by lease. Under the obedientiary system, Brinkworth rents and fees were paid not to the abbot but to the monk who held the office of kitchener. Brother John Wotton was the kitchener in 1494 and Culford's complaint was therefore directed against him. Culford claimed that in the two decades since he had become the kitchener's tenant he had made many improvements to the property, thereby increasing its value.

> Seeing that your poor liegeman hath done & made great buildings and costs upon & in the same messuage and lands in divers ways and hath employed his said lands to his most advantage & profit more than it hath been before by his great labour of husbandry to his great cost & charge [...][10]

Culford implied that Wotton had ordered his eviction, intending to lease out the improved property to a new tenant at a higher rent. Motivated by his 'covetous disposition' Wotton sent servants to Culford's cottage armed with swords, bows and arrows and clubs. The servants assaulted his wife and children and 'would have slain' him if he had not managed to escape. The outcome of Culford's complaint is not known.

Six years later, in 1500, the Abbey was again obliged to defend its behaviour in the Star Chamber when a Malmesbury man called Robert Carter claimed that he was falsely imprisoned by Abbot Thomas Olveston on the spurious grounds that he was a villein. Carter was clearly a relatively prosperous man, and his complaint stated that the abbot's men seized from him livestock worth £20: five bullocks, ten cows, nine calves and 109 sheep. In defending himself Carter and others recounted the story, told in the previous chapter, about how his grandfather has bought manumission from serfdom many years before. The abbot and his servants were accused by Carter of various nefarious practices, including the deceitful acquisition of his family's manumission documents, which made it difficult for him to prove his free status. At the time of his complaint, he was still kept in chains in the monastery prison.

> The said riotous and misruled persons by the Commandment of the said now Abbot then and there unto your Orator made assault and took and imprisoned him and so from his house carried him into prison as a thief into the said monastery and there put him both hands and feet in strait stocks and ponderous Irons and tied him to a great new chain and so yet keepeth him in that intolerable duress.[11]

10 Leadam, *Select Cases*, 45–6.
11 Leadam, *Select Cases*, 120. The original version was as follows: The seid riotouse and mysruled persons by the Commaundement of the seid now

The Tudor Abbey

Carter was not allowed bail and was not permitted visits from friends and family. However, he was resourceful enough to smuggle his complaint out of the Abbey prison, and had literate associates who were able to frame his statement of grievance in the correct legal form, and as a result Olveston was obliged to respond to the Star Chamber. The abbot did not dispute the facts of the imprisonment but claimed that the custody was justified because Carter was indeed an unfree tenant of the Abbey whose claims to the previous enfranchisement of his family were false. It is not clear what precisely Olveston hoped to achieve in this case: perhaps he wanted to force Carter to buy his freedom and thereby raise some much-needed cash for the Abbey. His attempt to establish that Carter was a bondman of the Abbey failed; although the Star Chamber papers do not record the outcome of the case, we do know that by Hilary Term 1502 Robert Carter 'yeoman' was a free man and was able to sue the abbot for defamation.[12]

The death of a poacher

The grounds of Cowfold, the abbot's country house, were still being used as a private hunting park at the beginning of the sixteenth century and continued to be of great interest to local poachers. Thomas Olveston clearly felt vulnerable and employed a team of guards to protect his park. These facts emerge from the records of a coroner's inquest held at Malmesbury on 26 February 1509.[13] The jury viewed the dead body of Andrew Ryche, a local blacksmith, who had been killed during a nocturnal poaching raid at Cowfold that had gone wrong. Park security was the responsibility of a man apparently named after the patron saint of Malmesbury – Aldelm Tovy – described at the inquest as 'keeper and parker of the park of Thomas, abbot of the monastery of the Blessed Mary and St Aldelm'. On the evening of 5 February 'around the eleventh hour after midday', Tovy sent out a team of three men to tour the grounds and look out for intruders. They came across a gang of four armed poachers.

> [...] and for the supervision, conservation and safe keeping of the same park and of the deer and rabbits [...] John Wytte, John Shyngels and Giles Saundyrs, had been perambulating around that park [...] and had found in that park a certain Richard Bayly [...] the elder, husbandman, Richard Bayly [...] the younger, husbandman, Thomas

---

Abbot then and ther in to your Oratoure made assaute and him toke and imprisoned and so from his howse carried him in prisoun as a theff in to the seid monasterie and ther put hym both handes and fete in strayte stockes and ponderous Irrons and tied hym to a great new cheyn and so yet kepyth him in that intolerable durese.

12   TNA CP40/959.
13   TNA KB 9/451.

Malmesbury Abbey 670–1539

Mey [...] weaver, and Andrew Ryche [...] smith, by force and arms, arrayed in warlike manner [...] without licence and against the will of the aforesaid abbot and keeper in driving and chasing the deer and rabbits of the same abbot, then being in the same park, and catching rabbits without the licence and against the will of the same abbot and aforesaid keeper [...][14]

The account of the members of the Cowfold guards was that they challenged the poachers and ordered them to leave, but the poachers stood their ground and attacked the abbot's servants. A fight ensued.

[...] the same Richard, Richard, Thomas and Andrew, carrying out and continuing their malice and wicked proposition with aforethought, and breaking the peace of the said lord king, by force and arms, aforesaid, and against the peace of the same lord king, made an assault upon the aforesaid John Wytte, John Shyngels and Giles, and beat, wounded and mistreated them, in such a way that they were in despair of their life, by which the same John Wytte, John Shyngels and Giles, both in defence of their life, and for the safe keeping of the park and the aforesaid deer and rabbits, defended themselves against the said Richard, Richard, Thomas and Andrew then and there.[15]

John Shyngels claimed that he was 'furiously assaulted' by Andrew Ryche, and so in self-defence took his bow and an arrow and shot Ryche, killing him instantly.

And the aforesaid Andrew then and there pursued the aforesaid John Shyngels so violently and furiously that the same John Shyngels, for the salvation of his life and for the defence of the aforesaid park, deer and rabbits against the said Andrew, thus furiously assaulted, shot an arrow and struck the same Andrew with one bow and one arrow, which he then held in his hands, the same hour, day and year, in his defence on the left side of the flank of the same Andrew, from which shot and blow of the arrow the same Andrew then and there died.[16]

The jury accepted the account given by John Shyngels who was not punished for the killing in self-defence of the blacksmith and poacher, Andrew Ryche.

An unhappy community

There were signs that all was not well in Malmesbury Abbey when the long abbacy of Thomas Olveston came to an end with his death in early 1510. The size of the community had shrunk considerably: we know that

14 Ibid.
15 Ibid.
16 Ibid.

The Tudor Abbey

in the abbatial election of 1462 twenty-nine monks had taken part as electors, but in the election of 1510 only eighteen monks participated.[17] The outcome was contested, indicating the existence of antagonistic factions among the community. One group claimed that a monk called Richard Frampton had been duly elected, and Frampton received royal approval as new abbot in June 1510. However, other monks considered that the election process was flawed, and they proceeded to elect John Codrington as abbot, while at the same time appealing for an arbitration to Pope Julius II. A protracted process of papal investigation began, and for many months there were two rival abbots of Malmesbury. Papal delegates eventually found in favour of Frampton, who obtained control of the Abbey's revenues in November 1511.[18] We know little more about Frampton, who died in February 1515 after just over three years in charge.

Richard Camme was chosen as abbot in March 1515, and he undoubtedly faced severe financial challenges. The great bulk of the Abbey estate had been leased out on extremely long leases at fixed rents: as a result, the monks played only a marginal role in the administration of their property, and there was little they could do to increase their revenues. The leasing out of the demesne lands in the early sixteenth century can be illustrated by the case of Purton. Documents submitted to the Star Chamber relating to a dispute in 1548 outlined the terms of the lease for Purton issued in 1515 by Richard Camme shortly after he became abbot. The manor was rented out to Richard and Margaret Pulley and their children: Ambrose, Edmund, Isabel and Giles. The lease would be held until the death of the person who lived the longest, and, for this period, control of the manor was completely handed over to the family. Richard Pulley and his immediate descendants had bought the right to act as lords of the manor; consequently the family was entitled to the rents and services of all those holding property in the manor, and all the 'appurtenances' including fines levied at the manor court and customary payments such as the 'heriot' due on the death of a customary tenant or 'merchet' levied when daughters of customary tenants were wed. All the tithes due to the church of Purton were to be paid to Pulley and his family. In return they paid £9 a year in rent for the manor and £7 for the 'spiritualities' due to the church. To all intents and purposes Malmesbury Abbey was removed from the day-to-day running of the manor.[19]

There are relatively few sources relating to the early years of Abbot Richard Camme's abbacy. We do know that in the early months of 1521 he welcomed a particularly distinguished pilgrim to the shrine of St Aldhelm. Edward Stafford, the third duke of Buckingham, was an obsessive visitor of holy places. His visit to Malmesbury took place shortly

---

17 Watkin, 'Abbey of Malmesbury', 183.
18 L. & P. Hen. VIII, i, 292.
19 Anonymous, 'Purton. A Case in Star Chamber', *WANHM*, 33 (1903–4): 146–7.

Malmesbury Abbey 670–1539

before his arrest for treason and execution in May 1521.[20] In September 1522 the Abbey was obliged to make a grant of £200 to the Crown to assist in the costs of the king's war against France. The demands were means tested with Malmesbury placed in a middling category in terms of wealth: the richer neighbouring house of Gloucester paid over three times as much while Bath Abbey paid only £66 13s 4d.[21]

In 1527 a great scandal occurred which was extremely well documented and sheds a piercing light on the internal life of the Abbey. In November of that year Abbot John Islip of Westminster, in his role as the senior president of the chapter of Black Monks of England, received news that violence had broken out at Malmesbury: Abbot Richard Camme had been attacked by some of his own monks. Islip called upon William Malvern, abbot of Gloucester, to investigate, and on 20 December a tribunal was held in the Malmesbury chapter house. Malvern's report has survived among the state papers of Henry VIII, and it portrays a community in deep crisis.[22] All members of the community were invited to make witness statements and the notaries recorded first the testimony of Abbot Richard Camme who claimed that many of his monks failed to give him due obedience.

> [The abbot] confessed that he does not command the obedience he is owed: many of his fellow monks are not obedient and are contumacious and rebellious against obedience, spurning authority in word and deed alike, and when they have committed serious sins they defend them obstinately and resist customary corrections. And that there are some owing obedience to him who favour and even defend [such people], who have defended the aforesaid monks in the aforesaid [practices]. And also that there are some owing obedience to him who have committed serious sins, and for the aforesaid reasons their [sins] still remain uncorrected and unpunished.[23]

The abbot then recounted how serious violence broke out in the Abbey on 10 November 1527.

> Recently, on the eve of the last Feast of St Martin, about seven after noon, it happened that eight monks of the said monastery, armed in a hostile manner, viz. with bows, arrows, swords, clubs and other offensive weapons, laid siege to the doors of the abbot there, intending to break them down and cruelly threatening the abbot aforesaid with the danger of death. They broke into the abbot's prison there, and snatched out two monks who had been thrust in there for their offences,

[20] G. W. Bernard, *The Late Medieval Church* (Princeton, 2012), 136.
[21] L. & P. Hen. VIII, iii, 1047.
[22] TNA SP 1/45 fol. 224–32. The manuscript was transcribed by William Pantin and published in 1937. See *Chapters of the English Black Monks*, III, 124–36.
[23] *Chapters of the English Black Monks*, III, 126.

The Tudor Abbey

and freed them from the aforesaid prison. And those who perpetrated the aforesaid wicked deeds are: the prime movers Thomas Gloucester and John London, with the aid and assent of Thomas Purton, Walter Bristow, William Bisley, Robert Sodbury, William Winchcombe, Thomas Frocester and Robert Cissetur and Richard Glastonbury.[24]

For the abbot this attack was the culmination of a long sequence of outrageous acts by his monks. Each rebel monk had a history of indiscipline and Camme proceeded to itemise their offences prior to the events of November 1527, starting with the worst two offenders

> And that the aforesaid Thomas Gloucester was often found breaking his vows, rashly putting off his habit, viz. twice at Gloucester and once at Dursley, and climbing the walls in full view more than forty times in the town of Malmesbury with illicit persons and whores, and committing open theft, viz. robbing his own master and surreptitiously taking clothes and bedclothes belonging to his fellow monks, and carrying weapons every day against his religious vows, and menacing his fellow brothers with death. And that John London aforesaid seriously raised violent hands against his fellow brothers, harming and wounding them both in church and in the dormitory. And that he committed the crime of vow-breaking three times in the last two years.[25]

'Vow breaking' was presumably a euphemism for a breach of the vow of chastity, and other monks were accused of sexual misbehaviour.

> [...] Richard Ashton and Walter Bristow, who took off their habits three or four times at their pleasure, without licence from the abbot, [at] their own monastery and [at] the town of Bristol and other places, for example at Braydon and other suspicious places, frequenting whores and having them in their company, to the scandal of the monastery aforesaid and the censure of their whole region.[26]

Richard Ashton was the almoner, and he is one of the few monks whose lives we can trace after the Dissolution. In 1548, several years after the closure of the Abbey, Ashton was called to be a witness in a Star Chamber investigation into the ownership of the manor of Purton, formerly part of the Abbey estate. He stated that he was eighteen or nineteen years old in 1515 and had been a professed monk of Malmesbury for about three years before that. From this we can calculate that he took vows at the extremely young age of fifteen or sixteen and was aged about thirty or thirty-one during the 1527 visitation.[27] Ashton and Bristow were accused of having prostitutes 'in their company at Braydon'. This is probably a reference to

24 Ibid.
25 *Chapters of the English Black Monks*, III, 126–7.
26 *Chapters of the English Black Monks*, III, 127.
27 Anonymous, 'Purton. A Case in Star Chamber', 145–68, 199–235.

Malmesbury Abbey 670–1539

the manor house at Purton which was located in the Forest of Bradon. As we have seen this was leased out to the Pulley family, and it seems that they often entertained the monks overnight at the manor house and perhaps turned a blind eye to their indiscretions. Two more monks were accused of sexual misbehaviour at Purton.

> And that Thomas Purton and Robert Elmore broke their vows at Purton for a day and a night without the licence of their superior, and that they committed theft, surreptitiously taking a gold piece from the purse of their fellow brother John Combe.[28]

The list of previous faults of the 'prime movers' who had participated in the riot concluded with accusations of indiscipline against Richard Glastonbury and Robert Cissetur.

> And that Richard Glastonbury was convicted of incontinence, and went round the town and left the precinct of the monastery without the licence of his superior, and is contumacious and disobedient, spurning the authority of his superior and altogether disregarding the injunctions laid on him, and that he hears confessions without the abbot's licence. And Robert Cissetur is similarly and habitually liable to get drunk.[29]

Having named and accused the worst offenders of an extraordinary range of breaches of discipline, the abbot turned on his lieutenants – the prior and subprior – and questioned their competence and rectitude.

> And that Philip Bristol the subprior is not suitable or fit for the aforesaid office, because he is weak and faint-hearted. And that Dom John Codrington the prior exercises his office slackly and negligently, often frivolously pleading his lack of power, and feeds and keeps hunting dogs.[30]

The abbot criticised by name about a third of the Abbey's monks, concluding his testimony with general comments on the lax and questionable behaviour of his brethren.

> And that the monks of the aforesaid monastery wear linen shirts and buckled boots. And that they do not eat in the refectory in the proper manner or have a reading there as the Rule lays down. And that suspicious women come in and are received into the infirmary.[31]

The abbot of Gloucester then turned to the other monks and invited them to testify. No one denied that violence had taken place against the abbot on

---

28   *Chapters of the English Black Monks*, III, 127.
29   Ibid.
30   Ibid.
31   Ibid.

The Tudor Abbey

10 November, and some monks agreed that there was a group of younger monks who were out of control. There was, however, little sympathy for Abbot Richard Camme. Not one monk spoke up in his support; instead, they portrayed him as an overbearing, capricious, incompetent leader who had, to some extent, caused the breakdown in discipline by his own behaviour. The prior, John Codrington (the man who had almost become abbot in 1510), did not challenge the idea that some monks were badly behaved and violent: he specifically accused Brother John London of throwing stones at the door of his chamber while he was in residence.[32] However, the main thrust of Prior Codrington's testimony concerned not the level of indiscipline but the failings of the abbot and the shortcomings of the religious life of the Abbey: the abbot wrongly kept the property of deceased monks for himself; chapter meetings were held in English rather than in Latin; monks were permitted to sleep in church; matins were rushed; the lack of a clock meant that services did not take place at the right time; the rule of silence was not observed properly either in the dormitory or the refectory. The prior implied that the blame for all these faults rested with the abbot. Other monks endorsed these points about the poor observance of the Rule and failure to respect Malmesbury traditions: the requirement for sacred readings in the refectory was not being met; monks saying mass lacked chalices and altar boys; the food in the refectory was inadequate, and junior monks were badly fed; on feast days there was a failure to provide extra bread and 'sufficient beer according to the old custom'. Several monks expressed unhappiness about the abbot's harsh discipline, which involved the use of arbitrary imprisonment and corporal punishment. One monk, John Horsley, described how in the past 'he had been unjustly imprisoned by the abbot'; several others complained about the abbot's use of violence against them.

> Thomas Gloucester: 'the abbot is over-cruel in the misericord, and [...] fights against his own people, wounding them with his staff.'[33]

> Robert Cissetur [...] deposes that the abbot corrects monks cruelly and in such a way as to cause offence to them.[34]

> Thomas Tewkesbury [...] deposed that [...] the same monks are threatened and otherwise troubled by the lord abbot. And that the abbot is harsh and [not] approachable, and that in correcting [monks] he is at times over-cruel, at times slack, and that the monks are quarrelsome and recalcitrant in chapter, and that the lord abbot does not treat the older [monks] well.[35]

---

32 *Chapters of the English Black Monks*, III, 127–8.
33 *Chapters of the English Black Monks*, III, 131.
34 *Chapters of the English Black Monks*, III, 129.
35 Ibid.

Malmesbury Abbey 670–1539

Several monks were keen to highlight the malign influence over the abbot of a local woman called Alice Taylor, who could frequently be seen around the Abbey and who gossiped about them with the abbot.

> Robert Frampton, steward, infirmarer, and gardener, deposed that 'Alice Taylor, who lives in the town of Malmesbury, is seditious and tells the abbot many idle tales to the detriment of the fellow brothers of the said monastery'.[36]

> Richard Glastonbury, sub-kitchener, stated that 'Alice Taylor possesses four bowls and the property of deceased monks'.[37]

> Thomas Stanley sub-sacristan described 'the cruelty of Alice Taylor in moving the abbot to anger with the brothers'.[38]

> Anthony Malmesbury, sub-sacristan and sub-almoner stated that Alice Taylor 'is quite often in the abbot's kitchen and brewhouse'.[39]

The monks' testimony sheds some interesting light on domestic arrangements in the Abbey in the 1520s. The dormitory was divided up by partitions into separate bedrooms, described as being not in keeping with the Rule because they were 'closed up and indecent'. The kitchener was criticised on the grounds that 'he does not take his repose in the dormitory'. The guesthouse was poorly maintained and as a result, guests were allowed to stay in rooms in the dormitory. The infirmary was also in a poor state and lacked suitable bedding. The system persisted of two main dining rooms: the meat-free refectory and the misericord where meat was permitted. In theory the rule established in the thirteenth century still applied that there was a minimum 'quorum' of monks who must dine each day in the refectory. The more conscientious brethren complained that this rule was not being observed.

It is difficult to know what exactly to make of this extraordinary document, but it would be simplistic to see it as evidence of institutional 'decadence'. Certainly, some monks were accused of behaving extremely badly, and the abbot's harsh discipline had, it seems, contributed to the riot of 10 November 1527. However, the picture was complex: several monks were conscientious and were clearly frustrated because aspects of religious observance were lax. They wanted more chalices and altar boys so that daily masses could be said properly and they were unhappy that the traditional quorum for monks in the meat-free refectory had fallen into abeyance. These observant members of the community called

---

[36] *Chapters of the English Black Monks*, III, 130.
[37] *Chapters of the English Black Monks*, III, 131.
[38] *Chapters of the English Black Monks*, III, 132.
[39] *Chapters of the English Black Monks*, III, 130–1.

The Tudor Abbey

for silence in the dormitory and refectory and proper sacred readings in the refectory.

We have the ruling of the abbot of Gloucester delivered to the whole community gathered in the chapter house on 20 December 1527.[40] It was an even-handed verdict. Abbot William Malvern excommunicated six monks for their breaches of the Rule, but at the same time, he severely admonished Abbot Richard Camme for his harsh and incompetent rule and obliged him to promise to change his conduct and address the legitimate grievances of the community. We do not know the names of the excommunicated monks, but presumably they included the two rebel ringleaders: Thomas Gloucester and John London. It is clear that the excommunications were lifted after a period of penance because some of the named miscreants took part in the abbatial election of 1533 and some received pensions at the suppression of the house in 1539.

Leland's visit in 1533

Abbot Richard Camme died in early 1533. Once again, the vacancy prompted considerable disharmony within the community as different factions vied to ensure the election of their favoured candidate. It was at about this time that the antiquary, John Leland, made his first visit to Malmesbury, as part of a regional tour of monastic libraries, and armed with a royal mandate allowing him to take interesting manuscripts for the king's library. He went first to Glastonbury, and from there to Wells, Bath, Malmesbury and Cirencester. Leland's notes from the visit portray the community in uncomplimentary terms, and he was particularly unimpressed that the monks had largely forgotten about William of Malmesbury. He asked where the great historian was buried, but nobody knew and only 'one or two' of them had ever heard of him.

> Yet when I was at Malmesbury recently and inquired for his burial-place, such was his obscurity among his own monks that only one or two of them even remembered his name.[41]

The monks had forgotten about William of Malmesbury but were keen to show Leland items connected with St Aldhelm: liturgical vestments, his book of Psalms and a curious altar.

> He [Aldhelm] lived under Ine, most powerful king of the West Saxons, and is buried at Maildunum, where the monks still display mementos of their patron: a holy vestment he wore when he used to celebrate mass; besides, the psaltery of David, written in rather long Saxon letters; third, an altar, though a very small one, of serpentine marble,

---

40   *Chapters of the English Black Monks*, III, 133–4.
41   John Leland, *Commentarii de* Scriptoribus *Britannicis* (Oxford, 1709), 196.

Malmesbury Abbey 670–1539

bound in silver, on which a Latin inscription may be seen. These things I recently saw at Meildunum.[42]

It is possible that the vestments and the altar on display were associated with the miracles that Aldhelm supposedly worked during and after his trip to Rome. William of Malmesbury recorded how a chasuble worn by Aldhelm in Rome had been saved from being dropped on the floor when it was caught miraculously on a sunbeam. The chasuble was still visible in William's day and was lovingly preserved by the monks.[43] Leland was unimpressed by the Aldhelm memorabilia, noting that he had 'discovered things far more remarkable' than these items in the form of several ancient and rare manuscripts.

The monks were in no position to challenge Leland's royal licence and he undoubtedly removed several rare manuscripts from the library during his 1533 visit. It is possible to identify four texts that were probably appropriated by Leland at this time; doubtless there were others. One item that he almost certainly took was a collection of the letters of Alcuin which survives today in a composite British Library manuscript, containing marginal notes in Leland's handwriting.[44] The same British Library manuscript also contains a work by Junilius, which may have been Aldhelm's own copy and could constitute an instance of a text that was in Malmesbury continuously from the seventh century to the sixteenth century.[45] We know that Leland had seen this work at Malmesbury and it seems likely that he took it away after his visit. A third item that Leland probably appropriated was a tenth-century copy of Milred of Worcester's *Sylloge*, a work which was known by Faricius and William of Malmesbury. Leland's *Collectanea* contains a set of extracts from the *Sylloge*, with a note that he had come across the work 'in a most ancient book of sacred epigrams when I recently visited Malmesbury, a monastery in the county of Salisbury, or, as it is now called, Wiltshire'.[46] A fragment of the *Sylloge* manuscript survives, with annotations by Leland, and is held by the University of Illinois Urbana Library.[47]

---

42 Ibid.
43 *GP* I V 218.5 (ed. Winterbottom 551).
44 BL MS Cotton Tiberius A. xv. Leland's extracts from this work were curated in *Collectanea*. See Leland, *Collectanea*, II 3.
45 Aldhelm's knowledge of this manuscript was discussed in Chapter Two. The manuscript also forms part of Cotton Tiberius A. xv.
46 Leland, *Commentarii*, 134
47 The history of the Urbana manuscript is obscure. It turned up, with no previous provenance history, in Berlin in 1934. Carley and Petitmengin considered likely that Leland removed this manuscript from Malmesbury in 1533 and eventually sent it to a scholar or publishing house on the continent. See Carley, James P. and Petitmengin, Pierre, 'Pre-Conquest Manuscripts from

The Tudor Abbey

Leland's fourth and best documented act of appropriation from Malmesbury Abbey in 1533 was of a manuscript of the works of the early Christian writer, Tertullian. The Malmesbury manuscript was sent by Leland to the humanist scholar, Beatus Rhenanus, who lived in Sélestat in Alsace. A covering letter has survived, in which Leland explained precisely how he had found the manuscript in Malmesbury, giving a summary of the early history of the monastery.[48]

> If, moreover, you desire to know where this copy was found, learn now. There is in the province Severia of *Britannia Prima*, close to the shores of the river Avon, a place formerly named Bladunum, a city of which the ramparts are still visible, although half destroyed. The Saxons, as Bede attests in his Ecclesiastical History, next called it Ingelburne. But once the Irishman Maildulph had opened a grammar school and built a monastery with the support of Ine, king of the West Saxons, and of Agilbert, bishop of Winchester, the city began to be called Maidulphsbyri, that is to say, the town of Maidulph, a name that it still retains today, although distorted.[49]

Leland was wrong to state that Bede gave the 'Saxon' name of the place as 'Ingelburne', and had forgotten that he had come across this information in another source, the *Eulogium*. He speculated as to how the Tertullian manuscript had reached Malmesbury in the first place.

> Here in the middle of other monuments of venerable antiquity I found the Tertullian that is now sent to you; as I deduce from various conjectures, it was brought from Italy to Britain, eight hundred years ago, by Aldhelm, the immediate successor of Maidulph as the head of the abbey, who then became bishop of Sherborne of the Durotriges.[50]

It seems unlikely that Aldhelm had brought the manuscript to Malmesbury from Italy; Leland was correct, however, to think that the manuscript was of great importance, as it contained material by Tertullian that was not otherwise known. In 1550 the Froben company published a new edition

---

Malmesbury Abbey and John Leland's Letter to Beatus Rhenanus concerning a Lost Copy of Tertullian's Works', *Anglo-Saxon England*, 33 (2004): 209.

[48] In 1983 the French scholar, Pierre Petitmengin announced that he had discovered a letter from Leland to Rhenanus in the Humanist Library of Sélestat. See Pierre Petitmengin, 'John Leland, Beatus Rhenanus et le Tertullien de Malmesbury', *Studia Patristica*, 19 (1989): 53–60. The letter was published in 2003. It is dated 1 June 1539, six years after Leland had removed the Tertullian. See Pierre Petitmengin and James P. Carley, 'Malmesbury-Sélestat-Malines: les tribulations d'une manuscrit de Tertullien au milieu de XVe siècle', *Annuaire des amis de la bibiothèque humaniste de Sélestat* (2003): 63–74.

[49] Petitmengin and Carley, 'Malmesbury-Sélestat-Malines', 63–74.

[50] Ibid.

of Tertullian's works, and the editor, Sigismond Gelen, acknowledged that this edition made use of the Malmesbury manuscript, and that he was indebted to John Leland. By this time Leland was suffering from serious mental illness, as Gelen clearly knew.

> At last John Leland, an antiquary who deserves better health, provided an exemplar from furthest Britain, found in the most ancient monastery of Malmesbury, in which you could wish for nothing more. It was so complete that it was lacking only a few [of the lost] books.[51]

Unfortunately, the Malmesbury manuscript that Leland sent to Alsace is now lost, but the additional Tertullian material it contained was preserved as a result of the Gelen edition. If Leland had not removed the text from Malmesbury, there is a good chance that it would have been destroyed in the aftermath of the Dissolution.

Thomas Cromwell and the last days of Malmesbury Abbey

Leland's visit in 1533 coincided with a succession crisis at Malmesbury Abbey following the death of Abbot Richard Camme in April or early May 1533. Thomas Cromwell took energetic steps to fix the abbatial election in order to ensure the appointment of a monk loyal to him called Robert Frampton. The election was acrimonious. A majority of the monks, including the prior, John Codrington, initially supported the kitchener, Walter Bristow, and opposed Frampton. Cromwell was not interested in their views, but Bristow had some influential supporters at court including the Lord Chancellor, Thomas Audley. In June Cromwell directed one of his key agents, Rowland Lee, to go to Malmesbury and force the monks to accept Frampton. Once there Lee encountered considerable resistance: the monks claimed that they were entitled to a free ballot and reminded Lee that they too had powerful friends. Cromwell's man had to make three visits before he was able finally to impose his master's will on the recalcitrant community. Fortunately for Cromwell, Lee found out about the visitation report of 1527 which identified Walter Bristow as a particularly ill-disciplined member of the community. Having obtained a copy of the report, Lee wrote triumphantly to Cromwell, informing him that the visitation findings were so shocking that they would 'stop the mouths' of the supporters of Bristow.

> I have sent you secretly a book sent me by the abbot of Gloucester, late visitor of this house, by which you will see the unthrifty and naughty

---

[51] Carley and Petitmengin, 'Pre-Conquest Manuscripts from Malmesbury Abbey', 219.

The Tudor Abbey

fashion of the cosynner[52] and his apostasy[53], whereby he is infamis, and infamibus non dantur dignitates. If this is shown to the Lord Chancellor, it will stop their mouths, and make them ashamed of meddling.[54]

Lee helpfully annotated the report so that Cromwell could see which of the monks, named and shamed in 1527, supported Bristow and which ones were the friends of Frampton. Armed with this information, Cromwell got his way and Robert Frampton was elected. Cromwell then demanded that the new abbot should pay a handsome fee for the privilege of having his appointment confirmed and that members of Cromwell's patronage network should be allowed to benefit from the Abbey's resources. The abbot understood what was expected of him: in May 1534 Frampton sent the first instalment of 100 marks in return for the ratification of his appointment, and in an accompanying letter he sought to ingratiate himself by offering sinecures to those in Cromwell's circle. One 'Mr Watkyns' was to be offered the position of 'receiver' in order to please Cromwell,[55] and in the same letter Frampton offered to provide Sir Thomas Arundell with a lucrative post. In another, undated letter the abbot discussed again how he could meet Cromwell's expectations relating to the distribution of sinecures at Malmesbury, concluding the letter with a commitment to follow Cromwell's in-person instructions at the forthcoming Parliament meeting where, 'I will wait on you to know your pleasure'.[56]

The *Valor Ecclesiasticus* survey of 1535 provides information about the economic situation of the Abbey during the abbacy of Frampton.[57] On the face of it, Malmesbury Abbey was a wealthy institution with an annual gross income of £891, which placed it in the top 10% of monasteries in terms of wealth.[58] However, all was not well. Since almost all the Abbey lands had been leased out, the Abbey had virtually no capacity to increase the productivity of its estates or increase their revenue by raising rents. Income from pilgrims had dried up: the total annual value of donations from visitors to Aldhelm's shrine amounted to a paltry 4s. 4d. a year. The *Valor* survey identified the Abbey's costs which included salaries paid to fifteen laymen, and some of these posts were clearly parasitic in nature. The *Valor* listed Sir Edward Baynton as the steward

---

52 L. & P. Hen. VIII, vi, 305. Bristow held the post of kitchener. Lee used the term 'cosynner' which was a version of the equivalent French word 'cuisinier'.

53 In 1527 Bristow was accused of taking off his monastic habit and dressing as a layman which was seen as temporary form of 'apostacy' or renunciation of his monastic vows.

54 L. & P. Hen. VIII, vi, 295–305.

55 L. & P. Hen. VIII, v, 459–70.

56 L. & P. Hen. VIII, x, 371–91.

57 Valor Ecclesiasticus II (London, 1814), 118–22.

58 Malmesbury Abbey was 36th out of 553 religious houses surveyed in the *Valor*.

Malmesbury Abbey 670–1539

of the monastery and Sir Thomas Arundell as the receiver general: each man was paid an annual salary of £6 13s 4d. These were sinecures paid from the Abbey treasury to absentee courtiers. Other burdens evident from the *Valor* include the requirement to pay Queen Anne Boleyn £20 a year as part of her dower and the need to maintain at the Abbey's expense three pensioners: two 'corrodians' designated by the Crown and another retired courtier.

Perhaps, at least in a small way, Abbot Frampton's personal life compounded the Abbey's financial woes. In a Star Chamber case heard long after the Dissolution several witnesses claimed that Abbot Frampton was on extremely friendly terms with a local woman, Margaret Pulley, a widow who held Purton manor under the long lease described earlier in this chapter.[59] Two witnesses hinted at an improper relationship. William Robbyns said that after the death of her husband Margaret 'grew in great familiarity with the last abbot of Malmersbury'.[60] Similarly, Thomas Eles claimed Margaret Pulley 'was very familiar with the last abbot of Malmesbury', and that once widowed she 'used to ride very often to the same abbey of Malmesbury'.[61] Both witnesses alleged that Margaret used her influence to obtain leases on properties in the town which she then sublet at a profit. The Star Chamber investigators also spoke to John Hayes, rector of nearby Lydiard Millicent, who knew Margaret Pulley and confirmed that she used her relationship with the abbot to obtain control of property in Malmesbury. He also told the story of how he had been approached by Margaret and was asked to make a substantial loan of £40 to Frampton. Margaret explained that the abbot was desperate: 'he then being destitute of money'.[62] She offered personally to provide security for the loan and promised that the abbot would eventually both repay the money and 'help him to a good turn' when a well-endowed benefice in the Abbey's gift became available. This story suggests that Frampton was in serious financial trouble.

Following the passing of The Suppression of Religious Houses Act in early 1536, most small monastic communities in England were seized by the Crown and closed. Pilton Priory in Devon, which was a Malmesbury dependent cell, was suppressed. The last prior, John Rosse, previously a monk of Malmesbury, acquiesced in the closure, refused to request a transfer back to Malmesbury and accepted a pension in June of that year.[63] The sense of growing financial crisis around this time is apparent in a letter sent to Cromwell by three prominent gentlemen with Wiltshire interests: Henry Long, Sir Anthony Hungerford and Sir John Bridges.

59 Anonymous, 'Purton. A Case in Star Chamber', 145–68, 199–235.
60 Ibid.
61 Ibid.
62 Ibid.
63 *Heads of Houses III*, 143.

The Tudor Abbey

The letter may date from 1537 when Bridges was sheriff of Wiltshire. The abbot had persuaded these influential local men to ask Cromwell for some relief from the financial demands of the Crown.

> We beg your favor for the abbot of Malmesbury for such payments to the King as he is behindhand for his temporalities. His predecessor left him little ready money. During the vacancy, part of the plate and much of the goods of the house were embezzled. It is sore decayed, and he must maintain it, or his friends would be blamed for his promotion. Considering these things, the subsidy and other charges, he can make no great payment at present.[64]

In December 1537 the abbot exhibited another sign of desperation when he attempted to have a local man called William Lane designated as the Abbey's bondman and villein. As in the case of Robert Carter several decades earlier, the plan was probably to force Lane to purchase his freedom, thus raising some cash for the Abbey. Bridges investigated the matter and wrote to Cromwell to explain that the abbot had failed to turn up during the investigation.

> Upon your letters to us, and others, to examine, between the abbot of Malmsbury and Will. Lane, the matter which was contained in a bill of complaint enclosed within your said letters, we, accompanied by Sir Henry Long, sent warning to the abbot to meet us at Myntye, two miles from his house, and then appointed another day to meet at Pyrton, because he would make no other answer then but demand a copy of the bill. But he did not come that day either, and made feigned excuses, and has kept no appointment since. We hear the abbot claims Lane as his bondman, and if he be not so the abbot does the poor man great wrong.[65]

The fundamentally predatory behaviour of the senior salaried lay officers of the Abbey was revealed again just weeks before the Dissolution. Sir Edward Baynton lobbied Cromwell, requesting that the last lands that were not leased out, namely the Abbey's two hunting parks with their associated pasture, should be handed over to him. Cromwell agreed to this and issued letters in October ordering the abbot to grant leases on the property to Baynton. Abbot Robert Frampton wrote plaintively to Cromwell asking him to reconsider this decision, which would reduce his income and impair his ability to provide hospitality in keeping with his status as a senior prelate. He wanted Baynton to be content with the substantial income he was already taking from the Abbey.

---

64 L. & P. Hen. VIII, v, 700–46.
65 L. & P. Hen. VIII, xii, 443–81.

Malmesbury Abbey 670–1539

[The abbot] has received Cromwell's letters for him to grant, under convent seal, to Sir Edward Beynton, the herbage and pannage, 'with the custody of the same', of Cowfold Park and Westpark. All the other demesnes having been leased out in his predecessor's time, he will not be able to maintain hospitality; even with the two parks, he has to spend 200 marks a year on grain and cattle. Desires Cromwell will urge Mr. Beynton to be contented with like profit Mr. Harmond and others have had. Malmesbury. 16 Oct.[66]

This request was rendered irrelevant by the decision, implemented just two months later, to close the Abbey as part of the general suppression of the larger monastic houses.

The end of Malmesbury Abbey

On 15 December 1539 Malmesbury Abbey was surrendered to the Crown, bringing to an end a remarkable story of institutional resilience and continuity. Máeldub had supposedly established his community in the 630s. Aldhelm was certainly the abbot of a monastery at Malmesbury by the late seventh century. Even at the height of the Danish disruptions of the ninth century there was some form of religious community engaged in worship at Malmesbury. Aldhelm and the relics granted by Æthelstan were venerated throughout the Middle Ages. All this came to an end in 1539: the abbot and twenty-one other monks accepted pensions, ranging from a generous allowance of 200 marks (£133 6s 8d) annually and a house in Bristol for the abbot to £6 a year for the most junior monks.[67] There is no evidence that any members of the community resisted the closure. The monks were doubtless aware of the fate of Abbot Richard Whiting of Glastonbury, who opposed the suppression and was executed on 15 November 1539, together with two of his monks. We do know that one member of the local community expressed opposition to the abolition of the monasteries. Richard Turner, vicar of the parish church of St Paul's since 1535, was reported to the authorities for criticising Henry VIII for hypocrisy. He had contrasted the king's order for solemn dirges and masses to be said for the soul of the Empress Isabella, wife of Charles V, when she died in 1539, with his policy of closing monasteries that reduced opportunities for intercession on behalf of other souls. Since the king appeared to believe that the intercessory prayers of monks could help the souls of the departed, he should be increasing the resources of the monasteries instead of closing them down. Turner's disloyal observations were noted and put on file.

[66] L. & P. Hen. VIII, xiv, 122–8.
[67] L. & P. Hen. VIII, xiv, 255.

The Tudor Abbey

These be the words of the vicar of Paul's in Malmesbury [...] 'I trow if the King's grace did think that masses and dirges did good to the souls departed he would not suppress so many houses or monasteries as he has done, and take their livings from them, but rather to have given them more'.[68]

---

68   L. & P. Hen. VIII, xiv, 303–58. The original version is as follows: These be the words off the vycar off Polles yn Maulmesbury [...] 'I trow yff the Kyng's grase dyd thynke that massys and dyryggys dyd good to the soles departyd he wolde nott subprese so many howsys or monasterys as he have done, and take there levynges from them, butt rather to have geve them more'.

Epilogue: After the departure of the monks

The last abbot of Malmesbury and twenty-one other monks were dismissed and granted pensions in December 1539. It took a little while for this information to reach all interested parties. Following the sale of the borough of Malmesbury to the Abbey in 1215, it was the tradition for the next three centuries to grant the feudal tax, the fee farm of £20, to the queen of England. When in January 1540 lawyers drew up the marriage contract between Henry VIII and Anne of Cleeves they specified that the new queen was entitled to the Malmesbury fee farm and that it was the responsibility of 'the abbot and convent of Malmesbury' to collect and pay this money. The lawyers had failed to notice that the Abbey no longer existed.[1] By the time of the marriage of the king and Anne, the monks were scattered to the winds and we know nothing about their subsequent careers, apart from two exceptions: Anthony Malmesbury obtained a post as a chantry priest at Frampton's Chantry in the church of St John 'on the Wall' in Bristol and Richard Ashton became curate of the parish of Churcham near Gloucester.[2] These were junior clerical positions. Anthony Malmesbury was paid only £3 a year as a chantry priest, and he lost this post in 1548 when the chantry foundations across England were suppressed.[3] By 1553 only seven former monks were alive and still receiving pensions: Walter Stacye, Richard Ashton, Thomas Frocester and Thomas Stanley who were by then married and Walter Sutton, Anthony Malmesbury and John Horsley who remained unmarried.[4] Some of these survivors can be identified as having been present during the scandalous visitation of 1527 and one had been a prominent 'rebel': Richard Ashton, who later became the curate of Churcham, had been accused of taking off his monastic habit on several occasions, donning secular clothes and consorting with prostitutes.

The fate of the Abbey property after the Dissolution was complex. The landed estate was broken up and sold off to different purchasers, who were a mix of courtiers of national standing and local people. Thus, Sir

---

1 L. & P. Hen. VIII, xv, 51.
2 Anonymous, 'Purton. A Case in Star Chamber', 227.
3 Sylvia May Gill, 'Managing Change in the English Reformation', Unpublished doctoral thesis, University of Birmingham (2010), 162.
4 John Mark Moffatt, *The History of the Town of Malmesbury and of its Ancient Abbey* (Tetbury, 1805), 180.

Malmesbury Abbey 670–1539

Edmund Bridges, Baron Chandos, acquired Purton, John Dudley, duke of Northumberland, obtained Brokenborough and John de Vere, earl of Oxford, bought Crudwell, while Garsdon, Lea and Cleverton manors were purchased by the Moody family from Malmesbury and the local clothier, William Stumpe acquired Brinkworth.[5] The courtiers in many cases re-sold their properties and several manors were eventually obtained by Stumpe. The core Abbey site and precincts were also acquired by Stumpe.[6] Most monastic buildings were destroyed, but some fragments were saved. The Abbey guest house probably stood on the site of the Old Bell Hotel, immediately to the west of the Abbey church, and part of the surviving fabric is medieval. The hotel possesses a fine thirteenth-century fireplace which was presumably one of the fixtures of the guest house. To the east of the Abbey church, the Tudor mansion, Abbey House, built by the Stumpe family, incorporates a substantial thirteenth-century under-croft that was part of the Abbey domestic buildings.

William Stumpe's greatest achievement was to ensure that the western end of the conventual church was saved, including the magnificent Romanesque porch, and converted into the town's parish church. The exact sequence of events is not clear. John Leland visited Malmesbury in 1542, and he recounted how Stumpe had taken over much of the site for the manufacture of woollen cloth and had initiated the campaign to convert the nave into a new parish church for the town.

> The whole lodgings of the abbey now belonging to one Stumpe, an exceeding rich clothier that bought them off the king. This Stumpe's son hath married Sir Edward Baynton's daughter. This Stumpe was the chief cause and contributor to have the abbey church made a parish church. At this present time every corner of the vast houses of office that belonged to the abbey be full of looms to weave cloth on, and this Stumpe intendeth to make a street or two for clothiers in the back vacant ground of the abbey that is within the town walls.[7]

One aspect of Leland's account was inaccurate: Stumpe had not bought

---

5   For Purton, see L. & P. Hen. VIII, XIX (I), 375. For Brokenborough, see Cal. Pat. 1550–3, 369–70. For Crudwell, see L. & P. Hen. VIII, xix (I), 286. For Garsdon, see L. & P. Hen. VIII, xviii (1), 257. For Lea and Garsdon, see L. & P. Hen. VIII, xv, 410. For Brinkworth, see L. & P. Hen. VIII, xix (2), 414.
6   L. & P. Hen. VIII, xix (2), 414.
7   Based on Leland, *Itinerary*, I 132. The original version is as follows: The hole logginges of th'abbay be now longging to one Stumpe, an exceding riche clothiar that boute them of the king. This Stumpes sunne hath married Sir Edward Baynton's doughter. This Stumpe was the chef causer and contributer to have th'abbay chirch made a paroch chirch. At this present tyme every corner of the vaste houses of office that belongid to th'abbay be fulle of lumbes to weve cloth yn, and this Stumpe entendith to make a street or 2. for clothiers in the bak vacant ground of the abbay that is withyn the toune waulles.

236

Epilogue: After the departure of the monks

the Abbey site from the king by 1542. On 13 June 1541 the Crown leased the site of the Abbey and the associated gardens to Edward Baynton, Stumpe's father-in-law.[8] Stumpe initially occupied the site as Baynton's tenant, and it was only in 1544 that Stumpe acquired the Abbey site. Leland explained how Stumpe was using redundant Abbey buildings for the manufacture of woollen cloth and how he intended to develop the area to the east of the church – 'the back vacant ground' – for his woollen business. This did not, in fact, happen and instead the Stumpe family built the mansion known as Abbey House amidst the ruins.

The historic parish church of St Paul's stood to the south of the Abbey and by the early 1540s was in a state of some considerable decay. Today all that survives of St Paul's is the tower and steeple. Leland recorded that St Paul's was ruinous and abandoned as a place of worship before the Dissolution.[9] It is possible that the practice of using the nave of the conventual church for parish services predated the Dissolution. Certainly, after the suppression a new parish church was created by sealing off the nave from the eastern end of the conventual church and blocking off the west crossing arch with an in-fill of stone. In 1542 the west end of the nave was still dominated by a large tower built in the late Middle Ages: Leland described how he observed this 'greate square toure' standing 'at the west ende of the chirch'.[10] At an unknown date after Leland's visit, the west tower collapsed, destroying the three western bays of the nave arcade. The congregation was obliged to construct a new west wall, truncating the space and leaving the original west end in a ruinous state.

Aldhelm's shrine and the Abbey relics were presumably destroyed shortly after the closure. Æthelstan's sepulchre, but not his skeleton, was rescued and moved from the eastern end of the conventual church into the new parish church. The bulk of the Abbey's library was also destroyed; as we have seen, some manuscripts had been removed a decade earlier by John Leland, and William Stumpe appears to have acquired the residue of the book stock. John Aubrey claimed that many manuscripts were still held by the Stumpe family in the early seventeenth century, and he told the story of how in 1633 he saw Abbey manuscripts in the possession of Stumpe's great-grandson, also called William Stumpe, who was the rector of Yatton Keynell near Aubrey's family home. Stumpe gave manuscripts to Aubrey and other schoolboys at Yatton Keynell to cover their exercise books, and also used them when brewing beer.

> The fashion then was to save the ferules of their books with a false cover of parchment, that is old manuscript, which I was too young to understand; but I was pleased with the elegancy of the writing and the

8   TNA E 328/257.
9   Leland, *Itinerary*, I 131.
10   Ibid.

Malmesbury Abbey 670–1539

coloured initial letters. I remember the rector here, Mr Wm. Stump, great grandson of Stump the clothier of Malmesbury, had several manuscripts of the Abbey. He was a proper man and a good fellow; and when he brewed a barrel of special ale, his use was to stop the bunghole, under the clay, with a sheet of manuscript; he said nothing did it so well: which methought did grieve me then to see.[11]

From Yatton Keynell Aubrey moved to a school in the nearby village of Leigh Delamere. Here, again, the tradition was to cover exercise books and other notebooks with Malmesbury parchment. The town was a centre for making woollen and leather gloves, and manuscript sheets were also used as shop wrapping by local glovers.

Afterwards I went to schoole to Mr. Latimer at Leigh-delamer, the next parish, where was the like use of covering of bookes. In my grandfather's dayes the manuscripts flew about like butterflies. All musick bookes, account bookes, copie bookes, &c. were covered with old manuscripts, as wee cover them now with blew paper or marbled paper; and the glovers at Malmesbury made great havock of them; and gloves were wrapt up no doubt in many good pieces of antiquity. Before the late warres a world of rare manuscripts perished hereabout.[12]

In 1647, by then a grown man, Aubrey sought out 'Parson Stump' to attempt to retrieve any remaining manuscripts, but to his disappointment he discovered that most had been destroyed.

Anno 1647 I went to Parson Stump out of curiosity, to see his manuscripts, whereof I had seen some in my childhood; but by that time they were lost and disperst. His sons were gunners and souldiers, and scoured their gunnes with them; but he shewed me severall old deedes granted by the Lords Abbotts, with their scales annexed [...][13]

The former monastery cast a long shadow over the life of the town. The abbot had dominated the town's local government for centuries, and the Dissolution initiated almost a century of debate and dispute about how the power vacuum should be filled. During the Middle Ages the large Abbey precinct was extra-parochial; it sat formally outside the parishes of Malmesbury St Paul's and St Mary's Westport. After the Dissolution both parish authorities refused to accept any responsibility for poor law provision within the Abbey precinct, and the area became something of a shanty town. By 1636 there were about 60 households living in the Abbey district, and many of the families were destitute but unable to obtain any

---

[11] Aubrey, *Natural History*, 78.
[12] Aubrey, *Natural History*, 79.
[13] Ibid.

Epilogue: After the departure of the monks

form of poor relief.[14] The county justices were petitioned and called upon to address this anomaly but the petition was not successful, and it was not until 1696, over 150 years after the Dissolution, that the corporation of Malmesbury accepted that it had any responsibility for the welfare of poor people living in the Abbey precinct.[15]

During the thirteenth century a series of enterprising abbots developed a substantial property portfolio in the town of Malmesbury. After the Dissolution the Abbey's urban property was claimed by the Crown and became known as the 'manor of Malmesbury'. By the 1590s the manor was leased to John Stumpe, a grandson of the clothier. The Crown sold the manor in the seventeenth century, and it was successively the property of the Danvers, Wharton and Rushout families during the following centuries. In 1896 Lady Elizabeth Rushout decided to sell off the manor in separate lots.[16] The result was that the property portfolio built up by the abbots of Malmesbury in the thirteenth century was finally broken up. A last thread connecting the town to the institution of the medieval Abbey had been cut.

14 B. Howard Cunnington, *Records of the County of Wilts* (Devizes, 1932), 117–18.
15 Donald Box, *Malmesbury Borough* (Malmesbury, 2007), 49.
16 Wiltshire and Swindon History Centre 622/1. *Sales Catalogue Manor of Malmesbury and Westport* (1896).

BIBLIOGRAPHY

Manuscripts

Cambridge

Corpus Christi College

23
330
361

Trinity College

O. 5. 20
R. 5. 36
R. 7. 2

University Library

Gg. 6. 42
Ii. 3. 20

London

British Library

Add. 38009
Add. 15667
Cotton Augustus ii. 38
Cotton Ch VIII 3
Cotton Claudius B. vii
Cotton Cleopatra B. iii
Cotton Otho B. x
Cotton Otho C. i
Cotton Tiberius A. xv
Cotton Vitellius A. x
Cotton Vitellius D. xvii
Harley 3140
Lansdowne 417
Royal 5 C. v
Roy. App. 85

Bibliography

Lambeth Palace Library

99
224

The National Archives

C 1/18/172
C 53/14.
C 66/150
CP 40/561
CP 40/664
CP 40/685
CP 40/724
CP 40/776
CP 40/959
E 164/24
E328/257
KB 9/45
KB 9/133
KB 9/134
KB 27/352
SP 1/32
SP 1/45

Malmesbury Parish Church

2

New Haven, Connecticut

Yale Beinecke Library

86

Oxford

Bodleian Library

Arch. Seld. B.16
Auct. F 3 14
Barlow 6
Bodley 852
Marshall 19
Rawl. G. 139
Rawl. liturg. g. 12
Wood Empt 5

Bibliography

Lincoln College

lat. 100

Magdalen College

lat. 172

Merton College

181

Oriel College

42

Sankt Gallen

Stiftsbibliothek

Cod. Sang. 26

Urbana–Champaign

University of Illinois Library

128

Vienna

Österreichische Nationalbibliothek

751

Published Primary Sources

Abbo of Fleury, *Passio S. Edmundi*, in *Three Lives of English Saints*, ed. Winterbottom, Michael (Toronto, 1972)

Aldhelm, *Aldhelm: The Poetic Works*, trans. Lapidge, Michael and Rosier, James (Woodbridge, 2009)

Aldhelm, *Aldhelm: The Prose Works*, trans. Lapidge, Michael and Herren, Michael (Woodbridge, 2009)

Annales Monasterii de Wintonia, ed. Luard, H. R., in *Annales Monastici II* (London, 1865)

Anglo-Saxon Chronicle, *The Anglo-Saxon Chronicles*, ed. and trans. Swanton, Michael (London, 2000)

Anselm, *The Letters of Saint Anselm of Canterbury*, trans. Fröhlich, Walter (Kalamazoo, 1994)

Aubrey, John, *The Natural History of Wiltshire*, ed. Britton, John (London, 1847)

243

Bibliography

Bale, John, *Scriptorum Illustrium Maioris Brytanniae Catalogus* (Basel, 1559)

Bede, *Historia Ecclesiastica Gentis Anglorum: Bede's Ecclesiastical History of the English People*, ed. and trans. Colgrave, B. and Mynors, R. A. B. (Oxford, 1969)

Calendar of Close Rolls, Edward I, 5 vols. (London, 1900–8)

Calendar of Close Rolls, Edward II, 4 vols. (London, 1892–8)

Calendar of Close Rolls, Edward III, 14 vols. (London, 1896–1913)

Calendar of Close Rolls Henry V, 2 vols. (London, 1929–32)

Calendar of Liberate Rolls II 1240–1245 (London, 1930)

Calendar of Patent Rolls Henry III, 6 vols. (London, 1901–13)

Calendar of Patent Rolls Edward II, 5 vols. (London, 1894–1904)

Calendar of Patent Rolls Edward III, 16 vols. (London, 1891–1916)

Calendar of Patent Rolls Henry VI, 6 vols. (London, 1901–11)

Calendar of Patent Rolls Edward IV 1461–1467 (London, 1897)

Calendar of Patent Rolls: Edward IV, Henry VI 1467–1477 (London, 1893)

Calendar of Patent Rolls. Edward IV - Edward V - Richard III 1476–1485 (London, 1901)

Calendar of Patent Rolls Edward VI, 6 vols. (London, 1924–9)

Calendar of Papal Registers relating to Great Britain and Ireland, 14 vols. (London, 1893–1960)

Charters and Documents illustrating the History of the Cathedral, City, and Diocese of Salisbury, in the Twelfth and Thirteenth Centuries, ed. McRay, R. W. Dunn (London, 1891)

Charters of Malmesbury Abbey, ed. Kelly, Susan (London 2005)

Charters of William II and Henry I Project, ed. Sharpe, Richard: available online at https://actswilliam2henry1.files.wordpress.com/2013/09/h1-abingdon-2013-1.pdf

Cogitosus, 'Cogitosus's Life of St Brigit', ed. Connolly, Sean and Picard, J.-M., *The Journal of the Royal Society of Antiquaries of Ireland*, 117 (1987): 5–27

Concilia Magnae Britanniae et Hiberniae III, ed. Wilkins, David (London, 1727)

Die briefe des Heiligen Bonifatius und Lullus, ed. Tangl, Michael (Munich, 1989)

Documents illustrating the Activities of the General and Provincial Chapters of the English Black Monks, 1215–1540, ed. Pantin, William Abel, 3 vols. (1931–7)

Eddius Stephanus, *Vita S. Wilfridi*, ed. and trans. Colgrave, B., *The Life of Bishop Wilfrid by Eddius Stephanus* (Cambridge, 1927)

Exchequer Domesday Book, ed. and trans. Fleming, Robin in *Domesday Book and the Law* (Cambridge, 1998)

English Benedictine Kalendars after A.D. 1100, ed. Wormald, Francis, 2 vols. (London, 1939–46)

Bibliography

English Monastic Litanies of the Saints after 1100, ed. by Morgan, N. J., 3 vols. (Woodbridge, 2012–18)

Eulogium Historiarum, ed. Haydon, Frank Scott, 3 vols. (London, 1858–63)

Faricius, *Vita S. Aldhelmi*, trans. Winterbottom, Michael, 'Faricius's Life of Aldhelm, Translation and commentary', *Wiltshire Archaeological and Natural History Magazine*, 115 (2022): 2–36

Geoffrey of Monmouth, *The History of the Kings of Britain*, ed. Reeve, Michael D., trans. Wright, Neil (Woodbridge, 2007)

Gerald of Wales, *Gemma Ecclesiastica*, ed. Brewer, J. S. (London, 1862)

Gesta Regum I, ed. Stubbs, William (London, 1887)

Gesta Stephani, ed. and trans. Potter, K. R. P. and introduction by Davis, R. H. C. (Oxford, 1976)

Gilbert Foliot, *The Letters and Charters of Gilbert Foliot*, ed. Morey, Adrian and Brooke, C. N. L. (Cambridge, 1967)

The Great Roll of the Pipe for the Eighteenth Years of the Reign of King Henry the Second (London, 1894)

Henry of Huntingdon, *Historia Anglorum: The History of the English People*, ed. and trans. Greenaway, Diana (Oxford, 1996)

Herbert of Bosham, *Epistolae, Patrologia Latina 190*, ed. Migne, J.-P. (Paris, 1854)

Hildebert of Lavardin, *Epistolae, Patrologia Latina 171*, ed. Migne, J.-P. (Paris, 1854)

Historia Ecclesie Abbendonensis: The History of the Church of Abingdon, ed. and trans. Hudson, John, 2 vols. (Oxford, 2002–7)

Ivo of Chartres, *Epistolae, Patrologia Latina 162*, ed. Migne, J.-P. (Paris, 1854)

John of Rupcissa, *John of Rupescissa's Vade Mecum in Tribulacione*, ed. and trans. Matthias Kaup (London, 2017)

John of Worcester, *The Chronicle of John of Worcester: Volume III: The Annals from 1067 to 1140*, ed. McGurk, P. (Oxford, 1998)

Leland, John, *Commentarii de scriptoribus Britannicis II*, ed. Hall, A. (London, 1709)

Leland, John, *De Rebus Britannicis Collectanea*, ed. Hearne, Thomas, 6 vols. (London, 1770)

Leland, John, *The Itinerary of John Leland I*, ed. Smith, Nancy Toulmin (London, 1907)

Matthew Paris, *Mathaei Parisiensi monachi Sancti Albani Chronica Majora IV*, ed. Luard, H. R. (London, 1877)

The Manuscripts of His Grace the Duke of Rutland, ed. Lyte, H. C. Maxwell (London, 1888)

Papsturkunden in England II, ed. Holtzmann, W. (Berlin, 1952)

Peter of Blois, *Petri Blesensis Bathoniensis archidiaconi opera omnia*, ed. Giles, J. A. (London, 1847)

Bibliography

Ralph of Diceto, *Radulfi de Diceto decani Lundoniensis Opera Historica: Volume 1*, ed. Stubbs, William (London, 1876)

Rauer, Christine, *Translation of the Old English Version of Pope Sergius's Bull for Malmesbury*, available online: https://www.st-andrews.ac.uk/~cr30/sergius/ [Accessed 18 March 2023]

Regularis Concordia; The Monastic Agreement of the Monks and Nuns of the English Nation, ed. and trans. Symons, T. (Oxford, 1953)

Richard of Devizes, *The Chronicle of Richard of Devizes*, ed. Bohn, James (London, 1841)

Select Cases before the King's Council in the Star Chamber, ed. Leadam, I. S. (London, 1908)

'Text of the Somerset Domesday: Part 2', in *A History of the County of Somerset: Volume 1*, ed. Page, William (London, 1906), 479–526

Thomas Becket, *The Correspondence of Thomas Becket, Archbishop of Canterbury, 1162–1170*, ed. and trans. Duggan, Ann (Oxford, 2000)

Thomas Walsingham, The St Albans Chronicle: The Chronica Maiora of Thomas Walsingham, I: 1376–1394, eds. Taylor, John, Childs, Wendy R. and Watkiss, Leslie (Oxford, 2003)

Wace, *Le roman de Rou et des ducs de Normandie II*, Tome 2, ed. Pluquet, Frédéric (Paris, 1827)

William of Malmesbury, *Polyhistor: A Critical Edition*, ed. Ouellette, Helen Testroet (New York, 1982)

William of Malmesbury, *William of Malmesbury: Historia Novella: The Contemporary History*, trans. Potter, K. R. and ed. King, Edmund (Oxford, 1998)

William of Malmesbury, *Gesta Regum Anglorum*, ed. and trans. Mynors, R. A., Thomson, Rodney M. and Winterbottom, Michael (Oxford, 1998)

William of Malmesbury, *William of Malmesbury: Saints' Lives: Lives of SS. Wulfstan, Dunstan, Patrick, Benignus and Indract*, ed. and trans. Winterbottom, Michael and Thomson, Rodney M. (Oxford, 2002)

William of Malmesbury, *Gesta Pontificum Anglorum: The History of the English Bishops*, ed. and trans. Winterbottom, Michael (Oxford, 2007)

William of Malmesbury, *William of Malmesbury on Lamentations*, trans. Winterbottom, Michael (Turnhout, 2013)

William of Malmesbury, *Miracles of the Blessed Virgin* Mary: *An English Translation*, ed. and trans. Winterbottom, Michael and Thomson, Rodney M. (Woodbridge, 2015)

Secondary Sources

Anonymous, 'Purton. A Case in Star Chamber', *WANHM*, 33 (1903–4): 145–68, 199–235

Barrow, Julia, *Hermann*, ODNB (2004)

Aberth, John, *Criminal Churchmen in the Age of Edward III: The Case of Bishop Thomas de Lisle* (Pennsylvania, 1996)

Bibliography

Baggs, A. P., Freeman, Jane and Stevenson, Janet H., 'Parishes: Dauntsey', in *History of the County of Wiltshire: Volume 14, Malmesbury Hundred*, ed. Crowley, D. A. (London, 1991), 65–75. British History Online http://www.british-history.ac.uk/vch/wilts/vol14/pp65-75 [accessed 7 April 2022]

Baggs, A. P., Freeman, Jane and Stevenson, Janet H., 'Durnford', in *History of the County of Wiltshire XV* (London, 1995), 79–93

Barker, Katherine ed., *Aldhelm and Sherborne* (Oxford, 2010)

Bartholomew, Ron, *A History of Malmesbury Abbey* (Malmesbury, 2010)

Bates, David, 'The Representation of Queens and Queenship in Anglo-Norman Charters', in *Frankland: The Franks and the World of the Early Middle Ages*, ed. Fouracre, Paul and Ganz, David (Manchester, 2020), 285–303

Bates, David, 'William the Conqueror and Wessex', in *The Land of the English Kin*, ed. Langlands, A. and Lavelle, R. (Leiden, 2020), 517–37

Bayliss, A. et al., *Radio Carbon Dates from Samples funded by English Heritage* (Swindon, 2013)

Bernard, G. W., *The Late Medieval Church* (Princeton, 2012)

Berry, Nigel, 'The Estates and Privileges of Malmesbury Abbey in the Thirteenth Century', unpublished doctoral thesis, University of Reading (1989)

Berry, Nigel, 'St Aldhelm, William of Malmesbury, and the Liberty of Malmesbury Abbey', *Reading Medieval Studies*, XVI (1990): 15–38

Billett, Jesse, *The Divine Office in Anglo-Saxon England* (Woodbridge, 2014)

Bischoff, Bernhard and Lapidge, Michael, *Biblical Commentaries from the Canterbury School of Theodore and Hadrian* (Cambridge, 1994)

Blair, J., *The Church in Anglo-Saxon Society* (Oxford, 2005)

Blair, J., *Building Anglo-Saxon England* (Oxford, 2018)

Bloomfield, Morton, *Piers Plowman as a Fourteenth-Century Apocalypse* (New Brunswick, 1961)

Borman, Tracy, *Queen of the Conqueror: The Life of Matilda, Wife of William I* (London, 2012)

Box, Donald, *Malmesbury Borough* (Malmesbury, 2007)

Bowen, John, *The Story of Malmesbury* (Malmesbury, 2000)

Bradford, Phil and McHardy, Alison, *Proctors for Parliament: 1248–1539* (Woodbridge, 2017)

Brakspear, Harold, 'Malmesbury Abbey', *Archaeologia*, 64 (1913): 399–436

Brooke, C. N. L., Knowles, David, London, Vera, Smith, David M., *Heads of Religious Houses in England and Wales*, 3 vols. (Cambridge, 2001–8)

Carley, James P. and Petitmengin, Pierre, 'Pre-Conquest Manuscripts from Malmesbury Abbey and John Leland's Letter to Beatus Rhenanus concerning a Lost Copy of Tertullian's Works', *Anglo-Saxon England*, 33 (2004): 195–223

Collard, M. and Harvard, T., 'The Prehistoric and Medieval Defences of

Bibliography

Malmesbury: Archaeological Investigations at Holloway, 2005–2006', *WANHM*, 104 (2011): 79–94

Coote, Lesley Ann, *Prophecy and Public Affairs in Later Medieval England* (Woodbridge, 2000)

Cowdrey, H. E. J., *Lanfranc: Scholar, Monk, Archbishop* (Oxford, 2003)

Cunnington, B. Howard, *Records of the County of Wilts* (Devizes, 1932)

Dent, Barry, 'The Royal Arms and the Frieze in Malmesbury Abbey', *WANHM* 117 (2022): 87–92

Dunning, Andrew, 'Alexander Neckam's Manuscripts and the Augustinian Canons of Oxford and Cirencester', unpublished doctoral thesis, University of Toronto (2016)

Dunning, Andrew, 'The Correspondence of Walter of Mileto at Cirencester Abbey, c. 1217', *Library of Digital Latin Texts* (2019) [online]. Available from https://andrewdunning.ca/the-correspondence-of-walter-of-mileto-at-cirencester-abbey [Accessed 18 March 2023]

Ecclestone, Martin, 'Mortality of Rural Landless Men before the Black Death', *Local Population Studies*, 63 (1999): 6–29

Esdaile, G., 'On the Roman Occupation of Britain', *Archaeological Journal*, 44 (1887): 51–5

Flood, Victoria, *Prophecy, Politics and Place in Medieval England* (Woodbridge, 2016)

Foot, Sarah, *Æthelstan: The First King of England* (London, 2011)

Fryde, E. B., *Studies in Medieval Trade and Finance* (London, 1983)

Gill, Sylvia May, 'Managing Change in the English Reformation', Unpublished doctoral thesis, University of Birmingham (2010)

Greatrex, Joan, *The English Benedictine Cathedral Priories* (Oxford, 2011)

Hand, Geoffrey J., 'The Common Law in Ireland in the Thirteenth and Fourteenth Centuries: Two Cases Involving Christ Church, Dublin', *The Journal of the Royal Society of Antiquaries of Ireland*, 97.2 (1967): 97–111

Hare, John, *A Prospering Society: Wiltshire in the Later Middle Ages* (Hatfield, 2011)

Hart, J. et al., 'A New Roman Villa near Malmesbury', *WANHM*, 98 (2005): 297–306

Harvey, John, *English Medieval Architects: A Biographical Dictionary Down to 1550* (Gloucester, 1987)

Harvey, John, 'Thomas of Witney', in *The Grove Encyclopedia of Medieval Art and Architecture*, Volume 2, ed. Hourihane, Colum (Oxford, 2012) [online] Available from https://www.oxfordreference.com/display/10.1093/acref/9780195395365.001.0001/acref-9780195395365 [Accessed 18 March 2023]

Heale, Martin, *The Abbots and Priors of Late Medieval and Reformation England* (Oxford, 2016)

Heale, Martin, 'For the Solace of their Advanced Years: The Retirement of Monastic Superiors in Late Medieval England', *The Journal of Medieval Monastic Studies*, 8 (2019): 143–67

Bibliography

'Hempsted', in *A History of the County of Gloucester: Volume 4, the City of Gloucester*, ed. Herbert, N. M. (London, 1988), 420–9

Herren, Michael W. and Sauer, Hans, 'Towards a New Edition of the Épinal-Erfurt Glossary', *The Journal of Medieval Latin*, 26 (2016): 125–98

Hinchliffe, John, 'An Early Medieval Settlement at Cowage Farm, Foxley, near Malmesbury', *Archaeological Journal*, 143 (1986): 240–59

Hinton, David, 'The Fortifications and their Shires', in *The Defence of Wessex: Burghal Hidage and Anglo-Saxon Fortifications*, ed. Hill, D. (Manchester, 1996), 151–9

Historia et cartularium monasterii Sancti Petri Gloucestriae I, ed. Hart, W. H. (London, 1863)

Holt, C., *Magna Carta* (Cambridge, 2015)

Horrox, R., *The Black Death* (Manchester, 2013)

Hoskins, Peter, *In the Steps of the Black Prince* (Woodbridge, 2011)

'Houses of Augustinian Canons: The Priory of St Oswald, Gloucester', in *A History of the County of Gloucester II*, ed. Page, William (London, 1907), 84–7

'House of Cluniac Monks: Priory of Monkton Farleigh', in *History of the County of Wiltshire III*, ed. Pugh, R. B. and Crittall, Elizabeth (London, 1956), 262–8

Huneycutt, Lois L., *Matilda of Scotland: A Study in Medieval Queenship* (Woodbridge, 2003)

Ihnat, Kati, *Mother of Mercy, Bane of the Jews: Devotion to the Virgin Mary in Anglo-Norman England* (Princeton, 2016)

Ireland, Colin A., 'Where was King Aldfrith of Northumbria Educated? An Exploration of Seventh-Century Insular Learning', *Traditio*, 70 (2015): 29–73

James, M. R., *Two Ancient English Scholars: St Aldhelm and William of Malmesbury* (Glasgow, 1931)

Johnston, E., 'Exiles from the Edge? The Irish Contexts of Peregrinatio', in *The Irish in Early Medieval Europe* (London, 2016), 38–52

Jurasinski, Stefan and Oliver, Lisi, *The Laws of Alfred: The Domboc and the Making of Anglo-Saxon Law* (Cambridge, 2021)

Keats-Rohan, K. S. B., *Domesday People* (Woodbridge, 1999)

Kemp, E. W., 'Pope Alexander III and the Canonization of Saints', *Transactions of the Royal Historical Society*, 27 (1945): 13–28

Ker, N. R., *Medieval Manuscripts in British Libraries*, 5 vols. (Oxford, 1969–2002)

Kerby-Fulton, K., *Reformist Apocalypticism and Piers Plowman* (Cambridge, 1990)

Keynes, Simon, 'The Fonthill Letter', in *Words, Texts and Manuscripts: Studies in Anglo-Saxon Culture*, ed. Korhammer, M. et al. (Munich, 1992), 53–97

Keynes, Simon, 'Edgar, *rex admirabilis*', in *Edgar, King of the English,*

Bibliography

959–975: New Interpretations, ed. Scragg, Donald (Woodbridge, 2014), 3–59

Keynes, Simon, 'The Fonthill Letter', in *Anglo-Saxon Kingdoms*, ed. Breay, Claire and Story, Joanna (London, 2018), 190–1

Kightly, Charles, 'The Early Lollards: A Survey of Popular Lollard Activity in England, 1382–1428', unpublished doctoral thesis, University of York (1975)

Knowles, David, *The Episcopal Colleagues of Archbishop Thomas Becket* (Oxford, 1951)

Knowles, David, *The Monastic Order in England* (Cambridge, 1963)

Knowles, David, *The Religious Orders in England*, 3 vols. (Cambridge, 1974–9)

Könsgen, E., 'Zwei unbekannte Briefe zu den Gesta Regum Anglorum des Wilhelm von Malmesbury', *Deutsches Archiv*, 31 (1975): 204–14

Lapidge, Michael, 'Some Latin Poems as Evidence for the Reign of Athelstan', *Anglo-Saxon England*, 9 (1981): 61–98

Lapidge, Michael, 'Beowulf, Aldhelm, the Liber monstrorum and Wessex', *Studi medievali*, 23 (1982): 151–92

Lapidge, Michael, *Aldhelm*, ODNB (2004)

Lapidge, Michael, *Máeldub*, ODNB (2004)

Lapidge, Michael, The *Anglo-Saxon Library* (Oxford, 2006)

Lapidge, Michael, 'The Career of Aldhelm', *Anglo-Saxon England*, 36 (2007): 15–60

'Lechlade', in *A History of the County of Gloucester: Volume 7*, ed. Herbert, N. M. (Oxford, 1981), 106–21

Lee, John S., *The Medieval Clothier* (Woodbridge, 2018)

Leedy, Walter, *Fan Vaulting: A Study of Form, Technology, and Meaning* (London, 1980)

Lenker, Ursula, 'The West Saxon Gospels', *Anglo-Saxon England*, 28 (1999): 141–78

Lennard, Reginald, 'Early English Fulling Mills: Additional Examples', *The Economic History Review*, 3.3 (1951): 342–3

Longman, T., 'Iron Age and Later Defences at Malmesbury: Excavations 1998–2000', *WANHM*, 99 (2006): 104–64

Luxford, Julian M., *The Art and Architecture of English Benedictine Monasteries* (Woodbridge, 2005)

Luxford, Julian M., 'The Seals of Malmesbury Abbey and Pilton Priory', *WANHM*, 115 (2022): 75–86

Miles, Brent, 'The "Carmina Rhythmica" of Æthilwald: Edition, Translation, and Commentary', *The Journal of Medieval Latin*, 14 (2004): 73–117

Moffatt, John Mark, *The History of the Town of Malmesbury and of its Ancient Abbey* (Tetbury, 1805)

Bibliography

Morgan, Nigel J., *English Monastic Litanies of the Saints after 1100 I* (London, 2012)

Niskanen, Samu, 'William of Malmesbury as Librarian: The Evidence of his Autographs', in *Discovering William of Malmesbury*, ed. Thomson, Rodney M., Dolman, Emily and Winkler, Emily (Woodbridge, 2017), 117–28

Nisse, Ruth, 'Prophetic Nations', in *New Medieval Literatures IV* (Oxford, 2001), 95–115

Orchard, Andy, *The* Poetic Art *of Aldhelm* (Cambridge, 1994)

Orchard, Andy, *Pride and Prodigies* (Toronto, 1995)

Orchard, Andy, 'Prudentius, Psychomachia', in *Anglo-Saxon Kingdoms*, ed. Breay, Claire and Story, Joanna (London, 2018), 258–9

Patterson, Robert, *The Earl, the Kings, and the Chronicler: Robert Earl of Gloucester and the Reigns of Henry I and Stephen* (Oxford, 2019)

Petitmengin, Pierre, 'John Leland, Beatus Rhenanus et le Tertullien de Malmesbury', *Studia Patristica*, 19 (1989): 53–60

Petitmengin, Pierre and Carley, James, P., 'Malmesbury-Sélestat-Malines: les tribulations d'une manuscrit de Tertullien au milieu de XVIe siècle', *Annuaire des amis de la bibiothèque humaniste de Sélestat* (2003): 63–74

Pfaff, R. W., 'The "Abbreviatio Amalarii" of William of Malmesbury', *Recherches de théologie ancienne et médiévale*, 47 (1980): 128–71

Reeve, Matthew, *Thirteenth Century Wall Painting of Salisbury Cathedral* (Woodbridge, 2008)

Richter, M., *Canterbury Professions* XL (Torquay, 1973)

Ridyard, Susan, 'Post-Conquest Attitudes to the Saints of the Anglo-Saxons', *Proceedings of the Battle Conference 1986*, ed. Brown, R. Allen (1987): 179–206

Rigold, S. E., 'Romanesque Bases', in *Ancient Monuments and their Interpretation*, ed. Apted, M. R. et al. (Chichester, 1977)

Roach, Levi, *Æthelred the Unready* (New Haven, 2016)

Robinson, D. M. and Lea, R., *Malmesbury Abbey: History, Archaeology, and Architecture to Illustrate the Significance of the South Aisle Screen* (London, 2002)

Rubenstein, Jay, 'Liturgy against History: The Competing Visions of Lanfranc and Eadmer of Canterbury', *Speculum*, 74 (199): 279–309

Shirley, Kevin, *The Secular Jurisdiction of Monasteries in Anglo-Norman and Angevin England* (Woodbridge, 2001)

Sims-Williams, Patrick, 'Cuthswith, Seventh-Century Abbess of Inkberrow, near Worcester, and the Würzburg Manuscript of Jerome on Ecclesiastes', *Anglo-Saxon England*, 5 (1976): 1–21

Sims-Williams, Patrick, 'Milred of Worcester's Collection of Latin Epigrams and its Continental Counterparts', *Anglo-Saxon England*, 10 (1982): 21–38

Bibliography

Sims-Williams, Patrick, 'The Settlement of England in Bede and the Chronicle', *Anglo-Saxon England*, 12 (1983): 1–41

Smith, Trevor Russell, 'The Malmesbury Continuation of the Anglo Norman Prose Brut, 1332–1357: Text and Translation', *The Medieval Chronicle*, 14 (2021): 234–67

Southern, Richard, *St Anselm: A Portrait in a Landscape* (Cambridge, 1990)

Summerson, H., *William of Colerne, Abbot of Malmesbury*, ODNB (2015)

Thompson, E. M., 'Offenders against the Statute of Labourers in Wiltshire', *WANHM*, 33 (1904): 384–409

Thomson, Rodney M., *England and the Twelfth-Century Renaissance* (London, 1998)

Thomson, Rodney M., *William of Malmesbury: Gesta Regum Anglorum: General Introduction and Commentary* (Oxford, 1999)

Thomson, Rodney M., *William of Malmesbury*, ODNB (2004)

Thomson, Rodney M., *Books and Learning in Twelfth-Century England* (Walkern, 2006)

Thomson, Rodney M., *Gesta Pontificum Anglorum: The History of the English Bishops 2: Introduction and Commentary* (Oxford, 2007)

Thomson, Rodney M., 'Malmesbury Abbey in the Time of William', *WANHM*, 115 (2022): 51–8

Thomson, Rodney M., Dolman, Emily and Winkler, Emily, eds., *Discovering William of Malmesbury* (Woodbridge, 2017)

Thornbury, Emily V., *Becoming a Poet in Anglo-Saxon England* (Cambridge, 2014)

Thurlby, Malcolm, 'The Romanesque Abbey Church of Malmesbury: Patronage and date', *WANHM*, 112 (2019): 121–55

Thurlby, Malcolm, 'Further Aspects of Romanesque Malmesbury Abbey', *WANHM*, 115 (2022): 58–75

Van Houts, Elizabeth, *Matilda of Flanders*, ODNB (2004)

Victoria County History, *History of the County of Wiltshire: Volume 14, Malmesbury Hundred*, ed. Crowley, D. A. (London, 1991)

Vincent, Nicholas, 'Isabella of Angoulême: John's Jezebel', in *King John: New Interpretations*, ed. Church, S. D. (Woodbridge, 2003), 165–219

Watkin, Aelred, 'Abbey of Malmesbury', in *History of the County of Wiltshire III* (London, 1956), 210–31

Whitelock, Dorothy, *Anglo-Saxon Wills* (Cambridge, 1930)

Williams, A., *Æthelred the Unready: The Ill-Counselled King* (London, 2003)

Winterbottom, Michael, 'Aldhelm's Prose Style and its Origins', *Anglo-Saxon England*, 6 (1977): 39–76

Winterbottom, Michael, 'William of Malmesbury: versificus', in *Anglo-Latin and its Heritage*, ed. S. Echard and G. R. Wieland (Turnhout, 2001), 109–27

Winterbottom, Michael, *Style and Scholarship: Latin Prose from Gildas to Raffaele Regio* (Florence, 2020)

Bibliography

Zutshi, Patrick, 'Images of Franciscans and Dominicans in a Manuscript of Alexander Nequam's Florilegium', in The Franciscan Order in the Medieval English Province and Beyond, ed. Robson, Michael and Zutshi, Patrick (Amsterdam, 2018), 51–66

INDEX

Abbey House, Malmesbury   154, 236, 237

Abbo of Fleury   49

Abingdon Abbey   47, 53, 68, 77, 85–8

Acircius *see* Aldfrith, king of Northumbria

Adam, abbot of Waverley   136

Adrian IV, Pope   124

Aedulf, abbot of Malmesbury   80–3, 89

Ælfheah, ealdorman of Hampshire   49, 52

Ælfric I, abbot of Malmesbury   39, 47–9

Ælfric II, abbot of Malmesbury   53

Ælfthryth, queen of England   52–3

Æthelhelm, ealdorman of Wiltshire   41–2

Æthelnoth   49

Æthelred, king of Mercia   15–16, 18, 20

Æthelred the Unready, king of England   52–4, 56–7, 65

Æthelstan, king of England   1, 44–5, 90, 103, 139, 196, 213, 232, 237

Æthelweard, abbot of Malmesbury   51

Æthelwold, St   47–9, 50, 52–3, 88

Æthelwulf, king of Wessex   40, 49, 52

Aidan, St   7

Alcuin   145, 226

Aldfrith, king of Northumbria   9–10

Aldhelm, St   1, 2, 4, 35–7, 48, 49, 111, 114, 123, 143, 155, 160, 177, 181, 213, 225–6, 227, 232

  Abingdon and Aldhelm's relics   68, 87–8

  Æthelstan and Aldhelm   44–5

  career   19–22

church building at Malmesbury   23–5

cult of   45, 46, 51–2, 61, 67–8, 71, 160

David, king of Scotland and Aldhelm   92

education   8–11, 28–30

endowment   4, 14–15, 49, 52, 66

family   8–9, 13–15

Faricius and Aldhelm   46, 47, 54, 63–4, 67–70, 72, 77–8, 86

fostering of students   25–7

Irish culture, attitude towards   12–13

library   32–3, 37

liturgical practice   27–8

Lullus and Aldhelm   36–7

Máeldub, Aldhelm's relationship with   5–7

Mercia, patronage of Aldhelm's monastery   15–19

miracles of   47, 63, 68–9, 71, 76–8, 80, 226

reputation after the Norman Conquest   61–72

shrine of   40, 46, 54, 72, 78, 107, 215, 219, 229, 237

teaching at Aldhelm's Malmesbury   28–31

translation of Aldhelm's relics   67–70, 72

William of Malmesbury and Aldhelm   45, 77, 78, 79–80, 81, 86, 89–90, 92, 103

works

  Aenigmata   31

  Epistola ad Acircium   9, 30, 31

  Carmen Rhythmicum   28

  Carmina Ecclesiastica   13

  De Metris   27–8, 31, 33

Index

De Pedum Regulis 31
De Virginitate (prose version) 10, 25, 33
De Virginitate (verse version) 25, 33
Wessex, patronage of Aldhelm's monastery 13–15, 17–18
Alexander III, Pope 127–34, 138
Alfred the Great, king of Wessex 8, 40–3
Amalarius of Metz 101, 106, 108
Ambrose, St 156
Anastasius IV, Pope 124
Andever, John, abbot of Malmesbury 139, 210–1
Anglo-Saxon Chronicle 3–4, 22, 41–2, 54, 56–7
Anne Boleyn, queen of England 230
Anne of Cleeves, queen of England 235
Anselm, archbishop of Canterbury 80–1, 82–3, 85, 99, 100, 101
Antisemitism 108
Arator 32
Aristotle 156
Arthur, Prince, son of Henry VII 214
Arundell, Sir Thomas 229
Ashton, Richard, monk of Malmesbury 221, 235
Assandun, Battle of 57–8
Astrology 29–30, 102–5
Astronomy 29, 102–5
Aubrey, John 198, 237–8
Audley, Thomas, lord chancellor 228
Audoenus, St 213
Augustine St 103, 156
Aumeney, Simon of, abbot Malmesbury 139, 194–5
Aust, William, monk of Malmesbury 204
Avignon 167, 175, 188
Avon, River 2, 118, 182, 227
Ayly, John, abbot of Malmesbury 211–2

Badminton, Henry of 168–75
Badminton, William of, abbot of Malmesbury 159–63

Bale, John 210
Balsham, William, renegade prior of Monkton Farleigh 173
Bangor (Ireland) 10
Bangor (Wales) 82
Barnet, Battle of 211
Basset, Alan de 144
Bayly, Richard, the elder 217
Bayly, Richard, the younger 217
Baynton, Sir Edward 229–30, 231, 236, 237
Beatus Rhenanus 227
Becket, Thomas, archbishop of Canterbury 120, 124–7, 145, 178
Bede 5–7, 8, 9, 11, 14, 16, 17, 22, 28–30, 102, 103, 227
Benedicite, Walter 169
Benedict, St 25, 27, 47
Benedict XII, Pope 199
Benedictine Order 25, 36, 46, 47–59, 126, 152, 156, 159, 160, 188, 193, 199
Beornwulf, king of Mercia 40
Berengaria, queen of England 141
Berhtwald, sub-king of Mercia 15–16, 20
Berkeley (Gloucestershire) 103, 166
Berwick, Gilbert of 165, 169–70, 173
Beteslegh, Adam de, monk of Malmesbury and later prior of Pilton 139
Birinus, St 8
Bisley, William, monk of Malmesbury 221
Black Death, the 176, 177, 179–80, 193–4, 201
Black Prince, the, (Prince Edward, son of Edward III) 1, 186–90
Blackland, manor of Malmesbury Abbey 148, 149, 151
Bladon Castle 180–3
Blankepayn, Richard 203–4
Bodleian Library, Oxford 51, 99, 102, 145, 213
Bohun, Humphrey de, third earl of Hereford 152–3
Bohun, Humphrey de, fourth earl of Hereford 160–2
Boniface St 6, 27, 35, 38
Boniface IX, Pope 202

256

Index

Boroughbridge, Battle of 162
Bradenstoke, John of 169–70
Bradenstoke Priory 144
Bradford-on-Avon (Wiltshire) 168, 210
Bradon Forest 73, 148, 222
Branscombe, Walter, bishop of Exeter 139
Bremhill, manor of Malmesbury Abbey 136, 138, 151, 168, 195
Bret, John le 153
Brétigny, Treaty of 189, 197
Bridges, Sir Edmund 236
Bridges, Sir John 230–1
Brihtric, abbot of Malmesbury 61
Brihtwold I, abbot of Malmesbury 54, 57, 58
Brihtwold II, abbot of Malmesbury 58
Brinkworth, manor of Malmesbury Abbey 151, 161, 169–70, 173, 199, 215–16, 236
Bristol 113, 144, 163, 179, 195, 221, 232, 235
Bristol, Philip, monk of Malmesbury 222
Bristow, Thomas, abbot of Malmesbury 201, 204–10
Bristow, Walter, monk of Malmesbury 221, 228–9
Brito, Geoffrey, canon of Cirencester Abbey 147
Brokenborough, manor of Malmesbury Abbey 151, 171, 180, 182, 236
Bromham, Thomas of, monk of Malmesbury 1, 2, 177–91, 195, 197
Broun, John 196
Brut (the Anglo-Norman prose version) 197
Burghal Hidage, the 41
Burton-on-Trent (Staffordshire) 61
Bury St Edmunds Abbey 82, 126
Buttington, Battle of 42

Cædwalla, king of Wessex 9, 13–14, 17
Caer Bladon *see* Bladon Castle
Calais 175
Camme, Richard, abbot of Malmesbury 219–25

Camme, Walter of, abbot of Malmesbury 190, 194, 195–200, 201, 202
Canterbury 9–12, 16, 19, 28–31, 33, 51, 79, 82, 100, 126, 152, 195
Carter, Robert 201, 215–7, 231
Carter, Thomas 207–8
Cartrai, Malger de 73–4
Catherine of Aragon, queen of England 214
Caynel, William 168
Celestine III, Pope 135
Cellanus 13
Centwine, king of Wessex 8, 13–14
Cenwalh, king of Wessex 9
Chaloner, John, the Elder 205
Chaloner, John, the Younger 205
Charlton, manor of Malmesbury Abbey 49, 151, 203, 205–7
Charlton, Walter 205–7
Charlton, Wybert 205–7
Chartres 85
Chastellayn, Richard 189
Chaucer, Geoffrey 202
Chausy, Joan 173
Chelworth (Wiltshire) 43
Chelworth, Thomas, abbot of Malmesbury 202–3
Churcham (Gloucestershire) 235
Christian Malford (Wiltshire) 149, 152, 193
Cicero 100
Cirencester (Gloucestershire) 3, 144, 145–7, 162, 181, 225
Cissetur, Robert, monk of Malmesbury 221–3
Clarence, George the Duke of 211
Clarendon Palace (Wiltshire) 164
Clement VI, Pope 175
Cnut, king of Denmark and England 57–9
Codrington, John, monk of Malmesbury 219, 222–3, 228
Cole Park, manor of Malmesbury Abbey 151, 168, 202
Colerne (Wiltshire) 171
Colerne, William of, abbot of Malmesbury 1, 139, 143, 148–58
Columba, St 7

257

Index

Columbanus, St 7
Columnis, Guido de 197
Combe, John, monk of
  Malmesbury 222
Common Pleas, Court of 202, 203,
  205, 207
Comyn, John, the Elder 153–4
Comyn, John, the Younger 153–4
Comyn, Margaret 153–4
Corpus Christi College,
  Cambridge 51, 102
Coumbe, Ralph of 171–3
Coumbe, Margaret of 171–3
Coumbe, Walter of 168
Cowage Farm, near Malmesbury 4,
  14–15
Cowfold *see* Cole Park
Crécy, Battle of 186
Cricklade, Robert of, canon of
  Cirencester Abbey 145
Cromwell, Thomas 228–32
Crudwell, manor of Malmesbury
  Abbey 136, 150–2, 195, 236
Culford, John 215–6
Cuthbeorht, abbot of Malmesbury 39
Cyneburg, abbess of Inkberrow 35–6
Cynegils, king of Wessex 8, 9
Cynewulf, king of Wessex 38–39

Daniel, monk of Malmesbury and
  later bishop of Winchester 6, 14,
  22, 27, 37
Danish threat to the monastery 41–2,
  54–7
Dauntsey (Wiltshire) 153
Dauntsey, Richard of 153
David, king of Scotland 91–3
Dealwine, monk of Malmesbury 36
Denise, daughter of John of
  Rodbourne 194–5
Despenser the Elder, Hugh 159–66,
  169, 174
Despenser the Younger,
  Hugh 159–66, 169, 174
Devizes (Wiltshire) 96–7, 111, 113,
  124, 142
Domesday Book 71, 72, 73–4
Dominic, St 147
Draycot Cerne (Wiltshire) 204

Dudig, thegn of Alfred the
  Great 41–3
Dumnonia 21–2
Dunstan, St 47–9, 52, 54
Dunwallo Molmuncius 2, 180–1
Dyer, John 208–10
Dyrham, Battle of 3

Eaba, abbot of Malmesbury 35, 38
Eadric 'Streona', ealdorman 56
Eadwig, king of England 45–6
Ealdgyth, possible name of the wife of
  Edmund Ironside 56–8
Ealhstan, bishop of Sherborne 90–1
Eastcourt (Wiltshire) 48–49
Eastry, Henry of, prior of Christ
  Church, Canterbury 152
Ecgberht, king of Wessex 40
Ecgfrith, king of Mercia 39–40
Ecgfrith, king of Northumbria 8,
  19–20
Edgar, king of England 47–53, 187
Edington, Battle of 41
Edith, queen of England and widow
  of Edward the Confessor 65
Edmund Ironside, king of England 1,
  56–8, 81
Edward I, king of England 148–9
Edward II, king of England 159–62,
  166
Edward III, king of England 164, 166,
  168, 175, 176, 186, 195, 197
Edward IV, king of England 211–12
Edward the Confessor, king of
  England 58–9, 71
Edward the Elder, king of Wessex 41,
  43
Edward the Exile, son of Edmund
  Ironside 58
Edward the Martyr, king of
  England 52
Eilmer, 'the flying monk', monk of
  Malmebury 55–6
Eleanor of Aquitaine, queen of
  England 116
Eles, Thomas 230
Ellandun, Battle of 40
Elmore, Robert, monk of
  Malmesbury 222

258

Index

Eorminburg, queen of
Northumbria 8–9, 20
Épinal-Erfurt Glossary 30–1
Eugenius III, Pope 114–16
Eugenius IV, Pope 210
Eulogium Historiarum 2, 8, 143, 176,
177–91, 195, 197, 227
Euridge, manor of Malmesbury
Abbey 151
Evenlode, River 182
Evesham Abbey 69–70
Evesham, Battle of 148

Faricius of Arezzo, monk of
Malmesbury and later abbot of
Abingdon 1, 17–18, 24, 45–6, 47,
54, 63–4, 67–70, 72, 77–8, 85–8, 106–7
Favel, William, monk of
Malmesbury 156
Flisteridge Wood, near
Crudwell 152–3
Foliot, Gilbert, abbot of Gloucester
and later bishop of London 112,
114
Foliot, Osbert, abbot of
Malmesbury 135
Fonthill (Wiltshire) 42–3
Fowlswick, manor of Malmesbury
Abbey 148–9, 151
Frampton, Richard, abbot of
Malmesbury 219
Frampton, Robert, abbot of
Malmesbury 201, 224, 228–32
Frampton's Chantry, Bristol 235
Francis, St 147
Franciscan order 185
Free Companies 189–90
Frenchwoman, Colette 205
Froben publishing company 227–8
Frocester, Thomas, monk of
Malmesbury 221, 235
Frocester, Walter, abbot of
Gloucester 166
Fursey 7

Garsdon, manor of Malmesbury
Abbey 64–6, 70, 151, 236
Gelen, Sigismond, editor of the works
of Tertullian 228

Geoffrey, abbot of Malmesbury 147
Geoffrey of Monmouth 2, 147, 181–3,
185, 188
Geraint, king of Dumnonia 21–2
Gerald of Wales 131–2
Gerard, archbishop of York 104–5
Gerbert of Aurillac (Pope Silvester
II) 102, 103–5
Gesta Stephani 109–10, 113–14, 115,
117–9
Giffard, William, bishop of
Winchester 88
Glastonbury, Richard, monk of
Malmesbury 221–2, 224
Glastonbury Abbey 47, 50, 75, 79,
152, 193, 201, 210, 225, 232
Gloucester 3, 44, 70, 82, 127, 195, 221
Gloucester, Thomas, monk of
Malmesbury 221, 223, 225
Gloucester Abbey 67, 112, 114, 135,
159, 166, 205, 220, 225, 228
Gloucester College, Oxford 159, 195,
196, 199, 210
Godfrey, abbot of Malmesbury 73–4,
77, 78–9, 80, 98
Godwin 72
Godwine, earl of Wessex 58
Grandisson, John, bishop of
Exeter 139
Gregory I (the Great), Pope 25, 100,
101
Gregory IX, Pope 144
Gregory X, Pope 155
Gregory, abbot of Malmesbury 125
Gregory, monk of Malmesbury 77
Grittleton (Wiltshire) 193
Gurmundus 2, 181
Guthlac, monk of Malmesbury 106

Hadrian, abbot of St Augustine's
Canterbury 11–12, 29–30
Hædde, bishop of the West
Saxons 22
Hailes Abbey 161
Handsex, Nicholas 194
Harold Godwineson, king of
England 58
Hasard, Roger, burgess of
Malmesbury 160

259

Index

Heahfrith 10, 12
Henry I, king of England 1, 58, 65, 76, 80, 82, 83–88, 93, 96, 109
Henry II, king of England 77, 115–121, 124–7, 135
Henry III, king of England 137, 144, 148
Henry IV, king of England 197
Henry VI, king of England 206, 209, 211
Henry VII, king of England 214
Henry VIII, king of England 214, 220, 232, 235
Henry of Blois, bishop of Winchester 112, 114, 123
Henry of Huntingdon, chronicler 109, 110, 116, 118
Herbert of Bosham, adviser to Thomas Becket 125
Hereford 163
Hermann, bishop of Ramsbury and Salisbury 67, 70
Hesdin, Ernulf de 76–8
Heywey, Robert 203
Higden, Ranulf, chronicler 178
Hildebert of Lavardin 85, 106
Hildelith, abbess of Barking 21
Hok, Adam de la, abbot of Malmesbury 163–4, 166–7, 172
Honorius II, Pope 93
Honorius III, Pope 136–8, 143
Horsley, John, monk of Malmesbury 223, 235
Hubald, archdeacon of Salisbury 67–8
Hubert Walter, bishop of Salisbury 135–6
Hungerford, Sir Anthony 230
Hungerford, Lord Robert 209

Illinois Urbana, University Library 226
Ine, king of Wessex 8, 13–14, 18, 21, 38, 66, 227
Ingelbourne Castle 180–3, 227
Inkberrow (Worcestershire) 36
Innocent II, Pope 123, 138
Innocent III, Pope 136–7
Interpretatio nominum Hebraicorum 51

Investiture Controversy 82
Iona 7, 10
Isabella of Angoulême, queen of England 141–3
Isabella of France, queen of England 163, 165–6
Isidore, St 102–3
Islip, John, abbot of Westminster 220
Ivo, bishop of Chartres 85

Jack Cade's Rebellion 208–10
Jerome, St 11, 51
Jocelin de Bohun, bishop of Salisbury 112–3, 124–35
John, abbot of Malmesbury 97–8, 112, 123
John, king of England 136, 141–3, 177
John Chrysostom, St 87–8
John Marshal, constable of Marlborough Castle 111, 112
John of Oxford 124
John of Salisbury 145
John Scotus Eriugena 62, 100, 106
John of Worcester, chronicler 56, 109, 110–1
Jordan, abbot of Durford 136
Jordan, constable of Malmesbury Castle 118–9
Julius II, Pope 219
Julius Firmicus 104–5
Junilius Africanus 33, 226
Juvencus 32

Kaylewaye, Thomas 169
Kemble, manor of Malmesbury abbey 136, 151
Kemp, John, Cardinal 206
Kenten *see* Centwine
King's Bench, Court of 168–9, 174, 205
Kington (Wiltshire) 193
Kingston-on-Thames 40
Knight, Thomas, monk of Glastonbury 210

Lacock (Wiltshire) 181, 208–9
Lane, William 231
Lanfranc, archbishop of Canterbury 66, 69–70

260

Index

Lateran Council (1215)   136

Lea (Wiltshire)   171–2, 236

Lechlade (Gloucestershire)   160–1, 163, 176

Lee, Rowland   228–9

Leiden Glossary   30–1

Leigh Delamere (Wiltshire)   238

Leland, John   2, 33, 183, 214–5, 225–8, 236–7

Leuthere, bishop of the West Saxons   11, 19, 29–30, 46, 89–90, 181–2

Liber Monstrorum   37

Lincoln's Inn, London   196

Little Durnford (Wiltshire)   210–1

Little Somerford (Wiltshire)   45

Llanthony Secunda Priory, near Gloucester   195

Lokyngham, John of, monk of Malmesbury and later prior of Pilton   193

Lollardy   199–200, 203

London   56, 57, 72, 83, 142, 161, 163, 165, 177, 195–6, 198, 214, 215

London, John, monk of Malmesbury   221, 223, 225

Long, Henry   230–1

Long Newnton, manor of Malmesbury Abbey   151, 153, 182, 207–8

Loring, Walter, abbot of Malmesbury   136, 141–3, 177

Louis, prince of France and later King Louis VIII   142

Lucan   32

Lullus, monk of Malmesbury and later archbishop of Mainz   6–7, 35–8

Lydiard (Wiltshire)   43, 230

Máeldub, reputed founder of the Abbey   5–9, 12, 23, 232

Magdalen College, Oxford   99

Malcolm Canmore, king of Scotland   58

Malmesbury, Anthony, Malmesbury   224, 235

Malmesbury Abbey

  Abbots *see* Aedulf; Ælfric I; Ælfric II; Æthelweard; Aldhelm; Andever, John; Badminston, William of; Brihtric; Brihtwold I; Brihtwold II; Bristow, Thomas; Camme, Richard; Camme, Walter of; Chelworth, Thomas; Colerne, William of; Cuthbeorht; Eaba; Foliot, Osbert; Frampton, Richard; Frampton, Robert; Geoffrey; Godfrey; Gregory; Hok, Adam de la; John; Loring, Walter; Nicholas; Olveston, Thomas; Máeldub, Pershore, Roger; Peter Moraunt; Robert of Melun; Robert Venys; Tintern, John of; Turold; Walsh, John; Warin

Agriculture   4, 14, 149–52, 194, 201, 202, 215–6, 219

Architecture and buildings   1, 23, 94–6, 102, 133, 154–5, 198, 213–5, 236–7

Cartulary   14, 40, 41, 42, 43–4, 45, 48–50, 59, 64–6, 71–4, 132, 136, 137, 143, 148–55, 158, 181–2

Library   1, 32–3, 36, 37, 50–2, 78, 98–9, 102, 106, 183, 226, 237

Liturgical practice   25, 27–8, 78, 98, 101, 107, 179, 198, 214

Manors belonging to the Abbey *see* Blackland, Bremhill, Brinkworth, Brokenborough, Charlton, Cole Park, Crudwell, Euridge, Fowlswick, Garsdon, Grittenham, Kemble, Long Newnton, Norton, Purton, Sutton Benger, Thickwood, Whitchurch

Monks *see* Ashton, Richard; Aust, William; Beteslegh, Adam de; Bisley, William; Bristol, Philip; Bristow, Walter; Bromham, Thomas of; Cissetur, Robert; Codrington, John; Combe, John; Daniel; Dealwine; Eilmer; Elmore, Robert; Faricius of Arezzo, Favel, William; Frocester, Thomas; Glastonbury, Richard; Gloucester, Thomas; Gregory; Guthlac; Horsley, John; Lokyngham, John of; London, John; Lullus; Malmesbury,

Index

Anthony; Purton, Thomas; Richard; Robert; Rodbourne, John of; Sodbury, Robert; Stanley, Thomas; Tewkesbury, Thomas; Tiderinton, Andrew of; Winchcombe, William; Wotton, John; Wulfwine

Malmesbury Castle 95, 96, 97, 109–19, 141–4, 177

Margaret, queen of Scotland 58

Marlborough Castle 111, 112, 144

Martianus Capella 102

Martin, representative of Pope Innocent IV 144–5

Matilda, Countess of Gloucester 153

Matilda, Empress 81, 91–3, 110, 113, 115, 124

Matilda of Flanders , queen of England 1, 64–7, 70

Matilda of Scotland, queen of England 1, 58, 77, 80–8, 89, 92, 93

Mearcdaeno 39

Melida, Walter de, canon of Cirencester Abbey 145–6

Merlin, prophecies of 147, 185, 188

Mey, Thomas 217–8

Milred of Worcester 226

Modesgate 71

Monkton Farleigh (Wiltshire) 149, 168

Moody family 236

Morcar, thegn of Mercia 56

Mortimer, Roger, earl of March 163, 165–6

Muhammad, the Prophet 177

National Archives, the 148

Neckam, Alexander, abbot of Cirencester 145–7

Nettleton (Wiltshire) 193

Neville, Robert, bishop of Salisbury 204

Newbold Comyn (Warwickshire) 72

Newman, John 207–8

Nicholas, abbot of Malmesbury 135–6

Nicholas ap Gwrgan, bishop of Llandaff 127–8

Nicholas of Malmesbury 149

Norton (Wiltshire), manor of Malmesbury Abbey 45, 151

Notton (Wiltshire) 171

Oaksey (Wiltshire) 152

Offa, king of Mercia 39

Old Bell Hotel, Malmesbury 236

Oldcastle, Sir John 203

Olveston, Thomas, abbot of Malmesbury 139, 213–8

Orchard, John atte 171

Ordlaf, ealdorman of Wiltshire 42–4

Osburga, Abbess 13

Osmund, bishop of Salisbury 67–71

Otteforde, Ralph of, monk of St Augustine's Canterbury 195

Ovid 32

Oxford 56–7, 96, 141, 159, 195, 199, 210

Pandulf (Pandolfo Verraccio), bishop of Norwich 137–8

Parker Library, Corpus Christi College, Cambridge 51

Parson, Edward 204

Paul, St 24–5, 158

Parvying, Robert, royal justice 168, 173

Paschal II, Pope 82

Paternus, St 44–5, 213

Paulus Quaestor 32

Pehthelm, monk of Malmesbury and later bishop of Whithorn 27

Peronne 13

Pershore, Roger, abbot of Malmesbury 202–4

Peruzzi bank 165

Peter, St 22, 23, 24–5, 116, 158, 213

Peter of Blois 128,

Peter Moraunt, abbot of Malmesbury 86, 88, 106–7, 112, 114–15, 116, 119, 123–4

Phelips, Robert 169–70, 173

Philo Judaeus 51

Pilton Priory 138–9, 193, 194, 204, 210, 230

Pius II, Pope 210

Podsmead (Gloucestershire) 195

Poitiers, Battle of 186, 188, 197

262

Index

Polonus, Martinus 197
Poore, Richard, bishop of
  Salisbury 136, 138
Prudentius 51–2
Pulley family 219, 222
Pulley, Margaret 219, 230
Purton, manor of Malmesbury
  Abbey 39, 133, 136, 151, 169, 203,
  219, 221, 222, 230, 236
Purton, Thomas, monk of
  Malmesbury 221, 222

Ramsbury (Wiltshire) 53, 58
Ramsbury, William 199–200
Reginald Fitz Jocelin, bishop of
  Bath 124, 127
Regularis Concordia 50
Richard I (the Lionheart), king of
  England 135, 141
Richard, monk of Malmesbury 99
Richard of Devizes, chronicler 135
Richard of Dover, archbishop of
  Canterbury 127–30
Robbyns, William 230
Robert, earl of Gloucester 109–10,
  113, 115
Robert, monk of Malmesbury 106
Robert Fitz Hubert 110–1
Robert of Lewes, bishop of Bath 109
Robert Losinga, bishop of
  Hereford 102
Robert of Melun, abbot of
  Malmesbury 135
Robert Venys, abbot of
  Malmesbury 126–32
Rochester (Kent) 16
Rodbourne (Wiltshire) 39, 52–3, 65–6
Rodbourne, John of, monk of
  Malmesbury and later prior of
  Pilton 171, 173–4, 194
Roger, bishop of Salisbury 83, 89–98,
  109, 110, 112, 113, 119, 123–4, 130,
  135, 137, 182
Rome 9, 12, 17, 24, 35, 41, 100, 123,
  124, 127, 129, 130, 136, 138, 143, 159,
  188, 198, 210, 211, 226
Rowdon (Wiltshire) 209
Rupescissa, John of 185, 188–9
Rushout, Lady Elizabeth 239

Ryche, Andrew 217

St Albans Abbey 126, 135, 144, 200
St Augustine's Abbey Bristol 166
St Augustine's Abbey Canterbury 11,
  126, 195
St Mary's Westport 133, 136, 238
St Nicholas Acon, London 72
St Oswald's Priory, Gloucester 127
St Paul's Malmesbury 232–3, 237, 238
Sankt Gallen, Switzerland 159–60
Saundyrs, Giles 217–8
Sedulius, Caelius 32–3
Sélestat, Alsace 227
Selwood, Forest of 22
Selyman, George 173
Seneca 32
Sergius I, Pope 17–18, 38, 89–90, 97,
  123, 138, 139
Serlo, abbot of Gloucester 67–8
Sherborne 22, 90, 96, 97, 227
Sherston, Battle of 57
Shyngels, John 217–8
Sigberct, king of the East Angles 7
Sigeferth, thegn of Mercia 56–7
Silvester II, Pope *see* Gerbert of
  Aurillac
Sixtus IV, Pope 212
Smyth, Thomas 194
Sodbury, Robert, monk of
  Malmesbury 221
Somerford Keynes (Gloucestershire)
  15–16
Stafford, Edward, duke of
  Buckingham 219–20
Stanley, Thomas, monk of
  Malmesbury 224, 235
Stanley Abbey 161, 165, 202, 212
Star Chamber, Court of the 207,
  215–17, 219, 221, 230
Statius 32
Stephen, king of England 96, 109–23
Stumpe, John 239
Stumpe, William, clothier of
  Malmesbury 236–7
Stumpe, William, rector of Yatton
  Kenynell 237–8
Sudbury, Simon, archbishop of
  Canterbury 198–9

263

Index

Sutton Benger (Wiltshire), manor of
Malmesbury Abbey   151, 193, 199,
204
Swein Forkbeard, king of
Denmark   56–7

Talbot, Richard   171, 173
Taylor, Alice   224
Terry, Thomas   194
Tertullian   227–8
Tetbury (Gloucestershire)   15, 181, 182
Tette, abbess of Tetbury   15
Tewkesbury, Thomas, monk of
Malmesbury   223
Theodore of Tarsus, archbishop of
Canterbury   10–11, 12, 15, 16–17,
19, 29–30
Thickwood, manor of Malmesbury
Abbey   148–9, 151, 171
Tiderinton, Andrew of, monk of
Malmesbury   195
Tintern, John of, abbot of
Malmesbury   1, 163–76, 193, 194
Tockenham (Wiltshire)   38–9
Tours   85
Tovy, Aldelm   217
Trinity College, Cambridge   177, 178
Trinity College, Dublin   187
Trowbridge, William of   168
Troyes, Bibliothèque Municipale   91
Trussell, William, royal justice   173–4,
176
Turgund   72
Turner, Richard, vicar of St Paul's
Malmesbury   232–3
Turold, abbot of Malmesbury   61

Uphulle, Richard   194
Urban VI, Pope   198–9
Ursinus, St   160

Valenciennes, Bibliothèque
Municipale   117
Valor Ecclesiasticus   229–30
Vastern (Wiltshire)   144, 161
Vere, John de, earl of Oxford   236
Vézelay   102, 124
Vienna   6–7, 35–7
Virgil   31–2, 82, 86, 146

Walsh, John, abbot of
Malmesbury   137, 143–4
Walter of Pinkney, constable of
Malmesbury Castle   112–5
Warin, abbot of Malmesbury   61–8,
70–3
Wells   66, 225
Westbury (Wiltshire)   210
Westminster Abbey   126, 220
Whitby, Synod of   12
Whiting, Richard, abbot of
Glastonbury   232
Wihtfrith   12
Wilfrid, St   8, 12, 19–20, 26, 28
William I (the Conqueror), king of
England   1, 59, 61, 64–5, 67, 70–1,
72, 73, 75
William II (Rufus), king of
England   73–4, 77, 119, 120
William of Malmesbury   1, 37, 39, 41,
42–3, 45–6, 47–9, 51, 52–3, 54, 57, 58,
73, 123, 145, 160, 225–6
Æthelstan, William's account
of   44–5, 213
Aldhelm, William and   8, 18, 19–20,
23–4, 45, 77, 78, 79–80, 81, 86,
89–90, 92, 103
Anarchy, the, William's account
of   109–11
Astrology, William's attitude
towards   102–5
Eilmer, William's account of   55–6
Faricius of Arezzo, William's
relationship with   77–8, 85–8
Friendship, importance of   105–7
Life and career   75–80, 98–101
Máeldub, William's account of   5,
23, 180–1
Matilda of Scotland, William's
relationship with   80–5, 87–8
Prejudices of William   107–8
Roger, bishop of Salisbury, William's
relationship with   89–98
Warin, William's account of   61–4,
67–70, 72
Works
Abbreviatio Amalarii   101, 106, 108
Gesta Pontificum   19, 23, 24, 43, 44,
45, 52, 61, 75, 76, 79, 80, 86, 89, 90,

Index

91, 97, 98, 99, 103, 104, 105, 106, 107, 180, 181
Gesta Regum   39, 44, 45, 53, 55, 57, 75, 79, 82, 83–4, 89, 90, 91–2, 95, 97, 103, 105, 181
Historia Novella   75, 95, 96, 97, 98, 109
Liber Pontificalis   89
Liber Super Explanationem Lamentationum   76, 101, 105, 108
Miraculis Beatae Virginis Mariae   75, 101, 103, 108
Polyhistor   104, 106
Willoughby, Robert   214
Winchcombe, William, monk of Malmesbury   221
Winchester   6, 22, 27, 37, 43, 45, 47, 48, 50, 53, 80, 88, 89, 112, 119, 135, 187, 227

Witney, Thomas of   162
Wodehill, Richard   210–1
Wolf, Richard   194
Woodville, Elizabeth, queen of England   211
Wootton Bassett (Wiltshire)   144, 161
Wotton, John, monk of Malmesbury   216
Wulfgar, bishop of Ramsbury   53
Wulfwine, monk of Malmesbury   72
Wyclif, John   199–200
Wyght, Ellen de   167
Wytte, John   217–8

Yatton Keynell (Wiltshire)   144, 168, 237–8